Martin Walker won the Brackenbury Scholarship to Balliol College, Oxford where he took a first class honours in modern history, and then went to Harvard University as Harkness Fellow. He later worked on the staff of Senator Ed Muskie before returning to Britain to join the editorial staff of *The Guardian*. He opened *The Guardian*'s Moscow bureau in 1984, was named Reporter of the Year by Granada TV's 'What the Papers Say' in 1986, and took advantage of *glasnost* to become the first western correspondent to contribute regularly to the Soviet Press, and to Soviet radio and television.

He has travelled widely through the Soviet Union, from Murmansk in the north down to the Iranian frontier in the south, and has swum in every sea that touches the Soviet coast, except the Arctic Ocean. He lived in Moscow with his wife and two small children until the autumn of 1988, when he took up a new posting as *The Guardian*'s Washington correspondent.

Martin Walker has published books on British politics, on the history of political cartoons, on newspapers around the world, and *The Waking Giant*, the first study of Gorbachev and the *glasnost* revolution, which was translated into six languages and published around the world.

**Other Collins Independent
Travellers Guides include:**

South-west France
Southern Italy
Greek Islands
Mainland Greece
Turkey
Spain
Portugal

COLLINS

INDEPENDENT TRAVELLERS GUIDE

SOVIET UNION

MARTIN WALKER

Series Editor Robin Dewhurst

Collins
8 Grafton Street, London
1989

Note
Whilst every effort is made to ensure that prices, hotel and restaurant recommendations, opening hours and similar factual information in this book are accurate at the time of going to press, the Publishers cannot be held responsible for any changes found by readers using this guide.

William Collins Sons & Co. Ltd
London · Glasgow · Sydney
Auckland · Toronto · Johannesburg

First published in 1989
© Martin Walker 1989

Series Commissioning Editor: Louise Haines
Maps by Maltings Partnership

Cover photographs: front Suzdal Monastery (Tass News Agency); back Uzbekistan (Zefa).

BRITISH LIBRARY CATALOGUING IN PUBLICATION DATA

Walker, Martin
Soviet Union.—(Collins independent travellers guide).
1. Soviet Union—Visitors' guides
I. Title
914.7'04854

ISBN 0 00 410980 5

Typeset by Ace Filmsetting Ltd, Frome, Somerset.
Printed and bound in Great Britain by Mackays of Chatham plc.

Contents

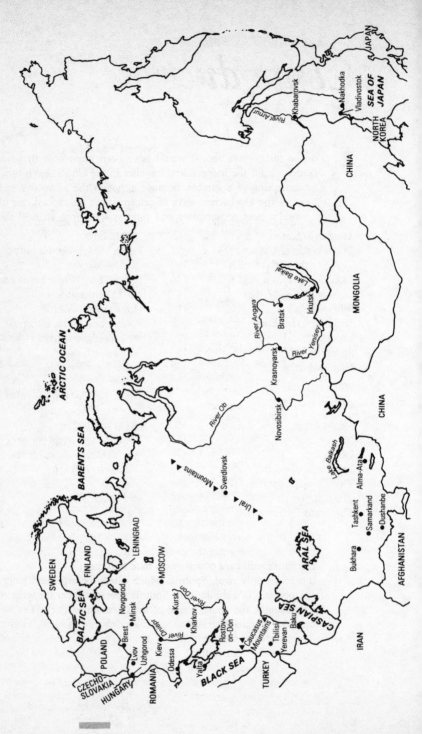

Introduction

Two or three years ago, it would have been impossible to write a guidebook for the independent traveller in the USSR. Even now, it is something of a gamble, because although the *perestroika* and *glasnost* of the Gorbachev wave of reforms have galvanised one of the world's most conservative and rigid systems into change, the Soviet Union remains a country in a difficult and uncertain state of transition.

The idea of letting foreigners roam freely around what has been the most security-conscious state on earth is enough to give the Old Guard the vapours. But partly because the Soviet economy needs our hard currency, and partly because they are a genuinely hospitable people, though mainly because of the new spirit of openness, tourism is going to grow, and is already breaking away from the traditional grip of the state-controlled tour.

Tourism is a state monopoly, almost wholly run and controlled through a single organisation, Intourist. Even if you go on a package tour through one of the large western agencies, they too have to operate through Intourist, whose official title is the State Committee for Tourism. A state committee is something rather different from a ministry, with rather less freedom of action, and is kept rather more closely under the eye of the Party and the Politburo. The KGB, for example, is the State Committee for Security.

Intourist arranges the visas and books the hotels and the internal travel on coach or train or Aeroflot. Intourist provides the interpreters and guides, plans the tour programmes around museums and collective farms, books the theatre and circus tickets, and when you go out to an ethnic restaurant like Moscow's Aragvi and pay by credit card, it is Intourist that will pay the restaurant (in roubles) and present the bill to your credit card company (in hard currency).

Intourist's only rival, Sputnik, which caters for organised youth travel, operates in a similar way. Sputnik operates under the wing of the Komsomol, the youth league of the Communist Party. Let me quote from Natalia Korolkova, Sputnik's deputy chairman, to give you a flavour of its mission: 'Young tourists are always eager to attend various international youth events. Among them are the Festival of Song in the Struggle for Anti-Imperialist Solidarity, the Peace and Friendship Centre whose annual meetings are sponsored by Sputnik; the Youth Peace Caravan that visited nearly all the European countries late last year, and the recent International Conference, "Youth in Society", dedicated to the seventieth anniversary of the Great October Revolution.' If this sounds like your sort of trip, and you are happy to sleep in shared rooms or dormitories, then Sputnik tours can be organised through western Students' Unions, or youth sections of Communist parties, or through some travel agencies like Britain's Progressive Tours.

Perhaps the most important single principle of the Gorbachev reforms in the economy is *khozraschyot*, which means standing on one's own financial feet, without depending on state handouts. It means having to make a profit to pay bonuses to staff, and to finance one's own investment. Intourist was one of the first state agencies to work on the principle of *khozraschyot*, and is now working enthusiastically to maximise its profits, and collect as much foreign currency as it can. In the days before Gorbachev, any foreign currency earned by Intourist or car factories or vodka sales simply went into the state exchequer, and if Intourist or the vodka producer needed some foreign currency to pay for imported cash registers or bottling machines, they had to make a separate application to the Ministry of Foreign Trade. These days, companies that earn foreign currency are entitled to keep a proportion – usually less than half – to spend as they choose. This means that Intourist has been given a real incentive to earn more, by providing more services.

This has been only partially successful. There are now many more roads open to foreign drivers, and more towns to which foreigners may go. But you still may not drive across the country, from the Polish to the Chinese borders. Almost one-fifth of the country remains formally closed to all foreigners; resident diplomats and journalists as well as tourists. And, in practice, a great deal more is closed whenever it is thought necessary. As soon as the mass demonstrations and strikes began in Armenia in February of 1988 over the disputed territory of Nagorno-Karabakh, Armenia and Azerbaijan, two of the major tourist centres, were closed to foreigners, and remained so for months. Tourism, like *glasnost* itself, can be turned on and off like a tap at the convenience of the state. It is worth thinking a moment what this implies about the nature of the Soviet state, and how few changes Gorbachev has really made. The French do not close Corsica, the Spanish to do ban travel to the Basque country, and Britain has never sealed off Northern Ireland from all travellers, in spite of very much more unrest and violence.

The Soviet Union is different, a country trying slowly to emerge from a police state, and thus Intourist still does not welcome individual travellers. The Soviet system is only really attuned to accommodate the group. Or as Alexandr Simchenko, Intourist's head of protocol, put it in an interview in 1988: 'We have to organise things for tourists, give them things to do. You cannot just have them arriving and being left to their own devices – they would not see anything, hear anything, or find anything out.'

But as part of its drive to expand and modernise, Intourist has gone in for joint ventures with western corporations, to learn how they handle the age of mass tourism. Most advanced is the deal with India's excellent Oberoi hotel chain, which will build and manage some new hotels in Central Asia. The foundations of the new hotel in Tashkent have already been laid, and when the place is finally built, we shall see whether Indian management proves any more successful at motivating and training Soviet staff than the Soviet managers of Intourist have been. The evidence of the joint venture on the Delhi Restaurant in Moscow is that Indian management is good, but that slowly, and perhaps inexorably, Soviet entropy takes hold, standards fall, the food starts to arrive cold, and the service loses its briskness and welcome. Gorbachev's reforms are meant to change all that, partly by using joint ventures to bring in western management skills and attitudes to service, as well as western technology.

More joint ventures are under way, with every western hotel chain from Trust House Forte to Hilton engaged in negotiations. Britain's Richard Branson, of Virgin Records and Airlines, has been made the first foreign director of Intourist after signing a contract to bring Virgin holiday-makers to the Oreanda Hotel in Yalta, on the Crimean coast. The Oreanda itself, having been restored and then managed by a Finnish company, is probably the best hotel in the Soviet Union. And in Moscow, the grim old Berlin Hotel, which never recovered the glamour it knew when it was the pre-revolutionary Savoy, is also undergoing a Finnish overhaul.

Why not use Soviet workers? You might as well ask why were foreigners brought in for the great Moscow spruce-up before the 1980 Olympic Games? The French built Moscow's Cosmos Hotel, the Germans designed the airport, and the Finns were brought in to help with the hotels and sports complexes on the Baltic coast. In order to get his *khozraschyot*-inspired new eye clinic opened on time, the great doctor Professor Fyodorov has imported Yugoslav building workers. Intourist will tell you that the foreigners are imported because all the Soviet construction workers are committed to solving the housing shortage, which is partly true, but begs the question.

Look at any Soviet housing estate, at the doors and windows that do not fit, at the balconies that sag away from the walls, at the cracked and crumbling concrete. In Leningrad, going round the restored palaces of the Tsars, you will see the most exquisite craftsmanship mixed with sloppy modern work, with gaping cracks in the relaid parquet floors. Every Soviet city looks as if it needs a thorough overhaul. They have little of the litter and graffiti that bedevil the west (although the graffiti are coming fast), but from public toilets to pavements, public catering to shopping, there is a constant sense of the makeshift, the jerrybuilt and the squalid. Russian workers have a saying, 'They pretend to pay us, and we pretend to work'.

Living standards here are low for a European country – only in Romania are they lower. And with the exception of the military-industries, the space programme and some high-tech sectors, productivity levels are also low – and have barely grown at all during the last twenty years. Gorbachev himself amazed the Soviet people when he told the Party's Central Committee in 1988 that over the past four Five-Year Plans, if one excluded the sales of vodka and the export of Siberian oil and gas, there had been no growth in the economy. The proud statistics of achievement that had been trumpeted throughout the Brezhnev years were so many lies.

Vladislav Sumochkin runs Intourist's huge construction department, and is in charge of the project to build another eighty hotels by the end of the 1990s. Interviewed in June 1988 about this growing dependence on western architects and builders, he said: 'The co-operation is so attractive to us primarily because of the speed and quality of construction work. However, our attitude cannot be described as consumerist; we do not just place an order with a foreign firm for the construction of this or that building. We draw into it numerous Soviet organisations, which receive in this way an opportunity to adopt modern experience right at the construction site.' There are five new hotels to be opened in Moscow alone by 1991, one of them the overhauled (Finns again) Metropol, a classic Art Nouveau building in a perfect location between Red Square and Bolshoy Theatre, which is reckoned to be the country's first five-star luxury hotel. The chances that they will all open on time are slim. Until they do, and with the Metropol being overhauled, Moscow is down to 12,000 international-standard hotel rooms – about one-tenth of the number available in the average major capital of the west. Half of these rooms are located in the Rossiya Hotel, just off Red Square, which is so vast, and so anonymous that I once met a young Italian couple sitting in one of the corridors sobbing at the sheer impossibility of finding their way back. Say each tourist stays a week, then fifty-two weeks times 12,000 rooms means Moscow can handle 600,000 tourists a year. In 1987, they received 5 million, and in 1988, the Gorbachev effect had boosted bookings by 30 per cent. With Armenia and Azerbaijan having to be declared off-limits, and the visit of President Reagan for the Moscow summit in the peak tourism period of late May bringing over 3,000 journalists in his wake, something had to give. Tourists found themselves bounced down from international-grade rooms in the centre to rather grimmer establishments like the outlying Sevastopol, designed for Soviet and Eastern bloc occupation. Other tourists found themselves sleeping in ferry boats tied up at the Rechnoy-Voksal, the river station. This promises to be the pattern of occasionally dislocated accommodation for some years to come.

Do not let this put you off. The Soviet Union is one of the great tourist destinations. The largest country on earth, with the largest range of ethnic cultures and climates and vegetation, it is at once safe enough for the most cautious tourist and exotic enough for the most adventurous traveller. In customs, manners and life styles, the place is hugely different. Parts of it are superpower and large chunks are Third World. Upper Volta with rockets, sneer American hard-liners, and there is an uncomfortable kernel of truth to the jibe. The remarkable thing about the country today is that it at last has a leader, in Mikhail Gorbachev, who is bold enough to admit it.

He has launched the Soviet Union on a remarkable experiment, an attempt to humanise the socialist system, and to invigorate its lumbering economy with a dash of private enterprise and initiative. Prepared to tell the ugly truths about Stalin's Great Terror, Gorbachev is seeking to recover some of the original democratic idealism of socialism that launched the 1917 Revolution. Rather like Ivan the Terrible and Peter the Great before him, Gorbachev has tried to impose a revolution from above. Even if he cannot succeed, the cultural and social ferment thrown up by his attempt makes the Soviet Union a fascinating place to visit.

In the last couple of years, western tourists have seen Mathias Rust's light plane land in Red Square, 300 Crimean Tartars stage a sit-down protest in front of Lenin's tomb, 800,000 Armenian demonstrators marching into the main square of the city of Yerevan, and heard hundreds of members of the new unofficial party, the Democratic Union, chant, 'Down with the KGB' on Moscow's Gorky Street. Everywhere is fizzing with new life.

And even though the length of your stay, your route and your hotel rooms or camp site are all in the hands of Intourist, you are then free to be as independent a traveller as you wish. You can poke around the Arbat courtyards, watch the used-car sales, join the football fans at their stadiums, go for a drink in the stand-up beer bars, or check out the prices of tomatoes in the peasant markets. You may go to a current affairs lecture or join the Russian kids at the animals' theatre, or attend a Buddhist ceremony or a heavy metal rock concert.

You can go fishing through the ice of the River Moskva, ski in the Caucasus, hunt wild boar in the Pamirs, windsurf on the Caspian Sea, cruise up the River Volga, enjoy a winter picnic in the Siberian Taiga, cling on to a wood and leather sleigh, while the Evenk hunters hold their reindeer races, or laze on a Black Sea beach. A country as big as the USSR can provide all the usual tourist attractions, and some more.

The purpose of this book is to tell you how to get the best out of a visit to the Soviet Union, even if you speak no Russian. *Schaslivavo puti* – have a great trip.

Republics of the Soviet Union

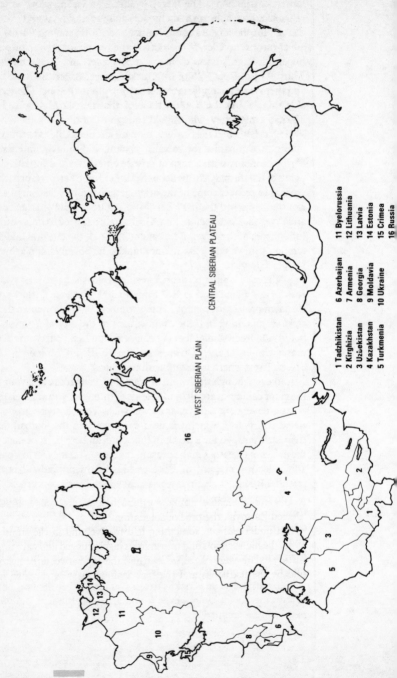

1 Tadzhikistan   6 Azerbaijan   11 Byelorussia
2 Kirghizia   7 Armenia   12 Lithuania
3 Uzbekistan   8 Georgia   13 Latvia
4 Kazakhstan   9 Moldavia   14 Estonia
5 Turkmenia   10 Ukraine   15 Crimea
                                      16 Russia

WEST SIBERIAN PLAIN

CENTRAL SIBERIAN PLATEAU

History

THE MAKING OF THE RUSSIAN EMPIRE UP TO 1917

The authorised version

The Soviet Union is a country that is slowly and painfully facing up to the reality of its own history. Adults and schoolchildren alike have been accustomed to an authorised version of the past that is tailored to the political demands of the present. History, for most of the last seventy years, has been what the state permitted the people to know. And dismantling this great machine of 'official history' has been a difficult process, because so much of it was based on lies and half-truths, and yet it was all bound up with the great sustaining myth of the state itself.

It is a tricky business, telling the citizens that the Party is always right and has the peoples' best interests at heart, when the people know how often the Party has been thumpingly wrong. One result is that the Soviet Union has become the land of political euphemism. Stalin's Great Terror against his people became known as the period of 'the cult of personality'. Nikita Khrushchev's disorganised but essentially well-meaning attempt to exorcise the Stalinist evil, close down the Gulag and improve the peoples' living standards became known (after his fall) as 'the period of voluntarism'. And the years of smug corruption under Brezhnev, when the economy was bankrupted to pay for a bloated military establishment, are today known as 'Period Zastoya', the time of stagnation.

But under *glasnost*, something had to give, and in the summer of 1988, the high schools and universities just shrugged and gave up. The history exams were cancelled, because the gap between the history as told by the textbooks and the real Stalinist past as revealed in the newspapers, magazines and television programmes was simply too wide to be ignored. At the same time, people were at last permitted to read again the classic and pioneering history of Russia by Nicolas Karamzin. Written in twelve volumes between 1818 and 1824, his *History of the Russian State* was a landmark in the development of a national consciousness. Karamzin's writing was also linguistically important, as he was one of the first men to devise a Russian prose that dispensed with the florid restraints of Church Slavonic.

The decision to allow his work to be republished in 1988 was essentially a political one. Karamzin, the keeper of the Tsar's archives, had been condemned by most Soviet historians as a reactionary monarchist. This was partly because of his famous phrase, 'The history of the people belongs to their Tsar', and partly because he sharply criticised Ivan the Terrible, who was something of a hero to Stalin and to the nationalist school of Russian historians.

The history of almost any period, and not just Stalin's brutal times, is a political minefield in the Soviet Union. It is not simply the rigorous Marxists who try to police the historians, but also the Russian (and other) nationalists. For example, when the Orthodox Church celebrated the thousandth anniversary of the introduction of Christianity in Russia in the year AD 988, the Ukrainians were furious that the main festivities took place in Moscow. They had a point. Kiev, then as now the capital of the Ukraine, was where the conversion to Christianity took place, when Prince Vladimir of Kiev instructed his people to topple their pagan idols and dive into the waters of the River Dniepr for a mass baptism.

The Dark Ages

But this tale of Kievan Rus, which was the pre-Mongol confederation of Russia based on Kiev, conceals a further controversy. Who exactly were the Russian people at this mysterious time, the Dark Ages of the tenth century? Many western historians say that they were composed of barbaric Slavic tribes, who were being knocked into shape by a new ruling class of warriors, the Varangians. Known in western Europe as the Norsemen or the Vikings, these adventurers from Scandinavia began by plundering, then started trading and finally returned to settle. There is some support for this theory in the Chronicle of Nestor, the eleventh-century monk of Kiev, whose lives of the saints and *Tale of Bygone Years* is one of the few written sources for the period. Nestor wrote of 'the beast-like life of the ancient Slavs', and praised the civilising, Christianising mission of the Varangian rulers of Kiev, like Prince Vladimir.

His Chronicle begins with a promise to explain 'the origins of the land of Rus', but what Nestor then gives us is a saga. Sometime around the year AD 860, three Varangian brothers, Truvor, Sineus and Ryurik, came in longships from the Northlands, in response to a curiously-worded invitation from the Slavic tribesmen: 'Our whole land is great and rich, but there is no order in it. Come to rule over us.'

'Thus was born the pernicious theory that the Russian people were not capable of independent creative work, and could not even launch their own culture and state without foreign help and influence,' complains the eminent Soviet historian and Academician Professor Boris Rybakov.

Certainly, there is archaeological evidence of sophisticated art works and ritual burials that suggest a complex social and religious system among the early Slavs. But equally, at about the time the Varangians started bringing their longships down the Russian river system, and opening what was to become a great trade route from Scandinavia to the Black Sea and the great Imperial city of Constantinople, something fundamental changed in the Slavic social system. They began to build towns.

But history does not begin with towns. The coming of the Varangians with their river trade, their towns, their laws and their system of land tenure, their organisation of armies and of taxation, helped to define the kind of state that Russia would become. But this was built on another, older tradition, of the nomad horsemen of the steppes. And over the centuries this was to prove an equally powerful factor in the creation of the Russian national identity.

Nomads

In 3–4000 BC, the great steppes between the Ukraine and the Altai mountains saw the emergence of a fairly efficient nomadic culture, based on the horse, the ox-cart and on herds of sheep and cattle. Above all, this culture produced the war chariot, which enabled the nomads to defeat in battle the richer, more stable communities based on agriculture and trade that were developing in the Caucasus, in Persia, in India and in China.

By the time that Greece and then Rome began to flourish, the steppes were dominated by Scythians, horsemen and archers. According to the Greek historian Herodotus, who spent some time in the Hellene colonies of the Black Sea, the Scythians ruled from the Danube to the River Don. They traded actively with the Greeks, produced marvellous gold ornaments and metalwork, and began a special cultural relationship between Greece and Russia that continued far beyond pagan times.

The arrival of the Slavs

What happened after the Scythians, and before the Varangians came, nobody is really sure. Nomadic tides of Goths and Huns and Avars swept back and forth, and somehow, the Slavs came and put down their roots. The first known references to them comes in the Roman writings of Pliny, and certainly by the time the Avars were flourishing in the sixth century AD, the Slavs were occupying the lands we now call the Ukraine and southern Russia, even if not ruling them. But what happened in northern Russia, we have very little idea. There are some burial mounds, notably the frozen tombs of Pazyryk, that suggest a barbaric and nomadic society rather like that of the Scythians.

The Khazars

But just as the Varangians came to join the Slavs and create the state we know as Rus, there was another and most unusual political development, the rise of the Khazars, who went on to establish the first Judaic Empire. The Khazars were another Mongol-Turkic tribe from Central Asia who swept across the steppes in the seventh century AD, and settled along the River Volga, where they began to build towns and trading posts, to prosper and to expand. Their capital of Itil, at the mouth of the River Volga, became rich on the 10 per cent toll they charged on every cargo that passed. But they provided a period of political stability that allowed Russian merchants to penetrate as far south as Baghdad, and Arabic coins to flow back north. Powerful enough to help stop the rising tide of Islam from lapping its way through the Caucasus and the Balkans and into Europe, the Khazar leaders converted to Judaism and established a state that was remarkable for its religious tolerance.

The city of Kiev was already growing when the Khazar Empire was at its peak, and as a tribute and symbol of political subordination, the Kievans sent to Itil a well-made sword, sharpened on both edges. The Khazar monarch tested the blade, and noted that a people who made a two-edged sword when the Khazars sharpened only a single edge, would soon be demanding tribute from other states, not paying it. He was right. In the year AD 965, the power of the Khazars was smashed by the Kievan Prince Svyatoslav, and within a generation, their Judaic Empire had disappeared.

The Varangians

Even before then, Rus under the Varangians had given proof of its vaulting ambition, mounting four military expeditions against Imperial Constantinople itself. Driven off by the famous Greek fire, and with serious losses, the Varangians still managed to sign trade treaties that allowed their merchants to live in the great city at the Emperor's expense, and to have free use of the steam baths.

Historians still dispute the nature of the Varangian state. Indeed, state is too grand a word for it. It was a riverine network, a loose agglomeration of trading towns held together by river communications. The main centres were Novgorod in the north, and Kiev in the south, and the support of one or the other centre was crucial in deciding the inevitable power struggles for the throne between the various princes. The same Svyatoslav who had defeated the Khazars had three sons. And after Svyatoslav was himself beaten by the Byzantine general, John Zimisces, in a doomed attempt to conquer Constantinople, his sons fought for the succession.

Thanks to the support of the northern town of Novgorod, Vladimir emerged victorious in 980, and celebrated his triumph with a ringing declaration of his pagan faith. He erected wooden statues of the old Slavic gods before his palace. There was Svarog, father of the gods, and his son Dazhd-Bog the sun god, Stribog the wind god and Perun the god of thunder, with moustaches of solid gold and hair of silver strands. The Slavic gods were close enough to the Nordic divinities of Wotan and Thor for there to be little conflict between Varangians and Slavs over religion. But Vladimir was to change all that.

Conversion to Orthodox Christianity

There is a delightful story that Vladimir thought long and hard about the available religions on offer. Recalling the Khazars, he first pondered Judaism, and then asked the Jews why their people was so scattered across the world. 'For our sins,' they replied, and he rejected that. Then he thought about Islam, the faith of the eastern Bulgars with whom Kiev both fought and traded, but rejected the Muslim faith on the sensible grounds that no man can be happy in Russia without alcohol. He turned down Roman Christianity, which had now spread to the Varangians' nordic homelands, because of the presumption of the Pope as spiritual leader claiming precedence over secular princes. This left Byzantine Christianity, the Orthodox faith which his own grandmother Olga had followed. There were also sound commercial and strategic reasons for the strengthening links with the Byzantine Empire that conversion would bring. Indeed, as part of the conversion agreement, Vladimir married the sister of the Byzantine Emperor. He brought bishops to Kiev from Constantinople, and ordered his deputies throughout the lands of Rus to continue the conversion. In far Novgorod it was done with fire and sword.

But it was done, and proved the crucial step that as much as any other single political decision was to define the future course of Russian history. Its implications were many. First, there was the way the Church was completely subordinate to the power of the state from the beginning. The conversion was a political decision by the prince, and the authority of the Russian state over the Church has never really been in doubt since. Second, there were the cultural consequences of choosing Orthodox Christianity. Roman Catholicism not only created political tension between Church and state, it also meant an aggressive commitment to conversion and to Crusade, whether against the Muslims who occupied the Holy Land of Palestine, or the Russian people themselves, as when the Swedes and the Teutonic Knights launched their northern 'Crusade'. But the choice of the Orthodox faith had other, even deeper implications.

There is something essentially restless about the faith of Rome, while there is a fundamental passivity, or a commitment to calm, about the Orthodox faith. These are loose and untidy concepts, but they help to explain why it was that western Europe, with the Roman faith, went through both Reformation and Renaissance and eastern Europe did not. This was to be a cultural cleavage point that has been at the root of the differences between Russia and the rest of Europe ever since. It is hard to think of any experience more fundamental than the Reformation, which redefined the way man saw his God and the spiritual world, and the Renaissance, which redefined the way man saw and responded to the flesh and the world around him. Clearly, other historical factors played their part in sealing off Russia from these tumultuous and formative European storms, but the embrace of Orthodoxy in AD 988 was the most important.

Golden age of Kievan Rus

The conversion began the golden age of Kievan Rus, a period which lasted some 250 years before the coming of the Mongol Hordes. Under Vladimir, and then Yaroslav the Wise, the great stone churches of Kiev began to rise. Yaroslav, following in the Imperial tradition, built the great Cathedral of St Sophia, erected his own set of Golden Gates, founded the Monastery of St George, established groups of scholars and began great libraries. Russian scholarship and written Russian history may be said to have begun with his reign, which saw the scholar monks begin to gather in the Monastery of the Caves, the limestone tunnels and caverns in the steep banks of the River Dniepr, which were to be the nursery of the Russian 'Chronicles'.

And out of scholarship grew the formal code of law, the 'Russkaya Pravda', whose precise distinctions between different kinds of loan and investment, between a seller's commission and a partner's share of profit, between deliberate and unfortunate bankruptcy, emphasise the importance of the trade that had produced Kievan prosperity. Through his dynastic marriages, Yaroslav took his place in the royal families and ruling houses of Europe. His son Vsevolod married the daughter of the Byzantine Emperor, and his sister married the King of Poland. He married his three daughters to King Harald Hardrada of Norway, to King Andrew of Hungary and to King Henry I of France.

After the death of Yaroslav, the usual battles for succession combined with a renewed threat from the Asian tribes to trouble Kiev's prosperity. Yaroslav had defeated the Pecheneg tribes who had dominated the northern shores of the Black Sea. But their defeat had opened the way for their replacement by a more disturbing tribal grouping, the Polovtsy. This tribe was to menace Kiev until the Mongols came, and the first great work of Russian literature, the 'Lay of the Host of Prince Igor', was written about a campaign against the Polovtsy. The Polovtsy, however, were more than simple barbarian raiders. Their command of the lower reaches of the Rivers Don and Dniepr threatened Kiev's crucial trade with Constantinople.

There were other, deeper social changes under way. More trade meant more and richer merchants, and in the cities of Novgorod and Kiev, the townsfolk began to agitate for some political power to match their growing economic muscle. The last of the great rulers of Kiev, Vladimir Monomakh, came to the throne in 1113 almost democratically, at the invitation of the *Veche*, or city assembly, although it was more a case of acclamation by riot than by sober parliamentary session. The *Veche* was to become rather more important in Novgorod than in Kiev, but the emergence of this political force of the townspeople suggests that twelfth-century Kiev had far outgrown its Varangian roots of Viking war leaders and Slavic forest-dwellers.

The prosperity was spreading. Other towns like Chernigov were beginning to rival Kiev in wealth, while the lands of Galicia and Volynia were becoming prosperous enough through the Polish trade to start going their own way. The rich northern towns of Pskov and Vitebsk were moving into the orbit of the even richer Novgorod. And where the tiny Yauza stream flowed into the River Moskva, a wooden fortification was being built on the top of the hill that was one day to become the Moscow Kremlin. A 160 kilometres further east, a new trading region was developing on the Upper Volga, around the towns of Yaroslavl, Kostroma and Rostov. And on the River Klyazma, the grandson of Monomakh, Prince Andrey of Rostov and Suzdal, was building his new capital of Vladimir. Not only did his splendid Uspensky Sobor, Cathedral of the Assumption, deliberately rival the great churches of Kiev, there was also an open challenge of power, which was settled in 1169 when Prince Andrey marched south to besiege and ruthlessly conquer the old capital.

The fall of Kievan Rus and the Mongol invasion

The sack of Kiev was more than just another tragedy of history, it was a symbol of the disunity of the state of Kievan Rus. By the time Prince Andrey's northern power base was ready to challenge old Kiev, the state had effectively divided into eleven separate principalities. The divisions went beyond simple geography. There were trading rivalries and there were different social systems. Novgorod called itself a Republic, and was ruled in effect by the *Veche*. Kiev was nominally ruled by its Grand Prince, but in fact an oligarchy of quarrelsome boyars, a hereditary aristocracy, was wielding increasing influence. Vladimir, which had been established by Prince Andrey so that he would be untroubled by the *Veche* and by the boyars of Rostov and Suzdal, was under the sway of an absolute monarch.

The endless wars of succession between the princelings sapped at the heart of Kievan Rus, as the Polovtsy gnawed endlessly at the eastern and southern flanks. Kiev itself became poorer and one reason for the steady rise in power of the northern principalities was the constant flow of refugees and settlers from Kiev heading north, away from the incessant frontier raids.

And thus it was a disunited, squabbling and weakened state that was hit by the Tartars in the year 1223 – the very year of the death of Genghis Khan, the man who gathered and unleashed the Mongol hordes. The first assault had been almost a reconnaissance, but was strong enough to make the Polovtsy band together with the forces of seven Russian princes, their traditional foes. Attacked by the Russians, the Tartars had been retreating when the Polovtsy panicked and fled. The Tartars returned to the attack, killing and capturing the Russian princes and bogatyrs, or knights. The Tartars then built a wooden platform like a vast raft, used the prisoners as rollers to roll the platform on to heaps of more prisoners, then dined atop the heaving, groaning mass below before crushing their captives to death. This, at least, is the Russian version.

But then the Tartars disappeared for fourteen years, while the Orthodox Church campaigned in vain for the Russian princes to cease their internal bickering and unite. And in 1237 the Tartars returned, this time to stay and conquer, under the leadership of a sub-Khan named Batu, who had been grandly awarded the vast lands between the Urals and Dniepr as his own. In a winter campaign, Batu struck directly at the strongest principality, Vladimir. Using a mobile siege train, he smashed down the walls, sacked the city, burned the Cathedral and then pursued and destroyed its army. He rode west to Novgorod, but when the thaw came the marshes around the city became impassable to the Mongol horses. Batu rode south to destroy and enslave the Polovtsy, storming the Russian fortresses of Chernigov and Pereyaslavl on the way. Next year, he rode back north to Suzdal, and in 1240, launched another winter attack on Kiev. The slaughter was almost total. Six years after the Tartar assault, a travelling monk reported only two hundred houses remaining in what had once been the proud and rich city of Kiev.

Batu rode west, storming through the principality of Galicia, into Poland to smash their army, and then turning south to defeat the Hungarians. But then came the Czech miracle, as King Vaclav and his troops stopped the now exhausted Mongols at Olmutz. The Tartars fell back to Hungary to regroup, and then invaded Austria, to be stopped again by King Vaclav and his Czechs. The Tartars turned back, to digest their Russian conquests.

The next two centuries of Russian history are the story of the Mongol yoke and also of the emergence of Moscow as the centre of Russian power. The balance of Russian power shifted away from Kiev to the north, as the great river trading route from the Baltic to the Black Seas simply dried up. Kiev's prosperity had been built on that trading route.

The trading routes that remained, like the connection between the city of Novgorod and the Hanseatic League, helped to shift the centre of gravity of old Russia. From being a riverine system, based on long-distance trade and communications, Russia became a far more enclosed entity, hemmed in by menacing neighbours. Whatever service Russia had done for the rest of continental Europe by absorbing and blunting the shock of the Mongol invasion was ill repaid. In the Baltic, the Knights of the Sword, an aggressively Crusading Order, took advantage of the Tartar disruption to launch a new Teutonic invasion from the west. Although defeated by Alexander Nevsky, Prince of Novgorod, at the battle on the frozen Lake Peipus in 1242, these Knights of the Sword were only one of the threats from the west.

The sacking of Kiev had isolated the kingdoms of Galicia and Volhynia, which were the prosperous districts of the western Ukraine. Although they retained a brief independence under Alexander Nevsky's great contemporary, Prince Daniel, they were quickly absorbed by the emergent new powers of eastern Europe. Volhynia came under Lithuanian control, and by 1321, the Lithuanians had taken command of Kiev itself. Meanwhile, Galicia had fallen under Polish control. In 1386, the unification of the Polish and Lithuanian crowns created a new great power on Russia's western frontier; a vast empire that stretched from the Black Sea to the Baltic. This was one by-product of the Tartar disruptions. But there were others, whose legacies were to last for hundreds of years. First, there was the powerful tradition of autocracy. The Tartars did not rule Russia directly, but through chosen Russian princes, whom the Tartars manipulated to raise taxes and to pay the huge annual tribute to the Khans. Second, was xenophobia, the mistrust of all foreigners. Tartar occupation on the one side, and raids and incursions by Lithuanians, Poles, Teutonic Knights and Swedes on the other, rendered the words neighbour and invader virtually interchangeable. Russia's welcome to foreigners has been cautious ever since. Third, was the rise of Moscow.

The rise of Moscow

Geography had much to do with this. The city was strategically placed on the river system that gave it access to the Volga to the east, to Kiev to the south and to Novgorod in the north. But Moscow was also far enough from the main invasion routes to be less vulnerable to Mongol raids. More important, it meant that Moscow became a magnet for Russian refugees fleeing from Tartar domination elsewhere. However, these advantages were not unique. The city of Tver, a week's march to the north-east, was similarly well-placed, and for most of the thirteenth century, the two cities were bitter rivals. In 1319, even the Tartars expressed disgust when this civic rivalry saw Prince Yury of Moscow murder his rival Prince Michael of Tver in the camp of the Golden Horde, where the two Princes had gone to pay tribute. Tver finally lost because it tried too quickly to break free from the Tartars, and the army of Moscow's Prince Ivan Kalita, known as 'Moneybags', joined the Mongol troops on the punitive raid which devastated Tver.

One crucial sign of Moscow's emerging role was the endorsement of the Church. In 1299, the Metropolitan Cyril and his churchmen left the wreck of Kiev. They went first to the city of Vladimir on the Volga, but dynastic wars and endless Tartar raids up the Volga drove them to seek security with Moscow's Prince Ivan 'Moneybags'. Money was the key to his power. It came from his careful husbandry of the taxes on trade and from the Tartars' trust in him as their tax collector from the surrounding towns and princelings. But it also came from the growth in population, swollen by the continuing influx of refugees into the Moscow region. There was no shortage of land, only of hands and labour to till it – and ultimately, to defend it. The more the population increased, the larger the harvest they produced from the newly-tilled virgin land, the larger the tax yield, and the larger the potential army.

Moscow's growing wealth and power depended on the stability of the ruling house. Authority passed from father to son, without the dynastic rivalries that had so weakened Kiev and Vladimir, thanks to the family tradition that the eldest son inherited the bulk of the family wealth. Thus, rather than divide his wealth equally among his five

sons, Prince Ivan 'Moneybags' left half of it to the eldest. This tradition was maintained, allowing one son to dominate the others, and to
have enough wealth to buy the support of the Khans.

However, as time passed, the nature of the Tartar control began to
change. From the aggressive nomad horde of 1237, the Golden Horde
of the year 1370 was becoming a civilised ruling caste, accustomed to
stability and the regular payment of tribute. And, while the Horde was
forgetting how to wage war, the Russians were learning. The Horde
was divided between rival Khans, when after a series of border
skirmishes, Moscow's Prince Dmitry Donskoy took the decisive step
of refusing the annual tribute.

The Battle of Kulikovo Field on 8 September 1380 was the first
time that the Russians had defeated the full strength of the Tartar
Horde in open battle. Behind him, Prince Dmitry Donskoy had the
forces of the princes of Serpukhov, of Tver and Vladimir, and the full
spiritual backing of the Church, through St Sergius, the founder of the
great monastery at Zagorsk. St Sergius had pronounced anathema
upon princes who rejected the prospect of Russian unification against
the Tartars. For the first time, one can begin to discern at the Battle of
Kulikovo something that can be called a Russian national consciousness. It was not, however, the end of the Tartar threat. After the defeat
at Kulikovo, Khan Mamay was replaced by Khan Tokhtamysh, who
launched a siege of Moscow, now protected by Dmitry's new stone
walls. Dmitry's heir Prince Basil travelled to the Horde to get the formal seal of Tartar approval upon his conquest of Nizhny-Novgorod.
In 1405, a new Mongol host had to be bought off from a siege of Moscow. As late as 1571, in the reign of Ivan the Terrible, Moscow was to
fall to an assault by the Tartars of the Crimea. But Kulikovo represented a fundamental change in the balance of power between Russians and Tartars.

Even the dynastic civil wars of the 1430s, as his uncle Yury tried to
take advantage of the youth of the boy-king Basil, could barely slow
the increasing authority of Moscow, which was now expanding to
include the proud trading city of Novgorod. The formal annexation of
Novgorod came with the reign of Basil's heir, Prince Ivan the Great
(1462–1505), who also extended Moscow's authority to the new township of Perm, in the foothills of the Ural mountains. Prince Ivan was
Russia's version of the Tudor monarchs in England (with whom he
was contemporary), a powerful and centralising king, who rewrote the
laws, established the beginnings of a state system of bureaucracy, and
who deliberately deployed nationalism and religion as political forces
to bolster his own authority. He succeeded in annexing Novgorod
largely because he persuaded enough of its citizens that the alternative to Moscow was Lithuanian rule, which was neither Russian nor
Orthodox.

Ivan the Great

The fall of Constantinople to the Turk in 1453 left a vacuum at the spiritual centre of the Orthodox Church that Ivan hastened to fill. He married Sophia, the niece of the last Emperor of Byzantium, took the title of Tsar (or Caesar), Sovereign of All Russia, and declared that Moscow was to be the third Rome, replacing Constantinople as the religious and political centre of the Empire. He formally threw off the Tartar yoke, but then forged a tactical alliance with the Tartars of the Crimea against the Poles and Lithuanians, to claw back Russia's lost lands of the west. It was Ivan's son Basil who finally reconquered the old frontier city of Smolensk in 1514, but the reign of Ivan saw the decisive transition from city to nation, from the principality of Muscovy to the Kingdom of Rus.

One striking feature of Ivan's reign was that he deliberately sought public support for his policies. He was an absolute monarch, but one who courted public opinion. Before launching the assault on Novgorod, and risking a general war with Lithuania, Ivan summoned a meeting of his boyars, the hereditary aristocracy, and also a general assembly of all sections of the population. This was a forerunner of the *Zemsky Sobor*, or fledgeling parliament, which was to be a feature of the reign of the grandson of Ivan the Great, who was to be known as Ivan *Grozny*, or Ivan the Terrible (1530–84).

Ivan the Terrible

Ivan became Tsar at the tender age of three, and for the next thirteen years, the country was misruled by contentious factions of boyars and by his mother who sought to rule with her lover Prince Obolensky. Power swung back and forth three times between the Shuiskys and the Belskys, two great boyar dynasties. Just across the western frontier, the once powerful Kingdom of Poland was steadily weakening as the Polish aristocracy undermined the authority of the King, and Ivan feared that Russia would share the same fate, unless the boyars were tamed.

At the age of sixteen, young Ivan asserted his power, had Prince Shuisky slaughtered by the Kremlin's kennel-stewards, crowned himself as Tsar, and chose a Russian, rather than a foreign princess, as his wife. He picked Anastasia Romanov, of a popular and not overgrand boyar family, which was destined to occupy the throne of the Tsars until toppled by the Revolution of 1917.

To counter the power of the boyars, Ivan chose his own governing council, composed of the Metropolitan Machary, the court chaplain

Sylvester, and a clever administrator and bureaucrat of humble birth, Adashev, whom he made court chamberlain. Like the English Tudor kings, Ivan outflanked the power of the nobles by promoting commoners who depended on his favour. Ivan went over the heads of the boyars to the Russian people with the calling of a full *Zemsky Sobor* in 1550. This assembly of the Church, the gentry, the merchants and the common people was convened for Ivan to hear petitions of all the abuses in his reign. In a flurry of reforming activity, the old legal codes were overhauled and the system of local government and taxation was replaced by elected officials – another blow to the authority of the boyars.

These early years of Ivan's reign were something of a golden age of efficiency and national expansion. He marched on the Tartar capital of Kazan, on the bend of the Volga, with an artillery train of 150 cannon and captured it with great slaughter. Impressed by Ivan's energy as much as by his guns, the other Tartar capital of Astrakhan, where the River Volga meets the Caspian Sea, asked for his nominee as their Prince. And by 1566, Astrakhan too was part of Ivan's Empire. It stretched now from the Caspian to the Arctic Ocean, and the way was open for the great wave of adventurers, merchants and settlers who were to add the whole of Siberia to the Russian Empire.

Expansion to the east and the south was matched, as a deliberate act of policy, by attempts to break out into Europe itself. Still blocked from the Baltic Sea by the power of Sweden, Poland and Lithuania, Ivan waged costly and incessant wars, much as Peter the Great was to later, in an attempt to open his own maritime outlet to the west. One of Ivan's first acts as Tsar, at the age of seventeen, was to send the Saxon savant Schlitte to France and Germany, to recruit scholars and craftsmen to come and teach in Moscow. But unable to break through by land, Ivan seized the dramatic and unexpected opportunity presented by the English merchant-adventurers in 1555.

Looking for a north-eastern passage to China and the Indies in 1553, the three-ship expedition of Willoughby and Chancellor saw two crews frozen to death when they were trapped by the ice, but Richard Chancellor survived to round the North Cape, sail past the ice-free inlet that was to become the great port and naval base of Murmansk, and into the White Sea. Welcomed by the Tsar, who saw the possibility of a direct connection with western Europe that outflanked the Polish and Swedish blockades, Chancellor returned to Britain carrying an ambassador to the Court of St James, with proposals for an alliance and highly favourable trading links. Ivan's hopes of an English alliance later extended to an offer to marry Queen Elizabeth I, and when that failed, he offered to make do with one of her maids of honour, Lady Mary Hastings.

It was not simply trade with the west that Ivan wanted, but also their knowledge and skills too. This was the first sign of what was to become a persistent inferiority complex, which still exists today, stemming from a fear of technological backwardness, and a hope that the west could remedy it. Ivan asked for English craftsmen to teach the Russians the arts of shipbuilding and gunnery. This seriously alarmed the Poles. King Sigismund Augustus of Poland begged Queen Elizabeth to refuse him. 'Up to now, we could conquer him only because he was a stranger to education and did not know the arts.'

The Polish reaction was not simply that of an alarmed neighbour who wanted to keep Russia weak and backward. It was also a rational response to the increasing irrationalities of the Russian Tsar. Like Peter the Great and Stalin after him, Ivan was one of those rulers of Russia whose achievements were matched only by the devastation they inflicted on their people. Ivan seems to have gone clinically quite insane at regular periods. Given his terrible childhood at the hands of regents and boyars, sanity might have been too much to expect, but Ivan's outbursts of sadism and atrocity reached horrific peaks. As a boy, Ivan was known for his wilful cruelty to animals, and as a Tsar, for his personal fascination with torture. But after a clash over policy with his advisors, Sylvester and Adashev, Ivan's perversions began to affect the realm. Following the fall of the Tartar capitals of Kazan and Astrakhan, the devout Sylvester urged the Tsar to conquer the last Tartar outpost of the Crimea as a war of crusade. Ivan refused, determined to devote his military resources to a drive to the Baltic Sea. This dispute led to the dismissals of Sylvester and Adashev when they sought the support of the boyars, to the defection of some leading boyars to Lithuania, and finally to a desperate sense of isolation for the Tsar. He seems to have been driven into madness by grief at the death of his wife, and the suspicion that she had been poisoned by boyars jealous of the growing influence of her family. So far, this is an almost everyday tale of the passions and jockeyings for power in medieval European court life, but Ivan was to go further.

Suddenly, in the mid-winter of 1564, without warning or explanation, Ivan abandoned Moscow together with all his icons and possessions. From the exile of the Alexandrovsky Monastery, he sent a strange letter to the Metropolitan, insisting that it be read out in all the churches. It was an attack on the boyars and the senior clergy for their threat to his absolute rule, and an appeal for the support of the ordinary people. It worked. The people appealed to the Metropolitan that their Tsar should be allowed, 'to rule however he pleased'. The Metropolitan led a deputation of boyars and bishops to the Tsar's monastic exile, where they found him transformed – his eyes staring, his hair and beard ripped out and white. Nonetheless, they begged him to return on any terms.

These terms were harsh, beginning with executions of some of the boyars, and proceeding to the demand that half of the country become his own personal estate, known as the *Oprichnina*, where his own laws and police held sway. The grimly familiar Russian pattern of an autocratic power sustained by a merciless secret police begins with the *Oprichniki*, the black-garbed servants of the Tsar. They carried the severed head of a cur on their saddle-bows, to symbolise their dog-like devotion to the Tsar, and a broom, as a pledge that they would sweep the land free of corruption and thieves. Ivan then nominated a Tartar convert to Christianity as the Prince of All Russia, those other lands outside the *Oprichnina*. (The *Oprichnina* is also the usual word to describe both the *Oprichniki*'s actions and Ivan the Terrible's reign of terror.)

He had no mercy on the Metropolitan Philip, who publicly condemned the reign of terror, first exiling him to the monastery in Tver, and finally putting him to death when Philip refused Ivan his blessing. Dressed in priest's robes, Ivan would take mock services in churches and plead for forgiveness before leading his cronies in another night of orgies and debauchery. He demanded ever more victims to be tortured to death in his salivating presence. He put the entire city of Novgorod to death in a massacre that lasted for five weeks. Those who jumped into the river were thrust back under to drown by teams of *Oprichniki* in boats. Ivan killed his cousin Prince Vladimir, murdered the leaders of the *Oprichniki*, and battered his own son to death with his Imperial staff. Unable to sleep, he stalked the palace at night, howling his epic rage until his death in 1584.

The Time of Troubles

With his death, began what the Russians call the Time of Troubles, as real and false heirs and the great boyar families vied for the throne, while Poles and Lithuanians occupied Moscow. But the Troubles had begun under Ivan himself, with the economic and social devastation he inflicted on the country. He spent his last two decades trying simultaneously to fight Tartars and Poles, to crush the power of the boyars and to establish the authority of his own *Oprichnina*. Unable to achieve all at once, he failed even to defend his capital. In 1571, he abandoned Moscow to the assault of the Crimean Tartars, and the chroniclers of the day record that they slaughtered 800,000 Russians, and carried off another 130,000 into slavery. Even allowing for the exaggeration of the day, it was a fearsome return of the Horde. A Jewish merchant who saw them return with their prisoners across the Perekop land bridge to the Crimea recorded that he saw so many slaves pass by that 'he wondered whether there were any folk remaining in Russia'.

Ivan pillaged the country to raise money to finance his wars and his armies. Without money to pay troops, he had to pay them with land. Ivan permanently distorted the Russian social structure to finance his armies. Long after the practice had died out in Europe, Ivan reintroduced military feudalism, a form of land tenure for military service. Ivan's gentry had little interest in the land itself, nor in improving its productivity. Their primary concern was in military service, and the state's concern was for the peasantry to stay as they were, a source of taxation, food and cannon fodder.

But many of them fled, to the border lands of the Ukraine and the Kuban where the Cossacks lived a kind of frontier freedom, or to the endless spaces of Siberia. The English traveller Fletcher records seeing fifty villages between Moscow and Archangel, each stretching up to a mile along the road, and each one deserted. 'The government officials come fresh and hungry upon them every year, to pull and clip them all the year long,' he wrote. Peasants became in such short supply that whole families were regularly kidnapped. The great Russian historian Klyuchevsky records that in the province of Tver in 1580, 17 per cent of migrating peasants travelled legally, 60 per cent were kidnapped, and the remainder had abandoned their homes and were fleeing the law. Although it was not finally to become entrenched as a system until the time of Peter the Great, the reign of Ivan the Terrible saw the coming of serfdom, the great social evil that was to burden Russia until the 1860s.

This was the rural setting to the Time of Troubles. But in the great city of Moscow, this was a time of surging growth. Just sixteen years after being sacked by the Crimean Tartars, Fletcher records that Moscow was bigger than London, and more than twice the size of Florence or Prague. Its very size and economic importance, as well as being the site of the Kremlin, made it the prize for the various armies of boyars, Poles and Pretenders who vied for Ivan's succession for thirty years.

The politics of the Time of Troubles are deeply confused, but they can all be traced back to the problem of finding a legitimate successor to the throne. Having killed his heir, Ivan left two more sons, neither of them able to dominate the turbulent land that Ivan had bequeathed them. The first, the feeble-minded Fyodor, succeeded to the throne, but the real power of regency was contested between the powerful boyars, the Shuiskys, the Romanovs and Boris Godunov. The second son, the child Dmitry, from a marriage not recognised by the Church and thus of dubious legitimacy, was later murdered in circumstances so obscure that in the next twenty years large numbers of Russians twice flocked behind the banner of separate Pretenders, who claimed to be this long-lost son of the Tsar. The first 'False Dmitry', who was briefly placed on the throne by the Poles, was finally slaughtered in the Kremlin, his body burned, and his ashes fired from a great cannon of the Moscow garrison, aimed vaguely in the direction of Poland, whence he had come.

The point about the various jockeyings for the throne is that each power group who wanted to rule had to justify their bid with a figurehead who could claim some legitimate title to the succession. Ivan and his ancestors had succeeded in creating a sense of Russian nationhood, and linking the fate of that nation to their ruling dynasty. The Poles and Lithuanians and Swedes, who each intervened to take advantage of the power vacuum in Moscow, had to do so through figureheads with at least a spurious claim to the throne. When the deaths of Fyodor and Dmitry left the throne vacant, the regent Boris Godunov required a *Zemsky Sobor* to proclaim him Tsar. Even then Boris waited for the Patriarch Job to lead a procession to Moscow's Novodevichy Monastery pleading for him to take the throne. But the Time of Troubles did not refer simply to the struggles for the throne. Everything began to go wrong at once. Famine broke out year after year and the boyars were forced to release the hordes of retainers and troops they could no longer feed. These bands of men became robbers, mercenaries and Cossacks, looting to live, and joining the regular outbursts of serf rebellions. The revolt of Ivan Bolotnikov was a straightforward appeal to class war, for serfs to take the wives, daughters and land of their masters.

The revolt failed and Moscow fell under Polish occupation and a decree was issued that said no Russian could lawfully bear arms. Only the great St Sergius Monastery at Zagorsk held out, a symbol and rallying point of Russian resistance. In 1610 the Patriarch Hermogen, imprisoned by the Poles until he died of starvation, smuggled out letters and appeals for national unity against the invaders.

The Patriarch's appeals, read out in provincial churches, helped to build a mood and a movement of national resurgence. In the Cathedral of Nizhny-Novgorod, the butcher and city councillor Cosmo Minin heard the Patriarch's letters and pledged all his goods to the cause of Russia. Other commoners and then other cities followed his example; he was joined by Prince Dmitry Pozharsky, and a national army gathered and rallied to win back Moscow from the Poles. Even the unruly Cossacks joined the last battle for the city.

Once successful, this popular uprising against the Poles turned from the business of national liberation to subjecting themselves once again to a new Tsar. They called a new national assembly to appoint a new monarch, which unanimously accepted the nomination of the late Patriarch Hermogen, and of the Cossacks. Their choice was Mikhail Romanov, the great-nephew of Ivan the Terrible through Ivan's first wife. In February 1613, exactly 304 years before the Romanov dynasty was to fall, Mikhail was elected Tsar of the All the Russias.

The coming of the Romanovs

Mikhail Romanov was not, it must be said, a very good Tsar, except that he and his successors throughout the rest of the seventeenth century did close off very firmly one important possible avenue of political development. Russia had been left hapless by her Tsar, betrayed by her boyars, plundered by her neighbours, only to be redeemed by the energies and talents of her people. The national assembly which elected Mikhail Romanov to the throne may not have envisaged that they were re-establishing the Tsarist autocracy. They may have believed, and with reason, that the role of the people in liberating the country had won them the right to a continuing voice in its government. Not so. Further national assemblies were called, but with less and less frequency, and to discuss a narrowing range of issues. The Tsar aligned himself firmly with the nobility and the gentry, tightening the bonds of serfdom to hold down the peasantry, and strictly limiting the role of the merchants and artisans, and the powers of the towns and cities. While western European countries were encouraging the growth of trade and technology that came with urbanisation, and thereby facilitating the emergence of a middle class that would eventually mount a political challenge to the power of monarchies, the Romanovs cleaved closer to the feudal backwardness of an economy based on serfdom. It was a very short-sighted policy indeed.

The greatest lesson of the Time of Troubles had been the vulnerability of Russia to her neighbours. The failure of Ivan the Terrible's attempts to establish a permanent connection with the trade and skills of western Europe had left the country a generation and more behind in the military arts and the industries which fuelled them. The great cannon and even the muskets which had fought the wars during the Time of Troubles had all been imported from the more advanced western countries. For twenty years after Mikhail Romanov was elected Tsar, nothing was done to improve matters. It was not until the 1630s that the first Dutch craftsmen were imported to establish the state ordnance factory at Tula, and the iron ore and copper deposits of the Urals exploited to make guns. It was not until the time of Peter the Great that a concerted attempt was made to force-feed backward Russia with the technologies of the west.

The few attempts before Peter to modernise the Russian system met furious resistance. The introduction of printed books (over a century after Gutenberg) meant that the texts of Bibles and prayer books had to be codified into agreed forms and spellings. This led to a bitterly fought schism in the Church. The traditionalists refused to spell the name of Jesus as Iisus, rather than Isus, as it had been mistakenly transcribed by some Greek scholar centuries before. Nor would they accept or give blessings with two fingers rather than three. These were but symbols of a deeply felt tradition, as much national as religious. The Old Believers fought hard for their faith. The Solovetsky Monastery on the White Sea had to be carried by military assault, and its leaders were hanged. Not that this ended their cause. Many fled to Siberia, seeking a new frontier for where they could worship as they chose, in much the same way as their contemporaries the Puritans set sail for the New World across the Atlantic. Many remained, some to take part in the incessant revolts of an increasingly exploited peasantry and some to serve in the Tsar's regiments of *Streltsy*, the nearest equivalent to a standing army.

The long century of recovery that followed the coming of the Romanov dynasty saw a bare minimum of the groundwork for modernising the most backward state in Europe. A handful of foreign traders, military advisors and craftsmen were invited to Moscow, where they lived in the 'German suburb', sealed off from their Russian hosts. Fortunately, it was near enough to the place where the future Peter the Great was brought up for it to become well known to him. His formative years were spent with the Swiss Lefort, the Scottish soldier Gordon, and the Dutchman Timmerman, who taught him how to navigate at sea.

Peter the Great

Peter lived for fifty-three years (1672–1725), was Tsar for all but ten of them, and was at war for all but two years of his reign. Longest and most bitter was the war with Sweden, to break out to the Baltic, and indeed to conquer the very land on which Peter built his great new capital of St Petersburg. His wars with the Turks were less successful. Although his first triumph as a youth of twenty-three was to capture the port of Azov, where the River Don flows into the Black Sea, he had to give it back again fourteen years later when he had to negotiate his way out of a Turkish encirclement on the River Danube. By the time Peter came to power, the freebooters and merchants had explored – and absorbed – the whole of Siberia. Only the peninsula of Kamchatka was formally claimed for his crown as late as 1696. It was the west, and the challenge of Europe, that fascinated Peter.

Peter caught the imagination of his contemporaries in western Europe with his youthful expedition of discovery to Britain and Holland. He travelled incognito, under the name Peter Mikhailov, in an embassy nominally led by Lefort, his Swiss advisor. He recruited over a thousand craftsmen and experts of various kinds, and studied shipbuilding and engineering, anatomy and commerce. This was the time when Peter learned the extent of Russia's need for modernisation, as well as a model of how to proceed. Planning to move on to

Venice, he had to cut short his trip because of reports of a new attempt at a palace coup in Moscow.

It was led by the *Streltsy*, the riflemen, who were the traditional regular troops of the Tsar. The *Streltsy* were a symbol of what was wrong with Russia. They were poor troops, brave but ill-disciplined, and ill-fitted for the modern methods of warfare of co-ordinated artillery, musketry and cavalry charges that Marlborough was perfecting in the wars against Louis XIV. The *Streltsy*, and the Russian armies, had no efficient commissariat, supply train, medical service nor training system. The *Streltsy* were financed in part from taxation, but also through their licences to trade on Red Square, and to have market gardens across the Moscow River from the Kremlin. They were more a Praetorian Guard than a regular army, too close to the Kremlin to stand aloof from Palace intrigues. They were a symbol of national backwardness, although they saw themselves as custodians of national tradition. Indeed, many of them were Old Believers, proudly wearing the flowing beards that signalled their faith.

The *Streltsy* had plotted a rising to replace Peter with his elder sister Sophia. But their attempted coup was typically incompetent, and had been crushed before Peter's return. He took the opportunity to execute hundreds of them as a warning to other potential rebels and to show his own ruthless determination. He cut off their beards, banned their traditional Russian uniforms, and launched a new modern army, dressed and drilled in western style. In effect, the *Streltsy* were disbanded, and the new army was modelled on the mock regiments of friends Peter had played with in boyhood. Named after the villages where they had drilled, the Preobrazhensky and Semenovsky Guards were to be the elite units of the Tsarist armies until the twentieth century.

The first half of Peter's reign was spent building and deploying the modern army and administrative base that would defeat the Swedes. The second was spent pushing through the mass of reforms which would allow that army and administrative machine to be paid for and sustained. Peter's passion for modernisation covered everything. Today's Russian alphabet is his invention. He edited the first Russian newspaper, produced lists of foreign books to be translated and published, brought the Church firmly under state control, launched a national education system, began a census, set up a postal service which used stamps, and issued rules of social etiquette that tried to teach Russians not to dance with their boots on.

Reform and administration

But the thrust of all Peter's reforms was autocracy, the fulfillment of the Tsar's will; his revolution, ordered and designed from the throne, was foisted on an unwilling and possibly unready people. Perhaps he had no alternative, and those stirrings of national consciousness and political responsibility that had saved Russia in the Time of Troubles had withered and died. But the only way that Peter could impose his reforms was by putting the country into a straitjacket. To build an administrative machine that could carry out his will, he created a national bureaucracy that was ordered like an army. Indeed, the status of the bureaucrats at various levels was directly equated to the ranks of military officers. All officers, and the top eight ranks in the civil service, were automatically ennobled. This, incidentally, explains why the revolutionary Lenin was enrolled at Moscow University as the son of a nobleman – his father, as a Schools Inspector, had been promoted into the requisite bureaucratic rank.

The system worked, albeit at the cost of freezing the future social system into rigid immobility. In return for the host of new civil as well as military services they owed, the nobles and gentry received extra powers over their long-suffering peasants. As the main source of revenue and military recruitment, the peasantry had to be forced to stay in place, rather than flee to the freedoms of Siberia. Under Peter's laws, no peasant was allowed to leave his squire's estate without written permission. Peasants could only travel with the head of their family, who had to be equipped with an official passport. They could be evicted at the squire's will, to provide accommodation for Peter's standing army, which was billeted in the very provinces that also provided the recruits. And the bulk of the additional taxes Peter raised to finance his army and his reforms fell on the peasantry, from the poll tax to the new taxes on their birth, their marriages, their hats, their baths, their scythes and even, lest they think death meant a release from taxes, on their coffins. Peter's achievement was colossal, but so was the burden he imposed on the Russian peasantry.

Like Ivan the Terrible before him, Peter bequeathed a chaotic succession, because he too killed his heir. The Tsarevitch Alexis, a mild youth whose doubts about Peter's religious reforms and chafings against Peter's stern parental discipline made him a focus of widespread disaffection, fled the country. He returned on condition that he could renounce the throne and live quietly. Accused of plotting rebellion, he was thrown into prison, and executed.

The result was that for the next forty years, Peter's reforms were left in the hands of three women, a babe in arms, a boy of twelve, and a mental defective. And the choice between them all for the succession increasingly fell to the Guards, the elite of Peter's standing army, based in the capital, and composed of the nobles and gentry. Although Peter's new nobles of the bureaucracy contained many Russian commoners, he had also elevated many of his imported advisors. And the marriages of his nieces and daughters into the Baltic and German aristocracy gave the court of eighteenth-century St Petersburg a distinctly Germanic flavour. Peter's new capital began as an alien imposition on the Russian people, and under his successors, it became more and more a city and a court apart from the land it ruled. But the German connection had one great merit. The only worthy heir to Peter and interpreter of his policies was the German spouse of a German-bred Tsar, the Princess of Anhalt-Zerbst, who became known to history as Catherine the Great.

Catherine the Great and Imperial Russia

Catherine came to power in 1762 after a Palace *Putsch*, in which her Guardsman lover deposed and later killed off the feeble-minded Tsar Peter, who was given to worshipping the bust of his contemporary, the Prussian King Frederick the Great. Worse than that, Peter threatened to overturn the basis of the Russian social contract, under which the gentry were given full authority over their serfs, in return for military and civil service to the state. While the gentry's authority over their peasants increased yet further in this period, with the power to do anything whatsoever to their serfs short of torture or murder, Peter issued a decree freeing the gentry from the obligation of state service. To pay for it, he appropriated the lands of the Church – one measure which Catherine did endorse, imprisoning the Archbishop of Rostov who had the nerve to object.

Catherine was named the Great because of her conquests. She extended the western frontier of Russia to the gates of Warsaw, coolly conspiring with Prussia and Austria to liquidate Poland and carve up its lands between them. She finally wrested Crimea and the northern coast of the Black Sea from the Turks, and advanced into the Balkans. After Peter the Great's Navy had fallen into neglect and was 'fit only to catch herring', Catherine rebuilt the fleet to fight the Turks and Swedes.

The real effect of Catherine's reign was to make Russia a factor not just in the diplomacy of eastern Europe, but an integral part of the balance of power in Europe as a whole. The elimination of Poland brought Russian troops to within striking distance of the European heartland. Before the end of the eighteenth century, Suvorov, her best general, was leading Russian armies to victories on the plains of Italy and in the mountains of Switzerland. Fifteen years later, Cossacks were watering their horses at the River Seine in Paris. The break-out from the remoteness of the east of which Ivan the Terrible had dreamed, and which Peter the Great had begun, became a triumphant achievement under Catherine, her son Paul, and grandson, Tsar Alexander.

This Russian advance into the affairs of Europe alarmed the other great powers as much as it impressed them. Fears of a Russian steam-roller, of an unstoppable military machine, were as common in nine-teenth-century Europe as they were to become in the forty years after 1945. Yet once again, history was to repeat itself. In each case, the mil-itary threat as perceived by the west was built on a faltering economic and social base back in Russia. The country could neither afford its ambitions nor sustain the army which was bankrupting the state while it frightened the neighbours. The Russian threat was, therefore, fundamentally unrealistic. Professor Bernard Pares, the outstanding British historian of Russia, once defined this phenomenon as: 'The monstrously unequal march of a great giant, whose one leg is sinking further and further into the morass created by serfdom, while the other stretches farther and farther afield, to covet new territory and to meet new problems with which the Russian government is increas-ingly incompetent to deal.'

Good intentions

Catherine is praised for her learning as well as her conquests. She cor-responded with Voltaire, became one of the French Encyclopedists, read Blackstone on law and Montesquieu on government, and was the very model of the thoughtful monarch of the eighteenth-century Enlightenment. Not much of this learning, however, actually trans-lated into the real political life of Russia. Her major attempt at consti-tutional change was the Nakaz, the principles of a grand new code of Russian law. Eighteen months in the drafting, with half of its 500 par-agraphs lifted directly from Montesquieu's celebrated *L'Esprit des Lois*, it was full of good intentions. It declared that serfdom was a bad thing, which ought to be accepted in rare cases only in the supreme interest of the state, and stated that agriculture could be productive only where the land was farmed by its owners. These admirable principles, however, were not put into practice. Catherine's Nakaz did not become law.

A similar, ultimately hollow monument to Catherine's enlightened concept of rule was the summoning of the Great Commission of the nation in 1766. Harking back to the *Zemsky Sobor*, the national assembly of previous centuries, it was a democratically chosen body. It comprised 564 members, 27 of them top government officials, and 150 representatives of the gentry. Then came the elected delegates. Two hundred towns were each authorised to elect one representative, from any social class. There were fifty representatives of the crown peasants (serfs on crown land and thus 'owned' by the reigning Tsar) and soldiers, and seventy elected from the frontier regions, predominantly the Cossacks. There were even fifty delegates from the non-Russian peoples of the Empire, including the nomads of Siberia. This was an assembly chosen by methods politically far in advance of their time.

It sat for eighteen months, with the delegates reading out the lists of complaints of bad government, corrupt judges, and ruinous taxation which the electors had given them. But it was no more than a talking shop, a safety valve for the complaints of the times, rather than a deliberative assembly that could actually change anything. Even though Catherine herself authorised the debate on the great and burning issue of serfdom, nothing was done. The powers and privileges of the gentry over their serfs, although discussed at length and condemned, remained in place. Indeed, five years after the great assembly was prorogued, it was made legal for serfs to be sold by their masters at public auctions, like the slave markets of the Americas, so long as an auctioneer's hammer was not used.

Frustration with the failure of reform helped provoke the most serious internal challenge of the century, Pugachev's revolt. A Cossack, and former soldier, Pugachev brought together all the disaffected of the land. His revolt began in a monastery of the Old Believers, who gave him their blessing, and spread to the Cossacks, to the runaway serfs and escaped prisoners from Siberia, and to the non-Russian minorities, the Bashkirs and Tartars. His plan was to despatch Catherine to a nunnery, to free the serfs, and wherever his growing armies went, Pugachev slaughtered the gentry. His disorganised host captured much of the Volga and the Urals, and began to advance on Moscow, to the great alarm of the nobility.

'It is not Pugachev that matters, but the general indignation,' reported Bibikoff, one of Catherine's most able officers. He said that the people were joining Pugachev because they had legitimate grievances, and blamed, 'the incompetent and dishonest officials, the weak and stupid officers.' Finally defeated, perhaps more by the outbreak of famine on the Volga than by the concerted attacks of Catherine's best generals, Pugachev was brought back to Moscow in an iron cage.

The rebellion was a warning which Catherine chose to ignore, probably because she judged that to tamper with the power and property of her gentry would put her throne at risk. Although from the evidence of her letters it is clear that she recognised the great evil of serfdom, she extended its sway to what had been the semi-free Ukraine. And in rewarding her favourites and lieutenants with gifts of crown lands, she transferred tens of thousands of relatively well-treated crown serfs to the slavish condition that she was the first to condemn.

Nor was she alone. Catherine's gentry were an increasingly sophisticated and cosmopolitan class. Peter the Great had decreed that their obligation to serve the state required that they be educated. French was the usual language at the schools for the Russian gentry, and travel to Europe became common. Exposed to the reformist writings of the Enlightenment, and later to the subversive ideas of the French Revolution, this class was nonetheless dependent for their wealth and status on the institution of serfdom which they knew to be Russia's bane. For over a century, the Russian ruling class was to be gripped by the psychosis this contradiction produced, a kind of civic schizophrenia which made them reformist in principle, but reactionary in practice. Catherine the Great was just an early example of the syndrome. Faced with a similar dilemma in our own day, the ruling elite of the Communist Party in the decades after Stalin fell victim to the same debilitating illness, and to the same paralysis of policy.

Napoleon's 1812 invasion

Serfdom's proponents had one great argument; how could one quarrel with a system which produced military success, and Russian greatness? Powerful enough in Catherine's day, it was an argument that grew in conviction after the defeat of Napoleon's invasion of 1812. Every other monarchy of mainland Europe had fallen before Napoleon's armies. However much serfdom inhibited the wealth and the productivity of Russian agriculture, however much it froze social mobility and precluded the growth of towns or industrialisation, however much it pained the sophisticated tastes of the intellectual gentry, a Russian army based on serfdom had beaten Napoleon's *Grande Armée* and marched across Europe to parade in triumph through Paris. (A century and a half later, equally conservative Soviet Communists were to justify Stalinism and resist change on the grounds that Stalin's methods had stopped Hitler's Wehrmacht.)

This was an argument that weighed heavily with Tsar Alexander I, who had come to the throne in 1801 an admirer of the French Revolution, a believer in the need for a liberal constitution and a critic of hereditary monarchies. Full of ideas for domestic reform, Alexander was overtaken by the war and by a financial crisis. His grand plans for wider education and a reformed judiciary were expensive, and so was the war. The only available source of taxation was the gentry. When his finance minister Speransky tried to impose a tax on the squires, the Tsar learned how potent the gentry lobby could be. Speransky was fired, and the tax dropped. And the Tsar's financial problems helped bring about the French invasion. Napoleon was trying to defeat Britain by a trade boycott. Although the Tsar agreed to join it on paper, his exchequer desperately needed the customs' dues paid by the importers in practice. At the same time, Russia introduced a new tax on the import of French wines.

The French invasion force of 1812 succeeded briefly in occupying Moscow, but never reached the capital of St Petersburg. And the French were never defeated in battle. It was the fierce Russian winter, and the lack of an efficient commissariat, that doomed the French armies, more than any great military skill of the Russians. The defeat of the French not only gave serfdom a new lease of life, but exposed the Russian armies to the far greater prosperity of the European countries across which they had marched. The instinct to reform among the Russian officer corps was strengthened by their victories. However, the instincts of the Tsar, like those of the restored French monarchy, and the Austrian Emperor, were increasingly to resist all political change.

Era of conservative absolutism

The death of Tsar Alexander in 1825 saw the last of the attempted military coups by the Guards regiments of St Petersburg. It was also the first such coup with a political programme, however vague, that included a call for a liberal monarchy and a constitution, and an end to serfdom. The uprising of the Decembrists, which lasted for a few hours on a St Petersburg parade ground, was cleared away by two volleys of grapeshot from loyal troops. Five of the leaders were hanged, the rest exiled to Siberia or to life service in the ranks of the army.

But the political significance of this botched coup was to make it clear that the traditional Russian ruling class could no longer be relied on to defend a system in which many of them no longer believed. Tsar Nicholas I refused to change. Indeed, as the absolutist monarchs of western Europe fell to the revolutions of 1830 and 1848, the Tsar took his conservatism to ludicrous extremes. Russia was ruled by censors. At the tightly controlled universities, philosophy was made a branch of divinity. All music had to be checked by the censor, in case the musical notation contained ciphers. All foreign travel was forbidden. Histories of ancient Rome were not allowed to say that Emperors were killed; only that they died. To take part in political discussion groups, the offence of the novelist Dostoyevsky, was to be sentenced to death, mercifully commuted in his case to exile in Siberia.

These extremes were the death throes of the system. In 1854, the British, French and Turkish armies invaded the Crimea, and finally put paid to the great myth of Russian military might which had overshadowed Europe since 1812. The bravery and endurance of the Russian troops were not in question, but their commanders were incompetent, and their supply services corrupt. More Russian troops froze to death on the march to the Crimea than ever died fighting the enemy, and more still died of disease. Florence Nightingale and the campaigning journalists of *The Times* showed that the British Army had little to be proud of, but at least the British failures were aired in the Press, provoked reforms and led to the fall of the government. In Russia nothing changed, except for the Tsar; Nicholas died in the winter of his defeat, 1855, the failure of his army to defend Russian soil against the invader finally discrediting the conservative absolutism he had maintained for thirty years.

Emancipation and reaction

Nicholas was replaced by his son, Alexander II, who was to be known as The Liberator for the final and long overdue emancipation of the serfs. Ironically, it took place within months of President Abraham Lincoln's emancipation of the American negro slaves, another measure of overdue reform that was eventually spurred by war. Defeat in the Crimea had not by itself made emancipation inevitable. The great step was preceded by an era of *glasnost*, a ferment in a Press suddenly liberated from the rigours of censorship. The newspapers exposed corruption, denounced the incompetent bureaucracy, and published open letters which called for the end of serfdom.

Reform too long delayed can lead to revolution. Serfdom was abolished in a complex, bureaucratic way that imposed a constant burden on the exchequer through trying to compensate the gentry for the loss of their serfs. And even before the inevitably slow procedures of the emancipation were complete, one of the great liberal reformers of the day, Alexander Herzen, had begun pressing for more sweeping political reforms. Herzen's Liberal Programme called for reform of the police and courts, trial by jury, free Press, free trade and a parliament to control legislation and the state budget. Alarming as this was to the new Tsar and his advisors, Herzen was already being denounced as too conservative by the young revolutionaries like Chernyshevsky and Pisarev.

Turgenev's novel *Fathers and Sons* is the classic expression of this curious relationship between the older liberals and the extreme young radicals that was to shape Russian intellectual life until the 1917 Revolution. Once allies against reactionary Tsarism, they were to become the most bitter of enemies. Indeed, the two revolutions of February and October 1917 can be seen as the successive and rival triumphs of the old liberals and the young radicals. Turgenev dubbed the young ones the Nihilists, and by 1862, pamphlets advocating open terrorism against the government, and the assassination of the Tsar were being distributed. In 1866, by which time many of Herzen's reforms in the law were being enacted, the Tsar was shot at by an isolated young revolutionary. In 1881, he was killed by a terrorist bomb.

But by then, the reaction had already set in. It had begun in 1863, two years after the emancipation, when the Poles launched a national uprising which was brutally put down. Alexander's reforms of local government, decentralising power to the new local councils or *zemstva*, were steadily undermined and their financial autonomy whittled away. New forms of administrative control over the Press replaced the old censorship, and the revolutionary campaigns of the Nihilists continued. The dining room of the Winter Palace was blown up. The chief of police was shot dead in the street. Young intellectuals went to preach revolution to the bemused peasantry, who usually turned them over to the local gendarmerie. In 1873, five shots were fired at the Tsar, but missed. Torn between repression and more reform to win over the moderates, Alexander appointed General Melikov as Supreme Commissioner. He abolished the notorious Third Section, the secret police, lifted Press censorship, and drafted plans for a modified form of parliament, and for elected representatives to join the council of state. The gamble on more reform seemed to be succeeding, as the *zemstva*, the embryos of a local democracy, came out in Melikov's support. But the Nihilists struck first. The bomb that killed the Tsar also ended Melikov's plans for constitutional reform. Under the new Tsar, Alexander III, a fresh era of reaction began.

But the country was no longer so easily controlled as it had been under serfdom. It had grown too big. Just as the Time of Troubles had hardly slowed the steady expansion of old Muscovy into Siberia, so the long debates about serfdom and reform had seen another, equally strategic, expansion into Central Asia. There was no great national policy, no coherent master plan to march on British India (which the British feared). The absorption of the Khanates of Bukhara and Samarkand and the expansion into Kirghizia and Tadzhikistan were the result of ad hoc decisions by ambitious generals on the spot, often far exceeding their authority. General Cherniayev stormed Tashkent after receiving orders to withdraw.

But Russia's Asian Empire was to be controlled by the steadily expanding railroads. The trains snaked across Siberia, opening the prospect of commercial exploitation of its mineral wealth. They began by bringing troops, and went on to create markets and trade. The building of the railroads provoked Russia's first great speculative boom, producing a stock market and a new financial system virtually overnight. There was little in the Russian administrative system to prepare them for the inflood and effects of unbridled capitalism, as French and British investors entered the market, and Russia's own new rich joined in. A striking proportion of them were emancipated serfs, many of whom were quick to seize the opportunities of freedom.

Emancipation had been designed to give half the land to the peasantry, reserving the rest for the crown and gentry. Within forty years, the peasants had acquired three-quarters of the land, mainly by purchase. The scene in Chekhov's play *The Cherry Orchard* of the former serf buying up the estate of the impoverished gentry could have been taken from life. The last three decades before the Revolution of 1917 saw a breakneck pace of economic growth impose dramatic strains on the social system.

Emancipation of the serfs had at last begun to unlock the chains that had kept the peasant fixed to the land, or had at least forced him to flee to Siberia or the Cossacks. The peasants could now move to the cities without fear of being caught and whipped. The populations of Moscow and St Petersburg began to swell. The growth of the railways demanded iron and steel for the rails and locomotives. The discovery of the huge coal and iron deposits of the Donets basin sucked in a hundred thousand workers where none had existed before. An industrial working class began to emerge. The railroads opened the huge cotton plantations of Turkmenia, and their cotton created a massive textile industry with yet more workers. Ill-paid, ill-housed, living at best in jerrybuilt tenements and at worst in shanty towns, a proletariat was being formed. In 1897, there were strikes to limit the working day to eleven hours.

The political debates between the Old Liberals and the Nihilists began to take on a new focus. The Russian peasants had ignored the appeals of the revolutionary intellectuals in the 1860s and 1870s. The children of those peasants, a new, alienated and hugely exploited working class in the cities, were more receptive to political argument.

Military defeat and the Revolution of 1905

Again, as with the decision to free the serfs, it took military defeat and national humiliation to bring about the political explosion. Russia was not alone in enjoying the fruits of industrialisation and modernisation in the later years of the nineteenth century. Imperial Japan had done the same. These two clashed over the control of Korea and Manchuria, and the Russians were defeated on land and humiliated at sea. Their Pacific fleet having been knocked out in the first weeks of war, in September 1904 the European fleet was sent around the globe on the long journey through the Indian Ocean to the Pacific, where the Japanese sank it on sight at the Battle of Tsushima the following May. The extreme reactionary Minister of the Interior Count Plehve had been alarmed by the growth of revolutionary sentiment in Russia, and had suggested the best way to prevent it was by 'a short, victorious war'. He had not reckoned with defeat.

But the full scale of the military humiliation was still unclear when the political crisis began. It started with the assassination of Count Plehve, in July 1904. He was replaced by a known liberal, Prince Mirsky, who authorised a conference of *zemstva* to discuss political reforms. In December, they met and called for freedom of speech and of the Press, elective local government, free and universal education, and for an elected national parliament – although they were divided over how powerful this should be. The Tsar, Nicholas II, signalled something like assent. Celebratory banquets were held by the professional classes of St Petersburg as the doctors, the lawyers, the journalists and the professors of the capital backed the *zemstva* programme and formed themselves into unions.

But it proved to be another false dawn of Russian liberal reform. Within days came the news of the fall of Port Arthur to the Japanese. And then Father Gapon led his working class supporters, women and industrial workers, on a march to the Winter Palace, carrying icons, singing patriotic songs and praying to their Tsar to grant the *zemstva* programme. Alarmed and unprepared, the Army opened fire. Prince Mirsky was dismissed, which dismayed the moderates and a wave of strikes spread across the country. The following month, the Tsar's uncle, Grand Duke Sergey, was killed by a terrorist bomb. The Revolution of 1905 had begun.

It is sometimes described as a dress rehearsal for 1917. The two revolutions had some things in common. There were Soviets, and in St Petersburg, one of the leaders was Leon Trotsky. The Navy proved radical, and in the Black Sea the battleship *Potemkin* declared for the Revolution. But in 1917, there had been three years of war, a succession of humiliating defeats and losses, desperate food shortages and the enemy was at the gates, rather than at the far end of Siberia. Above all, in 1905, the government did not lose its nerve. The Army, on the whole, obeyed orders. Some regional governors, like Peter Stolypin, who was promoted to be Minister of the Interior, proved able to maintain order. And in 1905, thanks to the able Count Witte, the government had a credible programme, which was able to command the support of the moderates.

An Imperial Duma, a formal national parliament, was authorised. It had strictly limited powers, and the first two Dumas were dismissed by the Tsar. But the third, dominated by the moderate reformist Oktyabrist Party, lasted for its full five-year term, and worked well with the reforming Prime Minister Stolypin. There was a real prospect of a transition from Tsarist autocracy to a representative parliamentary government. Three events aborted this last chance of constitutional change. The first was the assassination of Stolypin in 1911, and his replacement by a Prime Minister with little influence at court, and even less commitment to the principle of the Duma. The second was the rising influence of the mad monk Rasputin at court, which served to discredit the royal family as the great crisis approached. The final blow was mortal – the coming of the First World War. Undergoing the desperate strain of rapid industrialisation and social demoralisation, Tsarist Russia sank under the added strains of war.

The powerful and industrialised German Empire lasted for four years of war before its armies and its will cracked in the autumn of 1918. Russia simply cracked that much sooner. And given the endless delays of reform over the centuries, the price the Russian peasantry had too long paid for Tsarism, the appalling organisation of military supplies and munitions during the war, the food shortages on the home front, it is remarkable that the Tsarist system lasted as long as it did.

SOVIET HISTORY SINCE 1917

The collapse of the Tsarist regime

The Great October Revolution, complete with capitals, is the sustaining myth of the Party and the system. But in retrospect, you might say that the Soviet state was founded in 1917 by a coup d'état, or even a *Putsch*. There was no great popular revolution. The Russian state had virtually collapsed. Little food was coming to the cities. The government was losing control. Armies ignored their orders, policemen abandoned the streets. The resulting vacuum of authority was vulnerable to the first group determined, organised and ruthless enough to fill it. This turned out to be the Bolsheviks – one of many different revolutionary groups, who believed that the violent overthrow of capitalism and Tsarism by an industrial working class was inevitable – though there was nothing inevitable about their success. Lenin had to cajole and bully a hesitant Central Party Committee into seizing power. But then even Lenin himself, like most of Russia's professional revolutionaries, had been taken by surprise when the whole process began.

Far from bringing about a crisis, the early effects of the First World War were to make the Tsarist regime more popular. Across Europe in 1914, the British, French and German socialists who had vowed grandly that international worker solidarity made war impossible found themselves goosestepping to the trenches. Russia too was swept by this wave of patriotism, which was symbolised by changing the name of the old Tsar's capital from the Germanic St Petersburg to the Russian Petrograd. Even the first devastating Russian defeat at Tannenberg was compensated by a series of victories on the southern front against the Austrians. At home, the Russian economy which had been booming in peace before 1914 swiftly adapted to boom in war. By the end of 1916, the Russian military industries were able to supply almost all the Army's needs, which became no longer dependent upon British and French imports. Economically and logistically, it was a prodigious achievement. But there was a price to be paid. The pre-war political unrest had come from an economic and social storm that had taken peasants from the farms and into the factories and the instant slums of the exploding cities. Now a new surge of industrialisation put even greater stress on the social fabric. The land strained to produce enough food as the young men were conscripted off the farms and into the armies, to be killed and taken prisoner in their millions, and women and adolescents were sucked into the factories. Had the war proved victorious, Tsarist Russia might have withstood the social stresses. Had the social revolution not dislocated rural and urban life alike, Russia might have coped with defeat in war. The events of 1917 were the result of fighting on two fronts at once.

The collapse began with a victory. In the summer of 1916, General Brusilov, the best of the Tsarist military leaders, launched a huge assault on the Austro-Hungarian front in Galicia. It was the greatest Russian military success of the war. But it merely attracted better disciplined German reinforcements to the front and took the Russian troops far beyond the capacity of their overstrained supply services. When it finally turned out not to be the decisive campaign that would end the war, the morale of the Russian troops dropped like a stone. Driven back by German counter-attacks, the Russian armies began to lose cohesion, and the troops deserted in droves. In the winter of 1916–17, the disastrous effects of Brusilov's 'victory' brought the crisis closer. First, the disruption of the rail supply services, whose priority was to feed and equip the front-line armies, meant a steady reduction in the amount of food reaching the cities, and a dramatic increase in inflation as hunger turned into the real threat of starvation. Second, the desertions from the front, and the need for reinforcements to stem the growing pressure of the German advance, forced the Tsar's High Command to turn to the last trained military reserves that could be deployed – the unwilling garrison of the capital of St Petersburg and the crews of the naval base at Kronstadt.

In January and February of 1917 there was a series of spontaneous demonstrations for bread, and against food speculators. The demoralised garrison troops refused to quell the demonstrations and mutinied. The Tsar tried to return to the city to reassert control, but the Army would not join him, and he could not even command the railways to take him from his Mogilyev headquarters towards the city. On 2 March, the Tsar abdicated in favour of his brother, whose 'reign' lasted a single day. After more than 300 years on the throne, the Romanov dynasty had simply imploded.

In the absence of any other authority, the troops established their own. They, the Kronstadt sailors and the city's factory workers who had mounted the food demonstrations established a Soviet (or council) of Soldiers' and Workers' Deputies, similar to the structure which had emerged in the abortive Revolution of 1905. At the same time, the politicians from the Duma saw their opportunity to establish a Provisional Government. For the next six months, real political authority swayed uneasily between these two bodies. Authority, in the context of 1917 Russia, was the power to give instructions that the Army (or what remained of it after the desertions) and the railways would obey. And on the biggest single question, whether to continue the war with Germany or to sue for peace, a kind of political stability lasted as long as the Provisional Government and the Petrograd Soviet agreed. This was a fundamentally unstable system of government, ripe for exploitation by outsiders, whether political extremists or foreign powers.

The fall of the Tsar was much welcomed in the west. Britain and France, who wanted to be seen as the liberal democracies fighting the German warlord, had long been embarrassed by their absolutist ally the Tsar. Their attempts to bring the United States into the war against Germany were made incomparably easier by the Tsar's fall, and indeed, one month later, the American President Woodrow Wilson brought the United States into 'the war to end wars'. It was naturally of urgent concern to France and Britain that the new Russian Government stayed in the war. The alternative would be the transfer of millions of German veterans from the eastern front to the trenches of France and Belgium. So financial credits, new supplies of military material, or indeed anything that could be made available, were freely offered to the Provisional Government by the allies, to ensure that the battered Russian armies stayed in the field.

It is an oversimplification, but not a distortion, to say that the Petrograd Soviet represented the working class and the military rank and file, while the Provisional Government represented the middle classes and the liberal nobility. Certainly the key figure of the Provisional Government, the socialist lawyer Alexander Kerensky, saw Russia's future linked to the liberal democracies of the west. That meant remaining loyal to the alliance against the Kaiser's Germany, and steeling the nation to go on with the war.

The Bolsheviks and the social revolution

In the early weeks after the fall of the Tsar, the Bolsheviks were barely involved. Most of their leaders, including Lenin, were stuck in exile. Stalin, the senior Party figure in the capital until Lenin's return, had proved a hesitant figure, unwilling to break away from the reluctant consensus within the Soviet that the war should continue. Lenin did not arrive in Petrograd until April, and he travelled courtesy of the Kaiser's Government, who had provided a sealed railway carriage to bring the dangerous revolutionaries from Zurich. The Germans' motive was to promote political unrest on the Russian home front that might weaken their war effort. Although taken by surprise at the Tsar's fall, Lenin was quick to spot the opportunities that awaited him in Russia. The war was unpopular, particularly with the Army, and the Provisional Government supported it, so Lenin committed the Bolsheviks to a policy of immediate peace with Germany.

This was logical. The allies were never going to support Lenin, since his revolutionary politics also presented a threat to them. But this also pointed to Lenin's tactical genius as a politician. This most cerebral and prolix of political theorists, a pedantic veteran of endless philosophical disputes with other far-left exiles, broke down his message into three simple words: Peace, Bread, Land. Peace for the soldiers, Bread for the workers, Land for the peasants. It was a slogan brilliantly pitched at the biggest sections of his target audience, and it simply ignored the concerns and the interests of Kerensky's allies in the middle class. Lenin's campaign established the Bolsheviks as the effective opposition.

This early success led to an over-confidence which proved almost fatal. In June, the Bolsheviks mounted a badly-coordinated and half-hearted attempt to seize power. Lenin was forced to flee into hiding, the presses of *Pravda* were closed and many of the Red Guards were forcibly disarmed. The Bolsheviks were then saved by the right-wing forces in the Army. To help put down the Bolsheviks' attempted coup, Kerensky had appealed to the military commander General Kornilov. Realising the weakness of the Kerensky Government, General Kornilov then in August launched a coup attempt of his own. This was defeated, or rather sabotaged, by the troops who refused to march and by the railway workers who immobilised General Kornilov by freezing the rail network. But to defend the Revolution against the right, Kerensky needed allies on the left. The Bolsheviks were rehabilitated, and the Red Guards rearmed. By early September, the Bolsheviks, still stressing their increasingly popular slogan of 'Peace, Bread, Land', were the dominant voices in the Soviets of Petrograd and of

Moscow. There was now a direct clash of policy between the Provisional Government and the two biggest Soviets.

But at the end of October, the All-Russia Congress of Soviets was due to meet in Petrograd. This was a body in which the Bolsheviks would be in a minority, and at which Kerensky hoped to gain support. On 24 October, after imposing his will on a hesitant Bolshevik Central Committee, Lenin struck. The Red Guards occupied key buildings throughout the city, and on the evening of the next day, began the assault on the Winter Palace, the headquarters of the Provisional Government. The attack was signalled by a blank shell from the small cruiser *Aurora*. It was not a hard-fought affair. Indeed, more lives were to be lost in the subsequent restaging of the event for an Eisenstein film.

Civil war

The coup was, nonetheless, decisive. Having seized power in Petrograd, and in the course of a week of street fighting, taken control of Moscow, the Bolsheviks held on through three years of devastating war. It was a civil war made the worse by outside intervention. First, the Germans kept attacking, forcing the Bolsheviks to agree to the humiliating peace of Brest-Litovsk, signed in March 1918, which surrendered almost half of European Russia and the country's industrial base. Second, the Tsar's old allies launched their own offensives. Contingents of British, French, Japanese and American troops all took the field in what Winston Churchill grandiloquently described as an attempt 'to strangle the infant Bolshevism in its cradle'. Third, and most devastating, the various domestic enemies of the Bolsheviks – known as the Whites – also joined the fray. Admiral Kolchak from the east, Generals Denikin and Wrangel from the south were each at one time in command of more Russian territory than the Bolsheviks. But there was little coordination between their campaigns, and controlling vast tracts of territory was not like controlling the key cities of Moscow and Petrograd.

Nor was it clear what these White Armies stood for politically, whether a restored Tsarist absolutism, or a constitutional monarchy. About the only thing the various ambitious White leaders had in common was their hunger for western support, in gold or hard cash, as well as in arms and munitions. And as in most civil wars, many of the battles were highly localised affairs. In the Caucasus, the Red-White struggles were complicated by campaigns for local independence. In the Baltic provinces of Latvia, Lithuania and Estonia, where the British Navy was able to provide close support, the local patriots won their independence. But the three years of war had the effect of legitimising the Bolshevik Government, at least in the eyes of those who fought for it, or felt protected by it. Simply by surviving, the Bolsheviks proved their competence, and the outstanding example was Leon Trotsky's skill in organising the Red Army. But to survive, to subdue their enemies, to enforce loyalty and to ensure that the peasants gave up their grain to feed the troops and cities, the Bolsheviks had to resort to terror. The CHEKA, as the secret police were known, may have been inevitable, but they were to colour the future of the Soviet state, and to distort whatever idealism remained of the eager revolutionaries of 1917.

In the end, after three desperate years of fighting, the Bolsheviks won the Battle of Russia, but lost the campaign for Europe. The attempt by Budyenny's Red Cavalry to sweep across Poland and export the Revolution to Germany and France was stopped (with French assistance) at the gates of Warsaw. The long campaign of the Italian Communists through strikes and factory occupations was finally defeated by Mussolini's Fascists. In Hungary, the short-lived Communist rule of Bela Kun was replaced by what was to become one of the most right-wing regimes of Europe. Whatever the dreams of Lenin and Trotsky, the rest of the European working class was not prepared to rise and welcome the Red Cavalry in the name of the international revolution. British dockers were sympathetic enough to refuse to load munitions destined for the enemies of the Bolsheviks, but that was the limit of their solidarity. The Russians were on their own.

New Economic Policy

Victory in the civil war in 1921 faced the Bolsheviks with the problems of peace. The industrial base of the country was virtually destroyed. The famines and the depredations of the armies had devastated the countryside. The city dwellers had fled to the country looking for food. Moscow's population had halved to barely a million, and Petrograd's had fallen from 2.5 million to 700,000. Whole swathes of the country were controlled by peasant armies opposed to any outside authority. And in March 1921, even the sailors of Kronstadt, once a crucial Bolshevik base, revolted against the authoritarian style and terror of the Communist Government, and against the autarky of War Communism. They were bloodily crushed by the Red Army.

That March was the moment when the future nature of the Soviet system was fixed. As well as the Kronstadt rising of the sailors, and the peasants' revolt in Tambov, it also saw the 10th Congress of the Bolshevik Party, when Lenin established the way ahead after winning the civil war. To revive the collapsed economy, Lenin announced the

New Economic Policy, a return to limited private enterprise after the absolute state control of War Communism. Under the New Economic Policy, traders and private shopkeepers could grow rich by being middlemen, or by opening small factories to produce consumer goods. The state reserved to itself 'the commanding heights' of power and heavy industry and the railroads. Lenin authorised the issue of a new and stabilised currency to defeat inflation, and the country began, with remarkable speed, to recover.

But the other great decision of the 10th Party Congress was to out-law factions within the Party. The effect of this was to stifle what had been a remarkable open system of debate over policies, which even extended to non-Party members at special conferences, and to open the way for Stalin's dictatorship. The easing of the controls on the economy were matched by a tightening of political control. But the 1920s were hopeful years for the young Soviet republic. Although kept out of the new League of Nations, it began to gain international acceptance. Under the 1922 Treaty of Rapallo, the Germans began a pattern of discreet military cooperation that led to the tactics of blitzkrieg first being practised by German troops in secret ma-noeuvres in Soviet Russia. And in 1924, Britain's Labour Govern-ment opened formal diplomatic relations with the Soviet Union. Thanks largely to the New Economic Policy, the economy revived and by 1925 Russia was again a major grain exporter. The best fruits of the Revolution were seen in Central Asia, in the old Khanates of Bukhara and Samarkand, where it brought schools for children and literacy classes for their parents, basic health care and a beginning of women's liberation with the campaigns against wearing the veil.

In European Russia, the whole period of the Revolution and the civil war and the 1920s was an era of remarkable artistic creativity. Meyerhold and Stanislavsky in the theatre, Eisenstein in film, Kandinsky and Chagall in art, Blok, Yesenin and Mayakovsky in poetry, and indeed Mayakovsky in practically everything, made it a uniquely heady and exciting time, full of optimism and possibility. 'Everything is to be reinvented in the light of the Revolution,' announced Mayakovsky, who demanded a peoples' architecture, a peoples' art and a peoples' sensibility. Had Lenin lived, it is just con-ceivable that the Soviet system might have evolved into a mixed econ-omy within a relatively tolerant single Party system. But the CHEKA remained, and so did the ban on factions within the Party, and when Lenin died after a series of strokes in 1924, the pattern of authoritarian rule was well established.

The rise of Stalin

Knowing his death was imminent, Lenin wrote a testament, a review of the possible leaders and options open to the Party. He warned them against Stalin, but the warning was in vain. Stalin's control over the Party machinery, in his role as General Secretary, was too well established. He even managed to have the reading of Lenin's testament restricted to a closed meeting of senior Party officials. Lenin had represented the intellectual tradition of the Party, and his father's job as a senior Schools Inspector in the Tsarist bureaucracy was senior enough for him to have been an honorary aristocrat (see p. 33). Stalin by contrast was the son of a Georgian cobbler, a grass roots activist who had begun by campaigning among the tough oil workers of the Baku slums, and went on to raise Party funds through bank robberies.

Because of this background, most of the senior Party officials assumed that Stalin had little chance of leading the Party after Lenin's death. The Party was still apparently dominated by its intellectuals, and the history of the 1920s turns on Stalin's skill in isolating and eliminating each of these potential rivals in turn, while claiming each time that a fundamental issue of policy, rather than personal rivalry, was the reason.

The point was that the Party had begun to change, and its members had become more like Stalin, and less like the intellectuals and professional revolutionaries who had controlled the organisation in the years before it achieved power. In 1905 there had been only 8,000 members, and in April 1917, fewer than 100,000. But by October membership had leapt to over 300,000 and by the time of Lenin's death, to over 500,000. The Party had become a mass organisation. The new Party needed a governing body, and its administration, its system of promotions and appointments, were all controlled through the membership files located in Stalin's office.

Trotsky, the organiser of the Red Army, was easily outmanoeuvred. Stalin was able to allege that Trotsky was promoting a split within the party, over the policy debate whether socialism could be built in one country. Stalin argued that Russia could rely on no one but herself, that the Revolution must be built and defended within Russia's borders. Trotsky's complex arguments about the relative strengths and weaknesses of Russia and the capitalist world were over-simplified by his opponents into an absurd claim that Soviet Russia was doomed unless she could foment revolution in, or export it by force, to the rest of the world.

In this argument, Trotsky lost the support of the other prominent Party intellectuals – Bukharin, Kamenev and Zinoviev. Stalin then used similar tactics against them. He managed to isolate Bukharin over the question of collectivisation of agriculture. Bukharin argued that the country needed a prosperous peasantry, owning their own farms, rich enough to become a viable internal market for the consumer goods that would come from Soviet factories. Industrialisation would follow. Stalin countered that there was no time for such a relaxed programme, that a crash campaign of industrialisation must come first, to give the country the economic base that could build a military machine capable of withstanding a renewed invasion by the capitalist powers. The land itself should be industrialised, the peasants should become organised workers in collective farms whose job was to feed the cities and the factory workers.

This was another argument that Stalin won, and it would be a bold judge who claimed that Stalin was entirely wrong.

Collectivisation of agriculture

The collectivisation of agriculture, which took place progressively between 1928 and 1932, was ruthlessly done, with the most successful peasants pilloried as exploiting *kulaks* and dispossessed, exiled or killed. Even the poorest peasants slaughtered their livestock and ate them for one final feast rather than share their sheep and cattle and pigs with the collective. The first effect of collectivisation was a devastating famine in which millions died. Soviet farms have not yet recovered from this 'reform', which alienated the farmer from the land that he tilled. With the German invasion of 1941, Stalin's priority of building an industrial base, of ensuring that socialism within one country could be defended, took on a new plausibility, but with each new victory, his grip on the country and the Party tightened, and the authoritarian nature of Stalinism became more pronounced.

The Great Terror

Stalin's rivals from the ranks of the Old Bolsheviks had been defeated, but another generation was coming up. The new Party chieftain of Leningrad, as the former capital of Petrograd had been renamed, was the popular and charismatic Sergei Kirov. In 1934, in circumstances which suggest Stalin's involvement, he was assassinated, and Stalin used this as a pretext to launch the Great Terror. At the time, it seemed like a great madness, as successive heroes and leaders of the Revolution were tried and executed as traitors to the Revolution, or as British spies. In retrospect, there was a terrible logic to it all. Stalin was wiping out the Old Bolsheviks, and erasing from the Party the tradition of free debate and thought. Stalin wanted a Party built in his own image, a militarised structure of blind obedience to the Party's instructions, of highly efficient yes-men. His first victim was the Party itself, but the Terror went on to devour the creative intelligentsia, the poets and the free-thinkers, to terrorise the technical intelligentsia, and to purge the officer corps of the Army, perhaps the last institution capable of challenging his rule. To give an idea of the sheer scale of all this, by 1940, three out of five marshals, all three commanders of army groups, all twelve commanders of armies, and sixty out of sixty-seven corps commanders had been arrested and shot out of hand. Two-thirds of all divisional and regimental commanders suffered the same fate, as did all of the old Party rivals. Kamenev, Zinoviev and Bukharin were sentenced to death in show trials. Trotsky was assassinated in his Mexican exile.

With hindsight, the Soviet 1930s seem to be composed of nothing but horror. It did not seem quite that way at the time. Soviet propaganda trumpeted the achievements of the Five Year Plans, the building of the new dams and power stations and vast tractor factories. Although they gilded and exaggerated the picture, there was some truth in the image of a planned, socialist economy growing dramatically while the capitalist nations were still in the slump of the Depression with millions unemployed. And as Hitler's Nazism began to dominate the rest of Europe, the only obstacle to Fascism's triumph seemed to be the Soviet Union. In the Spanish Civil War, Hitler and Mussolini supplied Franco with troops and aircraft while Britain and France dithered over supporting the Spanish Republic. Stalin's Russia at least sent arms and military advisors, even if the price was the export of Moscow's purges to the Spanish comrades. If the democracies could not stop Fascism, Stalin seemed the only hope. Little wonder, then, that so many on the left in western Europe and the United States felt sympathetic to Stalin's great experiment, and dismissed the reports of the Terror as typical anti-Soviet propaganda.

The Second World War

The Soviet achievements of the 1930s were not entirely propaganda. The titanic battles between Hitler's hitherto invincible Wehrmacht and the Soviet Army were also a struggle between two industrial giants. When all due credit is given to the support and supplies that came from Britain and the United States through Lend-lease (the US law which allowed arms and munitions to be given to the allies was called Lend-lease in an effort to pacify Congress – a loan or a lease rather than an outright grant), the Soviet economy out-performed Hitler's. Even when reeling back in the first disastrous months of the war, they dismantled over 1,500 entire factories in the path of the advancing panzers, sent them to Siberia out of bombing range to be reassembled and start work again. In the T-34, the Soviet Union produced the best tank of the war, and over 100,000 of them rolled off the world's first tank assembly line. In the Stormovik, they produced the best ground attack plane of the war. And they bore the brunt of the war against Nazism. Soviet guides constantly claim that their country lost 20 million dead in the war. As a global figure, it may well be true. The exertions of the Russian people, and their losses, were prodigious. The war was the Soviet Union's finest hour.

But it had not always seemed that way. The Soviet war began as an exercise in *realpolitik*. In August 1939, when Britain and France were at last steeling themselves to stand up to Hitler, Stalin signed the infamous Non-Aggression Pact with the Nazis, under the terms of which Germany and the Soviet Union each took half of Poland, and Stalin was allowed to swallow the three independent Baltic States. The later justification was that Stalin believed Hitler's attack was inevitable, and this squalid deal bought time and territory. Against this charitable view must be set the fact that in the summer of 1941, Stalin simply refused to believe the intelligence warnings, from his own master spies as well as from Winston Churchill, that the German invasion of Russia was imminent. The surprise was complete. General Guderian relates in his memoirs that his advancing tanks kept passing Soviet trains filled with grain and oil and bound for Germany under Stalin's trade agreement. In those early months, the invaders were greeted as liberators by many of the collectivised peasants of Byelorussia and the Ukraine. But the organised racism of the Nazis which declared all Slavs as less than human, and the appalling brutalities of the SS, wasted this strategic chance to use the Soviet people against Stalin's regime. Even so, over 300,000 Soviet prisoners of war volunteered to fight on the German side under the turncoat General Vlasov. Whatever the unpopularity of Stalin in the first months of the war, by its end, he had become identified with the patriotism and the endurance of the Soviet people. Perhaps a government less ruthless than Stalin's might have been unable to exert that much discipline, but it nonetheless remains an open question whether more Russians were killed by Hitler or by Stalin.

The Cold War

When the Red Army finally rolled into Berlin in 1945, Stalin's case for socialism in one country had been proved right. The one socialist nation had indeed been attacked, but the industrial base Stalin built had withstood the challenge. With victory, the Soviet system was carried into the heart of Central Europe on the bayonets of the Red

Army. Ironically, this high point of Stalin's success was also the moment when the wartime alliance cracked, and the Cold War began. There is little point in allocating blame for this. Stalin's suspicions of the west, Britain's attempt to cling to a great power status it could no longer afford, France's determination to retain her Empire in southeast Asia, the inability of Chiang Kai-shek to keep Mao's Communists from seizing power in China and America's magnificent innocence in foreign affairs, all played a part.

The effect on the Soviet Union was to lock the country into a wartime mentality. Investment went into defence and not civilian consumption, factories continued in their quasi-military role, the secret police maintained their fixation with spies, and Stalin encouraged the spasmodic witch-hunts for the enemy within. The purges resumed as soon as the war ended, with those prisoners of war who had been 'polluted' by their stay in German hands the first victims. Then came the turn of the intellectuals, with the persecution of the poet Anna Akhmatova, and the musician Shostakovich, and of the 'rootless cosmopolitans', by whom Stalin meant the Jews. Whatever terrible method there may have been to his madness, Stalin took ruthlessness to the point of insanity.

His death in 1953 suggested, however, that he had retained his popularity, at least among those Russians who claimed their vast lands could only be ruled by a *Vozhd*, a tough and merciless boss. At his funeral, hundreds died as the grieving crowds pushed and trampled their way into Red Square. To this day, you can see his portrait on buses and in truck windows. The intellectuals loathe his memory, and what he did to the character of the country, but Stalin remains a hero to much of the working class.

It could have been worse. He might have been succeeded by his crony Lavrenti Beria, the secret police chief. Beria used his position to bully pretty women to his bed, while threatening or imprisoning their husbands. He cruised along the Moscow streets in his black limousine, picking up pubescent girls. The rest of the Politburo and the Army combined to stop Beria from succeeding Stalin. He was arrested at gunpoint by General Moskalenko during a Presidium meeting in the Kremlin, while Marshal Zhukov ordered tanks to occupy the key points in Moscow, to stop Beria's para-military troops from coming to his aid. A crucial moment for the regime, the defeat of Beria opened up the possibility that the Soviet system could slowly recover and free itself from the straitjacket in which Stalin had imprisoned it. Above all, it implied that in spite of everything, the Soviet system and the Party retained the capacity to improve itself from within.

The Thaw

With Stalin's death began the period known as The Thaw, after Ilya Ehrenburg's novel of that name, which condemned the vaunted 'New Soviet Man' as a self-serving toady, and the approved socialist realist artists as barely talented hacks. The new government of Malenkov and Khrushchev began shifting resources from heavy industry and defence to the civilian sector, and tried to moderate the tensions of the Cold War. The Red Army withdrew from its half of Austria, and a truce was agreed in Korea. The gates of the Gulag were opened, and millions of prisoners released, among them, the future novelist Solzhenitsyn. At the 20th Party Congress in 1956, the crucial event of The Thaw took place behind closed doors, as Khrushchev spelt out Stalin's crimes in detail: the decimation of the Party ranks, the mockery of all judicial procedure, the grim record of a reign of terror. It was a brave act, with Stalin but three years dead, and the top ranks of the Party machine still stuffed with men who shared in his guilt.

It was a dangerous signal to send to the unhappy subjects of the Soviet Empire in eastern Europe, whose local Communist Party leaders had been appointed for their loyalty to Stalin. In October 1956, the Hungarian uprising, which was bloodily put down with the help of Soviet tanks, showed that the Warsaw Pact was more of a Soviet military occupation than a free association of socialist states.

The Hungarian tragedy also emphasised the Soviet Union's own difficulty in trying to shake off Stalinism, while retaining the Communist Party system and its superpower status. Alarmed by the risks Khrushchev's Thaw involved, the conservatives on the Politburo mounted a Kremlin coup against him in 1957. They had a majority on the Politburo, but Khrushchev refused to accept their verdict, and demanded a meeting of the full Central Committee of the Party. Through Marshal Zhukov, the military backed Khrushchev, and supplied air force planes to fly in Central Committee members from all across the country to give Khrushchev the vote of confidence he required. After the defeat, one of the conservatives, Kaganovitch, telephoned Khrushchev sobbing, begging him not to treat them as Stalin would have done. They were humiliated, demoted to run Siberian cement factories or to become Ambassador to Outer Mongolia; but they lived.

This period of the later 1950s and early 1960s was perhaps the Soviet Union's happiest time. There was a new and liberating mood in the cultural world, with the journal *Novy Mir* publishing Alexander Solzhenitsyn's novel of life in Stalin's Gulag *A Day in the Life of Ivan Denisovitch* – a novel that was published with Khrushchev's support. The new generation of poets like Yevgeny Yevtushenko and Bella Akhmadulina were giving open-air readings to tens of thousands at

Mayakovsky's statue and in football stadiums. Khrushchev's journalist son-in-law Alexei Adzhubei was bringing a little touch of *glasnost* to the Press. In 1957, the first Sputnik showed the excellence of Soviet space science, and four years later, Yuri Gagarin became the first man in space. And also in 1961, the process of de-Stalinisation went a stage further, when the 22nd Party Congress (to which the young Mikhail Gorbachev was a delegate) voted unanimously to remove Stalin's corpse from its place of honour alongside Lenin in the Red Square Mausoleum.

Khrushchev's fall

These reforms were not universally popular. The armed forces never forgave Khrushchev for his dramatic cuts in the size of the Army. Some 1,200,000 men were demobilised in 1960–61, including 250,000 officers. The humiliation of the Cuban missile crisis in 1962, when Soviet ships turned back from the US naval blockade, lost Khrushchev what little military support he had retained. The Party bureaucracy never forgave him for the changes in the Party rules he pushed through in 1961, which limited Party officials to two five-year terms of office, and effectively ended their life-time job security. Although he deserved their support, the intellectuals found it hard to take seriously this tough Russian peasant who took off his shoe to bang the podium at the United Nations and who dismissed modern art as 'dogshit'. And for all his merits, Khrushchev was a poor administrator, too impulsive and too ready to go overboard with a new enthusiasm, like the passion he developed for growing maize after his visit to the United States, or his decision to divide the Party and the administration into agrarian and industrial branches.

The Brezhnev years

Khrushchev's fall in 1964 showed how far the system had been civilised since Stalin's death. Khrushchev was retired, with a pension, and a comfortable dacha outside Moscow. He was replaced by Leonid Brezhnev, the Party boss, with the support of the efficient technocrat Prime Minister Alexei Kosygin, and Mikhail Suslov, the puritanical head of ideology in the Party. The Brezhnev era had one great asset. Year after year, the economy seemed to be getting richer as the great oil and gas fields of western Siberia began to come on stream. By the time of Brezhnev's death in 1982, oil and gas accounted for 70 per cent of Soviet export earnings. The foreign currency went to fuel the consumer boom, to buy the new car factory from Fiat that mass-produced the Zhiguli car. The vast mineral wealth of Siberia helped sustain the myth that the Soviet Union had inexhaustible reserves of everything, that the solution to any economic problem was to open a new mine or build a new super-factory, or drill a new well. The result was waste. The OPEC price rise of 1973–74 forced the west into energy conservation, but the Soviet economy had no such incentive to efficiency. In the year of Brezhnev's death, one of the reform-minded economists, Dr Abel Aganbegyan, made a study of growth rates in the Soviet economy. Now Gorbachev's senior economic advisor, he found that each 1 per cent of growth in the Soviet economy required an increase of 1.4 per cent in investment and 1.2 per cent in raw materials. In short, the economy was sucking in more than it was producing. They were running faster and faster to stay in the same place.

At the same time, consumer appetites were growing sharply. The Brezhnev policy of détente brought an increasing number of western tourists and businessmen to the big cities. The example of their life styles, and the Beriozka hard-currency stores opened specially for them, spurred the growth of the black market and the corruption which was to become a distinctive feature of the Brezhnev years. Western jeans, western rock music on tape or record, western cigarettes and alcohol, and even plastic bags, all became status symbols in a society deliberately starved of luxuries. The black market expanded to embrace large numbers of ordinary citizens, and what had under Stalin been a strict and even puritanical society drifted into a state of moral decay. The corruption went right to the top, to Brezhnev's own family. His son-in-law, who was also deputy Minister of the Interior, went on trial in 1988, charged with having taken nearly a million roubles in bribes.

Police corruption was so endemic that every driver kept cash in his driving licence as a matter of course to pay small bribes. Shortly after Gorbachev came to power, 50,000 policemen were forcibly retired, and replaced by untainted new recruits drafted in from the Army and the Komsomol (Young Communists). But other kinds of social discipline were rigidly enforced. Almost as soon as Khrushchev had been overthrown, the controls on the arts and literature were reapplied. The trial of the writers Daniel and Sinyavsky, the harrying of Solzhenitsyn and the removal of the *Novy Mir*'s great editor Alexander Tvardovsky signalled not just the end of The Thaw, but the beginning of the rule of a new breed of Philistines. The KGB chief, Semichastny, joked at parties of the need to arrest 'a thousand intellectuals in Moscow'. In 1966, at the 23rd Party Congress, there was a serious attempt within the Party to rehabilitate Stalin. The liberal intellectuals organised a petition to the Central Committee, signed by leading scientists like Andrey Sakharov and Pyotr Kapitsa, by the Bolshoy prima ballerina Maya Plisetskaya, by the retired ambassador

Ivan Maisky, urging no rehabilitation. One of their supporters at the top was Yuri Andropov, who was to become the head of the KGB in 1972, and to replace Brezhnev as Soviet leader in 1982.

The widespread corruption of the Brezhnev years and the cultural repression began the disaffection of the intellectuals with the regime. In 1968, the dissident movement was born with a demonstration in Red Square against the Soviet invasion of Czechoslovakia to crush Dubcek's 'Prague Spring'. The *Samizdat* underground literature of painstakingly hand-copied books by banned authors like George Orwell or Solzhenitsyn expanded to include political journals like the 'Chronicle of Current Events', which recorded the arrests and the progress of the repression. The state responded with new catch-all laws to make 'anti-Soviet propaganda', or 'slander of the Soviet system' into criminal offences.

Brezhnev's state was ill-equipped to comprehend, let alone handle, this quiet revolt of the intelligentsia. Its policies became a mass of contradictions. In foreign affairs, it sought to woo the west into economic cooperation with détente, while its human rights violations and abuses of psychiatry intensified the west's suspicions of the system. And while administering the clamp down, there were signs that the KGB itself was becoming a force for reform. Yuri Andropov, who was to begin the process of cleaning-up after Brezhnev's death, carefully protected some of the liberal intellectuals, such as Yuri Liubimov and his Taganka Theatre, whose production of *Hamlet* symbolised the mood of Moscow in Brezhnev's closing years. A theatre under the patronage of the head of the KGB portrayed the Danish prince as an honest, if hesitant young man, fighting hopelessly against an evil ruler and the deadening grip of an entire society weighed down by corruption and hypocrisy. For a Soviet audience, the parallel could hardly have been more explicit.

One of the key words of the Brezhnev era was *pokazhuka*, or window-dressing. When a Party bigwig went on tour, new lavatories and guest houses would be built, luxury goods would be delivered to the supermarket that was on his tour itinerary, and so on. Things were supposed to look good. Brezhnev's foreign policy was rather similar. In the 1970s, détente began to wither as the Soviet Empire seemed to spread across the globe. The Vietnamese victory in Indo-China brought the Soviet Navy to the huge base of Cam-Ranh Bay. The end of the Portuguese Empire in Africa brought Cuban troops and Soviet advisors to Angola and Mozambique. The spread of Soviet influence in Ethiopia and in Central America revived western suspicions, and at the end of 1979, the invasion of Afghanistan finally killed off détente and revived the Cold War. But this spread of Soviet power was so much *pokazhuka*, concealing the weakness of a society drifting into economic crisis. Each new expansion cost the overloaded Soviet budget more money. Subsidising eastern Europe with cheap oil and gas on the one hand, and paying direct subsidies of over US$5,000 million a year to Cuba and Vietnam on the other, the Soviet economy then had to finance the highly unpopular war in Afghanistan.

Gorbachev and the second social revolution

By the 1980s, the Soviet political leadership was dangerously out of step with the society it ruled so clumsily. Brezhnev and his two successors, Yuri Andropov and Konstantin Chernenko, were all in their seventies, and each of them ruled the country from the Kremlin hospital's geriatric ward. They were all from the generation which looked back to the defeat of Hitler as the country's great achievement, a generation which remembered Stalin with nostalgia as well as with fear. But the forty years of peace since the end of Hitler's war had seen a quiet but profound social revolution take place. For the first time in the twentieth century, a generation was able to grow up without huge loss of life from war, civil war and purges, which had disproportionately affected the educated classes. Time after time, the Soviet state simply destroyed itself. But the long years of peace under Khrushchev and Brezhnev allowed the social system to heal and to recover, while a massive state investment in education helped create a new intelligentsia.

Mikhail Gorbachev was the first Soviet leader since Lenin to have a university education. He was a country boy who went from a collective farm near the Black Sea to the country's most prestigious university. Like many millions more, he was able to take advantage of the opportunities within the Soviet system, which is one reason why he still believes in it. The entire Gorbachev family is a classic example of this process. He is a lawyer who has made a career in politics. His wife is a sociologist and university lecturer. Their daughter is a medical researcher, and their son-in-law a rising young surgeon. This is the kind of professional family that could blend easily into New York or London or Melbourne. The Gorbachevs are Soviet Yuppies – and there are lots like them in Moscow.

For all the awful history of purges and Gulag, and today's grim reality of queues and shortages, Gorbachev's coming to power, and the reforms he has already introduced, suggest that the original ideals which inspired the Revolution have been neither forgotten nor betrayed. The social revolution which produced the Gorbachev generation, and remember that generation includes the dissident movement, may not have been intended by successive Soviet leaders. But it stands as one of their finest achievements.

ICONS AND SOCIALIST REALISM

It takes time to adjust your eye to the often hesitant beauty of icons, and to the proportions of Russian church architecture. The Russians themselves needed several centuries to appreciate their own culture. It was not until the seminal exhibition of early Russian Art in Moscow in 1913 (held to commemorate three centuries of the Romanov dynasty) that Russian artists, critics and intellectuals suddenly became aware that these things they had grown up worshipping as part of the church furniture were in themselves works of art.

The Byzantine tradition

Icons came to Russia with the Christian religion from Byzantium. In Greek the word simply means an image or a likeness, but after a number of Church controversies about whether or not icons were the kind of graven images that Christians were not supposed to venerate, the Byzantine Church had established some very strict rules about the way they should be painted. The Greek icons and painters that came first to Kiev to help decorate the St Sophia Cathedral were stylised and formal. Their icons illustrated the separation of the spiritual world from the physical by avoiding human models or expressions; usually, they showed God as the Pantocrator, the ruler of everything, remote and severe.

Emotion in Russian icons

The Russians, slowly but surely, began to soften and moderate this concept, and developed the 'kenotic' Christ, the merciful son of man, a Christ who had known suffering and was therefore gentle. It took a very long time for this process to develop, and it did not reach its peak until the fifteenth-century icons of Andrey Rublyov. But this development in different parts of Russia was marked, and the question really is not why the Russians stayed so long within the cultural and religious confines of the icon form, but how they managed to break away, when the Byzantine authors of the form remained locked within the old structure.

As well as softening the Pantocrator, the Russian icon painters modified the image of his mother, Mary. One rare form of the Byzantine icon was '*Umileniye*' – the image of tenderness. An example was brought to Russia where it became famous and particularly venerated as the Virgin of Vladimir. Said to have been painted by St Luke, it was later credited with saving Moscow from the armies of Tamburlaine. It made a powerful impact on Russian art because these qualities of gentleness and humanity became steadily more central to the Russian icon form – and thus increasingly distinct from its Byzantine origins.

These developments were probably accelerated by the Mongol invasions. Kiev had been the centre of icon painting and, after the city had been sacked, the surviving monks fled north for refuge, taking their skills to Pskov and Novgorod, which were relatively safe, while connections with Byzantium withered. The colours started to change, possibly affected by the traditions of Russian folk art. The Pskov icons started using green, albeit in dark and sombre tones, while the Novgorod painters began to mix golds and reds to produce a bright vermilion. And the icons started to look like real people, with expressions and personalities. The twelfth-century St George of Novgorod, clothed in bright red, now in the Kremlin's Cathedral of the Assumption, is a classic example. A steady shift towards portraiture was taking place, which meant that people were starting to see icons as paintings that were involved with life on earth, not just as symbols of life in heaven. The proof of that came in Novgorod when men started to paint icons of battles they had seen or heard of, without reproducing the stylised images of Jesus or Mary or Saint, except as bit-part players in the epic of the painting.

We will never know the identity of most early icon painters. They did not sign their work and indeed one of the clues to the way the concept of icons was changing was that this anonymity started to slip. Not much is known about the greatest icon painters, but at least we know who they were. Theophanes came from Byzantium in about AD 1370 to work in Novgorod. Its Church of the Transfiguration is his monument, although it was only during restoration work this century that his frescoes were found. His Pantocrator is as severe as the Byzantine pedants could wish, and yet the frescoes are of real people. His stylites, old men sitting on pillars, are actually witty, caricatures as well as genres. Theophanes used the sombre colours and forms of Byzantine style, but combined them with the new artistic flourishes and freedoms that he had found at Novgorod. Theophanes is credited with having painted the famous Virgin of the Don icon, said to have been taken by Moscow's Grand Prince Dmitry Donskoy to the great Battle of Kulikovo Field against the Mongols, the first Russian victory. Whether or not the legend is true, it is worth remembering that for Russian contemporaries, icons could have miraculous powers; they were still something more powerful than just paintings.

In about 1390, Theophanes moved to Moscow, where he began to work with a young Russian, Andrey Rublyov. A monk first in the Trinity-Sergei Monastery at what is now Zagorsk, and later at Moscow's Andronikov Monastery, Rublyov brought the humanisation of the icon to its culmination. His icons may be seen in the Kremlin's Cathedral of the Assumption, but his masterpiece, The Old Testament Trinity, is in Moscow's Tretyakov Gallery. Three figures are seated around a chalice, but with a dignity, a sense of shared humanity, a mutual sympathy and a reality of expression that transcend the icon form. The third great icon painter was the fifteenth-century Dionysius, who was not a monk but a layman, a professional painter

The three greatest icon painters

who used new effects, softer colours and tricks of perspective and proportion, to make the paintings somehow more elegant. His two best works, The Crucifixion and the Metropolit Alexei, are both in the Tretyakov.

This trend towards sophistication was to be intensified into a stylised mannerism in the next century. But the development of icons continued. In 1547, the great Moscow fire destroyed many of the Kremlin icons, and painters were summoned from other cities to Moscow to replace them. Somehow, the new icons were smaller, more crowded with real people, more like paintings of a contemporary Russian setting. Later in the century, the wealthy Stroganov family acted as patrons for a new school, which packed in a greater number of characters and additional detail and tended more towards the illustrative prettiness of Persian or Mogul miniatures than to the traditions of Orthodox art. The seventeenth-century Simon Ushakov even brought the long-forbidden arts of perspective and formal background into an icon that was increasingly drifting into the western European mainstream. Indeed, Ushakov has been described as Russia's 'Raphael'.

Development of western-style art

But Peter the Great wanted Raphaels of his own. Part of his bustling, westernising drive involved the arts. He established a school of drawing in St Petersburg with Dutch and French teachers, sent promising young Russian painters abroad and invited European artists to come to his court to make their fortunes. The policy was maintained by Catherine II, who gave Peter's painting school the status of a national Academy of the Arts in 1757. The results were not impressive, though there were some competent portraitists, of whom Dmitry Levitsky was the most successful. And in the nineteenth century, Karl Bryullov's dramatic Last Day of Pompeii (1833) made a great stir with its doom, disaster and toppling statues because the fashionably liberal St Petersburg intelligentsia saw it as a clever allegory of the imminent fate of Tsarism.

Well into the nineteenth century, Russian painters seemed forced to dedicate themselves by act of will to break away from the icon tradition. Alexandr Ivanov's Christ Appearing before the People was not only a Russian version of the fashionable pre-Raphaelite school, but was the first time in Russian painting that Christ had been portrayed in naturalistic form. Others committed themselves obsessively to landscapes: Ivan Ayvazovsky produced an epic collection of Black Sea scenes – over 5,000 paintings of waves and skies.

The influence of politics

Politics helped to galvanise Russian art into a new direction. The influential critic and commentator Nikolay Chernyshevsky argued: 'The goals of art are to understand reality, and then to apply its findings for the use of humanity.' A group of painters calling themselves the 'Wanderers' set out to do just that, to paint the plight of Russia under autocracy, to focus on the drunkenness and poverty, and also to take their paintings out of the fashionable salons of the big cities and into the provinces through travelling exhibitions. Their paintings carried clear political messages. Vasily Surikov's idealised paintings of the old Russia before Peter the Great's westernising reforms, or Ilya Repin's devastating indictment of the insanity behind autocracy, the painting of Ivan the Terrible killing his son – this was art with a conscience, determined to influence public opinion. As such, it bored or revolted the next generation, who rallied to the apolitical motto, 'Art pure and unrestrained'. In the 1890s Serge Diaghilev and Alexandr Benois launched the highly influential World of Art movement – a magazine, a series of exhibitions, a club. It brought Art Nouveau to Russia, and the Ballet Russe and the revolutionary stage designs of Leon Bakst to the west.

The modern movement

The west's contemporary taste in the arts in general was to a remarkable degree formed in Russia in the years before the Revolution, when an astonishing generation produced Eisenstein in film, Stravinsky and Prokofiev in music, Chekhov, Stanislavsky and Meyerhold in the theatre, Diaghilev in ballet, Schechtel in architecture, Chagall, Malevich and Kandinsky in painting, Mayakovsky and Blok and Yesenin in poetry. To a quite striking extent, the modern movement was a Russian inspiration.

It was too good to last. Although the first decade after the 1917 Revolution saw a flowering of creativity and experiment in Russia, the political controls soon began to slam into place. Chernyshevsky's words were quoted out of context to justify the grim disciplines of socialist realism. Art in the service of the Revolution was reinterpreted to mean lots of portraits of Stalin. However, there were some interesting works. Sergey Gerasimov seems to have been a believer and his bucolic scenes of happy peasants are pleasing, until you recall just how the peasantry was being persuaded to work in the collective farms. Isaak Brodsky went from painting flattering portraits of the Tsar before 1917, Kerensky during 1917, to Lenin after the Revolution. In the meantime, Marc Chagall (having begun enthusiastically with the Revolution) went into exile. Leaders of the avant-garde like Malevich, Filonov and Alexander Drevin faced persecution. The Philistines took over and have remained in charge ever since.

Khrushchev's view of art

From Khrushchev's secret speech to the Party attacking Stalin in 1956 to Khrushchev's fall in 1964 there was a thaw, enough to allow Solzhenitsyn to be printed. And it began to apply to the arts. There was a famous exhibition in the Manezh, the old riding school of the Tsar's opposite the Kremlin. Khrushchev came to look, and exploded with all the vehemence of an ill-educated peasant who suspects the intellectuals are trying to put one over on him. Dogshit, he said, a donkey could do better with its tail. The sculptor Ernst Neizvestny had the guts to argue back. Khrushchev might know about politics, but not about art, he said. Ten years later, long after Khrushchev's fall, and when Neizvestny was living in disgrace while awaiting an exit visa to leave the country, Khrushchev finally died. *Pravda* announced it in two lines: 'Death of a Pensioner'. Khrushchev's son-in-law came to the studio and said that the old man had asked in his will for Neizvestny to design the gravestone. It stands today in the Novodevichy cemetery, a striking work. Khrushchev's bald head, like a bronze cannon-ball, is suspended between one jagged white pillar and one equally jagged black pillar, as if to express the good and the bad, the dark and the light side of the man.

Wherever his sympathies lay, there was little Khrushchev could do about Soviet art. The Academy remained in the hands of the time servers who had done rather well out of a career of devotion to socialist realism. The patrons who bought works of art, the collective farm and factory chairmen and the men who ran trade union holiday camps wanted (or felt they ought to want) the traditional stuff, a statue of Lenin or a painting of the workers looking happy.

Revival in the arts

The re-emergence of a Soviet avant-garde depended on the arrival of a Soviet intelligentsia who had the taste and the money and confidence to buy something new. This has begun to happen in the last ten years or so. The clearest sign has been the appearance in the last year of the weekend open air art market at Izmailovo Park, Moscow. Much of the work on display is kitsch, but artists can now offer for sale what they want, not what the state galleries agree to take. Ironically, it was at Izmailovo Park in 1974 that the security police used fire hoses and bulldozers to clear away the first attempt at an unauthorised modern art exhibition.

Soviet modern art is reviving fast under the Gorbachev reforms. Try to visit one of the new art exhibitons run by Moscow's Hermitage Group at their exhibition rooms at Ulitsa Profsoyuznaya 100, or go to the new gallery on Ulitsa Akademika Millionschikova near the Kashirskaya Metro. The Hermitage Group sometimes puts on retrospective exhibitions of the underground avant-garde art of the 1950s and 1960s. Check also whether the Cultural Fund is organising one of its regular auctions of modern art, in its restored Golitsyn Palace on Karl Marx Street. It is only since Gorbachev came to office that the museum curators have started to delve into their basements and bring out the works of the artists who were previously frowned on for political reasons. When the Pushkin Museum held their exhibition of Falk's work, and then of Chagall, the queues stretched around the block.

It is an exciting time because the Soviet Union is rediscovering modern art, and it has a promising crop of painters. If the Moscow Graphic Artists are holding an exhibition at Kuznetsky Most, tear up the Bolshoy tickets and go. If you see the names Andrey Medvedev, Grisha Bruskin, Leonid Purygin, Ilya Kabakov or Yevgeny Dybsky on an exhibition poster, then go, because although they represent different schools and are known as primitive, or neo-classic, or formalist, or abstract, they are among the most exciting artists working now.

The sharp, almost generic difference between traditional Russian painting and the art of western Europe has tempted many visitors into an attitude of unthinking superiority, assuming that because this country did not live through the Renaissance, its artistic credentials are somehow weaker. Nothing could be more mistaken. The development of the icon as an art form refutes such an egocentric view from the west. But that is not all. The Russians have been for over two centuries the most acute and far seeing collectors and patrons of art – just look at the collection in Leningrad's Hermitage Museum. The reason that the Soviet museums have quite so many Impressionists is that two Moscow industrialists of the 1890s, Shchukin and Morozov, had the taste to enjoy them. Shchukin was also perhaps the first serious patron of Matisse and Picasso, and Morozov was an assiduous and methodical collector of the Impressionists and post-Impressionists, particularly Cézanne.

It was politics and prejudice that froze Russian artistic sensibilities as Stalin's regime tightened its grip in the 1920s. But then it was politics that kicked Russian painting back into life in the nineteenth century. Now the politics have changed, the artists are showing a bubbling new energy, and the Moscow public is showing its readiness for their work by flocking to the exhibitions. If you cannot read Russian, ask your Intourist guide to translate the list of exhibitions printed each week in the what's on supplement to the Moscow papers, *Dosug v Moskve.*

The Soviet Union Today

Glasnost, *Gorbachev and change in the USSR*

Post-war generation

The pace of political change in the Soviet Union has been so rapid in the last few years that it is tempting to give all the credit to Mikhail Gorbachev. But Gorbachev can also be seen as merely the standard-bearer of a social revolution that was already happening. Just as President John Kennedy symbolised the coming to power of a new American generation, so Gorbachev is the first Soviet leader whose adult life has been lived out of Stalin's shadow, and is thus untainted by the purges and by Stalin's Great Terror.

Gorbachev's generation, which came of age after the Second World War, was the first to have the opportunity of a formal education, and the first to have a sporting chance of staying alive to use it. Since 1914, the people of what became the USSR had known forty years of blood-letting. The three years of war before 1917 cost 4 million lives, and the civil war and famine that followed the Revolution took many millions more. The drastic famine of the early 1930s, the direct result of collectivisation, was followed by Stalin's purges with their millions of victims, and finally by the Second World War, which took another 20 million Soviet lives. But for the whole of Gorbachev's adult life, until the Afghan War, the country was at peace. And it was investing furiously in education. Gorbachev was just one of the 1.4 million lawyers and economists, the 7 million scientists and the 18 million engineers produced in those post-war years of peace. His coming to power, or the arrival in the Kremlin of someone of his age, background and education – and the essential optimism and faith in human progress that went with them – was simply a matter of time.

Gorbachev's background

Certainly, Gorbachev's own instinctive skill at public relations, at marketing his own image, and at selling his concept of Soviet democracy, has given his reforms an international credibility that would have been unthinkable for his predecessors. And the contrast between Mikhail Gorbachev and the three elderly invalids who ruled from the Kremlin before him was so sharp that it was almost cruel.

It was not that Gorbachev was a young man, although he seemed so, coming after three septuagenarians, who had each tried to rule the world's second superpower from the Kremlin hospital's geriatric ward. Gorbachev was fifty-four when he came to power in 1985. And although he was the first Soviet leader since Lenin to have had a formal university education, he was also a product of the system, a classic *apparatchik* from the Communist Party machine who had risen through the ranks of the Komsomol, the Party youth organisation. He had run propaganda departments, and then a city, and finally his home district of Stavropol before being promoted to the Central Committee, the Communist Party Headquarters in Moscow, in 1979.

The size of Ireland, rich and vastly fertile steppe country in the neck of land between the Black and the Caspian Seas, the Krai or district of Stavropol contains a series of clues to Gorbachev's character and to the brilliant success of his career. First, it is Cossack country, and Cossacks were always rebels. The Cossacks were neither race nor tribe, but Russians, Ukrainians and others who lived on the frontier, just out of reach of the Tsar's power. Originally, they were outlaws and pirates, many of them runaway serfs, who pillaged passing trade and raided their neighbours. At first, they fought against the Tsar rather more than they fought for him. When Peter the Great was fighting the greatest battle of his life against King Charles of Sweden, the Ukrainian Cossacks played both sides. The Cossacks of the Kuban, the frontier land before the Caucasus mountains where Gorbachev comes from, had fewer pretensions to statehood, but just as much pride and independence. Gorbachev has a proud claim to Cossack ancestry, and clearly relishes its traditional independence of spirit. The second important fact about Stavropol is the richness of the soil. The peasants in these parts were always prosperous. It is the kind of land that can show the advantages of collective farming with vast and fertile fields rather like the North American prairies, made for the huge fleets of combine harvesters which Soviet television loves to show.

Gorbachev was born into a relatively privileged family. His grandfather was the founding chairman of the local collective farm at Privolnoye, just north of the town of Stavropol. His father was a tractor operator, at a time when tractors were state of the art technology. The young Mikhail Gorbachev got his start in Soviet life in the late 1940s, just after the war, when he won an award for outstanding labour as a tractor driver during his school vacations. It was a distinction that helped win him a coveted place to Moscow University.

But he had been born into a nightmare. In the spring of 1931, the peasants of the North Caucasus where he was born were deliberately slaughtering their horses and cattle, eating them in a final feast rather than let their own livestock be absorbed into the new collective farms that Stalin's government was imposing at the point of a machine gun. The official Soviet history of collectivisation acknowledges that some parts of the Stavropol region were in open revolt against the policy in the year young Gorbachev was born. The Bolsheviks had come to power in 1917, in the second of the two revolutions, promising 'Peace, Bread, Land'. They secured a peace with the German armies (at the price of the surrender of vast tracts of land), but a bloody civil war followed that lasted for three more years. They brought little of the promised bread, with famine stalking the rich lands of the North Caucasus throughout young Gorbachev's childhood. And although the Bolsheviks had also promised land to the peasants, the policy of collectivisation in fact meant dragging the peasants from the small plots of land which they felt they had finally come to own after 1917, into the enormous and anonymous farms. These were where the most idle worker could claim to live as well as the most industrious, and where little could be passed on to one's children save an education and the modest influence with the local Party office that a collective farm chairman could hope to wield. But it was an experience that put Mikhail Gorbachev closer to the seat of a tractor than any other member of the Politburo he joined.

The third feature of Stavropol was that as well as the rich farmlands, it contained the lovely wooded foothills of the Caucasus Mountain range, and a wealth of cool hill resorts, health spas and sources of mineral water. These mountain resorts were always popular with the Soviet leaders, and in the 1970s, Yuri Andropov, the head of the KGB and from 1982–84 head of the Soviet state, was a regular visitor. By this time, Mikhail Gorbachev was first secretary of the Communist Party in Stavropol, which was rather like being the local Governor-General, and therefore the natural host of any top Moscow official who came to take the waters and enjoy the wooded walks around the privileged resort area of Krasniye Kamni.

To Yuri Andropov in the 1970s, Mikhail Gorbachev must have symbolised the kind of man that the 1917 Revolution was intended to produce: the son of a Cossack peasant, given the opportunity to take a university law degree, with a lovely wife who was herself an academic researching an impressive thesis on the sociology of peasant life styles, and a bright, pretty daughter who wanted to be a doctor.

Economic problems
Perhaps only the head of the KGB, with all the access to information about the realities of life in the USSR and in the west, could know just how serious the situation seemed to be in the Soviet Union in the 1970s. Although the discovery of the huge oil and gas reserves of Siberia had given the country a sudden transfusion of western technology as Soviet energy was sold abroad, the economy was in severe trouble. The impressive growth rates of the first Five Year Plans in the 1930s, and the years of post-war recovery in the 1950s, had given way to a progressive stagnation. At the same time as the capitalist west was becoming a computerised society, with robots in its factories and a steadily improving standard of living, and with even former colonies

like Singapore and Hong Kong becoming high-tech economies, the Soviet Union was stubbornly refusing to grow.

Mikhail Gorbachev had few illusions about the relative prosperity of the Soviet bloc and the west. His rank in Soviet life gave him the ultimate privilege of foreign travel, and in the 1970s he and his wife Raisa made two long motor tours, one of Italy, and the other of France. He knew too that whatever *Pravda* may have said about the mass unemployment and downtrodden workers of the capitalist world, the Soviet Union was in fact in danger of falling irretrievably behind. There were the exceptional sectors of defence and space, but the rest of the economy was paying a disproportionate price for the concentration of investment and research skills in these fields. While the United States was spending 7 per cent of its GNP on defence, the USSR was spending at least 15 per cent. And there were ominous signs that, even so, the Soviets were trailing behind. When Soviet and western technology fought by proxy in the battles between the Israeli Air Force and the Syrian Air Defence Command in the Beka'a Valley in the early 1980s, the western technology seemed a generation ahead, with the Israelis able to blast Syrian planes and radar stations with virtual impunity.

Rise to power   Gorbachev came to power in March 1985 not only aware of Soviet backwardness, but convinced that the only way to remedy the situation was by letting the Soviet people into what had hitherto been the biggest state secret of all. Some three months before he was elected to the Party leadership, in December 1984, he had given a remarkable speech which had sounded very much like an election campaign manifesto. At the time, his promotion to the General Secretaryship was by no means assured. Even though the hard drinking and quick temper of fellow contender Grigory Romanov had undermined the chances of this former Party chief of Leningrad who now ran the military-industrial complex, Viktor Grishin, the cunning old Party boss of Moscow, also had his own ambitions to succeed Konstantin Chernenko. In that speech, Gorbachev presented the succession as a simple choice between the future and the past, with himself as the man of the future. Many of the reforms and policies that were later to surprise the west and the Soviet people alike were clearly spelt out. 'Our Soviet contemporary is a well-educated person who has lived through a great deal, and who easily detects falsehoods, sloganeering, window-dressing and the like. We must speak to him only in the language of truth,' he had said, foreshadowing what was to become the policy of *glasnost*.

Gorbachev came to power, not as his own man, but as the representative of a coalition of powerful supporters that had gathered around Yuri Andropov. This coalition had emerged as a response to the increasingly close-knit clan associated with the rule of Leonid Brezhnev. Sometimes known as the Dnepropetrovsk mafia, after the Ukraine city where Brezhnev had begun his political career, it included Konstantin Chernenko, the Party boss of the southern republic of Kazakhstan, Dinmukhamed Kunayev, the Prime Minister Nikolai Tikhonov and senior officials throughout the upper ranks of the Party. In the late 1970s and early 1980s, these became the conservatives, while around Andropov gathered a group of reformers. The latter were by no means liberals in any western sense, they were products of the Party machine, jealous of its privileges and believers in the system. But they knew it was working badly and had to be made more efficient, and that the corruption and general stagnation of the Brezhnev system had to be changed. The problem was that this group included puritanical and tough-minded types like Andropov himself, or the Siberian Yegor Ligachev, who believed that the remedy was much more discipline, while people like the relatively young Mikhail Gorbachev believed in deep structural reform of the Soviet system. But in the years of the Brezhnev era, and during the brief reign of Chernenko, these fundamental differences in approach were masked by their mutual loathing of the legendary corruption of the Brezhnev clique, and their joint determination to do something about it.

Andropov's own brief sixteen months in power saw rather more of the puritanism, and not so much structural change. The first sign of the new broom came with the sudden invasion of the beer halls and the bath houses by the police, demanding to know why the customers were not at work. The second sign was the arrest of the corrupt Minister of the Interior, General Schokolov, a crony and neighbour of Brezhnev. They each occupied a whole floor of the government apartment block on Kutuzovsky Prospekt, a building in which Andropov had a far more modest home.

Conservatism versus reform

After Gorbachev came to power, his first promotions were of other members of the Andropov coalition. Yegor Ligachev was made a full member of the Politburo, and effectively the deputy leader, chairing the weekly meetings of the secretaries of the Central Committee *apparat*, and taking Gorbachev's place as chairman of the Politburo when Gorbachev was travelling, or on holiday. But the differences between the Gorbachev and Ligachev models of reform became glaringly apparent as the 1980s wore on. The tough-minded reforms of Gorbachev's first years, including the laws against unearned income, which tried to clamp down on the black market, and the strict controls on alcohol which seriously undermined Gorbachev's popularity, were Ligachev policies.

And yet the two men were locked into a symbiotic relationship. If Ligachev had not existed, Gorbachev would have been forced to invent him. Precisely because of Ligachev's known caution, his public defence of privileges for the Party elite, and his refusal to accept any western or free market role model for the economic reforms, his presence in the leadership reassured the Party faithful around the country. Gorbachev could not overnight replace the veteran bureaucrats of the

Party machine. Indeed, even though most of them owed their careers to Brezhnev, they were the men on whom Gorbachev relied to bring about his reforms.

In 1964, Nikita Khrushchev had been toppled from power because his policies aroused too much resentment and alarm among these Party barons. Gorbachev did not want to follow Khrushchev's fate, and for all the risks involved, Ligachev's presence and power on the Politburo was a reasonable price to pay to keep the grudging loyalty of the Party machine. Gorbachev was careful to move Ligachev sideways into the Politburo seat for agriculture, rather than to dismiss him during the Politburo reshuffle of October 1988. How long that situation will last, with these Party barons being steadily retired and replaced, and a new Gorbachev-era Party machine being promoted into place, is an open question. But the need for caution, to take account of the conservative factor in Soviet politics, seems to have slowed many of the key reforms that Gorbachev envisaged.

The Gorbachev revolution

It is worth looking in some detail at the main provisions of the Gorbachev revolution.

● *Glasnost.* So far, the promised law on *glasnost* has neither been published, nor debated, nor enacted. This means that the Press has no legal right to insist on going into factory premises to check safety levels, or to demand interviews or statements from Ministries or other bodies. The fact that the KGB has appointed a Press spokesman, and that the Ministry of the Interior holds a weekly Press briefing, is an act of internal reform by those bodies, not a legal requirement. Until the law is passed, *glasnost* could disappear as quickly as it emerged. *Glasnost* also has strict limits. You will not, for example, find articles criticising aspects of Soviet foreign policy. Until Mikhail Gorbachev's statement on Afghanistan, the Press did not publish the case for withdrawal, nor critiques of the decision by Leonid Brezhnev to send in the Soviet troops in the first place. After the Gorbachev announcement of the withdrawal schedule, there were no articles published in favour of the Soviet Army staying to complete the job they had begun. Similarly, though the Chernobyl disaster saw unprecedented criticism of the management of one nuclear power station, there was no public discussion of the dangers and benefits of nuclear power as a whole.

● **The law on enterprises.** This is the economic reform, which only came into force in 1988, and seeks to break the stranglehold of the central planners on the individual factories and managers. And even then, its main provision was being sabotaged. According to its main architect, the economist Dr Abel Aganbegyan, the law was supposed to take the state out of the economy. The plan was that, by 1991, independent wholesale trade between farms, factories and consumers should account for two-thirds of economic activity. Only one-third should be controlled by the state, through the mechanism of state orders for particular products, in defence, or the health service and so on. But by the end of 1988, it was clear that the bureaucracy was either unable to handle this reform, or was deliberately trying to disrupt it. Factories were reporting that all of their output was being pre-empted by *goszakaz*, or state orders, leaving them little or nothing to sell independently.

● **The law on co-operatives.** This began to take effect in 1987, and was intended to bring the flexibility and initiative of private enterprise into the service and light industrial sectors. Its beginnings, in restaurants and cafés and a mushrooming fashion industry, were impressive, although highly expensive and therefore unpopular with many Soviets. Rather than let competition bring down the prices, as Gorbachev suggested, the bureaucracy sandbagged the fledgeling co-op sector with taxes. The first plan was a progressive tax on co-ops that would take up to 90 per cent of their profits. An outcry followed in the Soviet Press, and in June 1988, the Supreme Soviet refused to pass this new tax plan, submitted by the Ministry of Finance, into law. Astounded by this almost unprecedented revolt of the elected deputies against their advice and draft laws, the bureaucrats retreated. But, in what seemed like deliberate sabotage of the spirit of the Gorbachev reforms, they came back with a new scheme, to tax all the income (not just profits) of the co-ops up to 50 per cent.

● **The electoral reform law.** This is still being drafted, although experiments in democratisation have been under way since 1987. The RAP minibus plant in Latvia was the first factory to try electing its new managing director. And in summer 1987, the elections for the Soviets, or local government councils, saw a number of reforms, again on an experimental basis. In Moscow, for example, the polling stations were redesigned so that the voters were genuinely able to cast their ballots in secret. Throughout Latvia, and in scattered cities elsewhere, voters were given a real choice among candidates, rather than being invited to rubber-stamp the sole name the Communist Party had already placed on the ballot paper. These principles of secret voting, and a choice among candidates, will be enshrined in the new law, when it eventually comes.

Perhaps more important, the local Soviets are also to be given the power to raise and to spend local money. Hitherto, to find the money to build a road, a school, a sports centre or to provide a new bus service, a Soviet anywhere in Russia had to apply to a Ministry in Moscow, or go cap in hand to a wealthy local factory. Under yet another proposed law, which is not yet even drafted, Soviets will have the right to pre-empt money from all local industries and farms. This means that for the first time Soviet voters will be electing deputies who actually have public money to spend, and thus real political choices to make. You can vote for the candidate who promises a new road, or the one who promises a pre-natal centre. This is the point at which the vote begins to have real meaning for the voter's own life.

In the long term, its effects on the Soviet political system will be profound, but it has yet to happen.

● **Human rights**. In December 1986, Dr Andrey Sakharov, the Nobel laureate and human rights campaigner who had also been the father of the Soviet H-bomb, was released from his sentence of internal exile in the industrial city of Gorky, some 320 km east of Moscow, and allowed to return to his home in the capital. During the telephone call from Mikhail Gorbachev which informed Dr Sakharov of his new freedom, the best-known victim of Soviet human rights abuses told the Soviet leader that he believed there were hundreds of prisoners of conscience still unjustly imprisoned. The month after Dr Sakharov returned to a tumultuous welcome in Moscow, over 300 more political prisoners began to return home. They included underground trade union activists, rebellious priests of the Orthodox Church, nationalists and political liberals. At least an equal number remained in prison, mainly those convicted of religious offences, whether giving unauthorised lessons in Hebrew or from the Koran, or refusing to do military service on religious grounds. Some convicted under the notorious Article 70, which made 'anti-Soviet agitation or propaganda' a criminal offence, also remained in prison, even though the official Soviet spokesman claimed that this law was itself under review.

So far, there is no sign that Article 70 has been scrapped, and it was used in spring 1988 to imprison one Armenian nationalist during the demonstrations of February and March. The attempt by the new self-styled independent political party, the Democratic Union, to hold its inaugural session in May 1988 was broken up by the police with a number of arrests. Again, the Democratic Union's attempt to hold regular demonstrations in Gorky Street on Saturday afternoons during June 1988 led to some reasonably restrained police operations to break up the demos and arrest the ringleaders. It also led to the striking sight of some hundreds of Soviet citizens shouting '*Doloi Ka-Gay-Bay*' ('Down with the KGB') in the heart of Moscow without being shot or arrested, or without the Kremlin walls crumbling.

The police state is trying to reform itself and the evident frustration and bewilderment of many police and KGB officers makes this a difficult, uneven process. It is still desperately dependent on the speeches of Mikhail Gorbachev and the occasional Politburo amnesty. Until the new civil rights law is enacted, liberalisation will be a delicate matter, capable of reversal at any time.

At least there is now a lobby of reformers, which includes not only the Democratic Union activists, Dr Sakharov and the old human rights groups, but also many members of the Soviet establishment. The best known is the new and avowedly independent Human Rights Council run by the political scientist, journalist, Gorbachev speechwriter and dramatist, Fyodor Burlatsky. This came to prominence in

1988 with its public call for all prisoners convicted of offences against the laws on religion to be released forthwith.

● **Foreign policy.** Mikhail Gorbachev is probably more popular abroad than he is in the Soviet Union and his extraordinary impact on western public opinion stems, in large part, from his foreign policies. He withdrew Soviet troops from Afghanistan, he has negotiated the INF Treaty which scrapped the medium- and shorter-range missiles of the Warsaw Pact and NATO, and he is widely perceived to be genuine in his constant calls for nuclear disarmament. However, a degree of caution is advisable. There is a great deal of circumstantial evidence that, despite the barrage of propaganda against the American SDI or Star Wars programme, the Soviet Union has been working on its own parallel programme for rather longer. The USSR first tested a primitive anti-satellite weapon in 1975. Moreover, while making some grandiose speeches about the need to cut conventional forces in Europe, the USSR is not exactly forcing the pace at the talks in Vienna about the amount of verification and inspection that will be required to monitor any agreement. The twenty Soviet divisions in East Germany alone outnumber the NATO divisions they face on the European central front, where the Soviet side (quite apart from the Warsaw Pact allies) has a powerful advantage in tanks, which are the classic weapon of attack. Mikhail Gorbachev's historic speech to the United Nations in December 1988, when he promised to withdraw six divisions from eastern Europe, and to cut the Army by 500,000 men, has reassured many sceptics. A dramatic and welcome new era of disarmament and détente may well lie ahead of us, but there will have to be a lot of diplomatic negotiation first. And while the cream of the Soviet Army is poised on the starting blocks in eastern Europe, and while the Berlin Wall continues to symbolise the kind of frontier the Warsaw Pact wants with the west, there are good reasons for caution.

The Soviet media

Glasnost

Glasnost means openness, or transparency, which is how the French translate it. It does not come from *glaza*, the word for eye, but from the Old Slavonic root of *golos*, or voice. It could be translated as outspokenness, but it also has a meaning in the Orthodox Church of speaking out collectively.

Even if you speak no Russian, you can still get a foretaste of *glasnost*. Before you visit the Soviet Union, buy one of the English-language versions of *Pravda* now available, or subscribe to *Moscow News*, *Soviet Russia*, *Soviet Panorama*, *Soviet Weekly* or to any one of the large number of Soviet English-language magazines now available. To read one is to realise that the Soviet motives for publishing quite so many English-language journals are not purely altruistic. In the words of Lenin, which *Pravda* cites every 5 May, Press day, 'The newspaper is an agitator and organiser on behalf of the Party'. But the quality of the Soviet media, whether for domestic or foreign consumption, has been transformed in the brief years since Gorbachev came to power.

There are several reasons why the media has been so important to Gorbachev's reforms. One major factor is that because so many of the senior journalists are of Gorbachev's generation and professionally and temperamentally inclined towards openness, the media was a natural ally. A second reason is that the media was one way to appeal to the Soviet public over the heads of the Party machine; an attempt to build something like a force of public opinion in the country. Indeed, many senior Party bureaucrats in the provinces have tried to ensure that *glasnost* is restricted to the Moscow Press, and is not available across the country. The best known case, in the Ukraine mining district of Voroshilovgrad, saw the editor of '*Soviet Miner*' framed and arrested by the KGB and interrogated round the clock for thirteen days. His offence was to have investigated local corruption, and the links between the police and top Party officials. He later died, as a direct result of his maltreatment. However, thanks to campaigning journalists on *Pravda*, the case was publicised, the editor vindicated, the regional KGB chiefs and Party baron sacked and disgraced, and the former head of the KGB, Viktor Chebrikov, wrote a letter of regret that was published on the front page of *Pravda* in January 1987. The third reason for the importance of *glasnost* is that by comparison with the economy, or the education system, or the Party machine, the media was a relatively simple institution to reform, because what you see is what you get. The Press allows its output, its reforming performance, to be monitored week by week.

The Press   It is striking how limited the impact of *glasnost* has been. As Gorbachev has complained, there has been little sign of it in the republican and provincial Press, with the exception of the traditionally liberal Baltic Republics. And even in the papers and magazines that are published in Moscow and distributed across the country, there are marked differences of enthusiasm for the new freedoms. There are two publications which can be described as the standard-bearers of *glasnost*. One is *Moscow News*, with a limited circulation of 600,000 copies a week in the Russian language. Published by the Council of Friendship Societies for foreign and tourist consumption, *Moscow News* comes in English, French, Spanish, Arabic and German versions. The second is the Russian-language weekly picture magazine, *Ogonyok* (Little Flame), edited by the Ukrainian poet, Vitaly Korotich. Its circulation of 4 million a week makes it an influential journal, but ironically, until Korotich became editor, it was known as a voice of conservative Russian nationalism.

Ogonyok took the lead in publishing long-banned authors. It was the first to reprint the poems of Gumilyov, who was shot as a counter-revolutionary in 1921. Its best campaign was to push for the rehabilitation of Nikolay Bukharin, the relatively liberal Bolshevik theorist shot by Stalin in 1938. Bukharin's theories on agriculture, critical of collectivisation and suspecting that the best guarantee of high productivity might be the prosperous farmer who owned his own land, were close to those of Gorbachev. And when *Ogonyok* published the letter to Gorbachev written by Bukharin's widow, pleading for his rehabilitation, there was little doubt that it had top-level approval. Similarly, when *Ogonyok* published the first-ever detailed figures of the numbers of Generals, Marshals and other senior military men shot during Stalin's purges, it cited Ministry of Defence figures. *Ogonyok* was not defying the Soviet establishment by printing such material, but was clearly carrying out the policies of the establishment's liberal wing.

Moscow News, although sometimes dismissed as 'a paper for foreigners' and thus not seriously engaged in the domestic political debate, has become the crucial symbol of *glasnost*. The first publication to report on strikes in Soviet factories, the first to question the decision to deploy SS-20 missiles, the first to give a platform to the artistic and literary exiles of the Brezhnev years, it has pushed forward the frontiers of *glasnost*, and the possibilities of Soviet journalism. (I should declare an interest here for it was *Moscow News* which asked me to be the first western journalist to contribute regularly to a Soviet magazine. Nor was I censored, even when I wrote that it was time for a public memorial to the victims of Stalin's purges.) Its importance in the domestic debate became obvious when the Kremlin's number two, the conservative Yegor Ligachev, singled out the 'ersatz journalism of *Moscow News*' as one of the excesses of reform of which he disapproved, during the 19th Party Conference in 1988.

No other newspaper or magazine has stuck its neck out quite so far, nor so regularly as *Ogonyok* and *Moscow News*. *Literaturnaya Gazeta*, the weekly journal of the Writers' Union, and known to the intelligentsia by the affectionate diminutive 'Literaturka' comes a distant but still respectable third in the *glasnost* stakes. This is thanks mainly to two outspoken and well-known journalists, the political commentator Fyodor Burlatsky and the legal expert Arkady Vaksberg, and their influence stems from their status as recognised Gorbachev advisors.

The daily papers are, perhaps inevitably, rather more staid. Until the vaunted new Press law is published, the ruling principle is that phrase of Lenin's which still shines out in bright neon over Smolenskaya Square, 'The Soviet Press is the strongest weapon in the hands of the Party'. As the official organ of the Central Committee of the Party, *Pravda* is restrained in its criticism. It has been losing readers in the *glasnost* era, and threatens to drop below a 10 million circulation. By contrast, *Izvestia*, the evening paper which is the voice of the

Supreme Soviet, or the 'elected' government, is going through its biggest circulation boom since the days when it was edited by Khrushchev's son-in-law, and was thus able to wangle more newsprint than *Pravda*. But in the 1980s, *Izvestia*'s rise in circulation in two years from 6.4 million to over 9 million has been based on the traditional newspaper virtues of news and campaigning. *Izvestia* was by far the most informative and critical Soviet newspaper on the Chernobyl nuclear disaster. And when *glasnost* was suspended throughout the Caucasus during the Armenian–Azerbaijani crisis over the disputed territory of Nagorno–Karabakh in 1988, *Izvestia*'s coverage was the fullest. The paper also led the campaign against the Ministry of Finance's attempt to tax the recently born co-operative movement into extinction. It also has a deservedly popular new section for outspoken letters, titled 'Bet you daren't print this'.

But in terms of circulation, it is not easy to argue that *glasnost* pays. As before *glasnost*, the biggest seller remains the trade union daily, *Trud* (it means Labour), which is the nearest the Soviet Press comes to sensationalism, with regular articles on UFOs, Atlantis, folk medicine, acupuncture and the like. As a result, it sells 18 million daily. *Komsomolskaya Pravda*, the official organ of the Komsomol, the Party Youth League, sells 17 million, helped along by the occasional rather token article on rock music, a newly interesting letters page, which has even acknowledged the existence of homosexuality, and a steady increase in its foreign coverage.

The literary journals

The other symbols of *glasnost* have been the 'thick journals', the heavyweight literary magazines, like *Novy Mir* (New World) which was the pioneer of the earlier cultural thaw under Khrushchev, the first Soviet journal to publish Solzhenitsyn's novel of Stalin's Gulag, *A Day in the Life of Ivan Denisovitch*. *Novy Mir* has now continued that tradition, publishing George Orwell's classic anti-totalitarian novel *1984* – and doubling its circulation, to 1.5 million copies a month in the process. One of the ways in which this new thaw under Gorbachev goes deeper and spreads wider than the Khrushchev thaw of thirty years ago is that these thick literary monthlies have been vying to publish the forbidden fruit of the past. *Oktyabr* ran Anna Akhmatova's long-banned poem *Requiem*, comparing the mothers of Stalin's purge victims (and she herself was one) to Christ's mother standing at the foot of the cross.

Kommunist, the theoretical journal of the Party, began reprinting the banned essays of the liberal Hungarian Marxist Georgy Lukacs, and articles by Bukharin even before his formal rehabilitation. And *Neva*, a Leningrad-based magazine, began in the summer of 1988 to publish the memoirs of Nadezhda Mandelstam, the most devastating personal account of what Stalinism did to the poets and writers and intellectuals of his time. All the other accounts of Stalin's terror explain how he wiped out the officer corps, killed off the Old Bolsheviks and deliberately murdered the best and brightest of his time. Mandelstam's memoirs make it clear that in targeting the poets and the dreamers, Stalin was trying to rip out the country's very soul. *Glasnost* was not something that happened overnight. It was always a gradual process, inching back the boundaries of public debate. And for many Russian intellectuals, one key test of *glasnost* was whether Mandelstam's wife's memoirs would ever be published. My own was whether Roy Medvedev's magisterial history of the Terror, *Let History Judge*, would be published, and arrangements for this are now under way. The big hurdle still to be cleared is whether Solzhenitsyn's *Gulag Archipelago* will ever come out in the long-suffering land in which he wrote it.

Equally reassuring, in a perverse kind of way, is that there are other magazines taking a very different political line. *Molodaya Gvardia*, (Young Guard), is the journal of the Komsomol (Young Communist League), and has for many years under the editorship of Anatoly Ivanov been the mouthpiece of a kind of national Bolshevism. For example, it supports the so-called conservation society *Pamyat* (Memory), whose members are keen to protect what is left of the old Russian heritage. *Pamyat*'s membership has increasingly been infiltrated by Russian nationalists so extreme they verge on neo-fascism. Their leader has a bodyguard who all wear black shirts, and they are openly anti-semitic. The journal *Molodaya Gvardia* claims that *Pamyat* is a worthy, patriotic and much misunderstood organisation and itself has a whiff of neo-fascism about it. It has sneeringly noted that many of the newly-published and long-banned writers were Jewish, attacked the fashionable liberalism of *Ogonyok*, and given a kind of theoretical and literary support to the cautious, conservative wing of the Party that says Gorbachev is going too far, too fast.

Other journals, like *Moskva* and *Nash Sovremennik* (Our Contemporary), take a similar line, and though the unpleasant way they state their views may be worrying, the fact that the once-monolithic Soviet Press is now arguing and speaking in different voices is heartening. *Samizdat*, (self-published), or underground journals still exist, even in these days of *glasnost*, although they no longer have the spread of distribution, nor the political weight, of the classic 'Chronicle of Current Events' of the Brezhnev years. One of the boldest of today's *Samizdat* is *Poedinok* (Duel), published underground on laboriously-typed carbon copies by some of the activists who later formed the Democratic Union. *Poedinok* has broken the bounds of censorship that still remain. When the exiled Soviet poet Josef Brodsky won the Nobel Prize for literature in 1987, *Poedinok* published his poems, when the mainstream media could not. It also published the secret clauses of the Nazi–Soviet pact of 1939, through which the Baltic States of Estonia, Latvia and Lithuania were to fall under Soviet rule. It comes out every two months or so, in an edition of sixty copies, and readers are supposed to type a new copy before passing it on. In the old days of the dissident movement and *Samizdat*, the late 1960s and early 1970s, people would do the retyping job religiously. These days, as one *Poedinok* writer once glumly told me: 'After reading *Ogonyok* and *Moscow News* and *Literary Gazette* and *Novy Mir*, people barely have time to read *Poedinok*, let alone recopy it.'

The trans-formation of Soviet TV

One of the great technical feats of the Brezhnev era was to spread television across the country. The Soviet Union was an early pioneer in the use of satellite television to give blanket coverage, and as an instrument of internal propaganda, the medium was obviously useful for the Soviet authorities, but it was not used to bludgeon this vast multi-ethnic state into monoglot Russification. Each Republic has a channel broadcasting in the local language, as well as the national channels from Moscow and Leningrad and the educational channel.

Before *glasnost*, Soviet television was very boring. One of its favourite programmes was 'Travellers' Club', which people used to watch for glimpses of life in the west. One reason for watching the news was to look behind the shoulder of the Soviet reporters speaking on the streets of London, New York and Paris and see the death-throes of capitalist society. Although there were some good entertainment shows, and some excellent drama series like the Leningrad studios' version of Sherlock Holmes, or the wartime spy thriller 'Seven Days in May', the news and current events programmes had little credibility.

One of the first job changes Gorbachev made when coming to power was to put a career KGB officer called Boris Aksyonov, who had also been Ambassador to Poland during the tricky time of Solidarity, in charge of *Gosteleradio*, the state broadcasting monopoly. And with a handful of new programmes, the world's biggest broadcasting system was hauled into the age of *glasnost*.

The first new programme to attract attention was 'Twelfth Story', a live discussion show which put Government Ministers and top officials in the hot seat, fielding questions phoned in from viewers across the country. We saw the Minister for Automobile Production being told by auto workers that the reason Soviet cars were so unreliable was that the Ministers and planners who set the production targets had never been on a shop floor in their lives, and also the Minister of Justice saying that yes, there was a serious problem of police corruption. 'To 16 and Older' was a youth programme that took cameras into the streets and discos to interview Soviet youngsters, and to hear their complaints about schools, their parents, the way that only the well-connected kids seemed to get into the best universities and even the threat of being called up for the Afghan War. 'To Midnight and After' produced the country's first late-night talk show host, Vladimir Molchanov. He ran film of Soviet punks rioting and of rock concerts and talked to sociologists about this alarming problem of youth alienation. *'Vzglyad'* (Glance) went further. In what became the most-watched programme in the country, they mixed western rock videos with investigative journalism, sending television cameras to film Soviet prostitutes and their clients, showing them breaking into bedrooms as trousers were hurriedly hauled on. Then came breakfast TV, a new programme called '120 Minutes', consisting of chat and interviews and a less than reverent look at that day's Soviet papers.

Vremya (Time), the 9 p.m. evening news, changed more than just the opening titles. The fleets of combine harvesters continued to sail proudly over the steppe, but now the commentator would ask how much of this grain was being made into bread, and how much was wasted in the rotten distribution and transport system. The news clips from the west began to look beyond the unemployed and the anti-war protesters. There was one celebrated story on McDonald's Hamburgers, with the Soviet reporter going into a Canadian store, and finally, mouth full of burger, saying plaintively to the camera: 'So cheap, so clean, so good – why can't we have restaurants like this in Moscow?'.

And after the news came the programme 'Spotlight on *Perestroika*', the flagship of televised *glasnost*. The cameras went into the warehouses to show hundreds of tons of vegetables rotting while the shops were empty. They filmed interviews with factory managers who claimed that the plans were being fulfilled, the products delivered on time – and then the interviewer accused them of lying and showed film to prove it. It was the kind of programme that sent shockwaves of alarm throughout the Soviet bureaucracy. Hitherto, to be invited to give an interview on Soviet television was a chance for self-glorification. Now it could be a trap. It was also unprecedented and riveting television for the viewers, and *Gosteleradio* claimed that 180 million people (out of a population of 285 million) tuned in every night.

But in the course of 1988, a series of television history documentaries was screened that had been long in the making. For the first time, the film makers were given access to the Party's film archives and programme after programme began to appear on Stalin and Stalinism. The clear political purpose was to rally support behind Gorbachev's reforms, by exploding the popular mythology about Stalin as a tough but necessary leader, the man who had won the war and the respect of the world. But it went further, with programmes that featured Nikita Khrushchev, an 'un-person' since his fall in 1964. It was an attempt to begin the long process of returning to the Soviet people their history. History used to be whatever the Party said it was, now the television documentaries suggested that there was enough historical evidence to let people decide for themselves. There was film of the prisoners building the White Sea Canal, which had been hailed as one of Stalin's greatest construction projects. There was film of Bukharin at his show-trial in 1938. There were scientists still alive who could recount how they had been put into concentration camps in Stalin's time. There was film of Khrushchev during the Cuban missile crisis.

Again, it was a gradual process, not a single leap from a censored society to media freedom, and there are still no public reassessments of the role of Soviet troops in crushing the risings in East Germany in 1953, in Hungary in 1956 and in Czechoslovakia in 1968. But the difference is that three years of *glasnost* on television, seen by tens of millions of people, has had a much greater impact on the Soviet public than the partial *glasnost* in the Press, whose effect has largely been limited to the intelligentsia. For the Ivan and Ludmilla in the street, and in the provinces far from Moscow, if you ask them about *glasnost*, they will talk about television, not *Izvestia* or *Moscow News*.

Talking peace and politics

You will often hear the words *'Mir i Druzhba'*. They mean Peace and Friendship and Soviet officials use them with what quickly becomes cloying frequency. Admirable as the sentiments are, one soon starts to nurture unworthy thoughts about their motives. A curious feature of the Russian language is that the word *Mir* means peace, but it also means the world. So the Russian toast *'Miru Mir'* means Peace to the World. And when the average Russian citizen says they want *'Mir'*, you can reckon that they are being pacific. But when a lot of Soviet officials use the word, what they really mean is that they would like to run the planet.

For the past seventy years, the Soviet state has run a very large propaganda department designed to make people at home and abroad support their point of view and oppose that of the capitalist world. They have scored some staggering successes, notably in the 1930s, when many European and American liberals and socialists closed their eyes to the horrors of Stalin's purges. Soviet propaganda has been rather less successful in our own day. But even when the shameful treatment of dissidents like Dr Andrey Sakharov and Alexander Solzhenitsyn left the west in little doubt that it remained a deeply unpleasant regime, Moscow's peace campaigns found considerable acceptance in the west.

The Soviet Peace Committee, a nominally independent body funded by public subscription, invited endless western peace delegations to conferences and on fact-finding tours. Some of the delegates were very woolly-minded, unable to realise that a system which built a Berlin Wall to keep its people in, or which would not give its citizens a chance to vote out the government, or which imprisoned its own unofficial peace campaigners, might not be altogether trustworthy. Oddly enough, the people who seemed most fooled by all the propaganda were the Soviet officials themselves, who became convinced in the early 1980s that the western peace movement would be able to stop NATO's installation of Cruise and Pershing missiles.

The Gorbachev thaw has brought some major changes to the work of the Peace Committee. Yuri Zhukov, the Neanderthal cold warrior and *Pravda* veteran who used to run the Committee, has been replaced by the bright and urbane Genrikh Borovik, a heavyweight Soviet television commentator whose son did some of the most impressive journalism from the Afghan War. Under Borovik, the Committee has begun to acknowledge the existence of the unofficial Soviet peace movement, like the Group for Trust, whose members were regularly arrested in the past. The Committee has not yet got to the point of criticising Soviet policy, but at least they are now prepared to agree that the Afghan invasion was a mistake, and that it might not have been a good idea to deploy SS-20 missiles at the end of the 1970s.

Whether you are a peace delegate, or a straightforward tourist, you can expect to come up against some part of the big Red machine that is the propaganda *apparat*. It may be an arranged discussion session with Soviet students or factory workers, or simply a rather loaded commentary by a tour guide – you can hear some bizarre versions of how the Baltic States of Estonia, Latvia and Lithuania became absorbed into the Soviet Union.

You should not let this worry you too much. The Soviet Union constantly propagandises its own people as well as its guests. Do not feel you have to defend the policies of the west, nor apologise for them. You are unlikely to make any converts, however well you argue the case for nuclear weapons, Star Wars, or the abolition of the Communist Party. Do not take the propaganda too seriously, because few intelligent Soviets do. But if you are put on the defensive – and I have seen a group of American adults reduced to tears by one 'friendly discussion session' – feel free to toss the following questions back.

• Britain and the United States have abolished military conscription. Why does the Soviet Union not do the same?

• NATO is a voluntary association. NATO troops withdrew from France in 1968 at French request and the US Air Force withdrew from Spain when asked to do so in 1988. Would Soviet troops withdraw from any eastern European country if asked to do so?

• Why was the Berlin Wall built, and why is it still there?

• The Communist Party has a poor record of government, with the terror under Stalin, the voluntarism under Khrushchev, the stagnation under Brezhnev. Why continue with the one-party system when it works so badly?

Religion

After seventy years of persecution, the Russian Orthodox Church seems to be entering into a new and highly promising relationship with the Soviet state. The year 1988 saw the thousandth anniversary of the introduction of Christianity to Russia, with Prince Vladimir of Kiev's decision to baptise his pagan subjects in wholesale batches in the River Dniepr. To celebrate this event on an international scale, the Danilovsky Monastery was returned to the Church as a new headquarters and centre for the celebration of the Christian millenium. The monks returned to Moscow for the first time since the 1920s, the Patriarch was given a well-publicised audience with Mikhail Gorbachev, the Church was given the right to name saints once more, and the great Monastery of the Caves at Kiev was also handed back to the Church authorities. At the same time, a new law on religion and Church rights was being prepared, in consultation with the Church. It was expected to increase the legal rights of the Church, to permit believers to avoid military service on grounds of conscience, and to allow parents to give their children a religious education – hitherto banned under the law which forbade religious propaganda.

These relaxations are characteristic of the general mood of reform under Gorbachev. But they can also be seen as a reward to the Church for its readiness to serve the interests, or at least the foreign policy concerns, of the Soviet state. Indeed, other religions fear that the new concordance between the Russian Church and Soviet state may lead to a kind of Orthodox imperialism over the other faiths, with the Church as an agency of Russian nationalism in the multi-ethnic empire. Certainly, it was through its essential patriotism that the Orthodox Church began the long haul back from persecution. At the outbreak of the Second World War, there was no Patriarch, no functioning seminary, only four bishops were left at liberty, and the Church was almost an underground body with barely 300 churches still left open on sufferance.

However, the instant espousal of the national cause against the Nazi invaders by the Metropolitan Sergei led to a new relationship. Sergei was elected Patriarch at the first permitted holding of a Church council, and monasteries, churches and ten seminaries were opened. After the war, in spite of the Church's complete identification with the Soviet line at international bodies like the World Peace Council and the World Council of Churches, Khrushchev launched a new persecution, closing over half of the 10,000 churches that were operating, and demolishing many of them. At the time of Khrushchev's fall in 1964, the three tiny but beautiful churches that now stand between Red Square and the Rossiya Hotel were to be demolished. They were saved, the first sign that the persecutions were ending, and that a mood for conservation was beginning to grow. Not only were the old churches a natural object of concern for the fledgling conservation movement, but the Church itself could rightly claim to embody Russian culture and to be a natural guardian of the Russian national heritage.

The fortunes of the Church prospered discreetly in the Brezhnev years. There were occasional examples of collective farm chairmen being fined for confiscating church bells, and one case of an official being imprisoned for refusing a priest admission to a dying believer in hospital. The Gorbachev reforms are thus intensifying an existing trend, rather than establishing a wholly new relationship. But Gorbachev himself comes from traditionally devout peasant stock. His mother is a believer, and regular churchgoer, who had the infant Mikhail baptised. Although a convinced atheist, Gorbachev reflects the maturity of a Soviet system which is now in its eighth decade; the Church is no longer an automatic enemy, the believer is no longer automatically suspect of potential subversion. During the Moscow summit of 1988, President Reagan made a much-publicised visit to the Danilovsky Monastery, just as Britain's Margaret Thatcher had gone to the great Monastery of Zagorsk in 1987. The lesson was clear; as far as the Kremlin and the Soviet diplomats are concerned, the Orthodox Church is these days more of an asset than a threat.

The law and you

Law reform

The Soviet Union is a police state, which is slowly, and with great difficulty, being tamed to abide by the rule of law. Officially, the courts and the judges are independent, and are charged with maintaining the rights of the citizen against unjust treatment by the police, or the KGB. Officially also, privacy of post and telephone is guaranteed by law. But don't count on it. Even Gorbachev noted that this remained a desirable goal to aim at, rather than an accurate description of the current situation, in his speech to the 19th Party Conference.

Russians speak of 'telephone justice', by which they mean that whatever takes place in the court-room, they assume that somebody somewhere will have discreetly telephoned the judge to indicate the desired verdict in all but the routine cases. This phrase first appeared in print in the weekly journal of the Writers' Union, *Literaturnaya Gazeta*, in one of a series of major campaigning articles for reform of the law written by Arkady Vaksberg.

A man who was promoting the cause of law reform even before *glasnost* made it fashionable, Vaksberg is one of that handful of well-connected and influential Soviet journalists whose articles tend to reflect the views of the reformer in the Kremlin. Since Gorbachev himself was educated as a lawyer at Moscow University in the early 1950s, the country's legal reformers are confident that dramatic changes are in train to increase the prestige and the independence of the judiciary. But it will be a long time before telephone justice is abolished for foreigners. If you as a foreign tourist get into trouble with the Soviet authorities, then for obvious political reasons, your fate will be decided at a rather higher level than the court-room.

There are a number of ways in which this could happen, and almost all of them will be your own fault.

Currency speculation

As you stroll the streets of the big cities, as you desend from your bus to take photographs, as you wait for a table in a restaurant or as you go shopping, you will be approached, not very discreetly, and asked if you want to change money.

Play it safe, and refuse. Nine times out of ten you would probably get away with it, and find yourself receiving three or four or even five roubles for your pound or dollar, instead of the roughly one rouble or eighty kopeks they give you at the bank. This may seem like a bargain, until you stop and ask yourself what exactly you are going to buy with these black market roubles. And even if you still want to dabble in the black market, think about getting caught.

If they decide to make an example of you, you will be hauled off to a militia station, photographed, possibly fingerprinted, and a *Protokol* or statement of facts according to the police will be written down in Russian, and you will be asked to sign this. Only do so if you have also written (in English) that you do not understand what this *Protokol* means, and do not agree with it anyway.

Do not stand on your rights and insist on seeing your consul. You are not under arrest (yet), and I can find no recent evidence of a tourist being imprisoned for minor currency offences. The policy seems to be to give the occasional tourist a bad fright with a few hours in a police station. But if too many tourists try to dabble in the black market, this relatively lenient policy could change. Play it safe, and change your money at the banks. After all, everything you want to buy can be bought legally with your own currency, with the one exception of meals at the new co-operative restaurants. But even these are now being allowed to accept western credit cards.

If the worst happens, and you are formally arrested and charged, refuse to say or sign anything until you have been allowed access to your consul.

Drugs

There are currently over a dozen foreigners serving stiff prison sentences for assuming that they could smuggle drugs into or through the Soviet Union. The relatively cheap air fares of Aeroflot to India and the Far East tempted some Dutch, British and American smugglers to fly back via Moscow, from where western customs men would not expect to discover exotic substances. This theory ignored the fact that all transfer baggage is checked by sniffer dogs at Moscow Airport, even when the bags are simply changing planes. You can expect at least a five-year term, usually served in the 'Intourist' prison camp not far from Moscow. Said to be rather less harsh than the usual Soviet camp, it is still a grim place.

Drug abuse is growing fast in the Soviet Union, to the very real alarm of the authorities, who tried for too long to brush the problem under the carpet. It has been made a great deal worse by the eight years of war in Afghanistan, which introduced an entire generation of Russian conscripts to a drug culture. *Ganasha* is the Russian word for marijuana, and it has been used for centuries in the traditionally Muslim republics of the south. It therefore finds its way to Moscow with great ease, and can be obtained without great difficulty at the Kazan Station, at the Lumumba University, and at various centres of the youth culture like the Zilyony Teatr, the rock music venue in Gorky Park. It is totally illegal.

Hard drugs are less common and heroin is very rare indeed, although hallucinogens, amphetamines, morphine and cocaine can be found. The hard drug culture was also spurred by the Afghan War. The Ministry of the Interior admits to some 24,000 addicts, who get their supply mainly, it seems, from hospitals and pharmacies, partly because the staff who work in this sector of the health service are so badly paid. A full-scale campaign is now being waged against drug abuse. The head of the Moscow drug squad recently told a conference at the Ministry of the Interior the situation was so serious that he personally believed addicts should be able to appeal for medical help, without the doctors automatically being obliged to call in the police and make it a criminal matter.

Religion   The Soviet Union is happy for you to bring in a Bible and prayer book and some religious literature for your personal use. Bring in rather more than that and you could run foul of the law which forbids religious propaganda. On the whole, this will mean simple confiscation of books and tracts at the airport, unless you are trying to smuggle in large amounts, which could lead to formal charges. The constraints on organised religion are being steadily relaxed and people who were imprisoned for religious activities are now being released.

Soviet Jews, who were being allowed to leave at the rate of barely 1,000 a year in the mid-1980s, were by 1988 leaving at the rate of 1,000 a month. So there are fewer *refuseniks* stuck in Moscow. But there still are some, and there are a lot of Soviet Jews who want to leave, and who remain deeply suspicious of the Soviet system. Their names and addresses are often circulated among Jewish or human rights groups in the west, and some tourists come planning to visit them.

There is no reason not to. It is not against Soviet law to visit people, nor to give them small gifts or souvenirs. It would not be wise to risk breaking the law by passing on foreign currency, nor by agreeing to take manuscripts out to the west on someone else's behalf.

Espionage

The Soviet Union has some strict laws about espionage, which should not affect the innocent tourist. However, if you photograph an airport, a bridge, or a military installation, you may find some pompous official wanting to confiscate your film. If you are photographing an obvious tourist sight, like the Kremlin, and a bridge just happens to be in the frame, refuse. You are unlikely to suffer anything worse than a wasted hour or two in a police station, and this will provide you with a wonderful anecdote for years to come. If you are simply photographing a bridge or army post or radar installation for the sake of it, you would be advised to hand over the film. Do not bother to explain how western spy satellites have already mapped every bridge in the country. Just accept that this is their country, even if they do run it in a very paranoid way.

Sex

Although not usually enforced, there is a law on the statute books against a foreigner spending a night in a Russian home, unless formally registered with the local militia and visa authorities. One prominent British businessman I know suffered some unpleasant harassment from the KGB after they turned up at his girlfriend's flat at 6 a.m. But that was in the grim days of 1984–85, before the recent thaw. Common sense should be your guide. If you are vulnerable to anything more than mild embarrassment, through your job or marriage or relationship back home, then you must decide whether the thrill of a Soviet sexual adventure outweighs the slim possibility that you may be deliberately compromised, or open to blackmail. It has happened before in the Soviet Union, and it will doubtless happen again.

The prostitutes you will find in every hard currency bar of every Intourist hotel are not all working directly for the KGB. But they would not be allowed to ply their trade unless they co-operated with the authorities when called on to do so. This kind of commercial sex will rarely attract the interest of the KGB, but if you are important enough, you will already have been assigned to a room that is wired for sound and vision.

There have been cases of tourists who have been slipped Mickey Finns in their hotel rooms, and have woken with a sick headache to find they have been robbed. There have also been incidents where tourists have travelled back to the girl's flat to be robbed there. It happens a great deal less often in the Soviet Union than in Miami or Paris, but you have been warned. Do not expect a great deal of sympathy from the Soviet police if it happens to you.

Homosexuality is illegal in the Soviet Union. This has not stopped it, but it would be unwise to test the tolerance of the Soviet police and public in this matter. Male homosexuality is commonplace in the arts world, in film and in the ballet, which helps explain why the main cruising ground has traditionally been the small park in front of Moscow's Bolshoy Theatre. When the AIDS scare first hit the Soviet

Union, a police car used to park alongside. Officially, the Soviet Union admits to one citizen with AIDS, and another fifty-eight cases affecting foreigners. They were all African students, and they have all been expelled. Believe those figures if you will. But bear in mind that the Soviet Union is at least averagely promiscuous and has an acute shortage of both condoms and disposable syringes. AIDS may not have hit them hard yet, but it could spread very fast.

Road accidents and traffic offences

There is a special traffic police, the GAI, which stands for State Automobile Inspectorate. These are the police who stand in the middle of the main roads, waving ordinary traffic off to the side of the road when the long black Zil limousines, reserved for Politburo members and top-ranking VIPs, zoom past in their reserved central lane. The GAI also man the police stations on all the main roads out of Moscow, and all other towns and cities. They check all foreigners' cars to make sure they are authorised to be on that road, and are supposed to monitor the pollution level of trucks and old cars, which they rarely do. Traditionally, the GAI were famous for their corruption, although they are now supposed to have been rigorously cleaned up. Even so, many Russians carry a small banknote inside their driving licence. It used to be 5 roubles, and is now 10, but it is a risky business to offer a bribe.

If you are driving through the Soviet Union, you will have an itinerary, saying which roads you will be using on which days. You should not diverge from this route, because the GAI will send police cars looking for you if you fail to go past the regular check points. We once stopped for an impromptu picnic just off the road to the old Russian city of Vladimir, and we had barely spread the rug on the ground and started cutting the salami before the GAI came down the road with loudspeakers, looking for the foreigners, and insisting that we move on.

Look on the bright side. This careful attention to your movements can be reassuring in the event of a breakdown. But do not expect the police to help. My wife was leaving our apartment one day, only to be informed by the policeman who manned the sentry box outside that her car had a puncture. He then stood behind her, commenting on how tightly the nuts seemed to be screwed on western wheels, as she struggled to change the tyre.

If you are involved in a car accident, do not leave the scene unless it is to help an injured person. Draw up your own account of the incident, including a diagram. The police will draw up their own *Protokol*. Again, sign it with the qualifying statement that you do not understand it. You should not be driving in the Soviet Union unless you are properly insured. And make sure the insurance is fully comprehensive, because there is no guarantee that the Russian drivers involved in the accident are also insured.

If they are not, you may have to go to court to sue them for the cost of repairs to your car. Even if you are armed with a Soviet police statement saying that it was all the other person's fault, this is very complicated. You have to hire Soviet lawyers, through an agency named Iniurkollegiya, to sue on your behalf, and you will have to pay them a retainer before they take up your case. If you win, and this process can take over a year, the defendant will pay off the damages in monthly instalments, in roubles.

Soviet attitudes to money

The Soviet attitude towards money is one of the main differences between east and west. Seventy years of Soviet economics have had an astonishing effect on the way people relate to hard cash. There are a number of reasons for this, and they go a long way to explaining what is different about life in the USSR.

Credit   Credit barely exists for individuals as it is, after all, essentially capitalist, an invention of the retail trade to stimulate more consumption, even when the consumer cannot quite afford it. Since the Soviet economy cannot satisfy the huge customer demand even without credit, it makes little sense to stoke up still more demand by making credit available. There are a handful of credit and charge card outlets, at the hotels, shops and restaurants that cater to foreigners with their hard currency American Express and Visa cards. As a foreign tourist, you can even pay for your drinks in the hotel bar with your plastic card, and see the charge translated into pounds or dollars turn up on your charge bill a month or so later.

A tiny number of the Soviet elite, very senior diplomats and travelling trade officials and journalists, and of course Mrs Raisa Gorbachev, are entitled to their own western credit cards. The handful of members belonging to this stratosphere of privilege is sometimes known as the *AmEx-niki*, after the ultimate symbol of their influence. And in Estonia, they have been experimenting with credit cards for petrol stations, except that it is the customer who extends credit to the state. You buy the card in advance, for cash, and when you get petrol, the attendant checks off how much money remains.

There is also a cumbersome form of hire purchase for expensive items like furniture or good winter overcoats, which can cost 200-300 roubles for woollen ones. Fur coats can cost thousands, but these count as luxury items, like cars, and hire purchase is not available for luxuries. It might encourage too many buyers. But, for a good woollen winter coat, costing 200 roubles, you can put down a deposit of 80 roubles, and pay off the rest at the rate of 10 roubles each month direct from your salary. However, it is all very complicated to arrange, requiring certificates from your place of work, character references, and a form of contract by which the money is deducted from your pay each month.

Banks

Cheque books were introduced in 1987, but they have not yet caught on. Soviet newspapers regularly run features complaining about the way shops and even government departments, like those of Telephones or Electricity, refuse to accept them, and insist on being paid in the traditional way by cash. Soviet people have savings banks, called *Sberkasse*, rather than current accounts. They are paid very low rates of interest, ranging between 1.5 and 3 per cent a year, depending on the kind of savings account, and the amount of money deposited.

There are various kinds of savings accounts, including one entirely anonymous form that reminds me a bit of the famous secret Swiss bank accounts. It is an account identified solely by the bank book, and whoever happens to be carrying it. Officially, it is designed for the wives of men who go off to work in the Siberian oil fields or on a temporary assignment. In fact, it is a pragmatic way of ensuring that at least some of the vast amount of black market money does come into the state's financial system. Regularly, when arrests are made in large-scale corruption cases, the Press reports that as well as the gold ingots, several dozen, or even several hundred, of these bearer bank books were found stashed beneath the floorboards.

Another interesting form of savings account is the lottery bond. You pay 105 roubles for a 100 rouble savings bond, and your 5 roubles, plus the annual interest you forego, go into the prize fund. There are monthly draws, and you can win a car, or a 10,000-rouble maximum prize. This is worth a great deal more than it sounds. Put the word around that you have won the cash prize and wait for the offers to come in. A certificate that shows you have legitimately acquired 10,000 roubles in cash is a highly valued commodity in a country with a large black economy. The lucky winner will be offered between fifteen and twenty thousand roubles in cash for the winning ticket. The offers will come from the criminal black market, from whores, from corrupt officials, or even from doctors who have made a lot of money through semi-legal private practice. A lot of Soviet citizens would like to be able to show the anti-corruption squads that they have legitimately acquired large sums of cash.

At last count, there were 260,000 million roubles in the savings banks, almost 1,000 roubles for every man, woman and child in the country. This makes the Soviet people among the thriftiest on earth, except that all of these savings really represent deferred spending, a great inflationary wave ready to swamp the economy just as soon as it starts producing sufficient consumer goods desirable enough for the savers to want to buy them.

Subsidies

The average wage in Moscow is 200 roubles a month. At the official rate of exchange, this represents £50 or US$80 a week, and at the black market rate, about £15 or US$25 a week. But most of the salary is genuinely disposable income, because of massive subsidies of rent and basic foods. Soviet income tax is 13 per cent of your earnings above the minimum wage. So on an average salary, tax would be about 5 roubles a month.

The average Moscow flat, consisting of a sitting room, a bedroom and a small kitchen–dining room, costs about 12 roubles a month, including the charge for heating and hot water. Electricity is extra, but still very cheap, about 1 rouble a week. Local phone calls are free and public transport, whether on the Metro, bus or tram, is 5 kopeks a ride.

The massive level of food subsidies is one of the country's biggest and most dangerous economic problems. They are currently running at over 60,000 million roubles a year – which means they are worth a month's extra salary for every man, woman and child in the population. It costs the state 5 roubles to produce the kilo of meat which is sold for 2 roubles. Bread is so cheap that the peasants feed it to their private livestock, rather than pay for more expensive fodder. In a speech in Murmansk, Gorbachev once publicly complained that he had seen boys playing football with big loaves of bread.

These subsidies are politically popular, because the population is accustomed to them, and the subsidies are also cited to justify the scandalously low old age pensions, student stipends and support payments for single parents and disabled people. But Gorbachev has already promised that the subsidies will have to be phased out, because the artificial price structure they have created is distorting the entire agricultural economy. As the state pays as little as it can to the farms for subsidised items, the farmers have a kind of warped incentive to under-produce, particularly since in the free markets, the peasants know they can get 8 to 10 roubles a kilo for their meat. Nonetheless, these subsidies mean that a basic diet is very cheap.

So after paying for housing, transport and food, the average Moscow worker could still have 100 roubles or more a month to spend. Education and basic health care are free, although all prescribed drugs must be paid for. Vacations, although they tend to be fairly grim communal stays in holiday camps, are heavily subsidised through the trade unions. Sports clubs are also subsidised by trade unions and you can go rowing, play football, or in Moscow, Tallinn and Riga even learn to sail, for less than a rouble a month. A newspaper costs 3 kopeks, and a theatre seat 2 roubles. An ice cream is 20 kopeks and a two-course meal in a public cafeteria, of macaroni and meatballs, will cost 75 kopeks.

By contrast, a slap-up dinner for two at the National Hotel on Gorky Street, with caviar, crab, champagne, chicken kiev and ice cream, will cost about 30 roubles. Not that the average Russian would be able to get past the stern-faced commissionaire and into the hotel (see *Blat*, p. 93). In one of the new co-op restaurants, where they have to buy their raw materials in the free markets rather than through the subsidised state outlets, you can easily pay 30 roubles a head without alcohol.

Salaries

There are people who can afford these prices, quite legally, and without benefit of the black market. To attract people to the grimmest jobs in Siberia, the state will pay two and even three times the standard salary, plus production bonuses, as well as one or even two all-paid holiday trips to the Black Sea sunshine resorts. The best paid man I met was a helicopter maintenance engineer in Magadan, the far north-east of Siberia. He cleared over 1,000 roubles a month. He had a car in Magadan and another back at the family home in Leningrad, where he had bought a co-operative flat (which meant he could leave it to his heirs). He also owned a dacha on the Baltic coast, wore a lot of gold jewellery, and still had more money than he could spend.

Authors, composers and actors can also become extremely rich. The thriller writer Julian Simyonov has one of the special 'bottomless' savings bank accounts, because the state judges he will never be able to spend what he is owed in royalties. The pop star Alla Pugacheva drives an imported black Mercedes limousine, an awesome status symbol in Soviet terms. Yet, if you travel on a Moscow bus you may see one of the small posters advertising jobs. In the summer of 1988, the pay scales were 300 roubles a month for a driver, 120 roubles a month for a cashier, and 90 roubles a month for a cleaner. This is not an egalitarian society.

There is little logic in the whole Soviet pay structure, except for a clear tendency to pay the skilled workers rather better than those in 'professional' white collar jobs. To this extent, there is just something to the claim that the USSR is a workers' state. Thus, while in 1984 the average pay of a Ukrainian coal-miner was 320 roubles a month, a Moscow museum worker earnt 110 roubles. Even after recent pay rises, schoolteachers and doctors are paid a basic 150 roubles a month, which is less than the average wage. However, many white collar workers make money on the side: doctors have private patients and teachers give private tuition.

A Soviet friend of mine, a prize-winning journalist on a big magazine, was on a basic salary of 150 roubles a month. But he could easily triple or quadruple that with bonus payments for every article he had published, freelance writing and television and radio appearances. He also had access to a country dacha not far from Moscow every summer, for less than 1 rouble a week.

Barter

There are ways in which today's Moscow is a bit like Berlin in 1945, with tourists playing the role of the occupying Allied armies. The local currency is almost valueless. You can buy just about anything with your own currency, or your own luxuries. You may not be able to buy a woman for a bar of soap, but a carton of Marlboros will go a very long way. The better brands of Soviet cigarettes, such as Kosmos, cost 60 kopeks a pack. On the black market, a pack of Marlboros can cost 5 roubles upwards. At the special duty-free store for diplomats on Gruzinsky Val, just off Gorky Street, where everything is paid for in a special paper currency called D-cheques, a carton of ten packs of Marlboros costs 5 hard currency roubles, or £5 or US$8. A bottle of Scotch whisky costs 3.15 roubles, and a bottle of vodka costs 1.30 roubles compared to 10 roubles in the ordinary shops, and that after two hours or more in a queue.

Diplomats of many a developing country have been quick to spot the opportunities this ludicrous system presents. Most western students doing their term or two at the Moscow language schools have quickly learned that the pair of jeans bought in the west for £15 or US$25 can be sold for 120 roubles in Moscow, and that a stereo tape-recorder can be sold for ten times the purchase price in a western discount store. Clothes, perfumes, tape cassettes, books, LPs, videos, cigarettes, alcohol, even western plastic bags carrying the right kind of label – they all carry a special value in Moscow. The trick is to find a way of selling or bartering safely. Diplomats and students who live in Moscow can do this more easily than short-stay tourists.

This is not a game to dabble in, because the Soviets have so little to offer you in return and attempting to export icons or antiques can lead to serious trouble. And if you are taking out jars of caviar or Palekh boxes, the customs will sometimes want to see the receipts from the hard currency Beriozka store where you are supposed to have bought them – particularly if they are not wrapped in the distinctive Beriozka paper.

Most bartering, however, takes place between the Russians themselves. Because so many desirable things are in short supply, and the subsidies of basic foods and living costs give many people a substantial disposable income, cash alone is not enough. You swap, or trade, or use influence.

So, for example, an apprentice dancer in the Bolshoy ballet can pass the tickets she gets to her hairdresser-beautician, who will in turn trade them to the teacher who gives her son private tuition in the evenings so that he can get into one of the elite schools where the teaching is in English, and the chances of getting into Moscow University or one of the prestige colleges like MGIMO, the Institute for International Relations, are significantly higher. This level of barter runs all the way through society. A shopgirl at a provincial foodstore will get regular supplies of good meat, or oranges, or tins of crab. These can be traded for a better place in the housing queue, or a better *Putyovka*, a voucher for a holiday camp, or some fancy Polish lingerie or Italian shoes, or a pair of Levi jeans that originally came in with a British student studying Russian at the Pushkin Institute. The black market, or the barter market, is probably the most efficient single part of the Soviet economy outside the defence sector.

Blat | This is Russian slang for influence or 'pull'. To get a hot meal when your coach arrives very late at a provincial hotel after a breakdown is evidence of big *Blat* wielded by your Intourist guide. To find a hotel room in a crowded city by telephoning a powerful local acquaintance is *Blat*. Getting seats for a gala show at the Bolshoy, or the hot new play at the Moscow Arts Theatre, is *Blat*. Booking a table at the window with a view of the Kremlin in the National Hotel during the week of the Reagan–Gorbachev summit is big *Blat*. Securing a decent flat in the centre of Moscow, or even getting a *Propusk*, which gives you the right to live in Moscow at all, is *Blat*. Finding a flight down to the Black Sea resort of Sochi in high season is *Blat*. Getting a regular supply of contraceptive pills, or a room in the right Abortion Clinic or Maternity Hospital (the Botkin), or a place in the best cemetery (Novodevichy) is *Blat*. The Russians even have a verb – *derzhat* – to describe the act of obtaining things with a degree of skill or difficulty.

It works at all levels, even for us foreigners. All Ambassadors are invited to the Kremlin reception after 7 November parade in Red Square. It is big *Blat* for Gorbachev to stop and engage you in conversation. For a foreign businessman, even if you do not get the contract, your ego can be stroked, and your big *Blat* proven, by the fact that the Minister of Foreign Trade comes to the small cocktail party you throw when your managing director is in town. To procure a seat in the relatively small room for a Gorbachev Press conference is big *Blat* for journalists. To be singled out to put a question to him is even bigger.

Blat is not just influence, it is also favours bestowed on you by somebody in a position of influence, and the unwritten rules state that the favours should always be returned. The *Blat* connection is sacrosanct, and the Soviets play the manifold subtleties of the *Blat* etiquette like grand masters. The only foreigners who really understand its intricacies are the Chinese and Japanese. I have heard Japanese colleagues spend hours agonising over the precise level of birthday gift to bestow on a treasured secretary. The rest of us see it as a crude system of you scratch my back, I scratch yours, all taking place in a deeply corrupt country where we foreigners have a monopoly of the dollars, the Levis, the Marlboros and the bottles of Scotch.

The Russian alphabet and language

Many people are intimidated by the very look of Russian street signs or newspapers. The Cyrillic alphabet looks at first so alien to an eye trained to read a Latin script that most tourists do not bother to make just the slight effort required to get at least a nodding acquaintance with the language. A few minutes' work will pay off handsomely, because even being able to decipher the Russian letters will at least enable you to make some sense of a Russian restaurant menu, to venture forth alone on the Moscow Metro, and to puzzle out the street posters and shop signs. And it is a great deal easier than it looks.

Look at these two words: Беф-строганов. That is the Russian for Beef Stroganoff, a dish you will find in most restaurants. So the Russian б is a Roman B. The Russian e is pronounced 'ye'. And the ф is F.

The Russian c is the Roman S. The т is common to both alphabets, as is the о and the а and the к and the м and the з or Z. The letter P often confuses people, because this is the Russian letter for R. But just remember the name of the cat at the British Embassy – Pectopah. Now put that into Russian script РЕСТОРАН. That is pronounced Restoran – or restaurant. The Russian г is the G in gun, the Russian н is the Roman N and the Russian в is the V in very.

There are some really tricky Russian letters, like щ. You will come across this in the menu in every РЕСТОРАН under the listing for soups. It is pronounced sch, and look for the Russian word борщ, *borsch*, the famous beet soup. Then there is cabbage soup, or щи, pronounced schee.

The backwards-looking И is a Russian I. It is easy to get this confused with the Russian letter Н, which is pronounced N. The best way to remember the difference is to think of Lenin's Mausoleum in Red Square, with his name carved into the stone. Lenin is Ленин.

Now apply these principles to the stations of the Moscow Metro. Проспект мира is Prospekt Mira, or Peace Avenue. ВДНХ is pronounced Vudunhah, with the emphasis on the 'hah'. This is the abbreviation for Exhibition of Economic Achievements, a large park packed with pavilions that give an exceedingly rosy view of the country. It is the site for the vast Cosmos Hotel where many tourists stay, and also of one of the city's great landmarks, the space statue, a rocket soaring into space on a parabolic curve of aluminium.

Дзержинская is Dzerzhinskaya. This is a useful station because it is so central. It is named after Felix Dzerzhinsky, the founder of the Soviet secret police. When you emerge from the station, in the middle of the square is his statue. Behind him stands the Lubyanka, the Headquarters of the KGB. Opposite the KGB is a shop called: Детский мир, which is pronounced Dyetski Mir, Children's World, the city's main toy shop. As you come out of the store, down the hill to your right runs a major thoroughfare called: Проспект Маркса. This is Prospekt Marksa, named after Karl Marx, and there is a Metro station of the same name that stands at the bottom of Gorky Street, where it meets the vast square that opens on to Red Square itself.

The word for hotel is *gostinitsa*: Гостиница. So we have *Gostinitsa* Rossiya: Гостиница Россия. *Gostinitsa* Intourist: Гостиница

Интурист. And *Gostinitsa* National: Гостиница Националь.

From the Проспект Маркса Metro station, take the train one stop north to a station called: Пушкинская. This is Pushkinskaya, named after Pushkin, the national poet, and when you come out on to the street again, his statue dominates the charming square. This is the nearest Moscow has to Fleet Street, a Press centre. To Pushkin's right is a large modern building, proudly blazoned with the word: Известия. This is *Izvestia*, which means information, or news and is the main evening paper. Opposite the *Izvestia* building is the office of *Moscow News*, which is written in English and several other languages on the façade. The Russian version is pronounced *Moskovsky Novosti*, and it looks like this: Московские Новости.

Around the square, which incidentally is the usual place for human rights demonstrations, you will see lots of small stands where the day's newspapers are displayed, a tradition that dates from Lenin's insistence that even people without the coppers for a paper should not be stopped from reading them. There is normally a small crowd around the display of the latest *Moscow News*, since that is the flagship of *glasnost*, but it is worth looking at the other papers to improve your Russian.

Правда is *Pravda*, which means Truth, hence the old pre-*glasnost* joke about there being no Izvestia in Pravda and no Pravda in Izvestia. Труд is *Trud*, which means Labour, or Work, and is the daily paper of the Soviet Trade Union Organisation.

And the two words you should be able to recognise are: гласность, which is *glasnost*. And перестройка, which is *perestroika*.

The Russian alphabet

А	а	a		Р	р	r
Б	б	b		С	с	s
В	в	v		Т	т	t
Г	г	g		У	у	u
Д	д	d		Ф	ф	f
Е	е	e, ye		Х	х	kh
Ё	ё	yo		Ц	ц	ts
Ж	ж	zh		Ч	ч	ch
З	з	z		Ш	ш	sh
И	и	i		Щ	щ	shch
Й	й	y, short i		Ъ	ъ	(mute), hard sign
К	к	k		Ы	ы	i
Л	л	l		Ь	ь	soft sign
М	м	m		Э	э	e, reversed e
Н	н	n		Ю	ю	yu
О	о	o		Я	я	ya
П	п	p				

The left-hand columns show printed capital and small letters and the right-hand column is the basis for the simplified transliteration.

The Weather and When to Go

As the biggest country in the world, the Soviet Union has every extreme of climate and vegetation, with the sole exception of tropical rain forest. In the Central Asian cities of Samarkand and Tashkent from May to September, it gets very hot indeed, often above 35°C (96°F). In mid-winter in Siberia, the temperature can fall to 50°C below freezing (−58°F).

Moscow   The temperature can range pretty widely in Moscow too, from 35°C below freezing (−31°F) in winter, to 35°C (96°F) in mid-summer. The first snows can come in mid-September, but they usually herald an Indian Summer, and winter proper, with permanent snow cover, normally comes in November. Snow can fall as late as May, but usually the grim season of filthy slush and thaw lasts from mid-March to late April. This is not the ideal time to visit Moscow. The best times are in mid-winter, anytime from December to the end of February, when you can appreciate how well this society has adapted to the cold, and learn to relish its bracing pleasures; or in spring and early summer. In May and June, you realise what a green city Moscow can be, the weather is warm without being baking hot, and without the humidity and thunderstorms which come in July and August. Although not quite far north enough to share Leningrad's famous White Nights of midsummer, around the equinox, Moscow is light until nearly midnight, and the new relaxations of the Gorbachev thaw are allowing evening street life to come into its own.

The most enjoyable time to visit Moscow in winter is late December, when the Moscow Stars Festival is under way, and Richter is organising the December Evenings at the Pushkin Museum, which are musical recitals in a delightful room that is also decorated with a special art exhibition. The first one I attended featured Richter's music and Matisse's late drawings. Also, the earlier in the winter you go, the cleaner the snow will be, and the more magical the city will appear. And winter is the time to understand the colours in which Russian buildings are painted, the warmth of the ochres of the university buildings, the Manezh (the Tsar's old riding stables) on one side of Moscow's great 25 Years of October Square, and the red stones of the Kremlin walls on the other.

Leningrad   Leningrad is one of the world's loveliest cities at any time, but in the brisk cold of winter, the lights of the buildings blaze against the ice and the slate-grey sky. Like Moscow, though, it is best to avoid Leningrad in the autumn rains of late October and November, during the thaw of early spring or in the peak of midsummer.

Central Asia and Caucasus

The time to avoid Central Asia is between June and September. But spring in Samarkand and Bukhara can be delightful. The trans-Caucasian cities of Tbilisi, Yerevan and Baku are at their best in spring and autumn. High summer in Yerevan is sweltering, and in mid-winter Baku, the wind sweeps bitterly off the Caspian Sea.

Crimea

One spot in the Soviet Union where the weather is almost always perfect is the southern coast of the Crimea, around Yalta, which the Tsars wisely made into a holiday resort. The Crimean mountains inland and the temperate effects of the Black Sea have combined to make a micro-climate which is almost identical to that of the French Riviera, but without the *Mistral*. It is excellent wine-growing country. Unfortunately, its popularity with Soviet holiday-makers has made the place increasingly over-crowded, and this is starting to have an adverse effect on the ecology of the beaches. New sewage works are planned, but until they are complete, bathe with caution. The beaches are gravel and tend to be narrow.

What to wear

Winter

Being accustomed to the cold of winter, the Soviets understand about central heating. It is always hot indoors in winter, even in vast public buildings. So unless you want to be uncomfortably warm, do not put on several layers of thermal underwear and sweaters. Rather you should have a very warm overcoat, and if relying on a thermal jacket, make sure it comes down low enough to keep your rump warm. You will need a good hat with earmuffs, a scarf and warm gloves, prefer-ably fur-lined, and also sturdy, warm footwear. For mid-winter, I would recommend Moonboots.

You do not have to dress formally, but you will be surprised by how often the Russians don jackets and ties. A night at the Bolshoy is enough of an occasion to merit a touch of formality, particularly if you join the parade around the formal halls during the interval.

Summer

Never go out without a plastic raincoat or umbrella; summer thun-derstorms can come out of nowhere. Evenings can be cool enough to need a light sweater or a jacket. Although few Moscow hotels boast a swimming pool, it is worth packing swimming clothes because you may be able to spend a couple of hours at the Moscow river beaches at Serebryanny Bor.

Autumn and spring

It can be sunny during the day and very cool at night. Until Novem-ber, or after April, you should get by with a good gaberdine raincoat, like a Burberry, with a scarf and gloves for insurance. It is also worth packing a thin woollen ski hat, just in case you are caught by a cold snap. Remember that as you will probably be doing a lot of walking, whether through museums or art galleries or in the streets, you should take a decent pair of comfortable walking shoes.

Pukh

Hay-fever sufferers and **contact lens wearers** should note that Moscow has a very high dust count in June, the season of *pukh*, sometimes known as Stalin's snow. Stalin once observed that he rather liked a certain kind of tree, the cottonwood poplar. So the man in charge of Moscow parks and greenery promptly ordered hundreds of thousands of these trees and planted them all over Moscow. Very nice too, except that at the end of spring, they shed "*pukh*", which is rather like miniature balls of cotton wool, and the city's streets fill up with acres of the stuff every year. It lies so deep that it can look like snow along the boulevards and can gather into drifts in the gutters. Small boys sometimes set light to these drifts and a thin sheet of flame will race down the street. *Pukh* and a rainstorm combine to cover up car windscreens with a opaque white mess. With Stalin safely dead for thirty-five years, the civic authorities are at last replacing some of these trees, but for the moment, the problem is still there.

Travel to the Soviet Union

Package tours

It is very much cheaper to go to the Soviet Union on a package tour than to arrange independent travel. A weekend booked in London can cost as little as £250, and a full week can come to less than £400, including air fares, hotels, meals and excursions. By contrast, to arrange the same trip independently would cost a minimum of £60 a night for hotel room alone. The disparity is so great that even businessmen sometimes travel on tourist visas and package tours.

From Britain In Britain, Intourist, Thomson Holidays and British Airways all offer various kinds of package tour, from weekend jaunts to a full week in Moscow, to three days in Moscow and three in Leningrad, which is probably the most inviting single package on offer. However, it is also frustrating to have so little time in each city for pottering around on one's own, and sometimes a whole day is wasted on the train journey from Moscow to Leningrad. However, if the train trip is by the excellent overnight sleeper, so that no sightseeing time is lost, it is an efficient, but exhausting way of packing a lot into one week.

The tour operators also have much longer tours that begin in Moscow, and then continue to the Golden Ring of old Russian cities, or to the Black Sea or Central Asia. And some include a trip down the River Volga and across to the Ukraine, or into the Baltic Republics, and back to Leningrad, taking as much as three weeks. Virgin Holidays operates a package tour to the coastal resort of Yalta in the Crimea, and there are other tours which fly directly into the Georgian capital of Tbilisi for a trans-Caucasian trip. In all cases, you are far more likely to get hotel and internal transport bookings by going on a package tour and you will pay very much less. Bear in mind that until Intourist issues you a confirmed tour or hotel or camp site booking, you will not be issued a visa by the Soviet Embassy.

This advice also holds good if you are joining a package tour from another European country, which can be competitive in price, though tricky on language as Intourist will not provide English- as well as French- or German- or Danish-speaking guides. France and Italy have big Communist Parties, and very cheap package tours for the comrades, which non-Communists often join. They do, however, tend to visit factories and collective farms rather more than art galleries. But the arguments between hard-line western Communists who have stuck by Moscow through thick and thin, and their now passionately anti-Stalinist Soviet guides can be riveting for the political neutral.

From the United States From the United States Pan-Am Holidays offers a variety of package tour holidays, each of eleven to thirteen days, and costing between $1,299 and $1,599 depending on the number of cities seen. General Tours does a good ten-day package, flying from New York to Helsinki with Finnair, and spending three nights in Moscow, two nights in Kiev and three nights in Leningrad before returning to Helsinki. This trip includes two nights in Finland and costs $1,249 in a low season month like January, but as much as $1,849 for the peak season like the Christmas and New Year period. It is worth shopping around for cheaper package tours, particularly if you have links with special interest organisations, like Russian study groups, or music and ballet appreciation societies.

The cheapest way to visit the USSR from the States is probably by combining your trip with a European holiday to another destination. You can buy a British Airways package holiday to Moscow, leaving from London, for under $500, but of course you have to get to London first and you must book well in advance in order to get your Soviet visa. British Airways does one particularly attractive package for American culture fans called 'Bard and Bolshoy'. This goes from the United States to London, includes theatre seats for the Royal Shakespeare Company in Stratford and London and then flies to Moscow for the Bolshoy.

In the United States, Intourist recommends booking at least two months in advance to give time for visas to be issued.

By air

Package deal
From Britain Most package tours go by air, into Moscow's Shermetyevo-2 Airport, which was built for the 1980 Olympics. Intourist and some of the smaller British agencies send you by Aeroflot whereas British Airways use their own planes and Thomson tend to use BA or British charter flights like Britannia. For duty-free goods, a western-style bar and in-flight meal, plus newspapers, pick a British carrier. One understandable, regrettable but doubtless significant feature of Soviet tourism is that western visitors frequently raise a cheer when the wheels of their plane lift off from Moscow Airport, or when the pilot announces that the plane has left Soviet airspace. Rude at the best of times, such

101

celebrations are strongly advised against if travelling Aeroflot.

Independent
From Britain

Even if you are not travelling by package tour, do not pay the full air fare unless you need an open return date, or can get no other flight. The complex agreements between Aeroflot and western carriers make the entire fare structure more of a nonsense than usual. An economy return fare booked from Moscow on British Airways or Aeroflot will cost roughly £650, because from Moscow there is only a business class. From London, which does accept the theoretical existence of economy class, it can be £400, and various cheaper options are available for early booking. Your travel or ticket agent will inform you.

Even that is too much to pay. Cheap fare agencies, which advertise in the travel pages of all newspapers and in magazines like London's *Time Out*, can get much better deals. In London, I have found Trailfinders (46 Earls Court Road, W8) to be reliable and cheap. From Britain, Trailfinders found me a Swissair return, that required changing planes in Zurich and going via Warsaw, for £200 return. Other cheap dog-legs, via Vienna or Copenhagen, are available. British Airways from London, Finnair from Helsinki and Austrian Airlines from Vienna all have daily flights to Moscow. The London–Moscow flight time is 3 hours 30 minutes.

The best way to travel from London to Moscow is to time your booking for a jumbo flight that is going via Moscow to Japan. British Airways and JAL each have flights with Moscow stop-overs, and you have the extra comfort of a big jet, with in-flight videos and a choice of meals.

From the United States

Both Pan-Am and Aeroflot fly to Moscow from New York. Aeroflot flies direct, but Pan-Am only has one direct flight, on Saturdays. The other Pan-Am flights, on Wednesday, Thursday and Friday each week, go via Frankfurt. The economy return fare is about $2,060. The APEX fare, booked in advance, is $980 if travelling on weekends, or $935 on weekdays.

By sea

Baltic ferries

The best approach to the Soviet Union is to arrive by sea at Leningrad. I once took a luxurious ferry from Stockholm, which was owned by a joint Swedish-Soviet company. It had a casino, swimming pool, sauna and an impressive vintage wine list, and the journey lasted eighteen pleasant hours. The last couple of hours are magical, sailing up the Gulf of Finland, past the island fortress of Kronstadt. This was the great naval base that was the bastion of the Revolution in 1917, and yet had to be stormed over the ice by the Red Army in 1921, when the sailors were agitating for a more democratic form of socialism, which sounds like the reforms being pushed through today.

These ferry boats still ply across the Baltic, with daily sailings from Helsinki to Tallinn in Estonia, to Riga in Latvia and to Leningrad. Most of these ships are carrying the Finns, who frequently visit their Soviet neighbour (370,000 in 1987). A strikingly high proportion are known as vodka tourists, coming for the cheap alcohol. They are also known as the 'two-jeans tourists', on the grounds that for one pair of jeans, a Finn can buy enough vodka to keep him blotto throughout the weekend, and the second pair will get him a woman. Drunken Finns can be the bane of Leningrad, not because they are violent or behave like hooligans, but for the leechlike amiability and total dedication of their drunks. I once encountered a stark naked Finn sleeping peacefully in the lift of Leningrad's Pribaltiyskaya Hotel in mid-afternoon.

Cruise ships Russian cruise ships have a good reputation, but make sure that you are on a modern boat, and that you are not going via a Third World port where the ship might suddenly fill to bursting with students bound for Moscow's Patrice Lumumba University. There are cruises to Odessa, the Black Sea port, that leave from Barcelona, and call at Marseilles, Genoa, Athens and Istanbul along the way. Other ships, often packed with Arab students, go from Alexandria, calling at Syria and Cyprus on the way to Istanbul and the Black Sea.

It is possible to take a car on your ship into Odessa. The return fare for a family of four plus car from Athens to Odessa is £1,700 and from Marseilles, £2,100.

From Japan The ferry and cruise ships are just about all that remain of sea travel to the Soviet Union, except for the Japan route. Unless you are taking the spur to China and Beijing, the Trans-Siberian railway stops at the Pacific port of Nakhodka, where there are regular passenger sailings back and forth to Japan. This can be booked and purchased in advance as part of your Trans-Sib rail ticket.

By rail

It is still possible to travel from London's Victoria Station to Moscow, or indeed, via the Trans-Siberian, on to China or Japan. But rail travel is recommended only for devotees. From Britain, through northern Europe and Berlin and Warsaw to Moscow, with a crossing of the Iron Curtain into East Germany (where they still take it seriously), and another slow crossing into the Soviet Union at Brest, the train journey takes the best part of three days, and is no cheaper than a charter flight. These days, thanks to the invention of adjustable bogeys, there is no need to change trains at the border, in spite of the different gauges (1.52 m between the tracks in the USSR, compared to 1.435 m in the west).

The customs guards at the rail crossings tend to be thorough, particularly on westerners coming back from Finland after a shopping or recuperative weekend. At the airports, they seldom bother to enforce the fairly strict regulations about importing foodstuffs, and one can bring in fresh fruit or bacon or British sausages with impunity. Some bright sparks have even brought in Indian and Chinese take-aways from Britain and warmed them up in a microwave. But at Luzhaika, the border point with Finland, the guards tend in winter to improve their diets through confiscating the fruit and vegetables brought back in suitcases. Not that they are always too familiar with western treats. One acquaintance, bringing back 2 kilos of avocado pears, was furious when she saw the guard take out his confiscation forms. But she got a sweet revenge when he asked her casually, 'And how do you prepare these things?'

She replied: 'You boil them, very slowly, for two hours.'

By car

See motoring, pp. 106–10.

Travelling around in the Soviet Union

Booking in advance

All of your travel inside the Soviet Union will have to be booked in advance. This is because you need a separate visa authorisation for each city you visit. All your internal travel arrangements, whether by rail or air or riverboat, must be made through Intourist. If you wish to change the means of travel you have booked while in the USSR, for example to fly to Leningrad from Moscow rather than to go by train, you must apply through the Intourist service bureau in your hotel. Again, if you wish to modify the route you had booked, ask Intourist. It is often possible to make certain unscheduled side-trips as excursions. Intourist, which these days has the incentive of *khozraschyot* to earn its own money, is very much more flexible than it used to be.

Without Intourist

If you speak Russian well enough to pass as a native, then you may be tempted to take your chances in the queues for rail or air tickets. But be warned. First, it is breaking the law for a foreigner to travel to a Soviet city without the relevant visa, or to take a route not authorised by Intourist. And the police do make occasional checks of train passengers for internal reasons, not to find errant foreigners. But a foreign tourist found where he has no right to be and not travelling on an Intourist voucher will have some tricky explaining to do. Second, it is common practice for train ticket sellers to keep tickets to popular destinations under the blotter, claim they are sold out and then wait for their petty bribe.

By train I like Soviet trains, which are designed for long journeys. I like the nostalgia of them, the smell of coaksmoke that comes, not from the locomotive, but from the tiny stoves under the samovars in each carriage. I like the way Russians relax on trains, take their street clothes off and don tracksuits, drink vodka and eat smoked fish and chicken, and play chess and chat happily to foreigners. Some of my most informative conversations came on train journeys.

You can travel soft class, with two-berth compartments, in semi-soft with four bunks to a compartment (which is very cramped for luggage), or in the dormitory sleepers, which can be a funky experience. For journeys longer than thirty-six hours, there will be a restaurant car, serving the Soviet standby menu of soup, chicken, meatballs with macaroni, cheese or salami sandwiches, very sweet fruit pulp drinks and mineral water. Except on Baltic overnight trains, I have never yet known a Soviet guard who was not able to conjure up a bottle of vodka if suitably persuaded. If there is no restaurant car, there will be a constant supply of tea from your guard, biscuits on the table in your compartment, and buffets in the stations that sell buns, chocolate and sandwiches.

By air If you have a non-Intourist air ticket, expect to be bumped off the plane. For Russians air travel is a hit and miss affair, with flights regularly delayed, cancelled and overbooked. As a foreigner travelling with Intourist, you will be on the beneficial end of a kind of transport apartheid. You have separated and uncrowded lounges and check-in facilities at airports. You will board before the Russian passengers, be greeted by Intourist receptionists as you disembark. In the event of overbookings or delays, you have priority and Russian travellers will be disembarked to make way for you.

Motoring and Camping

Motoring in the Soviet Union is not the way to achieve freedom of travel, nor to avoid the controls and restrictions that come with Intourist's package tours. Intourist remains the supervising organisation for your trip, and as a motorist, you will be given a strict itinerary, with pre-booked hotel rooms or camp site places each night. You won't be able to decide, on the spur of the moment, to linger in a city that takes your fancy, nor to drive on through the night if that evening's hotel or town looks too grim to tolerate. Nor may you turn off on to a side road to explore a pretty valley in search of a quiet riverbank for an impromptu picnic. The impromptu is a concept wholly alien to the Soviet bureaucracy.

Parking

However, once those restrictions are understood, there are some pleasures to motoring in the Soviet Union. The first is easy parking. There have been some rumblings about the need for parking meters in central Moscow, particularly outside the big hotels where the fleets of Intourist buses create a parking problem of their own. Parking is forbidden along main highways, and is indicated by the international sign of a blue circle with a diagonal red cross. Otherwise, you may park almost where you please.

You are advised to park overnight in the guarded areas recommended by your hotel, because while theft of a foreign car is most unusual in the USSR, souvenir hunting is common. You can expect to lose any of the chrome badges or identifying names fixed to your car. Hubcaps too seem to be fair game. Soviet drivers remove their windscreen wipers and wing mirrors whenever they park, because these accessories are in such short supply. A rain shower in a Soviet street is greeted by half the cars screeching to a halt while the drivers hurriedly leap out to fit their wipers. On the whole, though, your wipers will not fit Soviet cars and are therefore safe.

Rush hours

Although Moscow's inner ring road is increasingly becoming clogged with trucks and private cars, traffic is light in comparison with the west. There are distinct rush hours in most cities, but particularly in Moscow, Leningrad and Kiev. The whole of Moscow can be jammed on the morning of a Politburo meeting (usually Thursdays), when the police keep blocking the traffic pouring over the Kammenny

Bridge and along Prospekt Marksa to allow the Zil limousines a smooth, uninterrupted journey into the Kremlin.

Hazards

There are other distinctly Soviet problems about motoring. It is, for example, very difficult to make a legal left turn in the big cities. Usually, one must go on beyond the desired turn and find a place to do a legal U-turn, or *razvarot*, which is signalled by a curved white arrow on a blue sign. Then there are the trams, which always have priority, and whenever a tram is stationary with its doors open, cars are not allowed to pass and must wait until the tram clatters off again. The combination of bad winters and rotten maintenance fills Soviet roads with potholes, and the tramlines often stand so proud of the road surface that they start looking like tank-traps. The roads are so hard on tyres that any one driving a car with the usual tubeless ones is advised to get inner tubes fitted, because they are easier to repair.

Some of the roads, like the Georgian Military Highway through the Caucasus Mountains, are marvels of engineering. The Moscow Garden Ring Road has ten lanes in some sections and the main roads from the city centre to the airports are good. And there are decent dual carriageway roads in the Baltic Republics, where car ownership per head is the highest in the country. But mostly, the main roads between cities are bad enough to remind the traveller that long-distance transport in the Soviet Union depends on rail and rivers very much more than on roads. There are places on the Moscow–Leningrad road, which should in principle be the country's main arterial road, where it degenerates into a two-track highway. We drove it several times and one of the games devised to keep our children amused was to count up the numbers of different animals that would potter across this main road ahead of us: pigs, cattle, goats, chickens and so on.

Petrol stations

Apart from serving as a constant reminder of the difference between the Soviet Union and the highly motorised countries of the west, this lack of development also means that the motorist cannot count on regular petrol stations. On average, they are over 100 km apart, and on some longer roads, as much as 250 km apart. My own rule was to refill as soon as possible after the petrol gauge registered half-empty. And even when you find a petrol station, you cannot rely on its having 95 octane in stock. The standard Soviet grade is 76 octane, which is not recommended for western engines. In Moscow, the petrol stations by the Tishinsky Market, just off Bolshaya Gruzinskaya, and just beside the Frunze Military Academy, on Pervaya Frunzenskaya Ulitsa, just off the Frunzenskaya Embankment, are the most reliable stockists of 95 octane.

Most petrol stations want vouchers for petrol. Known as *Talon*, each of these vouchers is good for 10 litres, or roughly 2 gallons of petrol, and are paid for in advance at Intourist offices or hotels. Petrol costs about 2 roubles a gallon (4.5 litres). In most cases, if your plight is desperate enough, petrol stations will give you petrol for roubles.

Speed limits

Maximum speed is 110 kph on main roads in open country. In towns, maximum speed is 80 kph on the outer lane of the Moscow ring road and the main arterial roads into the city. Elsewhere in towns, the speed limit is 60 kph, but when going through small villages, where animals and people often seem unaware that the motor car has been invented, drop to 40 kph.

It is a criminal offence in the USSR to drive after consuming any alcohol, even a single vodka or beer.

What to take in

You will need an international driving licence, with an insert in Russian, a car registration document to show that it belongs to you, and an insurance document. You can buy Soviet insurance, through Ingostrakh, at the border for about £40 to £60 (US $70–100) per week, depending on how much you insure your own car for. Entering the country, you will also have to show the Intourist form for motorists, which shows your itinerary and bookings for camp sites or hotels. Your car should also carry a sticker indicating country of origin.

Your car should have been thoroughly serviced before you enter the USSR, with new filters and fresh oil. The brakes should be in perfect condition. One (or better still two) jerry cans for spare petrol will come in useful. Check that your tool kit and spare tyre and wheel changing equipment are in good order. You should take a reasonable selection of spare parts for your car, including a plastic windscreen for emergencies, a tow rope, jump start leads, fan belt, electric points and fuses, light bulbs, spark plugs, windscreen wipers, some engine oil and brake fluid. If you need to purchase more engine oil, the Soviet version of Multigrade, which can be used all year round, goes by the snappy and memorable brand-name M10GI (written М10ГИ). Soviet transmission oil is TAD-17I (written ТАД 17И) and anti-freeze is TOSOL A-40 (written ТОСОЛ А-40). If you do break down, you are required to place a reflective triangle in the road about 45 metres behind your car to warn approaching traffic.

If driving between October and April, have the radiator filled with heavy-duty anti-freeze, and you would be advised to fit a new battery and snow tyres. In winter, fill your windscreen washer reservoir with hot water and anti-freeze before setting out each morning and keep testing to ensure that the tiny nozzles on the bonnet of the car do not freeze up. If driving a fuel injection car, be warned that Soviet petrol is notorious for its capacity to clog up such systems.

Hiring a car

It is possible to hire a car once you arrive in the USSR, but it would be best to plan your itinerary well in advance since for each city you wish to visit, the regulations call for a separate visa authorisation, and applications for these should be made at least six weeks in advance. It is advisable to book the car at the same time. Remember that you will have to ensure there is an Intourist hotel or camp site wherever you wish to stop, and you do not exceed 500 km on any single day's driving.

Type of car
You will be given a recent Lada saloon model. This is a four-seater and a Soviet-built and modified copy of a Fiat design that is now twenty years old. To a driver accustomed to modern western or Japanese cars, the steering will seem spongy, the gears and clutch very imprecise, and the suspension like something that should be pulled by a horse. Ladas are, in fact, like most Soviet technology, very rugged. But if they are not 100 per cent reliable, they are easily fixed. Even if you are stuck by some rural roadside, you will find that many drivers will stop to help, and most will be able to solve the problem.

Cost
For the 1989 season the cost of hiring a car is 24 roubles a day, regardless of the length of time you are booking it for. This includes insurance for third party liability, servicing of the car and a map of permitted Intourist routes. However, it does not include full insurance for any damage done to the car you are hiring, and you are liable for the first 120 roubles of any repair bills, including paintwork damage. To get full insurance cover, you will have to pay an extra 1.5 roubles a day.

Also note that you have to pay 10 kopeks for each kilometre driven. At 1 rouble for every 10 km, this sounds cheap enough. But if you are planning to hire the car for the drive down to Armenia and back, that will cost you over 500 roubles in mileage charges. And if you have hired the car for thirty days to make the trip, and pay for the extra insurance, your total bill will leave little change from 1,265 roubles, before you even think about the cost of the petrol. The best plan is to hire a car for local journeys, and to use train or air travel for long trips.

Where to hire
You may hire cars from Intourist in Brest, Yerevan, Kiev, Kishinev, Leningrad, Lvov, Minsk, Moscow, Odessa, Sochi, Sukhumi, Tbilisi, Kharkov and Yalta. Apply to the service bureau to pick up a prebooked car, or to make a booking once you arrive. The car hire agreement and the insurance are valid for authorised Intourist itineraries only. Unless you want a car just to drive within the city limits, you will have to show your itinerary, issued by Intourist when you booked your holiday, before they will let you have a car.

Permitted routes
If you try to leave the city limits by road without permission, you will be stopped by the GAI traffic police. Intourist hire cars, like all cars driven by foreigners in the USSR, carry distinctive number

plates. A list of all number plates authorised to be on certain roads on certain days is sent to the traffic police along your route. The man hours and paperwork involved in this method of surveillance stagger the imagination, but this is the way the country is run.

If you wish to hire a car while you are in a city where there are no car hire facilities, you may arrange through Intourist for a car to be delivered to you at a cost of 1 rouble for each 5 km you are away from the nearest depot.

Car hire is not available in Central Asia, Siberia, nor in most Baltic regions, though ironically, the latter have the best road systems. As of 1989, the only route permitted to you is Leningrad–Tallinn, but plans are under way to open a new trunk road that will go from Tallinn through Riga and Vilnius to Warsaw.

Chauffeur-driven car hire

If you want to feel like a member of the Politburo for a day, it need only cost 70 roubles – the hire charge for a Chaika limousine for a day, plus driver, from Intourist. Chaikas seat six people, and inside the leg room is vast. The 70 roubles also includes 240 km free mileage and the petrol, so you could use the Chaika to visit the old monastery-fortress of Zagorsk. For an extra 50 roubles, you might try to go the 400 km and back to the old Tolstoy estate-museum at Yasnaya Polyana, though they like to restrict the Chaikas to short trips and city limits. The minimum hire time for a Chaika is one hour, which will cost 13 roubles. Chaika limousines may be hired only in Moscow, Leningrad, Kiev, Riga, Sochi, Tashkent and Tbilisi.

Rather less grandly, you may hire a chauffeur-driven Volga, which seats four people, for 44 roubles a day, with 240 km free mileage included. The Volga saloons, which are the official cars made available to all but the very high ranks of Soviet and Party bureaucrats, are authorised to take you on long trips on Intourist routes.

Camping

When you arrange your route with Intourist, you will have to book camp site places. Throughout the country there are twenty-four camp sites. They vary in size from 100 to over 1,000 plots. They all open on 1 June and close either on 10, 15 or 30 September. They are usually located just outside a town or city in a pleasant, wooded area, and the Odessa camp site is beside a beach. At Odessa, Kalinin, Kiev, Moscow and Pyatigorsk, there is a sauna, and at Pyatigorsk and Odessa, a petrol and service station. A few have small chalets for rent. The vast Kiev camp site boasts over 700. Most have restaurants, and if not, there will be a small shop that sells basic foodstuffs.

You can, in principle, hire everything, from tents to sleeping bags to cooking equipment. But if camping, you are strongly advised to take your own tent, your own sleeping bag and linen, your own cooking utensils and a supply of iron rations. Soviet camp sites tend to run out of things.

The best camp sites are those run by Intourist, where you can be sure that if they have mislaid your booking, your Intourist voucher will guarantee you a place. The Intourist camp sites are:

Kalinin: Tver, 130 Leningrad Highway; tel. 5-56-92. The camp site is attached to the motel, which is located as you enter the city on the main road from Leningrad. No restaurant. Fifty plots are available for customers' tents. Two hundred tents and chalets available. Closes 30 September.

Kiev: 1 Brest-Litovsky Prospekt; tel. 44-12-93. The camp site is attached to the motel, which is located at the entrance to the city coming from Lvov and Zhitomir. There is a restaurant, and a hard currency bar in the motel. A massive and rather grim place, with 300 free plots and 759 chalets. Closes 30 September.

Minsk: 16 km west of the city on the main road to Brest; tel. 29-68-219. The next turn-off after the camp site leads to a motel and petrol station. It has 100 free plots, and 500 tents and chalets. No services at this camp site, but food available at nearby motel. Closes 15 September.

Moscow: 165 Mozhaisky Highway, attached to the motel where Moscow's main outer ring road crosses the main road to the west; tel. 446-5141. (This should not be confused with the Butovo camp site, 24 km south of the city, which is not run by Intourist.) There are 300 free plots, and 200 tents and chalets available. There is a bar and restaurant and full Intourist services at the motel. Closes 15 September.

Odessa: 299 Kotovsky, Luzanovka; tel. 55-22-61. The Delphin camp site, on the outskirts of the city, in the suburb of Luzanovka, is perhaps the best in the USSR. It has a restaurant and bar and all facilities except a bank and international telephone link, which are available at the nearby motel in Pobeda Park. It has 120 free plots, 120 tents for hire and 110 chalets. Closes 30 September.

Sukhumi: located in the village of Gumista, on the Novorossiisk road, 5 km north of Sukhumi; tel. 295-68. It has 50 free plots, and 150 tents and chalets for hire. A pleasant location. There is a restaurant, but facilities are spartan. Closes 15 September.

Yalta: called Polyana Skazok, this camp site is located on the Yalta bypass, about 20 minutes' walk from the town; tel. 395-249. It has 100 free plots, and 240 tents and chalets. There is a restaurant, bar, telephone and Intourist service bureau. Closes 30 September.

Leningrad: there is no Intourist camp site in Leningrad, but the Repino village camp site, 48 km from Leningrad on the main road to Vyborg and Finland, is delightfully located in the village named after the great Russian artist Repin; tel. 231-6839. It has 250 free plots, 500 tents for hire and a restaurant. Bookings for the camp site can be made through Intourist. It closes early on 10 September.

Getting About in Cities

By Metro

The plan is to build Metros in all the biggest Soviet cities. The Moscow Metro is the most famous, but Leningrad, Kiev, Tbilisi and Tashkent also have their own Metros, and others are 'a-building', not always to the gratitude of the citizens. Indeed, in the Latvian city of Riga, a lovely old Hanseatic trading port, opposition to the Metro has become a symbol of Latvian nationalism.

The Moscow Metro

The Moscow Metro, a source of pride since its construction in the 1930s was organised by two young Stalin loyalists from the Party machine, Kaganovitch and Khrushchev, is now in trouble. Too little maintenance, too much traffic, and the general laxity and falling off of standards, which marked the Brezhnev years, have tarnished the showcase. There have been occasional accidents and one attempt at sabotage in 1973 when Armenian nationalists placed a bomb in a carriage. It remains, for most foreigners, the cleanest and most punctual Metro in the world, and probably the safest (I have heard of no case of mugging on the Metro). But the 6 million passengers daily also make it one of the most crowded. Try to avoid it at rush hours, from 7.30 to 10 a.m., and from 4 to 6.30 p.m. It closes at 1 a.m. and opens just before 6 a.m.

The Moscow Metro also encapsulates modern Soviet architectural history. The first line, 11.6 km long, was opened in 1935, running between Sokolniki and Park Kultury. The second line between Sokol and Ploshchad Sverdlova (Sverdlovsk Square, in front of the Bolshoy Theatre) was opened three years later. The finest looking stations all date from this period, when the vogue phrase said they were to be the palaces of the working class, and they were all deep enough to be used as air raid shelters during the war.

Mayakovskaya, Ploshchad Sverdlova and Kropotkinskaya are my own favourites. Mayakovskaya station was the site of Stalin's famous speech to the Moscow Party committee in November 1941, and Kropotkinskaya was originally named Dvorets Sovyetov, or Palace of Soviets. This had been the site of a huge nineteenth-century Cathedral of Christ Saviour, demolished by Stalin to make way for a new building to symbolise the power of the Revolution. Intended to be the biggest building in the world, it was to have been topped by a 61-metre high statue of Lenin, towering over the city. But the marshy soil by the river could not take the foundations, much to the delight of the faithful who believed the Bolsheviks were being punished for their blasphemous destruction of a cathedral. To this day, you can see elderly people cross themselves as they pass the site. It has now become the famous open-air heated swimming pool, identified in winter by the constant cloud of steam that hangs over it, and which is slowly rotting the paintings in the nearby Pushkin Museum.

The Metro never stops being built. The network already extends over 200 km, with 115 stations, and it is planned to reach 400 km by the end of the century. New lines are still being opened, the latest runs down to the south-east of the city, and its Tulskaya Station is handy for the newly-restored centre of the Orthodox Church, the Danilovsky Monastery. One of the signs of falling standards has been a design and tunnelling scandal. The extension of this line, which like the other new ones is more spartan than the classics of the 1930s, into the centre of the city, and the building of the new station Biblioteka Imeni Lenina, or the Lenin Library, has undermined the foundations of the Library itself. Some books and archives have been evacuated for safety and parts of the library have been closed to scholars. The scandal was exposed by one of the country's best female journalists, Olga Tschaikovskaya, on *Literary Gazette*, who blamed the politicians for bullying the engineers to push on and finish the line on time, at all costs.

Using the Metro

A Metro station is indicated by a large red neon 'M' by the entrance at the top of the steps. To pay for one journey you put a 5-kopek coin into the automatic barrier. There are change machines at every station which will give 5-kopek coins in return for a 20-, 15- or 10-kopek piece. The small window marked касса will change rouble notes, or sell 6-rouble Metro passes that are valid for a month. You may change trains as often as you like and ride as far as you wish for the 5 kopeks. But once you pass out of the barriers again, your ride is over.

From the platforms, there will be one or more exits leading out on to the street, which are marked: Выход в город or *V'hod v gorod*, which means exit to the city. At big stations, these exits can be a considerable distance apart, so if you want a particular street corner, ask another passenger. There will also be an exit which says: Переход на поезда до станций; this is pronounced, *Perekhot na poyezda da stantsiy...*, and means, Change for stations ..., and will give the names of those you can reach by changing to another line.

There is an illuminated sign at the end of each platform that tells you how long it is since the last train left. In rush hours the next train will be along in little more than a minute. Even late at night, I have never waited more than ten minutes.

The golden rule is to plan your journey before you enter the Metro, and to have written down the Cyrillic form of the station you are aiming for, plus the names of any stations where you have to change lines. It is then simply a matter of checking the *perekhot* (transfer) list for your station. When you get to the right platform, you should check the signs again to see which direction you want, and thus on which side of the platform to stand.

Just before the carriage doors close, a loudspeaker in each train announces: '*Astarozhna, dveri zakrivayutsa, sleduyushchaya stantsiya . . .*' – 'Attention, the doors are closing, the next station will be . . .' And as you arrive at the next station, its name will be announced, together with the *perekhot*, or transfer, to any other lines: '*Stantsiya Kievskaya, perekhot na Koltsivuyu Liniyu*', which means you are pulling into the Kiev Station and can change to the Circle Line. Sometimes, you have to walk a very long way. For example, if you are changing from Prospekt Marksa to Ploshchad Sverdlova, you face a 365 metres' walk along the well-lit underground tunnel.

By bus, tram and trolley bus

These also cost 5 kopeks a ride. Until Gorbachev came to power, trolley buses cost 4 kopeks and trams 3 kopeks. They run from just after 5 a.m., are all crowded and uncomfortable and follow complex routes that are of little help to the tourist. The exceptions are the buses that run up and down Gorky Street, and around the Garden Ring Road, though these are often the most crowded of the lot.

You should have small change ready to pay for your ride, dropping the 5 kopeks into the box provided, or, when as usual it is too crowded to do this yourself, hand your fare to somebody nearer the front and say: '*Piridayite, pazhalsta*', or pass it on, please. In return, you should get a thin paper ticket, which is meant to be stuck into one of the punches placed around the vehicle. You may also buy rolls of ten tickets from the driver.

To get off, start saying, '*Vy seychas vihoditye?*', which means, are you getting off now, and is the standard phrase to clear the way.

There are said to be plain-clothes inspectors who make very occasional and random checks of passengers to make sure that they have paid their fare. I have never encountered one, but am told that they are understanding with baffled tourists who speak no Russian.

I have a soft spot for trams and although the Moscow vehicles provide a very uncomfortable ride, during the day they are usually less crowded and there are worse ways to see the city. A tram-ride around the eastern boulevard ring, from Pokrovsky Boulevard into the centre past the Turgenevskaya Station, is a pleasant way to see one of the more charming quarters.

By taxi

There are minibus taxis, called Marshrutnoye Taxi, which take a fixed route between major centres, such as train stations or the big squares. They are usually crowded and cost 15 kopeks.

The yellow taxis have meters and if you catch one at one of the taxi ranks outside the main stations, the meter charge is what you will pay, plus the usual tip of 20 kopeks. But to get a taxi outside your hotel is to engage in negotiations with a driver who will usually be fluent enough in the broken English and sign language of international barter. A carton of western cigarettes or a bottle of Scotch should easily secure you a taxi for the whole day, to take you all around the city. For short rides, they will probably ask for dollars or Deutschmarks, or demand a very much higher fare than the meter. The sharks outside Moscow's Mezhdunarodnaya Hotel are the worst.

Taxis show whether they are free by a green light in the top right corner of the windscreen. This is rarely lit. At night, or in the rain, if you really need a yellow cab, hold up two fingers if you are ready to pay twice the meter fare. Four fingers, four times the fare, should get you a ride. Do not despair if the yellow cabs do not stop, somebody else always will. Every private car in Moscow, and all official cars with the exceptions of Zils, are ready to do a little moonlighting. I have been driven home by an ambulance, a police car, a black Chaika limousine which normally worked for the Moscow city council, a fire engine and a snow-clearing truck, as well as by lots of private cars.

The peoples' taxis

The new fashion for co-ops and private enterprise means that anybody can use their private car as a taxi, in return for buying a licence which costs about 400 roubles. There is also, this being the USSR, a vast amount of bureaucracy to go through to get a taxi permit, including medical checks, approvals from your usual place of work and trade union, and authorisations from offices all across the city. So, many drivers in Moscow do not bother. But in the rather more efficient Baltic cities of Riga, Tallinn and Vilnius, more than half of all the available cabs are now official co-ops, small family limousines with chequered signs fixed to their roof-racks.

Usually, the fare will be 2 to 3 roubles for the average Moscow journey during daylight or the evening. After midnight, it can rise considerably. To take a party of guests from southern Moscow where I lived to the Cosmos Hotel in the far north at 3 a.m., 10 roubles was too little. Two or three packs of Marlboros would have done the trick, but we were all non-smokers. However, a small bottle of vodka was found and won me the eternal gratitude of the driver. You should make sure that your destination is written down in Cyrillic, so that you can show it to the driver, otherwise you should have great faith in your spoken Russian. And, if using the peoples' taxis, have several small notes to hand. Do not expect the driver to give you change.

Where to Stay

Once you book a Soviet holiday, you just about surrender your rights as a capitalist consumer. You will be assigned a hotel and, if you do not like it, tough. The only way to beat the system is to be very rich and to book your holiday independently from the beginning. But you can expect to pay 70 to 120 roubles a night, and you will usually be assigned to the same hotels anyway.

Most of the hotels are of an acceptable standard, though they do not offer outstanding value for money. If anything does not work, complain. However, there is little to be done about the flimsy bath towels, the gritty soap, the abrasive lavatory paper, and the paper-thin and undersized curtains that will have the sun streaming into your eyes just after dawn. The person to complain to about broken lamp bulbs, blocked toilets and so on is the *dezhurnaya*, the floor manageress, who sits by the lift and hands out the room keys. She is also the person who will sell you tea and mineral water, and arrange for your laundry to be done.

But for all its faults, your hotel is your home, your rock of security in a bewildering land. It is the place where you will be expected to eat. It will contain everything the complaisant tourist requires, from souvenir shop to post office to hard currency bar. You need hardly leave the premises, except to follow your Intourist guide on the official excursions, and in the old days, this was the way the Soviet Union preferred its tourists to behave. These days, they are more welcoming, and you are positively encouraged to make forays into the town, to explore and to meet the locals. But bear in mind that the hotel is also a representative body of the Soviet system. It has a right to take away your passport and give you a flimsy room card in exchange. This is your substitute passport, which identifies you as a genuine guest of the hotel, will let you in and out of the hotel at will, and will mollify policemen should they demand your papers. Do not lose it.

Veterans of Soviet travel fall into two camps. There are those who prefer the modern hotels, where the lift works, there are private bathrooms and the rooms are all the same. And there is the rather smaller group who grimly tolerate these modern places without any character, and relish the discomforts and idiosyncrasies of the older hotels. There are hotels that date from before the Revolution, such as Moscow's National and the Metropol, where you can still catch a faint whiff of the grandeur of a long distant past, and there are the Stalin-era hotels, which sometimes seem older. My favourite is the Ukraina on the west bank of the Moscow River. Better to admire it than to stay in the place, the Ukraina reminds all its guests of the insignificance of mere mortals when set against the grandeur of Stalin's dreams. You should have plenty of time to ponder these philosophical matters as you wait for the world's slowest lifts. Still, I suspect that the older hotels will become increasingly popular as the hotels that were the height of modernity in the 1970s, like Moscow's Intourist, start to show their age.

Eating and Drinking

Although Intourist has begun offering 'Gourmet Tours' of the Soviet Union, it is a rare experience to dine really well, or to explore seriously the subtleties of food and wine, except in private homes, and in the Caucasian Republics. Eating in Soviet restaurants and hotels means that you will not starve, and you will rarely have a really bad meal. You are likely, however, to become increasingly bored with the general sameness of Russian food. You will not go wrong with a meal of *zakuski*, *borsch* and chicken kiev or beef stroganoff and, indeed, the first and second and even third tasting of such meals can still be a feast. But the repertoire of Soviet chefs is usually limited and the lack of variety becomes wearisome. The way to avoid this is to explore the many ethnic restaurants, which reflect the cultural diversity of the country. And although the prices are high, it is worth taking advantage of one of the most prominent symbols of the Gorbachev reforms by trying a co-operative restaurant. Do not settle every night for the food in your hotel dining room; this is package tour cooking.

On the whole, Soviet people do not go to restaurants frequently, and when they do it is not for the food. For them, the attraction is the entertainment, the music and dancing, the drink and the chance of a good time. Restaurants are for celebrations. Thus in the evenings, there will usually be a very noisy band, making conversation difficult. The service is often slow. Many of your fellow diners will be ebullient and noisy, brimming over with that assertive good fellowship that can be distinctly irritating for those who do not share the mood. Join in, and you are likely to have a splendid evening of toasts, dancing and international peace and friendship that may well end up with the party continuing in somebody's flat long after the restaurant has closed.

You will have a quieter meal at lunch, because there is no band, and the recent anti-alcohol campaigns mean that no alcohol is served until 2 p.m. Thus, the fashionable time to book a table in a Moscow restaurant is 1.30 p.m. But for foreigners with their hard currency, such rules are made to be broken. In Moscow's National Hotel restaurant, hand the waiters a few dollars at noon and ask them to stroll to the hard currency bar for a bottle of wine or some beers. In a co-operative restaurant, simply take in your own wine discreetly wrapped in some newspaper. It will magically reappear on your table in a large jug, pretending to be fruit juice.

Russian meals

Zavtrak (breakfast)

In a Soviet hotel, this will usually consist of fruit juice, tea or coffee, boiled or fried eggs, bread, butter and jam. But you should try some Russian specialities. *Kasha* is buckwheat porridge, by which the Russians swear, although you seldom see them eat it, except when prepared at home with lots of butter. Instead of the usual tomato or apple juice, try *kefir*, which is either a very thick buttermilk or a thin yoghurt. *Tvorog*, or deep-fried curds, are often available. Slightly sweet and highly nourishing, they, like the *kefir*, are very good for the stomach, and both may be confidently recommended if too much vodka has been drunk the previous evening. Russian coffee is not good, but then count yourself lucky to be drinking it at all. Few of the locals can afford to, with the latest price rise taking it to 20 roubles a kilo, while the average Moscow wage is 50 roubles a week.

Obyed (lunch) and oozhen (dinner)

These days, the two meals are very similar. Fashions change. Like eighteenth-century English squires, the Russian gentry used to sit down to a massive dinner in mid-afternoon and save the evening for dancing, cards and a light supper. The French influence brought in the formal seated dinner, but the Russians had their revenge by introducing the buffet, and by giving the word 'bistro' to the world. In Russian, it means 'quickly', and after Napoleon's defeat, the Russian troops in Paris would shout 'bistro' in the restaurants.

The Russian buffet is a great institution, and in the past often served as a splendid joke on the unwary foreign visitor. Dinner would be announced, and the party would advance on a huge table covered in delicacies, but without a single chair to sit on. The guests would happily stand to eat, going from caviar to crab to roast chicken, from devilled eggs to stuffed hams, from salads to salmon, and from pies to pickles. The foreign guest would eat with enthusiasm, and just as he was about to put down the plate, fold the napkin and declare himself well satisfied, the footmen would open the next set of doors and the party would stroll through to the real dining room for the sit-down dinner.

These traditional Russian buffets are still served by prior arrangement at the grander hotels, or in the state guest houses in the Lenin Hills on formal occasions. Most evenings will see such a *koktyel* in the Zerkalny Zal, the Mirrored Hall of the Praga Restaurant, or on the first floor of the National Hotel. If invited, accept with alacrity, even though in these days of the anti-alcohol campaign, there will be more Pepsi and mineral water on offer than vodka and wine.

Zakuski

At more humble occasions, the grand Russian buffet lives on in the *zakuski*. The word means snacks, or hors d'oeuvres, and for many people it is the best part of the meal.

Black caviar from the sturgeon	*ikra (chornaya)*	Икра (Черная)
Blinys (buckwheat pancakes) with caviar	*bleeny s'ikroi*	Блины с икрой
Blinys with soured cream	*bleeny s'smetanoi*	Блины со сметаной
Chicken and potato salad	*stolichny salat*	Столичный салат
Cucumber salad	*salat iz ogurtsov*	Салат из огурцов
Herring	*syeld*	Сельдь
Pickled mushrooms	*mareenovaniye greeby*	Мари鮮ваные грибы
Red caviar from the salmon	*ikra (krasnaya)*	Икра (Красная)
Smoked salmon	*kapchonaya syomga*	Копченая семга
Sturgeon	*osetrina*	Осетрина
Tomato salad	*salat iz pomidorov*	Салат из помидоров

Soups

Борщ
Borsch

Then comes the soup course, and 'Ruskrainian' soups (which is one way of avoiding the Russian–Ukrainian arguments over who invented which) can be magnificent.

To say this is beetroot soup is to say that they do a bit of dancing at the Bolshoy. Properly made, it begins with a large shin of beef, then the beetroot, followed by everything else. A naval *borsch* (*borsch flotskii*) will be based on a ham bone stock and contain bacon plus tomato purée. Some experts (including the chef at Moscow's National who makes a good one) maintain that it should be accompanied by a meat *pirogi* (pastry) as well as by soured cream.

Other wonderful soups are:

Cabbage soup, but often made as thickly nourishing as a good *borsch*. You should be able to pick out chunks of ham or salami	*shchi*	Щи
Cold vegetable soup, made with *kvass* (beetroot water), and very good in summer	*okroshka*	Окрошка

| Kidney and cucumber soup | *rassolnik* | Рассольник |
| Thick meat or fish soup, very filling | *solyanka myasnaya* or *ribnaya* | Солянка |

At this point in the meal, if you are lucky, you might be offered one of the great Soviet dishes:

| Mushrooms cooked with onions in soured cream, served in tiny silver pots, topped with cheese and toasted. Quite delicious | *greeby v'smetanye* | Грибы в сметане |

Another relic of the great old days when meals were feasts is that the main course is called both first dish (*pervoye blyuda*), which means the fish, and the second dish (*vtoroye blyuda*), which means the meat. In these feeble days, we normally choose one or the other.

Fish

Fried pike-perch	*Soodak free*	Судак фри
Poached pike-perch	*Soodak atvarnoy*	Судак отварной
Sturgeon, casseroled with tomatoes and vegetables	*osetrina pa-russki*	Осетрина по-русски
Fried sturgeon	*osetrina free*	Осетрина фри
Trout	*faryel*	Форель

Other fish are seldom available, save occasionally for carp, which is pronounced 'karp', and salmon (*syomga*), which is usually smoked and served with the *zakuski*.

Meats

Beef stroganoff	*beef-stroganoff*	Беф-строганов
Cabbage leaves stuffed with minced beef	*goloobtsi*	Голубцы
Grilled steak	*bifsteks naturalni*	Бифштекс натуральный
Goulash	*goolyash*	Гуляш
Pork, roasted with plums	*zharkoye iz svinir s'slivami*	Жаркое из свинины со сливами
Rice pilau with mutton	*ploff iz baranini*	Плов из баранины
Roast beef and vegetables	*rostbif s'garnisrom*	Ростбиф с гарниром

	Shish kebab or meat grilled on skewers, usually lamb	*shashlik*	Шашлык
	Veal cutlet	*shnitzel*	Шницель
Game and poultry	Boiled chicken	*kuritsa atvarnaya*	Курица отварная
	Chicken kiev	*kotlyeta po-Kievski*	Котлеты по-киевски
	Duck with apples	*ootka s'yablokami*	Утка с яблоками
	Goose with apples	*goos s'yablokami*	Гусь с яблоками
	Roast and pressed chicken, Georgian-style	*kuritsa tabaka*	Курица табака

The usual final dish is ice cream (*marozhenoye*), but occasionally you may be offered:

Puddings	Apple pie	*yablochny pirog*	Яблочный пирог
	Jam pancakes	*blinchiki s'varyenyem*	Блинчики с вареньем
	Rum baba	*romovaya baba*	Ромовая баба

Drink

The classic Russian drink is vodka, taken supercold – fresh from the freezer (or the gap between the double-glazed windows in winter) so that the bottle is frosted. In restaurants, it is normally ordered by the hundred grams (*sto gram*), the usual portion per head if other drinks are to follow. It is always served in a tiny glass, which is drained at a single swallow after a suitable toast.

At a meal, you will usually be served a plain vodka of export quality, a Moskovskaya or Stolichnaya brand, or even the cheaper Russkaya. It is also worth trying some of the other plain brands, such as Kuban or Pshenichnaya, to see if you can tell the difference. If you are prepared to splash out twice the usual price for a bottle of 'Golden Ring' vodka at 12 roubles in the Beriozka, then the difference should be apparent. The flavoured vodkas like Pertsovka (red peppers) or Limonnaya (lemons) are not drunk with meals.

Wine   Soviet wines suffer from state price control, which gives wine growers little incentive to produce anything special for the mass market. However, Georgian, Moldavian or Crimean wines drunk on the spot, having been bottled and cared for by somebody who knows and loves wines, can be quite splendid, unlike the very ordinary wines that reach the Moscow hotels and shops. Even the Bulgarian cabernet wines, which have won a good reputation in the west, are disappointing in the Soviet Union. The Bulgarians would rather earn hard currency from the west than roubles from Moscow, and so their Russian comrades get the plonk.

Still, if you cannot get one of the Georgian wines, then settle for a Bulgarian or Moldavian Kabernay. The Georgian Mukudzani or Saperavi reds are very drinkable dryish table wines. For historical reasons, you should try Stalin's favourite red wines, Hvanch'kara and Kindzma'aruli, though they taste sweet to a western palate. Pushkin claimed that the heavily scented and full-bodied wines of Kakhetia, of eastern Georgia, were like French Burgundies. They certainly are less rich and cloying than the Azerbaijani wines Matrassa and Shamkhor, which would probably be taken as dessert wines in the west.

The best dry white wine is again Georgian, Tsinandali, which is rather like an Aligote. It is usually served warm, but ask for ice cubes (*lyod*) to cool it down. Georgian Gurdzhani is also a good dry wine. Georgians are proud of their semi-sweet whites Tetra and Akhmeta, and the extremely sweet white Tvishi, but these are crude wines, whose rawness is not disguised by the abundant sugar. Table wines will cost you less than 2 roubles a bottle in the Beriozka, and 3 to 4 roubles in a restaurant.

The Massandra winery at Yalta, in the Crimea, was experimenting very successfully with some dry white wines. It still houses the Tsar's old cellars, and they contain some outstanding eighteenth-century Madeiras and nineteenth-century clarets. Since most Russian alcoholics drink the rotgut cheap fortified wines known as Barmatukha (babbling juice), Massandra was trying to educate the national palate into appreciating a light table wine to go with food. I tasted several of their attempts, which were getting better year by year, and the 1985 was very promising indeed. Sadly, it was also the year that the anti-alcohol campaign was announced in Moscow. The mindless bureaucrats ordered the experimental vineyards to be ploughed up, so they could report on their teetotal zeal to Moscow.

Sparkling wines

Russians are very proud of their champagnes, even though they have now been forced to rename them 'sparkling wines' by the French. Soviet taste is for a sweet champagne, which is very cloying. Western palates will prefer the 'brut', which is dryish, or the Sukhoy, or Polysukhoy, which are less sweet than the rest. Most of it is made (that is, the bubbles are added) in Moscow. But if you find a bottle marked Novi Svyet, which is from the Crimea, it will be rather good. Also, if you can obtain a bottle, try the rare but very good Georgian sparkling dry white wine called Chkhaveri. It is rather like a Portuguese Vinho Verde, and less likely to give you a thumping headache than Soviet champagne. The ordinary champagne will cost you 5 roubles in the Beriozka, and 8–10 roubles in a restaurant.

Brandies

Soviet cognacs are very good. Every Armenian will tell you that Winston Churchill, after being given a bottle by Stalin at the Yalta Conference, would drink nothing else thereafter. The Georgians tell the same story about their cognac, and add that since Stalin was a Georgian, it must be true. They certainly price it steeply. Cheap brands are available, but a decent bottle will cost at least 15 roubles in the state shops, and 8 roubles or more in the Beriozka. The best Armenian brands are Yubileiny, Ararat, Yerevan and Dvin, and the best Georgian are Tbilisi, Gremi, Vartsikhe and Eniseli. The cognacs of Azerbaijan also have their adherents.

Restaurants

There are several different kinds of public eating places in the Soviet Union, offering a wide range of prices and quality.

Buffets   *Boofyet* буфет

In stations, airports and hotels, theatres or large entertainment centres like Moscow's Tchaikovsky Hall or the Olympic stadiums, buffets serve tea and coffee, soft drinks and fruit juices as well as bars of chocolate, and a range of sandwiches (*booterbrod*), usually cheese (*seer*), salami (*kolbassa*) or smoked fish (*reeba*). In theatres, they usually offer open caviar sandwiches. Until the anti-alcohol campaign, you could also buy champagne by the glass. Indeed, when the Bolshoy Company was performing at the huge 6,000 seat Palace of Congresses in the Kremlin, one of the most impressive displays of mass catering was to watch the way 6,000 spectators could be whisked up to the top floor buffet on banks of escalators, fed champagne and caviar canapés and whisked down again all within twenty minutes.

Cafeterias   *Stolovaya* столовая

These are where most Soviets eat out. They are cheap and rather nasty. You can get a bowl of soup and bread, macaroni and meatballs or chicken croquettes, and a glass of fruit compote (like a watery jam) for a rouble. It is like all institutional food produced to a tight budget; think of school meals. They ought to be on every tourist itinerary, to give a quick insight into the Soviet quality of life. Intourist will not show you one, but in Moscow, you will find a classic example at the Tsentralny Rinok, the central market on Tsvetnoi Boulevard. The best ones I know, though, are in Tashkent (see p. 275).

There is another version of the *stolovaya* in residential areas called a *domovaya kukhnaya*, or a home kitchen. The original rather idealistic idea in the 1920s was to free women from housework and cooking through cheap, communal restaurants, whose ovens and cooking facilities were also available to locals for special occasions. The places have long since become cheap cafeterias. There is one on the southern side of Moscow's Serpukhovsky Val, about 300 metres from the Tulskaya Metro station.

Kebab bars | ***Shashlichnaya*** шашлычная

These vary in quality and decor. They can be open air barbecue stands, of the kind you will find in Gorky Park, where you can get a skewer of meat, bread and ketchup and still have change from a rouble. They can be rather brief, flimsy kiosks, with chest-high tables at which you stand to eat, like the one mentioned on p. 125 on the corner of Serpukhovsky Val and the Warsaw Chaussee. Or they can be proper restaurants which specialise in *shashlik*. In Moscow one of the best is on Ulitsa Dmitrova, opposite the large new toy store (see p. 183). For atmosphere, the best *shashlik* bars are in Tbilisi in Georgia. The mutton *shashlik* of Armenia, which are marinated for some hours in onions and spices before cooking, are also good.

Pelmeni bars | ***Pyelmennaya*** пельменная

Pyelmennaya are the Russian version of ravioli. They are small dumplings filled with meat, usually served in a *bouillon* sauce. A classic Siberian dish, it is somewhat bland to western tastes, although very filling. Like most Russian cooking, they are much better eaten in somebody's home, when individual cooks add different herbs or spices, than in the public bars.

Sausage bars | ***Sosiskaya*** сосиская

The sausages served in these traditional, small, dark and friendly bars are watery, filled with cereal, have tough skins and are chewy. But the excellent mustard makes up for it. The sausages come served with bread. If you could buy a beer at the same time, it would make a respectable snack.

Bliny bars | ***Blinnaya*** блиная

Take some hot blinys still oozing butter, smear them with soured cream and spread thickly with black caviar, fold over and then eat this heavenly dish, followed by a slug of freezing vodka and you will be a convert to bliny-culture for life. Sadly, your first experience of a Soviet bliny bar could well put you off again. The blinys come plain, leaking margarine, or spread with a miserly smear of plum jam, or shreds of smoked fish. And instead of being thin and crisp at the edges, the blinys are fat and stodgy.

Pie stalls | ***Pirozhkovaya*** пирожковая

The *pirogi*, or meat pie, is so honoured in Russian tradition that the Muscovites even named a street after it – Bolshoya Pirogovskaya, which leads to the Novodevichy Monastery. Do not listen to pedants who say it was named after someone called Pirogov; even if they are right, he was probably named after his mother's pies. There is a Russian proverb about the beauty of a home lying not in its furnishings, but in the pies baked by the hostess. They can be filled with meat, onions, mushrooms, fish, or a mix of meat and vegetables. In Kiev, they sometimes serve a delicious kind with pork and apple. They should be served hot.

Ice cream parlours	**_Morozhenoye_** мороженое

Soviet ice cream is excellent, varied and somehow they seem to sell as much of the stuff in winter as they do in summer. Sales average 187 tons a day in Moscow, all year round.

Outside almost every Metro station, on street corners and near bus stops you will find a small ice cream kiosk, selling Eskimo bars (a vanilla ice cream cylinder covered in chocolate ice cream) or blocks of plain ice cream. But the sit-down ice cream parlours make all kinds of exotic concoctions with blackcurrant syrup, nuts and chocolate sauce.

Beer bars   **_Pivnoy_** пивной бар

These are grim places, on the whole, the beer usually served by automat. But the snacks can sometimes be tasty, even if the shells and heads of the shrimps and the stale crusts of the sandwiches often end up in a foul stew beneath your feet.

Cafés   **_Kafay_** кафе

Soviet cafés are rather more ambitious than the name suggests. Since most of the places called restaurants usually offer dinner and dancing and live music, the café is often the place to go for simple food. The more ambitious ones usually serve soups, omelettes, steak or meatballs or roast chicken with basic vegetables. They are more expensive than the _stolovaya_, but cheaper than the restaurant. A three-course meal for two of soup, steak and ice cream with a bottle of wine should cost just under 10 roubles.

Ethnic restaurants

As a gesture to socialist solidarity, Warsaw Pact and other friendly countries have been invited to open restaurants which specialise in their own cuisine. With a handful of exceptions, this experiment has not been a success, mainly because of the difficulty of obtaining the right ingredients.

Co-operative restaurants

'When I eat pork at a meal, give me the whole pig; when mutton, give me the whole sheep; when goose, the whole bird. Two dishes are better than a thousand, provided that a fellow can devour as much of them as he wants.' Sobakevitch at dinner in Gogol's _Dead Souls_.

When Andrey Anatolovich Fyodorov opened a restaurant in the old aristocrat's town house on Moscow's Kropotkinskaya in the early spring of 1987, it was the first tangible sign that the Gorbachev reforms might change the quality of Soviet life. It was the first of the new crop of co-operative restaurants, in which the salaries of everyone from chef to doorman depended on pleasing the paying customers, and which might even be allowed to go bankrupt if the customers stayed away. And given the prices, the customers would have every justification. The co-ops were not allowed to purchase their raw materials from the state warehouses which supplied the state restaurants, and were thus forced to buy at the peasants' free markets, where they were paying 8 roubles a kilo for meat instead of the state price of 2 roubles. In the first few weeks of the Kropotkinskaya Co-op's existence, customers reeled out amazed after paying bills of up to 100 roubles for four, without alcohol.

Prices began to settle down as this first co-op, and then its successors, began to make arrangements with individual farms for regular supplies of meat and vegetables at more reasonable prices, and as competition began to bite. But even these entrepreneurial pioneers were strangers to the ways of free markets. Fyodorov was personally offended when the first rival co-op opened in Khimki, and when he went to the market at dawn one morning, he found that the Khimki manager had already bought up the meat. Well connected (and it took political influence to get the first co-op licence), Fyodorov then tried to have allocated to him a small collective farm in the Moscow district to guarantee cheap food supplies. There were also problems with the rule that forbade co-ops from selling alcohol and at least one of Fyodorov's co-op members was sacked for selling vodka.

Then the co-ops became something of a political football, their high prices leading to largely justified complaints that only foreigners and black marketeers could afford them. The complaints were directed more against the co-op *shashlik* stalls, where the meat was being sold at 2 roubles for 100 grams (or ten times the price of meat in state stores), and against the co-op clothing stalls than the restaurants. But conservatives in the Moscow City Council, in the Party bureaucracy and in the Politburo were able to cite public disquiet when they noted that these new-fangled co-ops seemed to be the kind of profiteering capitalism that the 1917 Revolution had overthrown.

This battle is not over, and the co-op boom could yet burst as fast as it grew. But partly because so many Soviet opinion-makers in the arts and the media have been to these places and enjoyed them, and partly because so many have now opened, the signs are that the co-ops are here to stay. By the end of 1988, there were over a hundred in Moscow alone, a dozen in Leningrad, but only two in Kiev, where the local council seemed more reluctant to experiment with these novelties. There are dozens in Georgia, but there, the principles of private enterprise and of taking pride and pleasure in good food, have never faded.

If the prices still seem too high, remember that competition takes time to work and that a hundred competing co-ops is not a lot for a city of over 8 million. Above all, bear in mind (as the co-ops do) that this experiment with private enterprise could be stopped at any time, as Lenin's New Economic Policy (see pp. 48–49) was stopped after his death.

It takes courage to set up on one's own, even in Gorbachev's Russia, and the high prices also reflect a determination by the co-op members to get their investment back within the first couple of years. So if you wince at the bill, console yourself with the thought that when you eat co-op, you are not only getting a better meal than elsewhere, you can claim to be doing your bit for the Gorbachev revolution.

Entertainment

Ballet

Intourist usually arranges at least one cultural evening for most foreign visitors, a night at the Bolshoy ballet in Moscow, or at the Kirov in Leningrad, or at the circus. The Soviets are proud of them, and it has somehow become an automatic part of the guided tour, a fixture on the itinerary for package tourists and official guests. Former British Prime Minister Harold Wilson once complained that he had seen *Swan Lake* seven times in the Soviet Union; moreover, the Soviet version insists on a happy ending. But however many times you have been to the ballet, you should not miss the Bolshoy.

For the next year or so, while its crumbling eighteenth-century building on Moscow's Sverdlovsk Square is being repaired, you will probably have to see the Bolshoy company in the massive 6,000-seat Palace of Congresses inside the Kremlin. The original theatre, which holds a maximum of 2,000 people, was half the pleasure of going to the ballet. The red plush and gold, the chandeliers and boxes are exactly how a grand theatre ought to look. Until the Gorbachev economic reforms gave the Bolshoy a direct interest in the box office receipts, it used to be one of the world's great bargains, at 3 roubles a ticket. These days, foreigners are charged up to 25 roubles in hard currency, but the experience is still cheap at the price.

The Bolshoy company, however, is not at its best. When Britain's Royal Ballet toured the Soviet Union in 1987, one of the leading Soviet ballet critics observed that what the world needed was a combination of British choreographers and Bolshoy dancers. The technical skills and training of the Russian dancers remain superb, but an increasingly tired and hackneyed repertoire is showing its age. The Bolshoy is run by and for the older generation. Maya Plisetskaya was a great ballerina, and it is sad to see her in decline, even though the new ballet of Chekhov's *Lady with a Dog* was written for her, and with her stiffening limbs in mind. The Bolshoy's director is Yuri Grigorevich, who introduced the fiery and dramatic *Spartakus* in the 1960s, and a very much less successful version of Prokofiev's *Ivan the Terrible* in the 1970s. *Spartakus* was his last real triumph.

The backstage controversies came out into the open in 1987 at angry meetings of the Bolshoy company, with the women dancers complaining that in the few new ballets that were being performed, all the best roles were going to the men. This is undoubtedly true, capitalising on the tradition of heroic leaps and superb Soviet training for male dancers which made Nureyev and Baryshnikov into superstars when they came to the west. However, the Bolshoy's new Georgian ballerina, Alla Khaniashvili, looks set to dance the men off-stage if she can learn to act even half as well as she dances. Meanwhile, the younger generation of the company complained virtually *en bloc* that the Bolshoy was stuffy, tired and too authoritarian.

At the same time, another scandal broke, of Bolshoy musicians complaining that they were having to pay backhanders to orchestra officials to ensure that they were taken on foreign tours. One of the great perks of Soviet artistic life is the regular foreign travel, which is a rare privilege for most of the population, and which can be a licence to print money. Shortage of foreign currency is so intense that most Soviet artists abroad get a pittance of local pocket money, around 10–15 roubles a week. Even so, when bulked out with some judicious sales of Palekh lacquered boxes or tins of caviar, it is usually enough to buy a cheap western video recorder or tape deck or even a personal computer, which can be sold back home for ten or twenty times its cost.

There has always been a rivalry between the Moscow-based Bolshoy company and Leningrad's Kirov. After all, until 1917, the Imperial ballet danced in St Petersburg. When Tchaikovsky's *Swan Lake* had its premiere in Moscow, it flopped. It took St Petersburg to make it one of the standard works of the repertoire. The legendary dancers, Nijinsky and Pavlova, had their débuts on the stage of the Mariya Theatre, now renamed the Kirov. And the great reputation the Bolshoy won in the 1950–60s came after Leonid Lavrovsky brought his choreographic genius down to the Bolshoy from Lenin-grad. *Romeo and Juliet*, set to Prokofiev's music, was his masterpiece. Now directed by Oleg Vinogradov, the Kirov is, in my view, a very much better and bolder company than the stodgy Bolshoy, and is now planning to bring into its repertoire the works of western choreographers like MacMillan and Ballanchine. The city is rightly proud of its Kirov company. Badly bomb-damaged in the war, the Kirov Theatre is so much a part of the city of Leningrad that by universal agreement, it was among the first buildings to be repaired. The new climate under Gorbachev now also makes it likely that the exiled stars of the Kirov, Nureyev and Baryshnikov, will be able to return as visiting directors. Nureyev has already been allowed to return to see his elderly mother.

There are ballet companies in each of the republics, of greater or lesser quality. The Vilnius ballet in Lithuania is one of the most original and impressive, and the Minsk company of Byelorussia has the enthusiasm and confident sense of attack that can convey some of the thrill of ballet even to tourists who are watching classical dance for the first time.

Opera and music

The origins of Russian opera and of their classical music are found in traditional Russian folk song and in the liturgical music of the Orthodox Church. But in the seventeenth century, Italian and German musicians began to perform and stay at the Tsar's court, and increasingly chamber orchestras spread from the colony of foreign merchants into the social life of the Russian aristocracy. The first stirrings of serious and non-religious Russian music emerged in the days of Catherine the Great, but it was not until the time of composer Glinka (1804–57) that Russian opera really began. His *A Life for the Tsar* is a flawed work, slow and mannered, but there is a distinctive musical voice, blended with a Russian historical theme.

Russia had joined the classical European mainstream, a country to which the leading composers from Berlioz to Wagner came to conduct their own music. The founding of the St Petersburg Conservatory under Anton Rubinstein in 1862, and subsequently of the Moscow Conservatory by his brother Nikolay established a firm foundation for the brilliant flowering of Russian music that was to follow. In the works of Borodin, Mussorgsky, Rimsky-Korsakov and Tchaikovsky, Russian history and nationalism became an inspiration. Borodin's *Prince Igor*, based on the great milestone of Russian literature, *The Lay of the Host of Igor*, is still one of the most characteristically Russian of operas, and a clear favourite with Russian audiences. Mussorgsky's *Boris Godunov*, based on Pushkin, created one of the great operatic roles, and established the chorus as a distinctive element of Russian opera. Tchaikovsky's classic contribution to the nationalist tradition of Russian music was his 1812 Overture. To commemorate the defeat of Napoleon's invasion, the piece combines cannon, church bells, hymns and Russian folk themes with enormous panache and gusto, and has become one of the best-known and best-loved pieces of classical music. His operas, *Eugene Onegin* and *Queen of Spades* and both based on Pushkin, are less well-known.

After this inspired generation of composers, Russia then produced another flowering of genius with Scriabin and Rachmaninov, Stravinsky and Prokofiev. But the Russian tradition was continued, with Stravinsky using Russian folk themes in *The Firebird* and *Rite of Spring* and Prokofiev celebrating Russian nationalism and the glorious Russian chorus in his music for the Eisenstein film *Alexandr Nevsky*, about the Prince of Novgorod who fought off the Teutonic Knights. Even the rigid Communist ideology, which decreed that art could function only as an arm of political propaganda, was unable to crush Russian music. But certainly it tried, and so lost many of its . finest talents to exile. Rachmaninov left for Hollywood in 1917, where his genius for romantic music was vulgarised, and Stravinsky and the great bass singer Chaliapin died abroad. Prokofiev died in Moscow in something close to poverty, after his music had been criticised as 'elitist' by Stalin's cultural bosses. Even Shostakovich, whose Seventh Symphony was written during the siege of Leningrad and became an anthem of patriotic resistance, came under Party attack.

The best place to hear orchestral and chamber music is the Moscow Conservatoire, named after Tchaikovsky, on Ulitsa Gerzena 13, or the Tchaikovsky Hall on Mayakovsky Square. Gala concerts are also given in the Rossiya Theatre, and if you are unable to obtain tickets for the Bolshoy, it is usually easier to get seats for the Stanislavsky and Nemirovich-Danchenko musical theatre on Ulitsa Pushkinskaya 17.

Leningrad has the Shostakovich Philharmonia, Ulitsa Brodskovo 2, and the Leningrad Concert Hall on Lenin Square, the Oktyabrasky Concert Hall on Ligovsky Prospeky, and the smaller Glinka Hall on Nevsky Prospekt 30.

Rock and jazz

Rock and jazz have had an uphill struggle in the Soviet Union though jazz has had a slightly easier ride, because it could be presented as the politically respectable music of downtrodden American blacks. But the innate rebellion against all authority that underlies rock music made it highly unpopular with many Soviet authorities until the more liberal Gorbachev era. There were regional differences, with Leningrad permitting the first experimental rock club to open at the beginning of the 1980s, a time when Moscow was still banning the outstanding Soviet band Time Machine from playing within the city limits. But in the last five years, Soviet rock has flowered with enormous energy, and gained a measure of respectability that was symbolised in June 1986 when the rock musicians themselves won official approval to organise the first Soviet charity rock concert – in aid of the fund for the victims of Chernobyl.

But the most of the time, it had been an underground activity. The first records were known as 'bones' because the state recording company would not produce them, and so the fans had to record their own on to the used negatives of hospital X-rays. In the 1960s, a castrated form of approved pop was grudgingly allowed, but the effect of state disapproval was simply to create a massive black market for western records, and a huge audience for western radio stations. Rock bands developed regardless, playing in private apartments, or giving the occasional concert at a factory social club or a youth club with a sympathetic manager. Rock was popular even with the children of the Soviet elite. So places like Moscow University or the Institute of International Relations, the Soviet Oxbridge or Ivy League, had their own home-grown bands for their discos. The best known was led by Stas Namen, grandson of the Politburo member Anastas Mikoyan.

There were also other ways for rock to prosper within the system. The first was in restaurants where loud, live music and dancing rather than dining had become a tradition by the 1970s. The customers wanted western-style pop, and the restaurant managers urged the Union of Musicians and the Ministry of Culture to provide VIAs, or 'Vokalni-Instrumentalni Ansambli'. The second route was through classic show business, in the big variety theatres like Moscow's 'Estrada' and on television.

This was the route taken by Alla Pugacheva, a brassy and big-voiced redhead who won a televised song contest in Bulgaria and went on to become the first Soviet superstar. A woman of huge talent, who writes much of her own material and has even put Shakespeare's sonnets to music, Alla had the popularity to bring together dancers and technicians and fill Moscow's Olympic Stadium with light shows and stage spectaculars even before Gorbachev came to power. It was also her name which ensured official backing for the Chernobyl charity concert. If Alla is performing, it is worth trying to get a ticket for one of her shows, but they are not easy to find. But there are a lot of excellent bands that now perform regular gigs in Palaces of Culture and clubs around the cities. The Green Theatre in Moscow's Gorky Park, under the careful stewardship of the rock musician Stas Namen, has become a regular forum for rock concerts, below a big logo that says this is all in aid of 'Musicians for Peace'. Heavy metal is all the rage and the best of its bands is Cruiz, but Ariya and Black Coffee are very popular.

The best Moscow band these days is Bravo, a post-punk group who combine a hillbilly guitar backing with a brilliant young woman vocalist called Anna who ran away from home in Siberia to be a rock star. Do not miss a chance to catch a band called Svuki Mu, who are worth seeing for the performance of their manic lead singer alone. Tsentr and Brigada S are also first-rate Moscow groups, and VABANK has a big punk following. Their lead singer, Sasha Skliar, used to be a diplomat in North Korea. Their concerts are announced on the big advertising hoardings for concerts, and in the weekly Press supplement of what's on in Moscow, in *Vechernaya Moskva*, the city's evening paper. The best restaurant bands are to be found at the Sofia, the Rus and the Uzbekistan, where the lead singer's miniskirt has become a city legend.

For jazz, the place to go is the Bluebird Café on Ulitsa Chekhova, tel. 299-8702, where a young Armenian jazz fan has created one of the most agreeable places in the city. Vartan Tonayan loves all jazz, but particularly Charlie Parker, and he persuaded the manager of the Bluebird Café to experiment with an occasional evening of jazz. Vartan books in the musicians, and pays them rather better than the state bookings' agency Goskonzert ever would, and the queues stretch right down the street. The variety is all. You can sit through thirty minutes of the most terrible experimental sounds from a tuba, and then go into a session of coolly cerebral modern jazz. Visiting western jazzmen and musicians now make a point of dropping in, and the jam sessions can be astounding.

The best rock bands are found in Leningrad: Avtograf and Televizor and Popular Mekanix. Avtograf is the vehicle for Boris Grebenshikov, who is probably the most talented single musician on the rock scene. The man is a musical polymath, a Russian Bob Dylan who is now experimenting with old Gaelic songs, and saga themes from old Norse. He is fascinated by the cultural links with northern Europe, the Viking traditions that stretch from Kievan Rus across Scandinavia to Scotland and the old Norse city of Dublin. A lot of young Soviet rock fans only began to take Gorbachev's reforms seriously when Avtograf was given a visa to tour the United States in 1987. Televizor is street-smart and savage, and it has been subjected to enough official pressure and harassment to know that rock is dangerous politics even now. It keeps being banned even from the permissive haunts of the Leningrad Rock Club. Its last offence was to dedicate a concert to Boris Yeltsin, the outspoken radical reformer who was sacked from the Politburo for criticising the Kremlin conservatives. Misha Borzikin, Televizor's lead singer, then launched into a number about modern Soviet politics called 'The fish is rotting from the head'.

Popular Mekanix is the vehicle for the group of free spirits who have gathered around Sergei Kuriokhin, one of the most gifted young musicians in the country. The PM group plays with buckets, crowbars, chunks of reinforced concrete and musical saws. This is heavy metal with a vengeance. They held one memorable concert with naked girls and wild goats. Sergei is a classical and jazz pianist of genius, a composer whose works are commissioned by orchestras in the United States, and a real original.

If you are seriously interested in Soviet rock music, *Back in the USSR* by Artyom Troitsky, published by Omnibus Press in London, is the only history, and the best guide.

The circus

The Moscow State Circus is world famous for its skill with animals and for its trapeze artists, clowns and tumblers. But because these are seen as rather old fashioned, the circus is increasingly emphasising some very different skills. So the standard evening at the Moscow circus these days consists of a first half which is a modern dance and light show backed by modernistic music. It is still a dazzling spectacular, and the dancers use the high wires and the props of the circus acts, but some western visitors are surprised and disappointed. Most adults enjoy it, and Soviet children tend to be too well disciplined to complain if they are lucky enough to get tickets, but western kids often complain volubly. The first half of the show, however, contains enough marvellous circus to satisfy most customers.

Sport

Tourists tend not to attend local sports events, but this is a mistake. A visit to the Moscow Dinamo stadium is just as much a part of the Soviet experience as the Bolshoy ballet. It can even be more fun. The team usually plays on Saturday afternoons from spring to autumn, and by taking a Metro to the Dinamo station you have a choice of two stadiums, Dinamo itself on one side of the road, and the TsSKA (Central Army Club) on the other. If you are really lucky, you might see these two top Moscow teams compete, and you will then see crowd control at work. The Soviet authorities take hooliganism seriously, and at a Dinamo–TsSKA match, soldiers will surround the pitch, shoulder to shoulder, facing the crowd. The crowd is only allowed to leave by sections, and your path to the Metro station will be through another gauntlet of soldiers.

Soviet football clubs are currently in a state of transition. Since the 1920s, they have been linked to a particular organisation or industry. So Moscow Dinamo was originally the sports club of the political police, just as Torpedo was the team for the automobile industry, and Spartak for aviation. For decades now, the star footballers have never seen the factory assembly line or the police station from which they ostensibly draw their pay. But Dinamo Kiev, which is currently the best team in the Soviet Union, has launched a new experiment by going *khozraschyot*, or standing on its own financial feet rather than depending on a parent organisation. As long as it keeps winning Soviet competitions and thus gets into the European cup matches, it should make enough from advertising and television to make ends meet. The same clubs play ice hockey in winter, but winter is also the time for participation sport, skating over the frozen paths of Gorky Park, or cross-country skiing in the woods of Sokolniki or Bitza Park. If you like horse-racing, try an afternoon at the 'Ippodrom' on Ulitsa Begovaya 22, where you can bet on the racecourse tote. The Russians are also now playing rugby, and are experimenting with baseball. The schedules of the games are to be found in the daily newspaper *Sovyetsky Sport*.

Shopping

At some point in your trip, you will be taken to a Beriozka store, where you can buy souvenirs for hard currency. Most of the package tours that visit Moscow are taken to the large Beriozka on the ground floor of the Rossiya Hotel, which has the widest selection, though the majority of them have a similar range of souvenirs and consumer goods. Looking at the goods on offer, it is clear that western tourists are expected to buy fur hats, vodka, caviar, a Palekh box, an amber necklace, a nest of the Matrioshka dolls which fit into one another, a few Soviet lapel badges and a Tchaikovsky record.

Vodka
The price of vodka in the Beriozka stores is higher than at a duty-free store in a western airport, or on a plane. Vodka is vodka, and it takes an expert to differentiate between the tastes, particularly when drunk ice-cold from the freezer, as it should be. The vodkas to take home as souvenirs are the exotic brands, which are less common in the west. The finest Bloody Marys are made with Pertsovka, the fiery red vodka flavoured with red peppers. It is also good for colds. Some people like the lemon-flavoured vodka. The brown-coloured Starka (which means strong) is a slightly higher proof, and Hunters' Vodka has a distinctive taste, a little like whisky.

Condiments
Soviet mustard is very hot, drab khaki in colour and very good. It is called 'Gorchitsa' and comes in small jars which cost 28 kopeks. 'Khrem', or pink horseradish, is also excellent, and these make unusual but tasty souvenirs.

Fur hats
If you want an expensive fur hat, then by all means buy at the Beriozka. If you are simply in the middle of a Russian winter and need something to keep your head warm and your ears from dropping off, go into ЦУМ, TSUM (Central Department Store), the Gothic-looking grey building to the right of the Bolshoy Theatre, and buy a cheap nylon and rabbit version for 8 roubles.

Matrioshka dolls
These are the classic souvenir, but you can buy really deluxe ones – and pay up to 315 roubles for a set – at the Izmailovo open-air art market. Rather than the mass-produced Matrioshkas on sale in the Beriozkas, these are works of art, with different dresses and faces on each doll. Some of the nests are of Russian Orthodox priests, or Soviet policemen in different uniforms.

Palekh boxes
A Palekh box is one of the outstanding examples of Soviet craftsmanship, and some of them are works of art. Exquisitely-painted lacquer boxes, made of papier-mâché, they come from a small group

136

of villages not far from Moscow. Palekh is the best-known village, but Fedoskino is where the craft began in 1796 when some lacquer painters were imported from Germany. The other villages are M'stera and Kholui, and each has its own distinct style.

After the Revolution and well into the 1970s, the artists were officially instructed to paint 'progressive' subjects and these small and delicate boxes would be decorated with scenes of a new tractor taking happy peasants to harvest. Increasingly, they are reverting to the traditional subjects of Russian fairy tales and folk legends, troikas driving through the snow, and even historical scenes which merge cleverly into religious themes.

By Soviet standards, Palekh boxes are hugely expensive. In a Soviet shop, such as Ruski Suvenir on Kutuzovsky Prospekt, a medium-sized box with a complex painting will cost over 1,000 roubles. You will be able to buy the same box for 315 roubles or so in a Beriozka. Tiny boxes from Fedoskino can be bought for 30 roubles or less.

Art

The most distinctive souvenirs are to be found in the ordinary shops, and not in the Beriozkas. Since the 1920s, Soviet poster art has been remarkable and quite unique. In Moscow, at Dom Knigi (House of Books) on Kalinin Prospekt, or in the Plakat (poster) Shop just beside the Praga Hotel at the eastern end of the Arbat, you will find a wide range of posters from as little as 10 kopeks. They make excellent gifts. And at 46 Gorky Street is an art salon, where they sell small etchings of Moscow scenes, already framed, for as little as 3 to 5 roubles. They also sell prints of modern art work, portraits of politicians and so on.

Books

Soviet art books are cheap and of excellent quality. The Beriozkas sell English-language versions of books on the classic art collections of Soviet museums, and these are good value. But go into Soviet bookshops to look at the art books in Russian, which are often cheaper and cover topics like nineteenth-century landscapes or watercolours, that you will never find in the Beriozkas. The collections of Soviet postcards are also worth studying. The best selections are to be found in the Knigi (Books) Shop on the northern side of Gorky Street, 400 metres up from the Intourist Hotel, or again, at Dom Knigi.

On the first floor of Progress Books, a large store right beside the Park Kultury Metro station, you will find a wide selection of Russian books in foreign languages. The English department is by far the largest, and they always stock cheap and good quality translations of the Russian classics, from Pushkin to Sholokhov, for less than 3 roubles a hardback volume. They also have translations of more modern Russian writers, which are worth exploring. There is a second counter, by the main windows, which contains political books. One end stocks the collected works of Marx and Engels, and the other contains some often fascinating books on modern international politics and on aspects of Soviet life from the way they organise chess, to an account of the building of the BAM, the second Trans-Siberian railroad. Fun to browse in, the Progress Bookstore should solve your Christmas present problem for the year.

Records

Do not buy Soviet records, unless you can make a decent tape recording the first or second time you play it. The quality of vinyl is poor and the records scratch very easily. After five playings, the deterioration is noticeable.

Hardware

I like Russian mailboxes, with the small slot for letters and the big one for newspapers and packets. They have *pochta* (post) written on the front, which should baffle your postman, and they can be found at *khudozhestvenniye* (hardware) shops. One of the best in Moscow is opposite the large column at Tishinsky Market on Gruzinsky Val, in the ground floor of the tall modern brick building. Here you can also find heavy, ironware cooking pots, which are good and cheap, and stacking light metal food containers, which are perfect for picnics. You can also sometimes find portable *shashlik* (shish kebab) barbecue sets.

Toys

Russian toys baffle me. The Soviets constantly quote Lenin on how 'children are our only privileged class', while continuing to produce toys which would be banned for their lethality in the west. Look inside the child-sized pedal-cars they sell at Dyetski Mir (Children's World) at Dzerzhinskaya Metro station. The sharp edges can do a lot of damage. Or examine the dangerous way that the eyes are fixed to the soft toys. But there is one prize to be found, the ultimate Russian souvenir, a Red Army remote-controlled electric toy tank.

General Basics

Documents needed to enter the Soviet Union

Passports and visas

To enter the USSR, you will require a passport that is valid for at least three months after your return date from the Soviet Union. It must be a complete passport. Temporary travel papers, or, say, a British Visitor's Passport, are not enough.

You will also require a Soviet visa. They come in several forms. There are diplomatic visas and there are *Mnogoshtatnaya* or multi-entry visas for journalists and businessmen accredited to a responsible Soviet ministry. Everyone else is given a visitor's visa, a small purple document of three perforated pages. One page is removed by the border guard on entry. The visa is valid for a specified period only, which you must state when you first complete your application form. Do not overstay your visa. Extensions can be arranged, by applying to the local OVIR, or visa office. The main office in Moscow is on Kolpachny Pereulok 10; tel. 924-9349. You will need a very good reason.

If you are travelling on a package tour, the travel firm will arrange your visa. If you do not have to hand over your passport, you will at least have to provide photocopies of the first five pages of it, as well as the standard visa application form and three passport-sized photographs. If you have relatives in the USSR, and complete that section, expect delays. If you are travelling independently, you should apply for a visa exactly ten weeks before you are due to leave. The surging growth in tourism to Gorbachev's USSR has put so much pressure on Soviet consulates abroad that they have developed a new form of Russian roulette and seem to take a sadistic pride in issuing the visa (and returning the passport) at the last possible moment before departure.

You should check what the visa says about permitted ports of entry and departure. Frayed nerves and hysterics have become a feature of Leningrad Airport since package tours began flying into Moscow and out of Leningrad, when the visa states entry and departure only via Moscow. Check everything, and particularly the dates. You can waste half a day at OVIR if a careless clerk has said your visa expires on the 4th when your package tour leaves on the 5th. This sort of accidental clerical error happens no more frequently with the Soviet Union than with the US visas, but untangling the Soviet bureaucracy is a great deal trickier. Keep your visa inside your passport, and preferably ensure it stays there with a paper clip. A lost visa or lost passport is a real headache, for you and for the local consul who has to help you through the resulting bureaucracy.

If you are driving through the Soviet Union, you must clear your route with Intourist, and your visa must reflect the route you have been authorised to travel. If you have a visa only for Moscow and Leningrad, you may not make a sudden decision one day to go to the rail station or to Aeroflot and buy a ticket for Kiev. You will first need to have your visa extended to include Kiev. Although they are relaxing quickly, the Soviet border guards, who check your visa on entry and departure, are an arm of the KGB. They take documents seriously. So should you.

Customs documents

Your customs document, or *Deklaratsiya*, is just as important as your visa. Paper clip it to your passport. And when you deposit your passport with the Soviet hotel for registration, do not forget that you will be needing it and the *Deklaratsiya* in order to change money.

The *Deklaratsiya* asks you to list all the foreign money or travellers cheques and other valuables you are bringing into the Soviet Union. You should list all jewellery, including St Christopher necklaces, wristwatches and items such as cameras or videos. This will be stamped by the Customs officer when you enter the country, and you will have to present that original *Deklaratsiya* when you leave. By that time, it should contain some bank stamps to show where and when you changed money. On leaving, you must also prepare a second and new *Deklaratsiya*, to say how much money you are taking out of the country. If the amounts of money on the incoming and outgoing *Deklaratsiyas* vary by much more than the sum you have legally changed, you may have some delicate explaining to do. The best way out is to explain that you drink a great deal, and the prices for whisky in the hard currency bars in the hotels are very high.

If you have bought some 'art' from the new open-air art market at Izmailovo, do not put this down in the section about exporting art and antiques. But do tell the Customs man that you have bought a painting from Izmailovo. If you are buying serious art, whether from one of the occasional auctions or salons, you will need a *Spravka*, or special export licence from the Ministry of Culture. This can take a week or more. Similarly, before going overboard in the Bukinist antiquarian book stores, and buying up several old volumes and prints, remember that you will need an export licence for each book that is more than fifty years old. You will also be liable to an export tax of 100 per cent of the price you already paid.

Permitted imports

An adult may bring into the country 200 cigarettes, a litre of spirits, 100 grams of tea, 250 grams of coffee, two watches, two still and one movie cameras, a radio, a portable typewriter, a musical instrument, sports equipment and reasonable personal effects.

You may not bring in pornography, which includes *Playboy* magazine. Books deemed harmful to the political or economic interests of the USSR are also liable to confiscation. In principle, this could include the works of Trotsky and Solzhenitsyn, copies of émigré magazines such as *Russkaya Mys'l*, and copies of many western books on modern Soviet affairs. These days, the Customs staff rarely search bags, relying on the X-ray machines to pick up the video cassettes they usually look for. Banned books are being permitted too fast for the Customs to bother any more.

On the way out, the Customs staff are often more watchful, particularly over the legal export of antiques. Although icons may be an example of popular superstition from the days when religion was Marx's opium of the masses, they are also a part of the national heritage and any foreigner trying to smuggle them out is in serious trouble.

Electrical current

The Soviet current is 220 volts AC, 50 cycles, but in some old buildings you may find the ancient 110 volt system. You are most unlikely to come across this old type in any Intourist hotel. You will need a continental plug adaptor with two small circular pins if your plug has square ones. Do not try to use too many appliances at once or you are likely to fuse a circuit that is designed for very much less intensive use than we westerners nonchalantly demand. Light bulbs are screw-in ones.

Embassies and consulates

If you need consular assistance, contact the embassy, in whose premises all consuls are located, with the exception of the US consulate in Leningrad and the one due to open in Kiev by 1990.

• **Britain**: 72 Naberezhnaya Morisa Thoreza; tel. 231-8511. The best site in Moscow, just across the river from the Kremlin. Built by a nineteenth-century sugar magnate for his mistress, when the British Embassy was located in St Petersburg. At some point in the 1990s, the British Embassy is supposed to relocate to a new riverside site near the Kiev Station, and the Politburo will no longer look out on a Union Jack fluttering cheekily across their best view. Should you be invited in, the white ballroom on the first floor and the carved fireplace in the drawing room are both worth a look. And naturally, the best view of the Kremlin may be obtained from the balcony. Pause at the top of the stairs. This is the spot where a fashionable young hussar officer blew out his brains on hearing that his mistress had found another gallant.

• **United States**: 19/23 Ulitsa Tschaikovskogo; tel. 252-2451. This should have been closed by now and the whole US Embassy moved into the new, purpose-built, red-brick Embassy compound to the rear. However, the nine-storey central block, looking rather like the keep of a medieval fortress, is so honeycombed with bugs and state of the art microphones that the sensitive sections of the Embassy, the defence and political analysts and the Ambassador, have refused to move in. The US Congress is still trying to decide whether to knock it all down and start again, with only American builders and materials. Defiant to the end, the US diplomats have written 'God Bless America' on the windows.

Do not pity them too much. Inside the compound, they have a hamburger bar, a western-style supermarket, a swimming pool, squash and basketball courts, and have done their level best to recreate Hometown USA in the heart of Moscow. They need never leave, and indeed, some of them boast of never venturing on to Soviet soil, save for the road that leads to the airport. Uncle Sam's is one of the best nightclubs in town, although the competition is limited.

The US consulate in Leningrad is at 15 Ulitsa Petra Lavrova; tel. 274-8235.

• **Canada**: 23 Starokonyushenny Pereulok; tel. 241-5882. This pleasant old building in the Arbat is famed for its hamburgers and Canadian beer basement bar early on a Friday night. You have to be taken in by a member, usually a Canadian or resident diplomat.

• **Australia**: 13 Kropotkinsky Pereulok; tel. 246-5011. This is one of the finest Art Nouveau (which the Russians call *Jugendstil*) buildings in Moscow, with the splendid original details, right down to the door handles. It is famous for its massive high fireplace in the main reception room. Suspecting that it was hollow at the top, one Ambassador demanded a ladder, climbed up, peered in, and saw a suspicious array of wires and electronics. Convinced he had evidence of a bug, he dived in and emerged, dusty but triumphant, with the machinery for the Embassy's front door bell.

After 7 p.m. on a Friday night, the Australian Embassy's basement beer bar, known as the Down-Under Club, is the social focus of expatriate Moscow, the point to which that day's British newspapers are brought. More Fosters lager is consumed in this one bar on a Friday night than in the whole of the rest of the USSR combined.

• **New Zealand**: 44 Ulitsa Vorovskovo; tel. 290-3485.

Health

Vaccinations | At the time of writing, travellers from most western countries no longer need health certificates to show that they have had certain vaccinations. As this may change quickly, check when booking your holiday or buying your ticket. If arriving from Asia or Africa, check with the local Soviet Embassy first. Visitors from African countries may face a compulsory AIDS test on arrival.

Drugs and medicines

If you need medication on a regular basis, take enough with you for the length of your stay. It is unwise to assume that any western drug or medicine, no matter how common, will be easily available in the Soviet Union. Even aspirin occasionally disappears from the chemists, known as *aptyekas*. Take your own supplies also of contraceptive pills, tampons or sanitary towels.

Food and drink

You need take no special precautions over food or drink in Moscow, but in Leningrad, do not drink the tap water, avoid ice in your drink, and unless acclimatised, it is advisable to brush your teeth in mineral water. Also, do not eat fruit unless you have peeled it yourself, or salads. Leningrad is built on a marsh and has a low water table. The water supply is therefore liable to contamination. In the Second World War, nearly 600,000 Leningraders died during the 900 days the city was besieged, most of them from starvation. Some 470,000 of them are buried in mass graves, now one of the most moving cemeteries in the world, at the Piskaryovka Memorial on the outskirts of the city. It is suspected, but not medically proven, that the corpses lie in uncomfortable proximity to the water table. In spite of all the sanitary precautions taken, many visitors succumb to *giardia*, a stomach bug that can cause nausea and dysentery. All Leningrad hotels keep Thermos flasks of boiled water for their guests. Use them.

In 1988, localised outbreaks of typhoid were recorded in Georgia and Armenia. And in Soviet Central Asia, remember that you are just across the mountains from Afghanistan and Pakistan and, although Soviet standards of hygiene are rather higher, many visitors suffer from stomach complaints. Take the same kind of anti-diarrhoea pills as you would take on a North African holiday, and also take the precautions advised for Leningrad, peel the fruit, and beware salads. All Soviet hotels keep plentiful stocks of bottled water, which are safe.

Medical emergencies

After decades of boasting about the free health service, *glasnost* has at last allowed the Soviets to admit that they have one of the most squalid, corrupt and inefficient health systems in the world. This is no place to fall ill. You should not travel to the Soviet Union without the kind of insurance that can fly you back to the west if something goes seriously wrong. Europ-Assistance has a permanent bureau and a doctor in Moscow, and can fly visitors out quickly if required. Their number is 254-6927.

The Soviet system is not sympathetic to stomach troubles, toothache or complex internal problems. But for something fairly straightforward, for instance if you break an ankle or sprain a wrist, you will probably be greatly impressed by the speed and efficiency and zero cost of Soviet medicine. A series of special facilities is available for foreigners. There is a whole ward set apart for foreigners at the Botkin clinic, the best public hospital in Moscow. Single rooms are available, some with TV, and although food is provided, it is best to follow the usual Soviet practice and arrange for family or friends to bring in supplementary dishes. The doctors and medical care are free. You will have to pay for any drugs prescribed. If you, or a friend are taken to hospital, ensure that a supply of one-rouble notes, or such items as packs of western cigarettes, are close to hand. Ward and nursing staff are so badly paid that to bring bedpans or clean bedding, to clean the space around the bed and to ensure prompt service, they are accustomed to daily tips from Soviet patients. Western patients will be better treated, but there is no need to test the system.

If you do fall ill, inform your hotel desk, or your tour guide at once. An ambulance, or visiting doctor, can be summoned by dialling 03. In Moscow, the central casualty department is found at the Sklifosovsky Institute, on the Sadovaya ring road just off Kolkhoz Square.

Laundry and dry-cleaning

In the grander Moscow hotels, laundry is done by the chambermaids, and should be arranged through the *dezhurnaya*, the attendant on each hotel floor. The maids will prefer to be allowed at least two full days to do it. They sometimes would rather be paid with small bottles of perfume, soap or western cigarettes than the roubles they are supposed to charge. In cheaper hotels, ask at the Intourist service bureau and make sure that they guarantee your shirts or whatever will be ready in time for your departure. Outside Moscow and Leningrad, you might be wiser to wash things yourself.

Dry-cleaning is available in all Soviet towns and cities. The shops are called *khimchistka*, but beware of fragile buttons and do not entrust them with delicate garments as the chemicals they use are crude.

Lavatories

Until the last year or so, the iron rule for Soviet lavatories was only ever to use the one in your hotel room. If the level of a nation's civilisation may be judged from the quality of its public lavatories (and there are worse criteria) then the Soviet Union is somewhere between Neanderthal and Cro-Magnon in its state of development.

But now we have the private enterprise loo. The first deluxe Soviet loo was provided in Leningrad, at the direct suggestion of Intourist, who were increasingly fed up at the way their coaches full of tourists were regularly returning to the hotels for a loo-break. Successive waves of western tourists had taken one look at the public lavatories available in the Hermitage, the Peter–Paul Fortress and the other great cultural symbols of this most scenic of cities, and rightly ordered the coaches back to the hotel. Coach and tourist schedules were being disrupted, and so Intourist authorised the first ever superloo on Nevsky Prospekt, with soft music, plastic flowers, lavatory paper, soap and running water and even doors on the cubicles. These items are seldom to be found in most public conveniences in the Soviet Union.

These superloos are run by co-operatives. The Leningrad pioneer makes its money from tips, but the co-operative is also guaranteed a high average income of 300 roubles a month. In Moscow, they have adopted a rather more classically capitalist system. The loo attendant makes his living from charging each user a modest fee. This does not always work. The first co-op loo in Moscow opened at the newly-restored Paveletsky Station as a decent 10 kopeks worth. Clean tiles, towels, soap and paper, even if one did have to use the paper to wipe the seats. Within six months, it was noisome, not quite back to Soviet normal, but with empty vodka bottles skidding round the floor, unattended leaks, paper in only one booth, filthy basins and no soap.

Other co-op loos are rather better. Moscow's Kiev and Kursk Stations each have a serviceable convenience. Other tourist sights should only be seen after thorough use of the facilities in your hotel. The trip to the marvellous monastery-fortress of Zagorsk takes half a day, and the public lavatories there are appalling, as indeed they are at the Novodevichy Convent. A useful rule of thumb is the more saintly the location, (with the sole exception of the recently-restored Danilovsky Monastery), the more foul the privy. The Lenin Museum convenience, by contrast, is reasonable, given the traffic.

(Incidentally, one of the world's most exclusive lavatories is to be found at the rear of Lenin's mausoleum on Red Square, installed for the obvious reason that the kind of elderly gentlemen who used to monopolise the Politburo on occasion required relief in mid-Parade. It is just alongside the world's most exclusive lift, which was installed to take the geriatric Mr Brezhnev from the postern gate in the Kremlin wall up to the reviewing platform above the mausoleum. In these energetic days of *perestroika*, Mr Gorbachev and his colleagues climb the stairs.)

If caught short in Red Square or the Kremlin, men should make for the rather foul lavatories in the basement of GUM by its western entrance. You will easily find them by the smell. Otherwise, head for the National Hotel. Any tourist can breeze past the doorman by saying 'Beriozka', and once inside, climb the stairs to the first floor, turn right past the bar, to find the very decent loos at the end of the corridor. Tip the ex-boxer who looks after this haven. In western Moscow, head for the Mezhdunarodnaya Hotel, where the loos are on the ground floor, straight across the lobby from the entrance, past the ornamental clock and the plastic trees.

Obvious advice: ALWAYS carry either some loo paper or tissues that can be used for the purpose, and some of the moist cleansing tissues that are given away on airplanes. Small travelling packs may be bought from chemists.

Post offices

Intourist hotels have their own post kiosks, where stamps, envelopes and postcards may be bought. There are postboxes in hotel lobbies. Stamps may also be bought at newspaper kiosks, as well as in post offices. Letters to Europe cost 45 kopeks, and to the United States 60 kopeks. Postcards to Europe are 35 kopeks, and to the United States 45 kopeks.

There are two international post offices in Moscow where English-speaking clerks are available, at 10 Komsomol Square and at 37 Varshavskoye Chaussee.

Public holidays

Each holiday is called a *prazdnik* and it is a time for giving gifts, throwing parties and drinking. Whenever possible, Russians link their day or days off to the nearest weekend to have a longer break. On each public holiday, banks, offices, museums and shops are closed, though some food stores stay open.

• **1 January**, New Year's Day is a national holiday, but the celebrations begin on New Year's Eve. If you are in Moscow, you can see the crowds start to gather on Kalinin Prospekt near the giant video screen from 9 p.m., but the place to be at midnight is Red Square, where the usual ban on drinking in public places is held in abeyance for the evening.

• **8 March**, International Women's Day is the one day in the year when the men do the cooking and buy their wives and girlfriends flowers. The result is a frantic inflation in the price of flowers sold in the street markets as the day draws near.

• **1 and 2 May**, May Day. In every town and city, there will be a May Day parade, when Soviet workers are expected to delay their departure for the dacha or the countryside until after they have marched. If you are in Moscow you should get as close as you can to Red Square in the morning and to Gorky Park in the afternoon.

• **9 May**, Victory Day, is the anniversary of Hitler's defeat. The soft pedalling on military manifestations under Gorbachev has ended the parades since the mammoth one in 1985, the fortieth anniversary of the war's end. But the fiftieth anniversary in 1995 will be the biggest of all. Military march past or not, every Victory Day sees veterans' reunions in Gorky Park. Some are squeezed into old uniforms, most of which are clinking with row upon row of medals. These old age pensioners who once beat the Wehrmacht, dancing and drinking together, are today a bizarre but oddly moving sight.

• **7 October**, Constitution Day. No one takes this holiday seriously except *Pravda*. A few token flags bedeck Moscow's bridges, but the constitution has little public popularity. Under Gorbachev, if the constitutional changes he has suggested become law, this may change.

• **7 November**, Anniversary of the Revolution. The October Revolution is celebrated on 7 November because the victorious Bolsheviks changed the calendar after 1917, so that Russia would keep the same dates as the rest of the world. Marked with a big parade in Moscow's Red Square, and in other cities, the holiday lasts for two days.

Shop opening hours

Most shops are open six days a week, from Monday to Saturday, though some food stores are always open on Sundays. Department stores like TSUM are open from 8 a.m. to 9 p.m. Food stores open at 9 a.m. and close at 8 p.m., and close from 1 to 2 p.m. for lunch. Some stores do everything one hour later, opening at 10 a.m. and closing at 9 p.m. But shops often shut on the first or last day of the month for stock taking and periodically close without warning for 'Sanitary Day'.

Telephoning home

If you have a telephone whose first three digits are 230, congratulations, you are on a special switchboard and you may dial the west direct. To do so, dial 8, wait for a new dialling tone, and then dial 10 followed by the country code and number. Here are some of the country codes:

• **Great Britain**: 44 (then leave out the initial 0 of the STD code)
• **United States and Canada**: 1
• **Australia**: 61
• **New Zealand**: 64

If you have another kind of phone, dial 8, wait for the new dialling tone, and then dial 194. This is the international switchboard, and English speakers are available. You will have to wait, usually up to two hours, for the call to come through. It costs 3 roubles a minute to Britain, and 6 roubles a minute to the USA.

If you speak Russian, by dialling 05, you get the Moscow theatre and cinema programme for the week.

Telegrams You may dictate a telegram by phone, although you will probably need the assistance of a Russian speaker, by phoning 225-2002.

Time difference

Moscow is three hours ahead of London and eight hours ahead of Washington and New York. At 9 a.m. in London it is noon in Moscow, 1 p.m. in Tbilisi, 3 p.m. in Alma-Ata, and 5 p.m. in Irkutsk.

Tipping

Officially, there is no tipping in the Soviet Union. In fact, foreign tourists are expected to give small tips in restaurants, usually about 5 per cent. Please do not give 10 per cent or you will raise the going rate. Give taxi drivers some loose change but, again, not more than 5 per cent, unless you negotiated a special price. Late at night or in bad weather, you can expect to pay two or even three times the metered fare (see p. 115). It is best to give small gifts, rather than cash, to people performing some personal service, like guides or helpful chambermaids.

Useful addresses and telephone numbers

Emergencies:

Fire	01
Police	02
Emergency medical aid	03

Travel information:

Intourist – general	203-6962
UK Dept	292-2697

```
        US Dept     292-2386
        Excursions  253-2362
```

Aeroflot – flight enquiries 155-0922
        Head office   245-3877
        Ticket office   253-8313 (This is the best of the ticket offices, for courtesy and for English-speakers. It is located on the second floor of the Mezhdunarodnaya Hotel.)

Rail enquiries   266-9900

Western travel numbers:

American Express   254-4495   Yes, a real Am-Ex office, with money-changing facilities, on 21a Sadoyaya Kudrinskaya, the Garden Ring Road, near the Planetarium.

Air France	237-2325	Japan Air Lines	221-6448
Air India	237-7494	KLM	253-2150
Alitalia	923-9840	Lufthansa	923-0488
Austrian Airlines	253-1670	Pan-Am	253-2658
British Airways	253-2481	SAS	925-4747
Finnair	292-8788	Swissair	253-1859

British travel agencies:

Thomson Holidays   203-4025   (Thomson is one of the most popular agencies for British package tour groups.)
Barry Martin Travel   253-2940   (Barry Martin Travel specialises in travel for businessmen and runs a courier service.)

Wildlife

In the winter of 1979, a wolf was seen walking down Moscow's Leninsky Prospekt well within the city limits, and in Bitza Park, joggers and cross-country skiers have been attacked by packs of dogs, abandoned by their owners, which have now gone wild. On the main road from Moscow to Leningrad, elk sometimes amble across the road and there are bears in the forests outside Suzdal and Vladimir. Ornithologists report that the countryside around Moscow is a birdwatcher's delight.

Apart from at the zoo and the circus, you are not going to see a lot of wildlife in the cities, but elsewhere the country teems with fauna. It is unlikely to prove dangerous, even on a Siberian picnic in the Taiga, or if you go winter fishing through holes in the river ice. In Central Asia you can find snakes and scorpions off-the-beaten track. But heed the advice of your Intourist guide and follow the example of the locals, and you shouldn't run into trouble.

Gazetteer

Introduction

The Soviet Union, the largest country on earth, covers eleven time zones, and runs from the Arctic north to the desert lands of the Turkmenian south. There are 110 official languages spoken within its borders, and some of its communities are so remote that they didn't know the Tsar had fallen until more than seventy years after it happened. In the 1980s, the readers of *Komsomolskaya Pravda* newspaper were entranced as week after week they read of the members of a sect of Russian Orthodox believers who had fled persecution in Tsarist times and retreated deep into the Altai Mountains in Siberia. In 1982, they were discovered by a helicopter carrying a geological survey team. They were entirely self-sufficient, spoke an antique Russian, and showed little interest in the events that had toppled Tsarism and the Orthodox faith back in 1917. But they caught the nation's imagination, bringing home to a modern, urban civilisation just how vast its country remains, so big that even today it is not fully explored.

The country is divided into fifteen republics, each of which has its own elected government, a Supreme Soviet which passes local laws, endorses local budgets and Five-Year Plans and, in theory at least, guarantees the rights of the minority nations of the Soviet Union. The fifteen republics vary widely in size and population, from the 1.5 million inhabitants of Estonia, to the 140 million people who live in the Russian Federation. The easiest way to keep track of the various republics is to break them down into the five groups:

The Baltic Republics: Lithuania, Latvia and Estonia, the most recent recruits to the Soviet Union, forcibly absorbed in 1940, and reconquered in 1944, and probably the least willing members.

The Caucasian Republics: often described in Moscow as if they were a single group. Georgia and Armenia are the two oldest Christian nations on earth. Their neighbour is Shi'ite Muslim Azerbaijan, and the simmering argument over the disputed territory of Nagorno-Karabakh which broke out in 1988 emphasised the power of ancient ethnic and religious feuds. Even after Armenia's devastating earthquake in December 1988, the enmity continued, with Armenians rejecting Azerbaijani rescue convoys, and Azerbaijani mobs attacking Armenian refugees. One of the loveliest parts of the Soviet Union, it remains the most tortured.

Soviet Central Asia: the traditionally Muslim republics of Turkmenia, Uzbekistan, Kirghizia, Tadzhikistan and Kazakhstan. The fastest-growing part of the Soviet population, it can claim one of the oldest cultural traditions, with the cities of Bukhara and Samarkand tracing their roots far back beyond Islam or Christianity to the time of Alexander the Great.

The Frontier Republics: Ukraine, Byelorussia and Moldavia. These march lands are inhabited by a predominantly Slav population, and yet they have distinct national traditions which both Tsarist and Soviet Moscow scorned and tried in vain to crush. The 50 million Ukrainians are the largest single national group after the 140 million Russians, and their capital of Kiev can claim to be the cradle of Slavic culture.

Russia itself: the largest republic of all, stretching from the Baltic Sea to the Pacific Ocean. Even without all the other fourteen Republics, it would still be the world's largest nation and, in raw materials, probably the richest. The possession of Siberia would make Russia potentially a superpower, even without its huge population and industrial base.

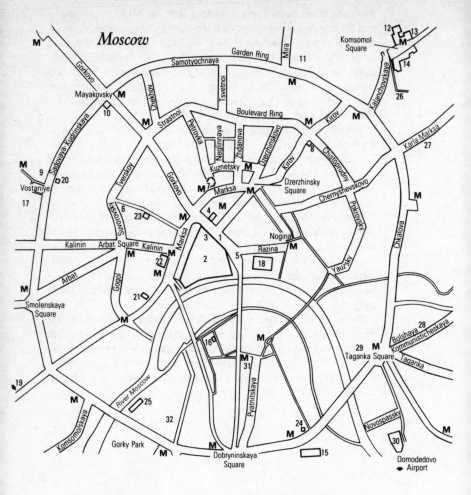

PLACES OF INTEREST
1 Red Square
2 The Kremlin
3 Lenin's Tomb
4 Central Lenin Museum
5 St Basil's Cathedral
6 Mayakovsky Theatre
7 Bolshoy Theatre
8 Post Office
9 Planetarium
10 Tchaikovsky Concert Hall
11 Sklifosovsky Hospital
12 Leningrad Station
13 Yaroslavl Station
14 Kazan Station
15 Paveletsky Station
16 Tretyakov Gallery
17 Narkomfin Building
18 Rossiya Hotel
19 Novodevichy Convent
20 Chekhov House-Museum
21 Pushkin Fine Arts Museum
22 Lenin Library
23 Tchaikovsky Conservatory
24 Bakhrushin Theatre Museum
25 State Picture Gallery

CHURCHES
26 Church of Saints Peter & Paul
27 Church of St Nikita the Martyr
28 Church of St Martin the Confessor
29 Church of the Assumption
30 New Monastery of the Saviour
31 St Clements Church
32 Church of St John the Warrior

M = Metro Station

Moscow

Introduction

In Russian, Moscow is 'Moskva', a feminine word, as opposed to the harsh masculine consonants of 'Petrograd' (Leningrad). Moscow is sometimes known as the Mother of the people as well as of the Russian cities. It was no accident that had Chekhov's tragic heroines wanting to go to Moscow, and not to St Petersburg. You went to Moscow for comfort, for solace, for another chance. It is a marvellous city, once you get to know it, under the grime, the potholes, the crumbling plaster and the smelly, half-empty foodshops. Moscow is as tough as old boots, but deeply sentimental; a city full of officials, but always ready for a party. Nothing is legal in Moscow, but everything is possible. Moscow looks both ways.

History   In Siberia, they call Moscow 'the west'. In the west, we think of Moscow as the beginning of Asia. We are both right. Moscow is a frontier city and melting pot, the Constantinople of our day. And not by accident. Moscow has been 'the third Rome' ever since the Tsars began to realise just how much potential power they ruled from the Kremlin. There was Rome herself, the great Imperial city, and then there was Byzantium, or Constantinople, the capital of the eastern Roman Empire. And when Byzantium fell to the Turks in the fifteenth century, there was the new Christian Empire of the north arising on the banks of the River Moscow – city of destiny, the third Rome. In fact, the city grew by accident. It began as a hunting lodge for Prince Yuri Dolgoruky (or 'long-armed George', which is how the name translates) who held a feast on what is now the Kremlin hill in AD 1147, when Kiev was declining and the new magnificence of the Russian north was rising in the cities of Vladimir and Suzdal. It was the Tartars who gave Moscow her chance of greatness, not just by devastating Moscow's potential rivals, but by favouring the intriguing and obsequious manners of the petty princeling house which ruled Muscovy. What the Tartars began, the Orthodox Church furthered, in the person of St Sergius, founder of the great monastery at what is now Zagorsk. He threatened with excommunication any prince who would not cleave to Moscow in the great struggle against the Tartars. And the symbiosis between Moscow and the Church was given shape in the astonishing energy of the religious builders, the monasteries that girded Moscow round, and the 'forty times forty' churches.

It took a Russian and Tsar to break Moscow's power, when Peter the Great turned his back on her Russianness, on her constantly open door to Asia, and tried to impose a European modernity upon the state by founding a new capital at St Petersburg. But the reversal of Peter's ambition, when Lenin moved the capital back to Moscow in 1918, makes the city as much a child of our own century as of the medieval age. The Moscow we see now is, above all, Stalin's city, defined by the neo-Gothic spires he loved and implanted all across the skyline, and by the vast parade-ground boulevards he pushed through the old chaos of Moscow's streets. The millions who live in the new high-rise suburbs are Stalin's babies, born of the peasants Stalin forced from the land with his brutal collectivisation of agriculture. And most of the excitement that is bubbling in Moscow today, in the *glasnost*-thrilled newspapers and magazines, in the newly bold theatres and television studios, in the street debates and political meetings, is best defined as a reaction against what Stalin stood for. The rules that are now being so joyously broken are rules that Stalin set. In Moscow, history moves slowly, but like the ice breaking up each spring, once it starts to move, watch out for the floods.

Intourist guided tours

All Intourist visits to Moscow include a half-day guided coach tour of the city. This is less useful than it sounds, but should not be missed by the newcomer: because of the language, the unfamiliar alphabet, the political system and its social priorities, the Soviet capital can be a confusing and even a forbidding place at first. So take advantage of the way Intourist gently breaks it to you. The coach will take you to Red Square and the Kremlin, and the delightful church of St Nicholas of the Weavers, past the big sports stadiums and across the river to the huge university. High up on the Lenin Hills (which used to be known as Sparrow Hills), this Stalinesque Gothic building is the best site from which to view the city. And you may be lucky enough to see a Soviet bridal party having their wedding photos taken at this traditionally lucky spot. Sometimes, they even feel lucky enough to defy the new ban on drinking alcohol in public and to toast the wedding with champagne. Even without the bridal groups, the view is memorable. The glinting domes of the Kremlin still dominate the city, in spite of the higher skyscrapers dotted around.

After this initial free tour, you should decide whether you really need the services of the Intourist guide again. They are competent, unimaginative and not very cheap. The Kremlin tour, for which they charge 5 roubles, can be done without escort for 60 kopeks, simply by buying the entry tickets to the Kremlin churches from the '*Kassa*' ticket kiosk in the Kremlin courtyard. Most of the inner city sights can be seen and enjoyed without a guide. And the pleasure of strolling through Moscow, pottering in and out of shops and discovering its pleasures at your own pace, is best experienced on your own. But for trips out of the city, or to places difficult to reach by public transport, it makes sense to go with Intourist. And for some popular sights, like the tour of the treasures of the Kremlin Armoury, the queueing and difficulties of trying to get a ticket without going through Intourist probably make it worthwhile paying the steep 10 roubles fee for their excursion.

Lenin's tomb

Finally, although Intourist will also help you jump the queue at Lenin's tomb, you can do this by yourself. The trick is to get your passport back from the hotel desk (they usually like to hang on to it for their own convenience). Once armed with your passport, head for Red Square, and walk up the queue towards the mausoleum. As you enter the square itself, show your passport to the first guard you see beside the queue, point to the tomb and say 'Lenin, *pazhalsta*'. You will then be inserted at the usual point for tourists, and can expect a twenty-minute wait in line, rather than the three or four hours most Russians face. Viewing the embalmed corpse is a brisk but somewhat ghoulish experience. There is an apocryphal story about one tour group seeing an ear fall from the body. Certainly, the place occasionally closes for repairs, but this probably refers to the building rather than the occupant. Being built upon the site of the old Kremlin moat, the building has a damp problem.

Each time I have been, at least one of the Russian women crossed herself as she went by. The mausoleum is also a useful reminder of the transience of human vanities. For eight years after his death, Stalin also lay here in honour, right alongside Lenin. In 1961, the 22nd Party Congress voted to remove Stalin from the mausoleum, and bury him under a plain stone slab at the back of the building.

When inside the tomb, do not try to take photographs, and remove your hands from your pockets.

Independent tours

Each of the following itineraries should last no more than half a day, but most can be done more quickly. I recommend that you get a good map of the city, which is best bought in the west.

The Falk maps, although infuriating to unfold, are the next most reliable after the ones produced by the CIA. Russian maps still include misleading bits, allegedly to baffle spies.

Tour one: the Kremlin

Note: The Kremlin churches and cathedrals, and the Museum of Seventeenth Century Life, are open daily from 10 a.m. to 6 p.m., closed on Thursdays.

We have been brought up to think of the Kremlin as quintessentially Russian. Not so. With its swallow-tailed battlements and towers, this is a classic fortress of the North Italian Renaissance, the type you see in the backgrounds of paintings by the old masters. Like many of the striking buildings to be seen in Russia, it was designed by Italians who were imported to Moscow by Tsar Ivan III at the end of the fifteenth century.

This was the third Kremlin on the site of the hill overlooking the long bend where the Yauza and the Neglinnaya flow into the River Moscow. The Russian word *Krieml* means fortress, and the first was a wooden stockade, built in the years after 1147 by Prince Yuri Dolgoruky. In the 1360s, in the time of Dmitry Donskoy who was the first Russian leader to defeat a Mongol army in the field, the second Kremlin was built. Its white walls were constructed from limestone.

A real fortress, the Kremlin has seen sieges enough. It last fell in 1917, after a six-day siege by the Bolsheviks. They finally broke through the Nikolskaya Gate at the north-west corner on Red Square, exactly the same place where the Russian levies under Minin and Pozharsky stormed the Kremlin in 1612 to liberate it from the Poles.

Getting there

You enter by another gate, at the Trinity Tower in the centre of the Kremlin's west wall. The best way to reach the place is to begin from the **Prospekt Marksa Metro station**, beside the National Hotel, where Gorky Street opens into the great square named 'Fifty Years of October Revolution'. There is a pedestrian tunnel beneath the square to the red-brick history museum at the western end of Red Square. Turn right and walk past the eternal flame to the Unknown Soldier, and through the Alexander Gardens along the Kremlin wall. These gardens are built above the River Neglinnaya, which now goes through an underground conduit. Ahead of you is a white and red brick gate tower, guarding a bridge which leads into the Kremlin itself. This is the Kutalya Tower, the last of these gate towers to survive. It guards the route to the Trinity Gate by which Napoleon entered the abandoned Kremlin in 1812, and it is also the entry for tourists.

Once inside the 4.5-m thick walls, to your right is a narrow lane where officers of the guard once lived. Lenin took rooms here when he first moved into the Kremlin in 1918 and Trotsky lived here throughout the civil war. Stalin's apartments were in the **Potyeshnii Palace** at the far end of the lane; it means Palace of the Amusements, after the royal theatre that was built there by the seventeenth-century Tsar Alexei. It was here that Stalin's wife Nadezhda, mother of his daughter Svetlana, committed suicide in 1932. Dominating the lane now is the modern glass building, the **Palace of the Congresses**, a 6,000-seat auditorium where major Party meetings are held, and the overflow theatre for the Bolshoy ballet.

To your left is the closed area of the Kremlin, where the Soviet government is based. There are three great buildings: the **Arsenal** alongside the Kremlin wall; the triangular **Senate** with its domed roof, formal meeting place for the Party's Central Committee; and then, furthest from the Trinity Gate by which you entered, the **Presidium** of the Supreme Soviet. In front of these buildings are hundreds of cannon, most of them captured from the French in 1812. Turn to your right, and ahead of you is the biggest cannon of all, the Tsar-Pushka, 5 m long, weighing nearly 41 tonnes, and almost certainly never fired since it was cast in 1586.

Museum of Seventeenth Century Life

Behind the cannon are two linked buildings, the **Patriarch's Palace** and the **Church of the Twelve Apostles**. Although they look of the same period as the rest of the main Kremlin buildings, they are in fact much later, dating from the mid-seventeenth century. They were built in the time of Nikon, the hard-line traditionalist who tried to take the Church back to its roots, in architecture as in theology. The two buildings are now the Museum of Seventeenth Century Life. Its best feature is the vast **Chamber of the Cross** (Krestovaya Palata), in its day the largest room ever built in Russia without columns to support the roof.

Cathedral Square

Proceed into the heart of the Kremlin, Cathedral Square, dominated by the tall bell-tower of Ivan Veliki, Ivan the Great, with its huge and broken bell lying beside it. The 200-tonne bell was cast in 1735, and broken two years later when cold water was thrown upon the red-hot bell during a fire. It had never been taken from the pit where it was cast. The 76-m bell-tower was built by Boris Godunov in 1600. Standing with your back to it, you are surrounded by the glories of Italian Renaissance architecture, adapted to Russian forms. To your right is the Cathedral of the Assumption, built by Aristotle Fioravanti in the 1470s. To your left is Alevisio Novi's Cathedral of the Archangel Michael, 1505–8. Straight ahead is the Faceted Palace (the Granovitaya), built by Marco Ruffo and Pietro Solario in the 1480s. The Palace is flanked by two Russian churches, both designed in the 1480s by architects from Pskov; to your left, the Cathedral of the Annunciation, and to your right, the Church of the Deposition of the Robe, which was the private church of the Patriarch, and later of the Tsar's own family.

Most of these churches were built on the foundations of older structures. The five-domed **Cathedral of the Assumption** was built on the ruins of an ambitiously-conceived cathedral that collapsed almost as soon as its architects had erected it, a disaster which prompted Tsar Ivan to import Signor Fioravanti from Bologna. The Tsar sent his

Italian to Suzdal and Vladimir to study the great tradition of Russian architecture, and Fioravanti found a way to bring delicacy to the ponderous dignity of the Russian style, to introduce light to the interior.

Few of the original frescoes, originally painted under the direction of the great Dionysius, have survived. The wall paintings date from the seventeenth century, and have been much restored. Two icons, St Peter on the south wall, and the Virgin on the first row of the iconostasis, are attributed to Dionysius. The 'Virgin of Vladimir', to the left of the royal door on the western side, is a fifteenth-century copy of the twelfth-century original from Byzantium which is said to have saved Moscow from Tamburlaine. The original is in Moscow's Tretyakov Gallery. The wooden throne of the Monomakh was carved for Ivan the Terrible, and the central silver chandelier was donated by the Cossacks, who recaptured some at least of the 300 kilos of gold and 5 tonnes of silver the French troops stripped from this cathedral during their occupation in 1812. They stabled their horses in this cathedral.

The **Cathedral of the Archangel Michael** contains the tombs of Tsars from the thirteenth century to the beginning of the eighteenth century, when Peter the Great shifted the capital to St Petersburg. Dmitry Donskoy, Ivan the Terrible, and Mikhail, first of the Romanovs, are all entombed here. The wall paintings are late seventeenth century, and the gold iconostasis dates from after the French occupation and looting of the Kremlin.

The **Faceted Palace** (Granovitaya), which contained the Tsar's banqueting hall and formal audience chamber, is now used by Mikhail Gorbachev for official state dinners. Not open to the public, it is a stunning room that seems roofed in pure gold; the relatively low ceiling and single thick supporting column bring the religious scenes intimately close. In the 1930s, the most distinctive feature of the Palace, the Red-Gold Staircase from where the *Streltsy* launched their massacre in 1682, and from which Napoleon watched Moscow burn, was demolished.

The **Cathedral of the Annunciation** became the chapel royal, the private church of the Tsar's family. Small, intimate and marvellously painted, it swiftly becomes the favourite of most visitors and is so rich and darkly glowing that entering the church is like being wrapped in golden fur. It is a church particularly associated with Ivan the Terrible. He added four domed chapels to its corners, and covered them with gold looted from Novgorod. After his fourth marriage, when church law forbade him to use the main portal, he built a private porch and chapel, and followed the services in seclusion. The frescoes, restored in the 1940s, are attributed to Theodosius, son of Dionysius. The iconostasis is judged to be the finest in Russia. Icons painted by Theophanes and Andrey Rublyov, thought to have been lost in the great fire of 1547, were rediscovered in the 1920s.

The **Church of the Deposition of the Robe** was built as the private chapel of the Metropolitan and then, after Moscow's refusal to continue to bow to the authority of Constantinople, of the Patriarch. After the building of the Patriarch's palace, it began to be used by the Tsar's family, and became associated with the Royal women. The seventeenth-century frescoes and iconostasis were restored in the 1950s.

Taynitsky Gardens

Beyond the Cathedral of the Annunciation are these gardens, overlooking the river and the south bank. To your left, looking along the gardens and past the statue of Lenin, is the great **Saviour Tower** (Spassky), the formal entrance to the Kremlin and bearer of the great clock whose chimes are the signature of Moscow radio and TV. The bells have been designed to play the tune of the Internationale. To the right of the Saviour Tower is the **Little Tower of the Tsar** (Tsarskaya), where Ivan the Terrible would stand to watch executions. Next, to the right, is the **Alarm Tower** (Nabatnaya), whose bell was the first fire warning. The next tower is the **Torture Tower** (Pyotoshnaya), used as a prison. Immediately before you, dominating the long south wall, is the oldest of the Kremlin towers, the **Storage Tower** (Taynitskaya), which contained food supplies for a siege, and also a water gate for access to the river.

Great Kremlin Palace

To the right stretches the 100-m yellow and white façade of the Palace, built in the 1840s. Closed to the public, it contains the formal great rooms of the government. When Mikhail Gorbachev received the world leaders paying their condolences after the funeral of Konstantin Chernenko, it was inside the Palace, in the vast **St George's Hall**, nearly 61 m long. In a building and a culture known for ornate magnificence, St George's Hall combines grandeur with restraint. White and gold, its walls are decorated with the names of the winners of St George's Medal, Tsarist Russia's highest award for gallantry. Beside St George's were the two smaller halls of St Alexander Nevsky, and the old throne room, the hall of St Andrew. In the 1930s, these two halls were combined into one great chamber where the 1,500 deputies of the Supreme Soviet, the nation's legislative body, now meets.

The north wing of the Great Kremlin Palace is the delightfully pretty **Terem Palace**, some of whose red and white tiles can be seen when you cross the Kamenny Most, the great stone bridge at the Kremlin's south-west corner. Built in the 1630s, above two much older churches, it is closed to the public.

The Armoury

Between the Great Kremlin Palace and the west wall of the Kremlin is the Armoury, which contains the stunning museum collection. Recently restored, the highlight of the collection is usually said to be the miniature Fabergé eggs made for the Tsar's family. They contain tiny models of the Trans-Siberian railroad, a miniature battlecruiser, and a music box model of the Kremlin. The museum also includes the world's finest collection of English sixteenth-century Elizabethan silver, sent to Ivan the Terrible by Queen Elizabeth during their abortive discussions of marriage. The best English collections were melted down in the 1640s to pay for the Cavalier–Roundhead armies in the English Civil War. The collections of royal dresses, and the Tsars' carriages and armour create a surfeit of magnificence after a while, and a great deal of the gold and silver, and the 800-diamond throne, are in such lavish taste they are almost vulgar. The Tsarist regalia are splendid, but the fourteenth-century fur-ringed crown of the Monomakh impresses by contrast through its very restraint. The Armoury must be seen. Unforgettable as a collection, its combination of wealth and bad taste, of magnificent and almost Asiatic decadence, carries important hints about the Russian character, as well as the nation's cultural traditions. Open daily from 9.30 a.m. to 5 p.m., closed on Thursdays.

Tour two: Red Square and around

Red Square (Krasnaya Ploshchad) has nothing to do with the Red Revolution. *Krasnaya* originally meant beautiful, and that description also hardly seems appropriate, however grand and imposing the vast expanse of cobblestones.

History

Known as Red Square since the seventeenth century, it has traditionally been a vast market place and a national theatre for the great moments of power and pageantry. Famous rebels were executed here, beside the Lobnoye Mesto, the raised circular dais near St Basil's from which state decrees were read aloud. It was here that Peter the Great slaughtered the *Streltsy* after their revolt, that Pugachev and Stenka Razin were put to death, and here that Ivan the Terrible declared his penitence before his subjects. The place reeks of Russia's history, which is to say that it also reeks of Russia's blood – and of another characteristic liquid. It was in Red Square that Ivan opened what might be called a Tsar's Bar and began the long tradition of declaring vodka a state monopoly, and taxing every bottle.

St Basil's Cathedral

Dominated on the west side by the Kremlin walls, and on the east by GUM, State Universal Store number one, the Square's most dramatic feature is the surreal masterpiece, St Basil's Cathedral, which was originally known as the Church of the Holy Veil by the Moat. It was dubbed 'St Basil's' after a new chapel was erected above the grave of the Holy Fool Vassily, a devout madman given to prophecy, who was known as Basil. This classic symbol of Moscow was built by Ivan the Terrible to commemorate the conquest of Kazan from the Tartars in 1552, and legend holds that Ivan blinded the architects so that never again could they design as fine a building. Legend is wrong. There was one architect, called Posnik Yakovlev, who was known usually by his nickname 'Barma', which is why people thought there were two of them. And he went on to design another church in Kazan later, so he can hardly have been blind at the time.

The church did not always look quite so psychedelic. Once painted all white and the domes simply gilded, it assumed its current multi-coloured appearance only towards the end of the seventeenth century. The statue near the entrance to St Basil's is of Minin and Pozharsky, who led the national uprising against the Poles in the Time of Troubles. It was erected in 1818, at a time of nationalist fervour in the wake of Napoleon's defeat.

Looking past St Basil's towards the river, to the right of the church, is the slight hill where the young German pilot Mathias Rust cheekily landed his Cessna light aircraft in May 1987. To the left of St Basil's is the vast and unappealing Rossiya Hotel. Along its north side runs a series of small churches, first **St Barbara's**, built just before the French invasion of 1812, then the late seventeenth-century **St Maxim's**, which became the centre for the Environment Protection Society. At no. 6 Razin Street is the **English Court** (Angliskoye Podvoriye), the house given to the English merchants by Ivan the Terrible.

Museum Built into the slope that falls down to the Rossiya Hotel is a remarkable museum, the **House of the Romanov Boyars**. Birthplace of the first Romanov Tsar, this house was restored in the nineteenth century as a museum of the way of life of the Muscovite nobility of the sixteenth and seventeenth centuries. It also presents occasional special exhibitions on particular themes, such as the history of the samovar, or Russian embroidery. Open daily from 10 a.m. to 6 p.m., closed on Tuesdays and on the first Monday of each month.

Continue down this street that runs along the north side of the Rossiya Hotel, and turn left up the hill into Ipatevsky Pereulok, following the lane around to the right, and the enchanting **Church of Nikitniki** comes into view. This seventeenth-century gem of Russian merchant architecture is now a museum with murals by Simon Ushakov. This district of the Zaryadye, which means 'beyond the market rows', leads into **Kitay-Gorod**, the commercial district that stretches from Red Square to Ploshchad Nogina, the square which houses the headquarters of the Party, the Central Committee *apparat*. The dominant building of the Kitay-Gorod is the GUM store, nationalised by Lenin in 1921. Built in the 1890s, it housed over 1,000 individual shops, and the great merchants kept their offices on the top floor. These days, small craftsmen have ateliers on the top floor. You can in principle arrange for a pair of handmade boots, or a bespoke suit, but the quality of work is disappointing. GUM itself is a fairly depressing place. In the summer, the western entrance, above the public lavatories and near the meat section, smells badly. The ice cream is good, the central fountain a pleasure and, leaning over the first floor balcony, the architecture is charming. But the endless stalls of cheap textiles, the plastic briefcases and tacky souvenirs, are a grim reminder of the failure of Gorbachev's reforms so far to improve the quality of consumer goods.

25 October Street

This street, to the west of GUM, is still one of the finest and most interesting in the city, in spite of the demolitions of the 1920s and 30s, whose greatest casualty was the Chapel of the Iberian Virgin, which dated from Tsar Fyodor's time. But the **Slaviansky Bazaar Restaurant** remains, one of Chekhov's old haunts. The lonely tower is the only remnant of the thirteenth-century Bogoyavlensky Monastery. But the old **Royal Mint**, and the **Old Printing House**, home of the first printed book in Russia, survive, just alongside the seventeenth-century and splendidly named **Monastery of the Saviour Behind the Icon-sellers' Stalls**. Immediately behind the GUM, along Ulitsa Kuibysheva, is the former **Stock Exchange**, a stolid building, but with a fine carved door. It now houses the Chamber of Trade. Just beyond this stands a very fine Art Nouveau building, the **Ryabushinsky Bank**, designed by the architect Fyodor Schechtel in 1904. One of the greatest (but least known) architects of the century, Schechtel's buildings are themselves worth a Moscow tour. His use of tiles to control and vary the texture of the bank building was echoed further up the street at his **Merchants' Association Building**, completed in 1909.

Tour three: The Boulevard Ring Road (Bul'varnoye Koltso)

Having seen the Kremlin, if I had but one day or half-day to enjoy the rest of the city, I would forgo all the rest and embark on the 8-km hike around the Boulevard Ring. Moscow's inner ring road, it follows the line of the sixteenth-century white city wall. Much of it is similar to a Parisian tree-lined boulevard.

Gogol Boulevard

The best place to begin is at the **Kropotkinskaya Metro station**, just across from the open-air swimming pool. Head north, away from the pool, and up the long thin park of Gogol Boulevard, named after the writer. This was the wealthy quarter of the nineteenth-century cultured bourgeoisie. Herzen lived near here, and the Tretyakovs who founded the great art gallery, and so did Chekhov's widow Olga Knipper. **Ulitsa Ryleyeva**, off to the left, contains one of the last private houses, surrounded by a private garden, in the city. It is owned by the veteran and legendary American journalist Mr Ed Stevens, and his Russian wife Nina. Ed can claim to have met every Soviet leader since Stalin, and to have been the man who persuaded Nikita Khrushchev to stop censoring western correspondents in Moscow. The

Luxembourg and Canadian embassies are located here, and in Starokonyushenny Pereulok is a fine example of a wooden house – the ornately carved **Porokovshikov House**.

Gogol Boulevard continues up a slight hill to the junction with the Arbat Square. The statue of Gogol is the summer meeting place for Moscow's hippies. In the summer of 1987, the city police responded to public complaints with a quick raid, a series of arrests and beatings. Nothing unusual about that, except that the hippies formally complained, and the incident provoked angry enquiries by the newspaper *Izvestia*; an investigation by neutral policemen brought down from Leningrad; and the dismissal of several police officials. After much initial scepticism about *glasnost*, the Gogol hippies became converts.

To the right of Gogol is the **Moscow Pentagon**, the Defence Ministry complex, and even before the Revolution it was the Officer Cadet Academy. To Gogol's left is the **Praga Restaurant**, with the old **Arbat** stretching away to the west. Now Moscow's first pedestrian precinct, it boasts pavement artists, hordes of instant portrait painters, buskers, political debates and constant crowds. Moscow's version of fast food, the *shashlik* stalls selling barbecued chunks of meat on a skewer at the equivalent of 20 roubles a kilo, gather round the door to the delicatessen counter of the Praga Restaurant, probably the best take-away food counter in the city.

Suvorovsky Boulevard

Across the wide modern thoroughfare of Kalinin Prospekt, which runs east past the massive **Lenin Library** to the Kremlin wall, the Boulevard Ring continues with Suvorovsky Boulevard. This is named after the legendary eighteenth-century general. At no. 7a, Gogol died, and the house is now a rather poor museum. Opposite stands **Dom Zhurnalistov**, the centre of the Journalists' Union, and since the coming of *glasnost* one of the livelier places in the city. Just beyond it is a small unnamed café where they serve rather good macaroons. But for the road underpass beneath Kalinin Prospekt, which makes Soviet drivers think they are in a Grand Prix, this would be a charming boulevard on which to stroll back and forth, admiring the architecture and enjoying the children playing on the wooden toy structures between the boulevard trees. As it is, you take your life in your hands to cross the road. This boulevard ends at the junction with Herzen Street (Ulitsa Gerzena), a corner which saw some of the most bitter fighting of the 1917 Revolution, changing hands several times.

The modern building to the right with the curved windows is the HQ of **TASS**, the Soviet news agency. The large white **Church of the Ascension** to the left is where Pushkin was married. On the corner beyond the church on Kachalova Street is the best-supplied textile store in Moscow, where silks and crepe de chine can sometimes be found. The first street off to the right from Kachalova is named after the writer **Alexei Tolstoy**, and Mikhail Gorbachev lived in a discreet enclave on this street before he became Soviet leader. He still maintains a private apartment there, and hosts the occasional dinner party for foreign guests whom he wants to pay the compliment of entertaining away from the formalities of the Kremlin. Mrs Thatcher was the first to be so favoured. This corner of Kachalova and Alexei Tolstoy Streets boasts one of Fyodor Schechtel's finest buildings, the Art Nouveau **Ryabushinsky House**, designed for the banker of the same name.

Herzen Street to the right leads down to the Kremlin wall. Almost immediately on its right stands a red brick building that looks as if it should have been carved of wood back in the sixteenth century. This is the **Mayakovsky Theatre**, and in the crazy months after the 1917 Revolution, he tried to run it as the official theatre of revolutionary satire. Mayakovsky was to commit suicide in 1930, probably because he finally realised how impermissible satire had become under the heirs of the Revolution. Further down the hill on the right is the white and yellow **Moscow Conservatory**, now named after Tchaikovsky. Almost opposite is Ulitsa Nezhdanovoy, which leads to a red brick and unmistakably English church of the late Victorian period. It was indeed the church for the English community; it is now a recording studio, but its most exciting moment came in the 1917 fighting when its tower contained an artillery observation post and a machine gun nest.

Tverskoy Boulevard

Go back up Herzen Street and turn right to continue on Boulevard Ring, this next stretch being the famous Tverskoy Boulevard, known for its theatres. The **Pushkin** and **Malaya Bronnaya** theatres are here, and the new **Moscow Arts Theatre** (MKhAT) is the modernistic building on the western side. The boulevard then crosses Gorky Street, with the vast **Izvestia** building dominating the junction from the left, and the **Moscow News** building from the right, and becomes Strastnoi Boulevard. This corner is the nearest Moscow has to a Fleet Street. Just behind the vast Rossiya movie house are the offices of *Novy Mir*, the monthly literary journal. It was in the forefront of Khrushchev's thaw a generation ago by printing Solzhenitsyn, and now in the Gorbachev thaw it published George Orwell's *1984*. To the left of Strastnoi Boulevard runs Chekhov Street, after the playwright who liked the street so much he lived in three separate houses there (nos. 11, 12 and 29). The white and green **Church of Our Lady of Putinki** dates from 1652. The **Komsomol Theatre** at no. 6 used to be the Merchants' Club.

Strastnoi Boulevard

Further east along Strastnoi Boulevard are the remains of **St Peter's Monastery**, founded in the fourteenth century. The young Peter the Great fled here for safety during the *Streltsy* revolt of 1682. The surviving monastery buildings all date from this period. The monastery gave its name to the wide street that crosses the boulevard here, the Petrovka, and like Scotland Yard, this has become a synonym for Police HQ. The huge building to the right as you look north up Petrovka is the main militia building, and the police operations

Petrovka Boulevard

centre. On the left of Petrovka running northwards are the old **Hermitage Gardens**, now very run-down. But the Hermitage modern art group seems to have won the support of the Mossoviet local authority to spruce up the gardens, and to recycle their buildings into a permanent exhibition of modern Soviet art. In the corner between Strastnoi Boulevard and the old Hermitage Gardens is the **Gagarin Mansion**, the English Club of the years before 1812, where Tolstoy set the scene for Pierre's challenge to a duel in *War and Peace*.

Petrovka runs south alongside the old monastery to the back gate of the **Bolshoy Theatre**, along one of the busier shopping streets of Moscow. Just before the Bolshoy, the Petrovka opens into a large square, the downhill end of the fashionable Tsarist shopping street of **Kuznetsky Most**. It retains a rather faded echo of its grander days, with some fashion shops to the left, and a series of bookstores to the right. To the left of the Bolshoy is a modern glass building called TSUM, the Central Universal Store, which is not to be confused with GUM. TSUM is more recognisably a department store, has a decent range of cheap fur hats, and is still known to elderly Muscovites as 'Muir ee Merrowleas', which is what the Scottish-owned store was called before the Revolution. At the far side of the store, you may still see the grey stone Gothic-revival façade of the original building.

Petrovsky Boulevard

Returning to our Boulevard, after crossing Petrovka it becomes Petrovsky Boulevard and runs down into **Trubnaya Ploshchad**, the heart of the old brothel quarter. Trubnaya Ploshchad can be translated as Pipe Square, after the great conduit that carried the River Neglinnaya through the old city walls at this point. Off to the right down Neglinnaya Ulitsa are the **Sandunovsky Baths**, now sadly run-down but still quite magnificent. No visit to the Soviet Union is complete without attending a Banya, a public bath-house, and this is certainly the best.

Tsvetnoi Boulevard

Up to the left from the open square, another boulevard runs north past the old circus and the **central market** on the left. This is Floral (Tsvetnoi) Boulevard, and the ground floor of the large public market in the glass-fronted building still offers the biggest selection of flowers in the city, although it is expensive. Behind the flowers, the fruit and vegetable market shows how well Soviet farmers can produce when they sell on their own account and have the incentive of turning a profit. Walk through the vegetable market, and into the two smaller buildings at the rear, the meat market and the dairy department. The honey will be the best you ever tasted – and the peasant women will offer you endless tastes scraped on to bits of wax paper.

There is more to all this than meets the eye. In the post-Brezhnev corruption crack-downs, the entire market police force was arrested, along with half the market management and several of the stall holders, accused of running a Mafia-style protection racket under which fat bribes had to be paid to get a guaranteed stall. The police did not push matters too far. The polite fiction says that these markets are available for the peasants to sell the surplus from their private plots; in fact, you will see the same faces selling the stuff day in and day out for years. It is a full-time job, and very lucrative too. You do not see these 'peasants' eating at the market cafeteria, which is just up the stairs at the right of the market entrance, and a depressingly typical example of Soviet public catering.

From Trubnaya Ploshchad, the Boulevard Ring becomes less attractive, and the footsore tourist may choose to break off here, having explored the central market. The Boulevard continues up a steep hill, the north slope of what had been the Valley of Neglinnaya. To the right are the remains of the **Rozhdestvensky Monastery**, named after the birth of the Virgin when it was founded in the late fourteenth century as one of the ring of monastic fortresses that protected the capital. The small sixteenth-century cathedral is the most striking building. At this point, the boulevard seems to narrow, but in fact what had been the narrow park is here replaced by some undistinguished buildings. Across the far side of the boulevard and to the north are the offices of *Literaturnaya Gazeta*, familiarly known as Literaturka, the house magazine of Soviet intellectuals.

Where Ulitsa Dzerzhinskovo enters from the right is another of the late fourteenth-century monasteries, the **Sretensky**. All that is left is the seventeenth-century green domed cathedral. (To continue down Dzerzhinskovo brings you to the rear of the headquarters of the KGB on Dzerzhinsky Square, see below.) The boulevard opens out into a large square, dominated by the **Kirov-Turgenev Metro station**. The Soviet Metro infuriatingly gives two names to one large station, simply because it serves two lines. To the right, or south of the square, **Kirov Street** is Kirov Street, the most pleasing route back to the centre for those who have had their fill of the boulevards, and certainly, you have now seen the best of them. Kirov Street was named after the energetic young Leningrad Party leader whose assassination in 1934, possibly at Stalin's instigation, launched the purges. In the old days, it was called Myasnitskaya or Butchers' Street, which might have been appropriate, considering what was to be the role of the KGB building during the purges, when it was nicknamed the Lubyanka, after another of the small old streets behind it. Kirov Street begins with the main **Post Office**, and the pink eighteenth-century building almost opposite is the **Yushkov House**, where the Painting Academy was established in the 1840s. Further south is the wonderful mock-Chinese tea shop, which dates from the 1890s. Kirov Street runs on, past the still functioning **Catholic Church of St Ludovic**, and then to the KGB building on **Dzerzhinsky Square**. Dzerzhinsky, known to his friends as Iron Felix, was the Pole who founded the Soviet secret police, known in his day as the CHEKA, the Extraordinary Commission.

To the left, or north of the Kirov-Turgenev Metro, Kirov Street continues as a wide and modern street where a series of striking new buildings are being erected, most of them attached to the vast and growing bureaucratic empire which is the State Statistical Service, few of whose figures are believed by anybody. Back in the 1920s, there was a plan for a grandiose new avenue to sweep north from Dzerzhinsky Square to Komsomolskaya Square, further north still. This wide new street is what is left of the plan, but on the left is the only Le Corbusier building in the city, built in the 1930s to house the main trade union organisation, but then taken over by the State Statistical Service, which *Pravda* once revealed produces 30,000,000,000 forms a year.

Chistoprudny Boulevard

Back on the Boulevard Ring, after the Kirov-Turgenev Metro, comes the delightfully named Chistoprudny, or clean-pond, Boulevard. The butchers used to toss their offal here until the place was cleaned up in the eighteenth century by Peter the Great's favourite, Alexander Menshikov, who was given a tract of land nearby and who built the boulevard's tall **Church of the Archangel Gabriel**. The pond remains, and seems the most popular place in Moscow for model boats. The boulevard houses the **Sovremennik Theatre**, in a classical building that used to be a cinema, and next door but one at no. 23 was the home of the film-maker Eisenstein.

The next junction is dominated by the splendid blue Baroque **Apraksin House**, a grammar school before the Revolution, and the Industrial Academy thereafter, where the young Nikita Khrushchev went to school with Stalin's wife Nadezhda as the Party organised crash courses to make its keen young militants into trained engineers.

Pokrovsky Boulevard

Across Ulitsa Chernyshevskovo is Pokrovsky Boulevard, site of one of the great Tsarist barracks, and now on Sundays a place to hear marvellous choral singing from the Baptist church. Beyond it and to the right at the building with the worker and peasant statues is **Podkolokolny Pereulok**, which leads to the area once known as the Khitrov Rinok, the city's worst and poorest slum quarter in Tsarist days. Stanislavsky went through it to absorb atmosphere before staging Gorky's devastating drama of slum life, *The Lower Depths*.

Yauzsky Boulevard

The last of the boulevards is called Yauzsky, after the River Yauza which flows into the River Moscow here. The boulevard ends suddenly at a junction marked by a wine shop. To the right of the junction is the ancient **Solyanka Street** which leads back to the centre of the city at Ploshchad Nogina. On the left up Solyanka is the vast orphanage of Tsarist days, now a barracks and military engineering academy. The last street on the right of Solyanka before the square is Ulitsa Arkhipova, site of the working synagogue. To the left of the junction, just before the River Yauza, is the bright blue eighteenth-century **Trinity Church**, which used to serve the local silversmiths who lived in this quarter. Beyond the river is one of Stalin's huge wedding cake buildings, a rather grand 33-storey apartment house. The road just before the river leads down to the River Moscow.

If not exhausted by the long stroll around the boulevards, the energetic may cross the River Moscow by the **Great Ustinsky Bridge**, and then walk back to the centre along the south bank, which gives an excellent view of St Basil's Cathedral and the Kremlin. It is not in fact the south bank of the River Moscow, but the north bank of the 'island' that appeared when the drainage canal was built in the 1780s to protect the city from floods. The weary should walk back to the centre along Solyanka Street.

Tour four: The Garden Ring Road (Sadovoye Koltso)

History

Moscow's eight-lane wide middle ring road looks as if it were built for the age of the motor car. Not so. It dates from the sixteenth century, when it was the site of an earth rampart and a wooden palisade, the outer defences of the city. After the French fled and left the city in flames in 1812, the ruined old ramparts were replaced by a new Boulevard Ring, planted with trees. Hence the 'Garden Ring' name.

This outer boulevard also served as an unofficial boundary between old Moscow and the new slums and industrial estates that were developing. The textile industry that grew along the banks where the Presnya stream flowed into the River Moscow to the north-west of the Kremlin spawned a slum district which became a hotbed for radical politics and rose in the 1905 Revolution. The workers tried to storm old Moscow across the Garden Ring at the place now called Uprising Square (Ploshchad Vostaniye). Beaten back, they set up their barricades at what is now the site of the Zoo, and the Barrikadnaya Metro station, until the Army brought up artillery and shelled the district now known as Red Presnya (Krasnaya Presnya) into submission.

In the 1930s, Stalin had the trees felled and the Garden Ring made into a grand thoroughfare. Nearly 16 km in circumference, usually packed with trucks and of limited architectural interest, this is not a route to stroll. There is a ring road bus, marked Б, which makes the full circuit for 5 kopeks (see p. 114). Each section of the ring road has a different name. The nearest Metro station to our starting point is Barrikadnaya.

Getting there

Starting on the western side from the 22-storey Stalin-era apartment house on Ploshchad Vostaniye, and travelling clockwise along the road called Sadovaya-Kudrinskaya, a two-storeyed red and white house on the right stands out. This is the house-museum of **Chekhov**, a disappointing place, where he practised as a doctor in the 1880s and wrote his first play *Ivanov*. Open daily from 11 a.m. to 6 p.m., closed on Mondays and on the last day of each month. **The Planetarium** is on the opposite side of the road, near the shop named 'Kabul' which sells Afghan goods, including the occasional decent carpet.

The next major junction is **Mayakovsky Square**, marked by a large statue of the poet after whom the square is named, where the Garden Ring crosses Gorky Street at an underpass. The tall hotel building on the left is the **Hotel Pekin**, with its 'Chinese' restaurant on the ground floor. To the right, just before Gorky Street, is the **Tchaikovsky Concert Hall**, one of the city's main performance stages, and the **Satyr Theatre**. Just behind the theatre is the formerly church-run district known as 'The Freedom of the Patriarch'. Focused around a small lake called the **Patriarch's Pond** (Patriarshii Prud), this became the rather Bohemian students' quarter in the nineteenth century, and is now a favourite spot for urban joggers.

After the Gorky Street junction, the Garden Ring runs alongside an area of major redevelopment on the right, by the old Hermitage Gardens, where both the Writers' and the Artists' Unions are building huge new apartment blocks for their members. On the left, the large white office block is GAI traffic police HQ, and on the right where the flyover begins at no. 12 Sadovaya-Samotyochnaya, is the main western Press building, the base for Reuter, the BBC, the *New York Times*, *Daily Telegraph*. In the block alongside, and not by accident, is the **Kolkhida** co-operative restaurant, specialising in Georgian food. Just across the street is the world famous **Central Puppet Theatre**, where in the bad old days before *glasnost*, western reporters and dissidents would arrange to meet. To the right of the flyover is Tsvetnoi Boulevard and the central market, and to the right, the valley of the Neglinnaya leads to the new Olympic Sports Complex.

The Ring Road continues to the major junction at the **Kolkhoznaya Metro station**. To the left here is Peace Avenue (Prospekt Mira), which runs north for a mile to the green and white Riga Station, site of the biggest of the new co-operative markets. Places on overnight trains from the Baltic Republics are hard to find, with the members of the co-operatives making their fashionable clothes in Riga, and then bringing them up to Moscow to sell at high prices.

Just beyond the Prospekt Mira junction on the left is one of Moscow's finest classical buildings, the **Sklifosovsky Hospital**, with its distinctive curved colonnade designed by Quarenghi. Further along this Sadovaya–Spasskaya section of the ring road is a junction dominated by the tall spire of the **Leningradskaya Hotel**, the Stalin-era building which most sacrificed content to form. Only 19 per cent of this building's interior space is actually used. On the opposite corner is an aggressively modern building of the inter-war years, Shchusev's

Constructivist **Ministry of Agriculture** building with its distinctive cylindrical corner. This road, Kalanchovskaya Street, leads north into the huge Komsomol Square, which used to be known as Three-Stations Square.

Komsomol Square

In some ways more characteristically Russian than Red Square, Komsomol Square sees thousands of provincials and peasants pouring into the capital every day, most coming to shop in the (relatively) well-stocked shops, but many also coming to sell foodstuffs and handicrafts. They clog the waiting rooms of the main stations and, late at night and in the early morning, present a scene that seems little changed since Tolstoy's day. However, it is more modern and less innocent than it appears. Kazan Station is notorious as one of the main drug dealing centres, and all three stations see a brisk but squalid night-time trade in alcohol and cheap prostitution. The parked trains in the marshalling yards are grim places at night, the underbelly of Gorbachev's Moscow.

The three stations that dominate the square reflect three quite distinct architectural styles and make it an instant introduction to the splendid oddities of Moscow architecture. The **Leningrad Station** on the north side is a classical 1850s building, but the **Yaroslavl Station** alongside is a bizarre Art Nouveau masterpiece by the architect Fyodor Schechtel, with odd Tartar echoes, built from 1902–4. The station for the Trans-Siberian trains, its steep roof and the grandeur of its main entrance have led more than one country bumpkin to stumble off the train and enquire if this is the Kremlin. On the far (southern) side of the square is the even stranger **Kazan Station**, designed by Shchusev in 1912 in old Russian style, but finally completed in the 1920s. Its 61-m tower was indeed based on a kremlin – the fortress in the old Tartar capital of Kazan. Immediately south of Kazan Station, on the way back to the Garden Ring, is the early eighteenth-century church of **Saints Peter and Paul**, which Peter the Great is said to have designed, grafting a Dutch-style spire on to a dumpy Russian body.

The next section of the Garden Ring is the Sadovaya-Chernogryaskaya, after the river whose name means 'black and dirty'. Ulitsa Karla Marksa to the left leads eventually to the Orthodox Cathedral, but the first church on the right, the semi-ruined and large **St Nikita the Martyr**, is a better building. It stands opposite the Bauman Gardens and the old Golitsyn Mansion, which is now used as the exhibition rooms for the Soviet Cultural Fund.

The Garden Ring then leads into Ulitsa Chkalova. Dr Andrey Sakharov, the veteran human rights campaigner and father of the Soviet H-bomb, lives in a humble apartment block on the right. The huge and modern Kursk railway station lies on the left, as the road drops down to cross the River Yauza. Across the Yauza, the Garden Ring goes into a long underpass beneath Taganka Square, a distinctive area of the city which has been given character by the nearby **Taganka Theatre**.

In the Brezhnev years, under its director Yuri Liubimov and the leading actor Vladimir Vysotsky, the Taganka became a cultural centre of importance, with a dangerous but exciting hint of political subversion. Vysotsky's songs of an eternal Russia, decent and brave even if drunk and running foul of the law, made him into a public figure. He has been called Russia's Bob Dylan and its John Lennon, and his death during the Olympic Games in 1980 was seen as a national tragedy. The authorities frowned and ignored him, but half the city turned out for the funeral.

Just along from the modern red brick theatre is a place now called **Vysotsky's Bar**, where he used to do a lot of the drinking that finally killed him. The tiny bar-restaurant contains an indoor pond with frogs, and a chicken that pecks among the tables; it serves a kind of Sangria, and stages floor shows that can be jazz jam sessions or a female contortionist. Russians need connections to get in. Foreigners can usually squeeze in with their passports.

From Taganka Square, Bolshaya Kommunisticheskaya Ulitsa runs east past the ruined eighteenth-century church of **St Martin the Confessor** to the vast **Hammer and Sickle Works**, and the main road to the north-east, known as Enthusiasts' Highway, from all the political enthusiasts who were sent that way to Siberia in Tsarist times. Just to the west of Taganka Square is the splendidly-tiled seventeenth-century church of the local potters, the **Church of the Assumption**.

To the south on the river bank, the white fortress walls are the defences of the **New Monastery of the Saviour** (the Novospassky), built in the 1640s and closed to the public because of restoration works that have been proceeding slowly for over twenty years. The Garden Ring, which is particularly un-garden-like along this stretch, then crosses the River Moscow. A better testimony to the restorers' skills is the **Paveletsky Station**, which was designed in the late nineteenth century to look like a French château on the Loire, and serves the southern Volga region down to the Caspian Sea. Situated just south of the drainage canal, it was the home of Moscow's first co-operative public convenience. In a small park alongside is a museum which displays **Lenin's Funeral Train**.

On the opposite (northern) side of the Garden Ring, at 31/12 Ulitsa Bakhrushina, is the **Bakhrushin Theatre Museum**. The country's premier theatre museum, its contents are displayed with shameful lack of imagination. Nijinsky's dancing shoes, models of sets from Stanislavsky and Meyerhold, and Chaliapin's costume robes as Boris Godunov are all there, amid the dust and gloom. Open daily from 12–7 p.m., closed on Tuesdays and on the last day of each month.

The next major junction is at the **Dobryninskaya Metro**

station, where the road south is the Warsaw Chaussee leading to the newly restored **Danilovsky Monastery** and the **Domodedovo Airport**. Just before the junction to the north, or turning right, is the delightful **Pyatnitskaya**, one of the best streets for strolling in Moscow. It runs from the Garden Ring due north into the heart of the Zamoskvarechiye, the city's left bank, and contains examples of all that is best about Russian architecture, from stout log houses to classical palazzi, and from churches to street markets, along its route. The street is dotted with churches; the two best ones are the eighteenth-century **St Clements**, halfway along Pyatnitskaya, with a central golden dome and four blue domes, and the seventeenth-century **Saints Michael and Fyodor** at the north end of the street, where the road swings left to the bridge which leads across the River Moscow and into Red Square. If the weather is too cold for any other stroll in Moscow, take the Metro to Dobryninskaya, and then walk the 1.5 km or so up Pyatnitskaya and into Red Square. In summer, it is the kind of district that cries out for the commercialisms of the west – an open-air café or a wine bar where one could sit surrounded by agreeable buildings near a pretty humpbacked bridge over a canal and watch Moscow go by.

Back on the ring road, **Dobryninskaya Square** also boasts a regional GUM Department Store, which is often better stocked than the main stores, because it is not known to the incoming shoppers from rural districts who descend upon places like TSUM like hordes of locusts. From its entrance, to the left you can see the statue of Lenin which dominates Oktyabraskaya Square. This is one of the main junctions of the city, where the Garden Ring goes beneath Leninsky Prospekt in a large underpass. The vast long building that dominates the southern flank of the square is an apartment block reserved for foreign diplomats. To the north, on Dmitrova Street, is the French Embassy. Opposite the French Embassy, and usually distinguished by a queue, is a café that is known for its hot chocolate. The glass-fronted shops alongside are Kommissioni, antique shops that specialise in glass, samovars and pottery, and a gallery that sells contemporary art. Just beyond them is the magnificent eighteenth-century church of **St John the Warrior**.

The Garden Ring continues across **Gorky Park** to the River Moscow, past the huge and imposing gates that guard the entrance to the Park on the left, and the new **State Picture Gallery** on the right. Most of the paintings of the Soviet period in the Tretyakov Gallery are being moved to this new building, or will be when they can stop the walls and ceiling from leaking. Almost all of them may safely be ignored, save for some of the canvases of Petrov-Vodkin and Sarayan, who is sometimes called, not without justice, the Armenian Matisse. The bulk of the collection is the worst form of socialist realism, happy collective farmers and noble proletarians under the benign eye of

Lenin. Open daily from 10 a.m. to 6 p.m., closed on Tuesdays.

Across the bridge on the left is the **Park Kultury Metro station** and the foreign language bookstore of Progress Publishers, and opposite is the **Press Centre** of the Ministry of Foreign Affairs, where Press conferences are held. The **Foreign Ministry** itself is the vast 27-storey Stalin-era building further along the Garden Ring on **Smolenskaya Square**, opposite the two wings of the Belgrade Hotel. Immediately beyond the Foreign Ministry and to the right is the western end of the **Arbat** pedestrian precinct, marked by a Gastronom that is one of the better foodshops in Moscow. The next underpass goes beneath **Kalinin Prospekt**, the wide modern thoroughfare lined with skyscrapers that Khrushchev built across the ruins of much of the picturesque old Arbat district. To the right, it leads to the Kremlin, and to the left, across the Kalininsky Bridge, past the Ukraina Hotel and out to the dachas of the powerful in Zhukovka. This is the road that Mikhail Gorbachev's Zil limousine takes to work most days.

After the underpass, the Garden Ring becomes Ulitsa Tschaikovskoyo, and passes a nine-storey yellow building on the left, the old **US Embassy**. It should have been empty by now, and the diplomats all moved into the vast new red brick compound behind. But, declaring that the new building was stuffed with bugs and electronic microphones built into the very brickwork, the Americans have refused to move in, and now say it must be demolished. A new embassy office block, built under secure conditions by specially-imported Americans only, will cost over $100 million. The diplomatic wrangle over this goes on, but should not divert you from the delightful single-storey classical building just past the embassy on the Garden Ring. This was the house of the opera singer Chaliapin, which is now being restored and will eventually open as a museum to the late singer. Immediately behind Chaliapin's house you can see one of the characteristic buildings of the Constructivist era, known as Narkomfin, the finance ministry, when it was completed in 1927. The next tall building to its right, in hideous Stalin style, is the Ploshchad Vostaniye apartment house back where this tour of the Garden Ring first started.

Museums

Moscow is filled with museums, which range from some of the world's finest collections to embarrassingly amateur 'home-museums' devoted to preserving the faded possessions of some obscure painter or actor. And the cultural revolution in the way museum exhibits are presented, the new user-friendly museum style which is now widespread in the west, has yet to reach the Soviet Union. The symbol of Soviet museums is the dusty glass case, guarded by a grim-faced and ageing woman whose glare insists that the public has no right to be in there. But even some of these should be braved. The following list is broken down into self-explanatory categories.

Must see
Tretyakov
Gallery

10 Lavrushinsky Pereulok. Nearest Metro: Novokuznetskaya. Open daily from 10 a.m. to 7 p.m., closed on Mondays. Tel. 231-1362.

The Tretyakov is not only one of the world's great galleries, it is a symbol of the Russian nationalist and cultural revival of the late nineteenth century, symbolised by the façade of the gallery itself, designed by Viktor Vasnetsov. There were two Tretyakov brothers, both wealthy merchants. Sergei collected Old Masters and French paintings, which he presented to the Pushkin Gallery, while Pavel created this finest single collection of Russian art, and also acted as the patron of one of the great Russian artistic movements, the Peredvizhniki, or Wanderers. Two of the prominent nineteenth-century portraits, Perov's painting of Dostoyevsky, and Kramskoy's portrait of Leo Tolstoy, were painted at Tretyakov's request.

There were two wings to the Peredvizhniki – the almost mystical discovery of the Russian landscape, and the passion for reinterpreting Russian history from the point of view of a late nineteenth-century reformer. The finest of the landscape artists was Isaac Levitan, rivalled only by Shishkin, but the movement really began with Savrasov's 'The Arrival of the Rooks' in 1871. The historic wing of the movement is by far the more dramatic. Vasily Surikov brought a touch of Hollywood to the Russian past; his paintings have their stars, like the 'Boyarina Morozova', and simplistic, Technicolor passions. Ilya Repin was a very much more subtle painter, and a far greater artist. You can breathe the very air of nineteenth-century Russia in his 'Religious Procession in Kursk', and feel the madness of Ivan the Terrible in the painting of his murder of his own son.

The other two great Russian artists of the period were Valentin Serov, whose portrait of the actress Maria Yermolova is an outstanding exhibit, and Mikhail Vrubel, whose half-sane visions and utter commitment to art heralded a departure from the quasi-political ambitions of the Peredvizhniki.

The Tretyakov also has an outstanding collection of early twentieth-century masters. Chagall and Kandinsky are well known to western art-lovers, but it is worth examining the less familiar works of Kazimir Malevich, Martiros Sarayan, and Kuzma Petrov-Vodkin. The later collection of Soviet period art is predictably uninspired, but look for Yuri Pimenov's 'The New Moscow'. A striking image of the new buildings and streets of the Moscow of the 1930s, seen from the back seat of an open car driven by a pretty girl, it suddenly reminds you of the confident self-image of Stalin's Moscow, whatever we now know of its dreadful reality.

The Tretyakov contains the world's finest collection of Russian icons, including the famous 'Novgorod St George', and perhaps the finest icon of all, Andrey Rublyov's 'Trinity'. It also contains the two celebrated historic icons, 'The Virgin of Vladimir', which tradition holds was painted by St Luke (more likely by a twelfth-century Byzantine master) and 'The Virgin of the Don' by Theophanes, which accompanied Dmitry Donskoy to the great victory over the Mongols at Kulikovo.

Pushkin Fine Arts Museum

12 Ulitsa Volkhonka. Nearest Metro: Kropotkinskaya. Open daily from 10 a.m. to 8 p.m., Sundays 10 a.m. to 6 p.m., closed on Mondays. Tel. 203-7998.

Founded by Professor Ivan Tsvetayev, the father of the great poet Marina, the museum was opened in 1912. It has a notable collection of Egyptian antiquities, and well-balanced examples of the Old Masters. There is a fine Botticelli 'Annunciation', six Rembrandts, a Rubens, and examples of Cranach and Veronese. But the Pushkin is outstanding for its Impressionists, collected mainly by two Russian merchants, Morozov and Shchukin, while the canvases were still wet and long before the French had begun to realise their importance.

Even if you hate museums, and paintings leave you cold, spare a few minutes to stand in rooms 17, 18 and 21 of the Pushkin. Room 21 has Monet's 'Boulevard des Capucines', some of the Rouen Cathedral and London series, and the water-lilies. These jostle with Manet's 'Déjeuner sur l'Herbe', 'Le Café' and his portrait of Proust, with Degas, Renoir and Pissarro.

Room 18 is Cézanne and van Gogh, Gauguin and Toulouse-Lautrec. Room 17 is Matisse, Bonnard, Henri Rousseau, Rouault, Léger and a marvellous collection of pre-1914 Picassos.

Novodevichy Convent

1 Novodevichy Proyezd. Nearest Metro: Sportivnaya. Open daily from 10 a.m. to 5 p.m., and from 3 May to 31 October, to 6 p.m., closed on Tuesdays and last day of each month. Tel. 246-8526.

This is my favourite single building, or rather complex of buildings, in the whole of Russia. It is best seen from the far side of the river, the domes and bell-towers rising magically from the trees, almost floating above the water. The approach by land from the Metro station or from central Moscow along Bolshaya Pirogovskaya brings you hard up against the grim brick walls and takes half of the beauty away.

The New Virgin Convent was built in 1524 to commemorate the conquest of Smolensk, and stands by the old road to Smolensk and the west. Although it looks like a fortress and occupies a strategic position on the river, it was not part of Moscow's fourteenth-century ring of monastery forts. Lavishly funded by Tsars and nobles, by the seventeenth century it had become one of the country's great landowners, with some 15,000 serfs. The convent has seen some historic moments. Boris Godunov was proclaimed Tsar here in 1598. It became the place to send women from the Royal family when their protectors died, or they became a political embarrassment. Peter the Great's sister Sophia was imprisoned here after her abortive coup against him. A scaffold was built outside her room, so close that the heels of her hanged associates drummed against her windowpane. Their bodies were left to rot her air for months. In 1812, the French used the convent to store supplies, and they left the place ready primed for demolition. The nuns found and extinguished the burning fuses. The small **Church of the Assumption**, attached to the large central Refectory, is still open for worship, but the rest of the complex is a state museum.

The **Cathedral of the Virgin of Smolensk**, modelled on the Kremlin's Cathedral of the Assumption, contains some excellent and very rare sixteenth-century frescoes. The gilt and wood-carved iconostasis is magnificent, and the church now presents an interesting exhibition on the convent's history. The late seventeenth-century six-storeyed bell-tower, the finest in Moscow and the structure which nails together the rest of the monastery complex, is probably the most painted single building in Moscow. Artists are obsessed by its proportions.

Although the convent grounds are filled with ornate ecclesiastical graves, the main cemetery is outside the convent walls, immediately to the south. Long closed by the authorities, who were apparently fearful that an informal shrine might develop around the grave of Nikita Khrushchev, it is now open again, and many of the headstones are remarkable. My favourite is of the inventor of the Katyusha, the Second World War lorry-borne rocket system, which struck terror into the Wehrmacht. The gravestone shows one of the trucks firing a salvo, all carved from marble. Gogol, Chekhov, Eisenstein, Stanislavsky, Scriabin and Prokofiev are all buried here. Khrushchev's grave is marked by Ernst Neizvestny's headstone, a cannonball bronze of a head, supported by an arch of black and white stones, to symbolise the good and the bad he did. On 14 October each year, the anniversary of his fall, the grave is heaped with flowers laid by old men and women who were freed when Khrushchev opened some of the gates of Stalin's Gulag in 1955.

Try hard to see
Andronikov Monastery

(Now called the Andrey Rublyov Museum of Old Russian Art.)

10 Ploshchad Pryamikova. Nearest Metro: Ploshchad Ilyicha. Open daily from 10 a.m. to 6 p.m., closed on Wednesdays and on the last Friday of each month. Tel. 278-1489.

One of Moscow's ring of fourteenth-century monastery forts, the Andronikov Monastery's central **Cathedral of the Saviour** was built in the 1420s and is the oldest surviving example of stone-built architecture in Moscow. The greatest of icon painters, Andrey Rublyov, lived and worked here, and is buried somewhere in the grounds, although the exact site of the grave is not known. Only two fragments survive of his paintings for the Cathedral of the Saviour, and his best-known works here are represented by copies. The museum holds one of the finest collections of icons in the country, its main strength being in the fifteenth- to eighteenth-century Moscow school.

Church of the Intercession at Fili

7 Novozavodskaya Ulitsa. Nearest Metro: Fili. Open same hours as the Andronikov Monastery, to which it is affiliated.

Along with the bell-tower of the Novodevichy Convent, this church is one of the finest examples of Moscow's distinctive Baroque style. Built by Peter the Great's uncle, Naryshkin, in the 1690s, it was well restored in 1980. Intourist has a magnificent poster of the Fili Church which manages to cut out the grim industrial surroundings. Once inside, the iconostasis is very fine, and the acoustics excellent; concerts of ancient music are sometimes given, and enquiries should be made through Intourist.

Museum of Folk Art

7 Ulitsa Stanislavskovo. Nearest Metro: Pushkinskaya. Open daily from 11 a.m. to 5 p.m., Tuesdays and Thursdays 2–8 p.m., closed on Mondays. Tel. 290-2114.

This museum houses the best collection of Palekh, the finely painted miniatures on lacquer. You will be struck by the way folk art was localised in Russia, with particular styles limited to small regions: the blue and white pottery from Gzhel, the brightly painted art of Khokhloma, the carved wooden toys of Zagorsk and the intricate carvings of bird feathers from Archangel. The collections of lace and embroidery are renowned, although poorly displayed.

Tropinin Museum

10 Shchetininsky Pereulok. Nearest Metro: Novokuznetskaya. Open daily from 10 a.m. to 5 p.m., Tuesdays and Thursdays 1–8 p.m., closed on Mondays. Tel. 231-1799.

This small and delightful two-storey museum near the Tretyakov Gallery houses some interesting eighteenth- to nineteenth-century portraits, as well as the works of the celebrated serf-artist, Tropinin. There is also a fine collection of nineteenth-century landscapes of old Moscow.

Vasnetsov House-Museum

13 Pereulok Vasnetsova. Nearest Metro: Kolkhoznaya. Open daily from 10 a.m., to 6 p.m., closed on Saturdays and Sundays. Tel. 281-1329.

Most of the house-museums in Moscow are a disappointment, wasting their collections through unimaginative display. The Vasnetsov home is an exception, because it is decorated with the artist's own works, and he also designed and painted the house and furniture. Viktor Vasnetsov was a key figure in the late nineteenth-century revival of Russian history, folk tales and folk arts. He was a member of the Peredvizhniki, and the designer of the façade of the Tretyakov Gallery.

Kuskovo Estate-Museum

2 Ulitsa Yunosti. Nearest Metro: Zhdanovskaya. Open daily from 11 am. to 7 p.m., Saturdays and Sundays from 10 a.m. to 6 p.m., closed on Mondays. Tel. 370-0130.

The summer estate of the aristocratic Sheremetyev family, this is a marvellous example of a whole series of eighteenth-century styles, all grouped in a park alongside a small lake. The main house is built of wood, carved and painted to look like stone. There are smaller houses in the Dutch, and the Italian styles. The pretty domed Hermitage was a private dining room, with the kitchen on the ground floor linked by a small lift to serve the diners above. The lakeside Grotto, decorated with shells brought from the Mediterranean, was opened with a famous banquet for Catherine the Great.

The estate now houses the **State Museum of Ceramics**, and contains some works by the father of Russian pottery, Dmitri Vinogradov. It also displays the famous Sèvres china service commissioned by Catherine the Great.

Ostankino Palace and Museum of Serf Art

5 Pervaya Ostankinskaya Ulitsa. Nearest Metro: VDNKh, and then take tram 7 or 11. Open daily from 10 a.m. to 3 p.m. from 1 October to 3 May, and from 10 a.m. to 5 p.m. in summer, closed on Tuesdays and Wednesdays. Tel. 283-4575.

In the shadow of the huge radio mast at the Soviet TV centre, the Ostankino Palace was built at the end of the eighteenth century by the son of the noble who built Kuskovo. Although first planned by the Italians, Quarenghi and Camporesi, the palace was finally designed and built by a family serf, Pavel Argunov. Ostankino's centrepiece was a large hall that could be converted from ballroom theatre complete with a revolving stage. The actors and stagehands were also serfs – including the opera singer Kovalyova, who was later to marry Count Sheremetyev. Built of wood for its acoustic qualities, Ostankino Palace is a jewel of craftsmanship, and a salutary corrective to the image of the Russian serf in Gogol's portrayal of the downtrodden peasantry. The five-domed **Church of the Trinity** was built for the estate's previous owners in the 1680s by another serf architect.

Kolomenskoye

31 Proletarsky Prospekt. Nearest Metro: Kolomenskoye. Open daily from 11 a.m. to 5 p.m., closed on Tuesdays and last Monday of each month. Tel. 112-5394.

This old country estate of the Tsars occupies a commanding bluff above a long curve in the River Moscow, and throughout the winter is one of the best places in Moscow for tobogganing and skiing. In summer, its architectural park, which includes examples of old wooden buildings from Peter the Great's hut to a seventeenth-century watchtower dismantled and brought here from Siberia, is a delightful spot to picnic. The tall white **Church of the Ascension** dates from the 1530s. The Tsar had a throne in the upper gallery which allowed him simultaneously to 'attend' the service and watch the military manoeuvres and falconry in the fields across the river. The museum contains an exquisite model of the huge old wooden palace of the Tsars that stood here until Catherine the Great demolished it. The seventeenth-century church of the **Kazan Icon of the Mother of God**, with its distinctive blue domes, was the Tsar's domestic chapel, and linked to the palace by an underground tunnel. Peter the Great spent most of his childhood here, and gave his royal protection to the park's grove of ancient oak trees, which are now up to 800 years old.

Gorky House-Museum

6/2 Ulitsa Kachalova. Nearest Metro: Arbatskaya. Open daily from 12–6 p.m., closed on Mondays and Tuesdays. Tel. 290-0535.

The attraction is not the over-rated writer Maxim Gorky, who lived and entertained here in the years that he was helping wrap the 'socialist realism' strait-jacket around Russian letters, but the house itself. Designed by the brilliant architect Fyodor Schechtel, it is an Art Nouveau classic, built for the banker Stepan Ryabushinsky in the 1890s. The porch and the interior staircase are superb.

Leo Tolstoy Estate-Museum

21 Ulitsa Lev Tolstova. Nearest Metro: Park Kultury. Open daily 10 a.m. to 5 p.m. to organised tour groups only. Closed on Mondays and last day of each month. Intourist organises guided tours for individuals at 11 a.m., 1 p.m. and 4 p.m. Tel. 246-9444.

Unlike Moscow's Pushkin Museum, which had nothing to do with the man, this Tolstoy Museum is the real thing, where the family lived and where the old man worked each winter from 1882 to 1901. The table is still laid for dinner, and the piano is the one Rubinstein, Rimsky-Korsakov and Rachmaninov played here and where Chaliapin sang for the family. At the end of the corridor is the writer's tiny room, where he exercised with dumbbells, and made shoes in the evening. His study is the next room, where he wrote *The Kreutzer Sonata*, *Resurrection* and his reply to the Church after his excommunication.

Worth a look if you have time
Central Lenin Museum

2 Ploshchad Revolutsiyi. Nearest Metro: Ploshchad Revolutsiyi, Ploshchad Sverdlova, Prospekt Marksa are all three stations on the same vast square. Open daily from 10 a.m. to 6.30 p.m., except Monday to Friday between 15 May and 15 October, when open 11 a.m. to 7 p.m. Closed on Mondays and last Tuesday of each month. Tel. 295-4808.

The Lenin Museum, at the western end of Red Square, beside the History Museum, is a disappointing place, the hagiography overwhelming the man. But the reconstruction of his Kremlin office is worth a look, and so is his immaculate 1914 Rolls Royce Silver Ghost, which is kept in working order by the RR mechanic who comes out every couple of years to service the British Ambassadorial limousine. Russian schoolchildren stare with reverence at the bullet-holed overcoat Lenin wore when he was shot by Dora Kaplan in 1918.

Borodino Panorama

38 Kutuzovsky Prospekt. Nearest Metro: Kutuzovskaya. Open daily from 10.30 a.m. to 8 p.m., closed on Fridays and last Thursday of each month. Tel. 148-1967.

The Borodino battlefield, where the retreating Russian armies inflicted serious damage on Napoleon before letting him occupy Moscow in 1812, is 125 km west of Moscow. It can be visited, but there is little enough to see except on the first Sunday of September each year when the Soviet Army stages a small re-enactment of the battle in costume dress. But you can make do with the Borodino Panorama, just a few Metro stops from the Kremlin. A circular depiction of the battlefield at the crisis of the fight, you stand inside the painting, in the heart of the village of Semyonovskaya, while the battle rages around. You can pick out Napoleon in the distance by his white horse.

Memorial Museum of Cosmonautics   Prospekt Mira, Cosmonauts' Alley. Nearest Metro: VDNKh. Open daily from 11 a.m. to 7 p.m., closed on Mondays. Tel. 283-7914.

In the base of the soaring obelisk, and so close to the VDNKh exhibition that it seems part of it, this separate museum contains the first-ever satellite, the Sputnik of 1957, and the Vostok spaceship which made Yuri Gagarin the first man ever to leave earth, back in 1961.

VDNKh   (USSR Exhibition of Economic Achievements)

Prospekt Mira. Nearest Metro: VDNKh. Open daily from 10 a.m. to 9 p.m. Tel. 181-9162.

The difference between the Soviet Union and the USA is that between this soulless, pompous 324 ha of arid state didacticism, and the fun of Disneyland. I hate the VDNKh Exhibition, but you may enjoy it. Its various pavilions are a series of self-serving and often mendacious pats on the back for Soviet science and technology, often claiming that everything worthwhile, from electricity to miracle wheat to AIDS cures, has been invented by Russians. *Glasnost* has yet to reach this fantasy land, where you would never think a queue or food shortage or any other problem has ever been seen in the workers' paradise.

It is worth visiting in winter, from 25 December to 8 March, when VDNKh holds a winter festival and you can go for troika rides. The Hunting Trail, a kind of walk-through zoo, the nearest Moscow gets to the Siberian taiga, is also fun for children.

Where to stay

The following hotels are in descending order of pleasantness:

National, 14/1 Prospekt Marksa (tel. 203-6539); nearest Metro: Prospekt Marksa. The best location in Moscow, where Gorky Street meets the big square by the Kremlin, and a very pleasant pre-revolutionary building with high rooms and decent restaurants. There are some much grimmer rooms at the back, and on the inside courtyard you will be awakened early by the kitchen noise, but it is still the best hotel in town. The suites are 200 roubles a night, including the one that Lenin slept in. If you can get in for independent travel, and they are usually heavily booked, it will cost 85–120 roubles a night.

Metropol, 1 Prospekt Marksa (tel. 225-6677); nearest Metro: Ploshchad Sverdlovskaya. Still being restored but, even when run down, it was a lovely-looking hotel, with grand corridors and Art Nouveau tiles and decor. Situated on the main square between the Bolshoy and the Kremlin, it is in a perfect location, and when re-opened will be the most expensive place in town, starting at 100 roubles a night.

Berlin, 3 Ulitsa Zhdanova (tel. 925-8527); nearest Metro: Dzerzhinskovo. Still being restored by a Finnish company, and will then be managed by Finns. This is the old pre-revolutionary Savoy Hotel, with an amazingly ornate dining room, and some grand suites, which run to 170 roubles a night; rooms from 80–95 roubles.

Intourist, 3 Ulitsa Gorkovo (tel. 203-4008); nearest Metro: Prospekt Marksa. A bland and modern skyscraper, visibly run down, with patched sheets, smeared windows, and the busiest lobby in Moscow. Good location, but rooms often narrow and pokey. The suites are fine, but the refrigerators usually fail to work. Suites 120–170 roubles a night; rooms from 80–120 roubles.

Mezhdunarodnaya (universally known as the **Mezh**), 12 Krasnopresnenskaya Nab. Nearest Metro (but still a walk of over 450 m): Ulitsa 1905. This is the hotel the Russians think is the most luxurious and most modern. It is inconveniently located and overpriced, but it has the boldest call-girls, the best phone and telex system, and is close to the International Trade Exhibition Centre. It is therefore useful for businessmen. As a tourist, avoid it; the taxi drivers think you are a rich businessman and overcharge. Suites from 150–250 roubles a night; rooms start at 100 roubles.

Ukraina, 2/1 Kutuzovsky Prospekt (tel. 243-3021); nearest Metro (but still a walk of over 450 m): Kievskaya. A real Stalinist wedding cake of a building, on the river just opposite the Mezh. Slowest lifts in the known universe. Suites 175 roubles a night; rooms from 80–95 roubles.

Kosmos, 150 Prospekt Mira (tel. 286-2123); nearest Metro: VDNKh. The best looking and best built of the modern hotels, designed by the French in time for the Olympic Games. Good public rooms if you need to hire space for a presentation, and good banqueting facilities. Far from the centre unless you are very confident about using the Metro. Has a disco which attracts trendy young Muscovites. Suites 170 roubles a night; rooms from 80–95 roubles.

Rossiya, 6 Ulitsa Razina (tel. 298-5409); nearest Metro: Ploshchad Nogina. Take a compass or you might get lost in the world's largest hotel. The rooms are small and pokey, but the views and location stunning, overlooking Red Square and the Kremlin. There is a big Beriozka on the ground floor. The food is poor, there is no hard currency bar, and the phone service is famous for its incompetence. Suites 170 roubles a night; rooms from 80–120 roubles.

Sovyetskaya, 32 Leningradsky Prospekt (tel. 250-2342); nearest Metros (but a long walk to either): Belorossiya or Dinamo. Congratulations, you have *Blat* (influence) to be assigned a room here. This is where they put guests of the state; Stalin's daughter, Svetlana, was here before leaving for the west for the final time, and western politicians and their senior aides stay here. Wonderful staircase, good suites, small single rooms. Unusually efficient room service, but this is a dry hotel. Suites from 170–250 roubles a night; rooms from 80–140 roubles. Bring your own booze.

Warning: from now on, you are entering the grim zone:

Moskva, 7 Prospekt Marksa (tel. 292-1000); nearest Metro: Prospekt Marksa. Great location and good sized rooms, but terrible service, poor lifts, no tolerable bar, and the worst food in any Moscow hotel. Rarely used for foreigners, which explains the low standards. Rooms from 80–95 roubles a night.

Belgrade, 5 Smolenskaya Ploshchad (tel. 248-7848); nearest Metro: Smolenskaya. Try very hard not to be put into this place. The food is so bad that in 1988 Intourist took away the hotel's right to charge a 'foreigner's bonus'. Rooms small and very dingy, with cockroaches. Suites 110 roubles a night; rooms from 80–85 roubles.

Druzhba, 53 Prospekt Vernadskovo (tel. 432-9629); nearest Metro: Vernadskovo. So far south out of town you might almost check into a hotel in Kiev. Used mainly for tourists from eastern Europe, and it shows in the standards. Western tourists are only put here in times of overcrowding, which means every peak season. Terrible food, service non-existent, light bulbs sometimes do not work. Rooms from 40–55 roubles a night.

Sevastopol, 1 Bolshaya Yushunskaya (tel. 119-6968); nearest Metro: Kakhovskaya. Very remote, and the hotel where they accommodate Intourist guides who come to Moscow for conferences and training sessions; in short, designed for Soviets, not westerners. Western student groups travelling cheaply often put up here. Rotten food, no service, only limited number of English speakers. Rooms from 40–50 roubles a night.

Where to eat

See also Eating and Drinking, pp. 125–8.

Whether you want simply a quick snack, or dinner with dancing or something in between, Moscow has a wide variety of eating places from which to choose.

Informal eating

Buffets, such as the one in the Tchaikovsky Hall, are found in most public places, and there is a classic example of a **Stolovaya** (cafeteria) at Tsentralny Rinok, the central market on Tsvetnoi Boulevard. There is also a **domovaya kukhnaya** ('home kitchen' cafeteria) on the southern side of Serpukhovsky Val, near Tulskaya Metro station. However, cafeterias are cheap and generally nasty and you would do better to eat at the grill bar in the converted red brick church on the other side of Tsvetnoi Boulevard, or even at the *Shashlichnaya* on the corner of the Val opposite the Metro station.

Shashlichnaya (kebab bars) can be either open-air barbecue stands such as the one in Gorky Park, or proper restaurants like the one mentioned above. Another to try is on Ulitsa Dmitrova opposite the large new toy store. The restaurant is on the same side of the street as the French Embassy but 200 metres further on; the *shashlik* are served with a small side salad, but they also do good soups and ham sandwiches. The nearest Metro station is Oktyabraskaya.

The **Pelmeni** (dumpling) bar on Ulitsa Lusinovskaya is reasonably good as these bars go; the nearest Metro station is Dobryninskaya. Or try one of the small, dark and friendly **Sosiskaya** (sausage bars) such as the one at Tishinski Rinok, on Bolshaya Gruzinskaya, in the shadow of the tall column composed of the letters of the Georgian alphabet.

There are also **Blinnaya** (bliny bars) and **Pirozhkovaya** (pie stalls) throughout the city. The *Blinnaya* opposite the entrance to the Zoo Park near Barrikadnaya Metro station is better than most, while there is a good *Pirogi* bar at Moscow's Dinamo football stadium out on the Leningrad Road.

In the 1960s and 1970s **Cafés** became fashionable among Moscow's gilded youth. In the 1960s, the **Café Mars** on Gorky Street was the place to go – hard to explain when you see it now. Then in the '70s the **Bluebird** (tel. 299-8702), or Sinnaya Ptitsa, on Ulitsa Chekhova, took over and it has now become more famous as home of the Moscow Jazz Club (tel. 129-3926). Today, try the **Four Seasons** café in Gorky Park, or the modern cafés along Kalinin Prospekt – the **Angara**, **Valday** or **Pechora**. In the Olympic Village the **Café v Fontane**, or Fountains Café, is the home of Moscow's breakdancers. Also try the trendy new co-operative café, the **Olymp**, in the basement of the Lenin Stadium.

If you're just in need of a drink, try one of the **Pivnoy** (beer) bars. The **Keramica** open-air bar by the pond in Gorky Park can be pleasant in summer, and there is a decent, modern beer hall, where the large glass windows discourage fighting, behind the Kievsky Voksal, the Kiev rail terminal. It is on Mozhaisky Val, just off Dorogomilovskaya Ulitsa, on the way to the Dorogomilovsky Market. In the centre of Moscow, try the **Yama**, a basement bar just behind the Bolshoy Theatre, on the corner of Pushkinskaya and Stoleshnikov.

Another favourite with the Russian people are the **Morozhenoye** (ice cream parlours). Three worth visiting are the **Sputnik**, on Gorky Street almost opposite the Intourist Hotel; a huge one called simply **Morozhenoye** on Lusinovskaya, south of Dobryninskaya Metro;

and the best, for hard currency only, is in the **Mezhdunarodnaya Hotel**, on Krasnopresnenskaya Nab., serving Italian ices as well as the Soviet brand.

Formal restaurants – state-run Hotels

The best is the **Russki Zal** at the National Hotel, with a splendid view of the Kremlin and the best *Borsch* in the city. The chicken kiev comes with the vegetables served in tiny pastry dishes. If you cannot get into the Russki Zal, or want to avoid the noise of the band, try the smaller hard currency room next door, but note that they charge you twice as much for each portion of caviar. (1 Ulitsa Gorkovo; tel. 203-5595.)

Almost as good is the **Praga Restaurant** in the hotel of the same name, although you should choose the Zimny Sad (Winter Garden), or Cheshky Zal (Czech Hall) for their decor, or the roof terrace in summer. They often have the excellent Czech Pilsner beer, and Czech specialities for *zakuski* (hors d'oeuvres), such as stuffed hams. Often boisterous in the evenings with wedding parties. (2 Ulitsa Arnat; tel. 290-8171.)

Tsentralny Restaurant, ground floor of the Tsentralny Hotel. Seldom visited by foreigners, this amazingly Baroque dining room provides sound Russian cooking. The poached sturgeon (*Osetrina po-Russky*) is good, and even if you cannot get one of the small private booths along one wall, it is interesting to see which Bolshoy dancer or TV personality has been dining so discreetly. In the 1930s, this used to be the Hotel Luxe, where the guests of the Comintern, the international wing of the Party, were housed. Memoirs by Italian and Yugoslav Party members have spoken of the terrible atmosphere in the dining room at the time of the purges, with no one daring to speak to his neighbour, and each evening old comrades saying 'goodnight' as if it were goodbye for ever, because every night there were the secret police black limousines at the door, the footsteps along the hotel corridor, the arrests and disappearances. (10 Ulitsa Gorkovo; tel. 229-0241.)

The **Restaurant Berlin** is being redecorated, as part of the very thorough overhaul of the Berlin Hotel itself. The food is standard Russian, although they try to push allegedly German specialities like Schnitzel and knuckle of pork. And you can sometimes get East German beer. This used to be the Savoy Hotel when the Tsar was on the throne, and was a very fashionable dining room, tricked out in blowsy opulence, lots of gilt and generous bosoms on the frescoes. More frequented by Russians than foreigners. (Current address: 3 Ulitsa Zhdanova, but expect that to change as Zhdanov [one of Stalin's nastier henchmen who took great pleasure in persecuting Shostakovich and the poetess Akhmatova] sinks into disgrace; tel. 925-8527.)

The **Mezh**, or **Mezhdunarodnaya** (12 Krasnopresnenskaya Nab.), contains a number of restaurants: the **Sakura** (Japanese) is hard currency only (tel. 253-2894); as is the **Bierstube** which serves

German beer, roast chicken, wurst and pork knuckle. (Tel. 253-7708.) The **Russky** is classic Russian food in over-stuffed Russian decor, rather tamed down for international tastes. Never known to run short of caviar or Georgian wines, and on some evenings there is a gypsy band. Good *pyelmennis*. (Tel. 253-2373.) The **Continent** cannot make up its mind whether it is a Russian or an international restaurant. It does neither cuisine well, but the atmosphere is quiet and relaxed, with a tinkling piano rather than a band. The service is very good for Moscow. (Tel. 253-9798.) The Business Club or Mercury restaurant was so outrageously expensive, the food so dreadful and the whores so persistent that even the captive businessmen in the Mezh began to object. The floor show, however, was usually rather good. The place is now regularly handed over to foreign organisations for food festivals. There was an interesting season of Chinese food, and during the Moscow summit an American restaurateur presented Louisiana Cajun dishes. Italian, French, Spanish, Mexican, Philippine and Indonesian seasons are all promised. The British offered, but were fobbed off with a dreadful mock-pub elsewhere in the hotel. Since only hard currency is accepted, these food festivals do not benefit the local Soviets (except for those trade and other officials being wined and dined by western contacts). (Tel. 253-1792.)

The Intourist Hotel (3/5 Ulitsa Gorkovo) also contains several restaurants: the **Intourist Restaurant** does a half-way decent 'Swedish table' at lunch where you can eat all you want for 3 roubles, with soups, salads and *zakuski*, plus a choice of main courses. (Tel. 203-4007-8.) I have never had an edible, let alone good, meal in the **Zvyezdnoye Nebo** (Starry Sky). Avoid it unless desperate, but it does stay open later than most. (Tel. 203-9608.) For the decor, rather than the food, try the Intourist Hotel's **Valyutni Zal** (it simply means hard currency room) which can be hard to find. Take the lift to the third floor, turn left to a grim-looking dining room where package tourists eat (instead of right to the hard currency bar). Walk past the spiral staircase, and then go through the double doors to the left, where a delightfully decorated 'old Russian' room awaits. (Tel. 203-4008.)

The **Metropol**, when the restoration work is complete, will be trying to establish itself as the best restaurant in the city. Given the competition, this should not prove too difficult. The **Chainaya**, or tea-room, used to be the place for a late supper of blinys and champagne after a ballet at the Bolshoy across the street, one of the few places in town where one could hope to eat that late. With luck, the tradition might continue. (1 Prospekt Marksa. The old telephone number was 225-6677, but this may change.)

The **Sovyetski Restaurant**, at the Sovyetskaya Hotel, is built on the site of the highly fashionable Yar Restaurant of Tsarist days, where Rasputin once became so erotically and scandalously drunk that there were complaints to the Tsar. These days, in spite of the proximity to the Gypsy Theatre, it is extremely prim, the hotel for state guests who do not quite rate an official guest house. The food, however, is good, with some of the best quality meat and fish in Moscow, and it often has fresh fruit and salad even in winter. (32 Leningradsky Prospekt; tel. 250-7449.)

The **Rossiya Hotel** is the world's largest, but it has no restaurant to boast of. But on a fine day, the 'Top of the Rossiya' restaurant will give an unmatchable view of the Kremlin and central Moscow. (6 Ulitsa Razina; tel. 298-0532 or 298-5478.)

Restaurants   **Aragvi** (Georgian food). This is probably the most famous restaurant in Moscow, although the service is slow, the food sloppily prepared, the dining room far too small for the band, and the bills steep. There have lately been attempts to control the legendary corruption of the doormen, but a pack of Marlboro should still persuade that locked door to squeeze ajar. The main dining room has marble walls, vaguely pre-Raphaelite murals and a minstrels' gallery for the band. Regulars tend to use the smaller room to the left, but the Georgian Mafiosi who once made this place their headquarters used the private banquet rooms to the rear. In the late 1960s and '70s, the Aragvi served wonderful food, because in those days of flagrant corruption, the Aeroflot planes were flying up the best wines and fresh foods from Tbilisi. By Soviet standards, the prices were outrageous, but the black marketeers were happy to pay. The parties would go on all night behind closed doors, and at dawn the revellers would be served the classic Georgian breakfast pick-me-up of *Khashi*, a soup of tripe, cow-heels and minced garlic. These days, the Aragvi is paying the price for the new Puritanism, half the clientele and some of the staff are in prison, and the food has lost its flair. For 20 roubles a head in advance (wines extra), Intourist will book you a Georgian feast. (6 Ulitsa Gorkovo; tel. 229-3762.)

Baku. Pleasant decor of marble, a fountain and several rooms where conversation may be heard above the band. Azerbaijani food is spicy, often flavoured with cinnamon and saffron. The *Lyulya-kebab* (grilled mutton sausage) and *Dyushbara* dumplings and *pilaus* are good, and Azerbaijani rosé champagne is a real discovery. (24 Ulitsa Gorkovo; tel. 299-8506.)

The **Uzbekistan** can be great fun. The singer in the band wears the shortest mini in Moscow. The fights sometimes have the waiters joining in, wielding the fearsome sword-like skewers for the *shashlik*. In summer, you can dine in the garden. The place is run down, the lavatories unspeakable, the food no more than acceptable, but the restaurant does have atmosphere. (29 Ulitsa Neglinnaya; tel. 294-6053.)

The **Slavyansky Bazaar** is large and noisy. Chekhov used to dine here, and in this room Stanislavsky announced his plan for the Moscow Arts Theatre. A stone's throw from Red Square and GUM, it claims to serve the best blinys in Moscow, and the *myaso v gorshichke* (a beef and vegetable stew served in individual earthenware pots) is recommended. The band is not. One of the few Soviet restaurants to ban smoking. (13 Ulitsa 25 October; tel. 221-1872 or 228-4845.)

The **Syedmoe Nebo** (Seventh Heaven) is a three-storey restaurant on top of the Ostankino TV tower. The food is a fixed menu and very similar to a package tour meal in your hotel. But on a fine day, the view is worth it. The place takes forty minutes to revolve. (15 Ulitsa Akademiki Korolyova; tel. 282-1238.)

Ethnic restaurants

The Vietnamese **Hanoi** is probably the most unpleasant. Spring rolls should not contain beetroot. (Ho Chi Minh Ploshchad; tel. 124-4740.)

The **Budapest** serves what it calls Goulash and Balaton Fish and Wild Cherry soup, but they ought to be sued for misrepresentation by the Hungarian Tourist Board. Still, there are usually Hungarian wines. True to Hungarian entrepreneurial tradition, the Budapest was one of the first places to try opening an all-night café in 1987. Drunks, drug dealers and finally the police soon forced it to close at midnight. (2/18 Petrovskiye Linii; tel. 221-4044.)

The quasi-Italian **Crystal Pizzeria** sometimes runs out of cheese, sometimes out of tomato purée, sometimes out of red wine, and on really bad days it runs out of all three. One dreadful night I was offered yoghurt and beetroot pizza washed down with a bottle of Hungarian vermouth. However, it can be better; but wait until the Pizza Hut chain finally opens in 1990. (17 Kutuzovsky Prospekt; tel. 243-4576.)

The **Bombay** Indian restaurant is appalling. (91 Ryublovskoye Chaussee; tel. 141-5502.) But its awfulness helped speed the arrival of the **Delhi**, a joint venture between the Indian Tourist Board and the Moscow Restaurant Trust, which serves real Indian food. The cooks and spices are Indian, and in the hard currency room, so are the waiters. In the rouble room, the waiters are Russian. Standards and quality have declined slowly but surely since the place opened in 1987, but it remains recognisably Indian. The decor is amazing; not so much Mogul, more Elvis Presley's bathroom. (23-b Ulitsa Krasnaya Presnnaya; tel. 252-1766, rouble room, or 255-0492 hard currency room.)

Gavana is the way the Russian language spells Havana. The only reason to go to this grim and often smelly restaurant miles out on Leninsky Prospekt is that they always have white rum and Pepsi for a Cuba Libre, and sometimes they have lobsters. It is worth phoning in advance to check. Even so, the ground floor lavatories before you get to the first floor restaurant may put you off in summer. (88 Leninsky Prospekt; tel. 138-0091.)

The **Pekin** restaurant, in the Pekin Hotel, was once one of the best restaurants in Moscow, and should be so again when the slow but steady improvement in Sino-Soviet relations finally allows the

Chinese cooks and ingredients to return to the kitchens. But in the late 1960s, 1970s and early 1980s, the Russians tried to make do. The result was dreadful, but there was compensation in the amazing decor, more Cecil B. de Mille's view of the Heavenly Kingdom than anything Chinese. It was also one of the few places where you could buy bottles of Scotch or French brandy for roubles. If the Russians are still cooking, avoid the *Druzhba* salad or the *Kisloye-Sladkoye Myaso* (sweet and sour meat). Order Russian-style food instead. If the Chinese cooks are installed, it should be worth a try, and there are plans for a take-away place on the corner. (1/7 Ulitsa Bolshaya Sadovaya is the address, but the hotel in fact dominates Mayakovsky Square; tel. 209-1865.)

Country restaurants

The **Russkaya Izba** (Russian Log Cabin), just by the bridge at Ilinskoe village, on the road to Uspenskoe, about 30 minutes' drive from the centre.

The best way to go is out on Kutuzovsky Prospekt and left on Ryublovskoye Chaussee to the outer ring road, and then left again on the Zhukovka road, past the private roads and dachas of the privileged. The picturesque effect of the wooden restaurant is spoilt by the corrugated iron roof. Excellent *zakuski* – the pickled mushrooms are locally picked – and soups thick enough to walk on. In summer you can stroll by the river or bathe, and this is a good area for cross-country skiing in winter. (Ilinskoe Village; tel. 561-4244.)

The **Rus** is a country restaurant to the east of the city, set in its own estate, and in summer there are horses and traps. The food is very ordinary, but the atmosphere is good – except that it sometimes seems to attract KGB types from their vast modern HQ that was modelled on the lines of the CIA building in Virginia, and is apparently known to its intimates as Langley-East. (Set well back from the road down a lane on 12 Krasnozyozdmaya Ulitsa, near Saltykovskaya Station; tel. 528-0778.)

The **Skazka** (Fairy Tale) is the carved wooden construction you pass on the way to the Zagorsk Monastery. As you pass the 40th kilometre post on the way out on Yaroslavskoye Chaussee, you will see it. Standard Russian dishes, and good soups, but it does often have the Zhiguli Russian beer, which is worth a try. (Tel. 184-3436.)

Co-operative restaurants

The following list is not exhaustive, because new places are opening all the time. But these are the co-operatives where I like the food:

Ulitsa Kropotkinskaya 36 is the name and also the address of Fyodorov's pioneering place. It serves classic northern Russian food, with a heavy emphasis on meat, pastry and dumplings. The blinys are very good, but the vegetables usually overcooked and the salads limp. The service is not fast but it is courteous. The bills average 15–20 roubles a head for three courses. (Tel. 201-7500.)

For consistent quality, the best of the co-operatives is probably the **Lasagna**, which naturally specialises in Italian food. Advised by an

Italian businessman who lives in Moscow, checks the menu daily, and who supplied the pasta machine, the place is run by Georgians. Small, with two rooms and a dozen tables, you have to book. The pasta dishes are first rate, the veal dishes acceptable. Take your own wine. (40 Ulitsa Pyatnitskaya; tel. 231-1085.)

The **Mei-Hua** is a very brave attempt to run a real Chinese restaurant with Soviet ingredients. It is run by a Chinese family who were on the Russian side of the border at the time of the Sino-Soviet split. Mama does the cooking, and Valodya is manager and head waiter, and he also puts in a full week's work as a schoolteacher. Valodya speaks a little English. Not all the dishes show much Chinese influence, but the ingredients are so hard to find; even the soy sauce has to be obtained from the Korean community who live in Kazakhstan. However, the Mei-Hua has friends and sympathisers in the foreign community who bring back spices from the Chinese supermarkets in London's Covent Garden. The salads are good, and mushroom soup excellent. The *Kisloye-Sladkoye* (sweet and sour) is the most recognisable of the main dishes. (Just under the railway bridge at the Krasnosyelskaya Metro station, behind a discreet wooden door; tel. 264-9574.)

The **Kolkhida** is a thoughtfully decorated Georgian restaurant which seems to prosper, although it is never crowded. It serves excellent Georgian *zakuski*, but you get very bored with the huge dish of *shashlik*, which seems the inevitable main course. (On the ring road, at 6 Sadovaya-Samotyochnaya; tel. 299-6757.)

The **NIL** is really a club, whose initials stand for Nauk, Izkustvo and Literaur, or Science, Art and Letters. But you can book a table for lunch or dinner, and wonder whether your neighbours in the dining-room write for *Pravda*, sculpt busts of Lenin, or are planning the next space launch. Standard Russian fare, but the steak is among the best you will get in Moscow. (13 Ulitsa Gottwald; tel. 251-8419.)

You cannot miss the **Atrium**; it boasts the only neo-classical portico on Leninsky Prospekt. The food is sort of Greek, too, with lamb kleftiko, dolmades and taramasalata on the menu. In fact, the cuisine is all-purpose Middle East, with dishes whose origins can be traced back to Uzbekistan or Armenia just as well as the cradle of democracy. (Tel. 137-3008.)

The **Rasgulyai** is the best decorated restaurant in town. The decor is Old Russian, with one room in the delicate blues and whites of Gzhel pottery, another in the bold reds, golds and blacks of the spoons and bowls you find in Russian souvenir shops, and another in plain wood, carefully carved. It serves the best traditional Russian fare of any Moscow restaurant. The stuffed and forced meats of the *zakuski* are excellent, but those plump-looking tomatoes could well be perfectly pickled, rather than fresh. The soups are a meal in themselves. (On Ulitsa Startakovskaya, just outside the Patriarchal Cathedral; tel. 267-7613.)

U Iosefa is the only Jewish restaurant in Moscow. (11 Dubininskaya, way up north on the Dmitrovskoye Chaussee. No phone at the time of writing.)

The **Hard Rock Café** is in the basement of the Green Theatre (Zilyony Teatr) in Gorky Park. It is part of the growing empire of Stas Namen, the ageing rock star grandson of the former Politburo member Anastas Mikoyan. Stas formed his first rock-and-roll band at the prestigious Foreign Affairs Institute where he studied, and his family name and connections were enough to keep him safe even during the harshest anti-rock campaigns. Under the umbrella of the Soviet Peace Committee, Stas has formed a body called Musicians for Peace, whose logo may be dimly discerned on the back of the stage at the open-air Green Theatre while Moscow's young heavy metal bands belt out raucous chords to a thrilled audience of head-banging Moscow teenagers. In effect, he has opened Moscow's first semi-permanent rock venue. The basement café serves quasi-Greek food like moussaka and stuffed peppers. Although good, the bill can mount up and as a result the place has won a tricky reputation. I was once in a party for six that was hit with a bill for 380 roubles without alcohol. We negotiated it down, but it was still excessive, even though we could go backstage to watch the rock acts between courses.

The **Stolishniki** is not a co-operative, but this excellently-restored basement of the gatehouse of an old Moscow palace is not your usual Soviet restaurant. It serves a standard meal of a plate of *zakuski*, including red caviar and smoked fish, and then a main course of beef, vegetables and plums stewed in a small earthenware pot, all for 5 roubles. You cannot book, so you will recognise the place by the queue under the copper porch halfway up Stolishniki Alley on the way to the statue of Yuri Dolgoruky on Gorky Street. (Tel. 229-2585.) (The decrepit old palace behind was the headquarters of Marshal Murat, head of the French cavalry, during the 1812 occupation. Anatoly Krapivsky, the one-man conservation campaign who restored the basement, planned and opened the restaurant, is about to start work on restoring Murat's palace into a restaurant complex for the 1990s.)

Outside Moscow but worth the excursion

See also The Golden Ring on pp. 294–304.

Arkhangelskoye Estate-Museum

You will be advised to go by car, 23 km west of Moscow along the Volokolamsk Highway. It is possible, but tedious, to go by Metro to Tushinskaya, and then take bus 541 or 549. Open daily from 11 a.m. to 5 p.m., between 3 May and 30 September, and from 11 a.m. to 4 p.m.

in winter; closed on Mondays, Tuesdays and the last Friday of each month.

Built originally by Prince Golitsyn in the eighteenth century, the place was devastated by the French in 1812, and then by a serf uprising and a great fire in 1820. It was rebuilt by the fabulously wealthy art collector Prince Yusupov, but in classical Enlightenment style. 'I feel suddenly transported to the days of Tsarina Catherine,' wrote Pushkin. A fine building, set in a lovely park with a serf theatre, colonnades and pavilions in the garden, it makes a pleasant excursion, particularly if combined with a lunch at the nearby Russkaya Izba restaurant (see p. 188).

Abramtsevo Estate-Museum

By car, 70 km along Yaroslavskoye Chaussee, and the route is then marked at the junction where the road signs point left to Khotkovo.

By train, direct to Abramtsevo from Moscow's Yaroslavl Station. Open daily from 11 a.m. to 5.30 p.m., closed on Mondays, Tuesdays and the 30th of each month.

This charming rural retreat was an important cultural centre at two separate periods of the nineteenth century. The progressive writer Sergei Aksakov was a friend of Gogol, Turgenev and the influential critic Belinsky, and they each came to stay with him at this picturesque village. In the 1880s, the estate was bought by the wealthy industrialist Savva Mamontov, who established the place as an artistic colony for the painters and writers that he helped subsidise. Abramtsevo became a centre for the Russian nationalist-historical revival and its associated arts and crafts movement. Most of the artists whose work is represented at the Tretyakov Gallery worked at Abramtsevo. The fairy tale **'House on Chicken Legs'** was designed by Vasnetsov, as was the charming small neo-Russian church, with some help from Repin Wood. Pottery workshops were also established, and the local peasant children were taught new crafts. The museum has a room devoted to the Abramtsevo Theatre, where Serov and Vrubel designed the costumes and scenery.

New Jerusalem Monastery

Located at Istra, north-west of the city, the monastery is just inside the 40 km city boundary, beyond which tourists would need an extra visa to visit. Almost impossible to reach by public transport, Intourist now arranges excursions.

The Cathedral of the Resurrection was begun in the seventeenth century, and is said to copy the design of the oldest Christian church on the Hill of Golgotha in the Holy Land. The church was completed in the nineteenth century, and has been much restored in the last twenty years. The interior is famous for its five-arched iconostasis, and the shimmering ceramic tiles round the vaults and archways. From the outside, this single building offers an example of almost every kind of dome known to Russian architecture.

The whole monastery complex is now a museum, with special exhibitions of Russian porcelain and medieval arms and armour.

Leningrad

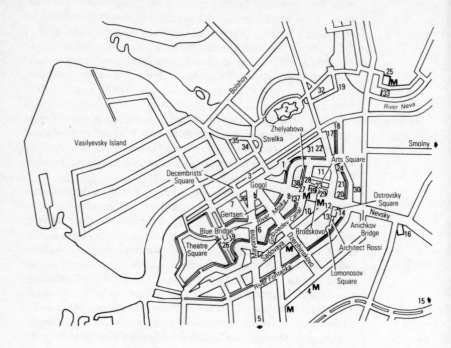

PLACES OF INTEREST

1 The Hermitage
2 Peter-Paul Fortress
3 Admiralty
4 Vitebsk Station
5 Warsaw Station
6 Marinsky Palace
7 Post Office
8 Stroganov Palace
9 Glinka Hall of the Philharmonic
10 Gostinny Dvor
11 Russian Museum
12 Saltykov-Schedrin National Library
13 Pushkin Theatre
14 Pioneers' Palace
15 Nevsky Monastery
16 Moscow Station
17 Summer Gardens
18 Summer Palace
19 Battleship Aurora
20 House of Peace and Friendship

21 State Circus
22 Field of Mars
23 Shostakovich Concert Hall
24 Engineers' Castle
25 Finland Station
26 Kirov Theatre
27 Dom Knigi
28 Maly Theatre
29 Passage Department Store
30 Catherine Institute
31 Pavlovskiy Barracks
32 Cabin of Peter the Great
33 Statue of Lenin
34 Central Naval Museum
35 Literary Museum

CHURCHES

36 St Isaac's Cathedral
37 Cathedral Of Our Lady of Kazan
38 Church of St Peter
39 Church of St Catherine

M = Metro Station

Leningrad

Introduction

The maps call it Leningrad; the locals still call it 'Peter', after St Petersburg, the name it was given by its founder, Peter the Great. In 1914, on the outbreak of the First World War, with Tsar Nicholas much embarrassed by the criticisms of his German wife, this 'Teutonic' name was changed to the Russian 'Petrograd'. Ten years later, with Lenin dead, the city was given his name, by right of conquest.

There was something deeply fitting about the name Leningrad, because the city Peter built to force Russia into the modern world and Lenin's Communist Party have a great deal in common. They were both bitterly contested strategies to modernise the country from on high. Like the city itself, the doctrine of Communism was an alien imposition upon an ancient, conservative and deeply religious land. The Party preached industries and proletariats to a largely peasant country, just as Peter had preached trade and navies to an introspective land. The roots of Communist ideology lay in Karl Marx's studies of the sufferings of the English working class and the complexities of German philosophy, just as the roots of St Petersburg lay in Peter's visits to the docks and shipyards of London and Amsterdam. St Petersburg and Communism were not just windows to the west; they were the west, in all its furious commitment to change.

Leningrad is not a Russian city at all. It is a fantasy, an alien growth, and it has no right to be where it is. The location itself is a great mistake, a port and naval base that is ice-bound for a third of the year. Peter the Great decided in 1703 to build his new capital at this furthest, most remote arm of the Baltic Sea because almost all the rest of the coastline was dominated by his Swedish enemies. Within the decade, victory over the Swedish Army at Poltava, hundreds of kilometres inland, was to bring much of the southern Baltic coast within his realm. The established ports of Reval (Tallinn) and Riga were at his mercy. But St Petersburg had already been begun. With that implacable will which was the key to his character, Peter continued with his city, at monstrous cost. Swedish prisoners of war, put to work sinking foundations into the marshy ground, died in their thousands. In Peter's lifetime, the naval base was shifted to the island of Kronstadt, and St Petersburg was theoretically redundant.

But by then, the city had put down its roots. The Peter-Paul Fortress on the north bank, and the Admiralty on the southern, were built in Peter's day. The needle-thin spire of the Admiralty, with its sailing ship weather vane, is a symbol of the city, and remains its heart. The Admiralty is one of the few great buildings of the city to have been designed by a Russian, Ivan Korobov, although he learned his trade in Holland. The Peter-Paul Fortress was by Domenico Trezzini, who also built Peter the Great's Summer Palace. The great palaces in and around the city were built by Rastrelli, Quarenghi and Charles Cameron.

The foreign sensibilities they brought to the city are an important component of the unique mood of Leningrad. It is like no other city, with its White Nights of summer when the sun never seems to set and the entire city seems bathed in silver. Muscovites tend to sneer at the 'museum city' and, having been built as a capital and the seat of an Imperial court, it now seems to ring a little hollow, bereft of the power that has been moved to Moscow. But Leningrad remains a great city, very much more than the sum of its museums, palaces and great buildings. More than any other city I know, it has a soul. I do not mean the mood that can be felt along its canals, the ghosts that one stirs in the Winter Palace, or by the Yusupov Palace where they killed Rasputin or even in the dungeons of the Peter-Paul Fortress. The soul of Leningrad is to be found at the Piskaryovka memorial cemetery, where over half a million Leningraders lie in mass graves. They all died in the 900 days of siege, and most of them were victims of starvation. Each of the great mounds represents a year of dead. There is nothing like this anywhere else on earth. Other cities suffered in war, but none so intensely. The single city of Leningrad lost more dead in the Second World War than Britain and the USA combined. But Leningrad survived, and rebuilt and restored its shattered palaces. Never tested in his own time, the city fulfilled Peter the Great's founding vision of a great northern fortress.

Tour one: The Hermitage

Open daily from 10.30 a.m. to 6.30 p.m. Tuesday to Friday, 10 a.m. to 6 p.m. Saturday and Sunday, closed on Mondays.

One of the world's great art collections, the Hermitage is part of that select group of museums, like the Louvre or the Prado, where the history and magnificence of the building match the importance of the paintings within. Even without the art collected by successive Tsars since Peter the Great, the three buildings of the Hermitage would still be a major attraction. But the place is so big, and the internal layout so confusing that you are best advised to begin with a half-day Intourist tour, which takes you through the main collections and rooms at a brisk pace. You may then return to examine particular exhibits at your leisure, but some of that leisure may be spent waiting outside, because the Hermitage is so popular that you must expect a lengthy queue. This is not a museum where you may stroll in and out at will. If you want to go back to look at the Rembrandts or the Matisses at some length, then either be prepared to walk to the head of the queue, flourishing your passport and ignoring the grumbles of the Russians, or pay an extra 5 roubles' guide fee to Intourist through your hotel service bureau.

One endearing feature of the Soviet Union has been a lack of commercialism, which is fast giving way to Mikhail Gorbachev's economic reforms and urgings towards profitability. But the Hermitage is almost unique among great art galleries in its lack of self-marketing. However, there is a bookshop, and the fat art books that will strain your coffee table are remarkably good value by western standards. Intourist sometimes takes western visitors in through the gate at the south-west corner, because it is more convenient to park the buses there. The hard currency bookstore, and a souvenir stand with postcards, is at the main entrance, immediately beneath the Nicholas Hall on the northern (river) side of the building.

Getting there

The buildings now known as the State Hermitage were the Palaces of the Tsars since the eighteenth century. They occupy a commanding position on the south bank of the River Neva, with the Admiralty alongside and the Peter-Paul Fortress on the far bank. The nearest Metro station is Nevsky Prospekt, from where it is a fifteen-minute walk.

The Hermitage Complex

There are three buildings in all, and from west to east they are: the **Winter Palace** itself, built in the 1750s by the Empress Elizabeth and designed by Rastrelli; the **Small Hermitage** built in the 1760s by Catherine the Great; and the **Large Hermitage**, built in stages between 1770–1860. Across the small but architecturally perfect Winter Canal (Zimnaya Kanavka), with its roofed bridge and echoes of Venice, is the magnificent **Hermitage Theatre**. Designed by Quarenghi in the 1780s, and one of the architect's favourite buildings, it is now used mainly for lectures, and public access is restricted. It is built on the site of the far more humble first 'Winter Palace', built by Peter the Great, and the building in which he died in 1725.

The Winter Palace

Part of the sheer force of the Hermitage complex lies in the contrast of relative sizes between the three buildings, which are carefully kept in proportion by intricate juggling with the scale of columns and pediments. The Winter Palace is a massive construction, of 1,050 rooms, 117 staircases, 1,886 doors and 1,945 windows. The main cornice is over 1.6 km long, and yet it seems smaller because of the huge statues which break up the roof line and diminish its height. The architect, Rastrelli, wrote that he was building the Palace 'solely for the glory of all Russia'. The building appears almost magically different depending on the viewpoint – seen afar from the other side of the river, or closer from the small gardens by the Admiralty, and then again from the Palace square to the south, across which the Red Guards made their celebrated but much exaggerated 'storming' of the Winter Palace in the October Revolution of 1917.

The **Palace Square** itself, with the great arcs of the General Headquarters, was also the scene of the massacre of 'Bloody Sunday' which began the Revolution of 1905. The central 47.5-m Triumphal Column, commemorating the victory of 1812, was quarried from a single cliff in Finland over a three-year period. The Tsar insisted that his column be taller than the one in the Place Vendôme, Paris (43.5 m), and taller than Trajan's Imperial Column in Rome (38 m). It took over 2,000 soldiers hauling on pulleys to lift it into position, and is held in place entirely by its own 610-tonne weight. The palaces were all built with remarkable speed, and Russia's vast forests were mercilessly pillaged for the great fires that allowed the work to continue through the winter. After the great fire of 1837, the place was virtually rebuilt in fifteen months. In the winter, with the temperature 20°C below zero, the palace was heated to 30°C inside, to speed the drying. The plasterers and artists working on the ceilings, where the heat was most intense, fainted so often that they were given caps filled with ice.

History of the collection

The art collection was begun by Catherine the Great, who built the Small Hermitage for her private gallery. 'Only the mice and I can enjoy it all', she wrote to Voltaire. The Large Hermitage was built in two stages. The northern half, along the river, dates from the eighteenth century, and was used for most of the nineteenth century as the seat of government, where the State Council and the Ministers would meet. The southern wing, sometimes called the New Hermitage, was built in the 1840s as Russia's first purpose-built public art gallery, and the Imperial collection began to be open to public view from 1852. Tsars Alexander and Nicholas, like their grandmother Catherine, were great collectors, and their purchases form the core of the collections. In the late nineteenth century, the Tsar's curators were given the funds to buy some of the great private collections of western Europe that came on the market, and after the 1917 Revolution, many of the finest Russian collections in private hands were confiscated for the benefit of the State. Treasures from the aristocratic houses of the Yusupovs, Shuvalovs, Sheremetyevs and Stroganovs may all be found in the Hermitage, and the Impressionist collections of Shchukin and Morozov were shared between Moscow's Pushkin Museum and the Hermitage.

A basic guide to the collection

Although I know the Hermitage well, and have a range of maps and guide books, I still get lost there. One famous Russian art historian never goes in without her compass. The way to keep your sanity is to follow this rough guide of what is where, and remember that if you look out of the window and see water, it is the River Neva to your north.

Winter Palace, ground floor, western wing

The **northern end** contains primitive cultures and art from the USSR, from Stone Age peoples to the Scythians to Siberian nomads. The sixth-century Golden Stag from Kostromskoi is the star of the collection. The **southern end** of this western wing contains the arts of the Soviet East, which includes Central Asia and Trans-Caucasia. Do not miss Tamburlaine's huge 1.5-metre high bronze cauldron, weighing 2 tonnes, in room 48.

Winter Palace, ground floor, eastern wing

This section is run by the Department of Oriental Culture and Art and contains treasures of antiquity from Egypt, Babylon and Assyria. It claims to have the oldest example of writing on earth – a Sumerian pictograph at least 5,000 years old. Between rooms 84 and 85 is the passage to the east that leads into the Small Hermitage, through the very large room 100, which contains ancient Greek art from the Black Sea colonies.

Small Hermitage, ground floor

This holds more Greek antiquities, including a copy of the Altar of Zeus frieze from Pergamon. The original has now been returned to the Pergamon Museum in East Berlin, from where the Russians looted it in 1945.

Large Hermitage, ground floor, eastern wing

This contains more classical antiquities, but finding your way around needs care. As you enter from the Small Hermitage, you have a choice of three directions. To your **left** is the splendid **Hall of Twenty Columns**, the heart of the great collection of Etruscan art. To your **right**, through room 107, is room 108, designed to look like the courtyard of a Graeco-Roman house, which contains the **Tauride Venus**, Russia's first classical statue, obtained from the Pope by Peter the Great. **Straight ahead** is room 121, which is the entrance for the **Special Collection**. Intourist will charge you an extra 5 roubles to see this, unless your Hermitage excursion specifically includes it. This is the ancient gold and jewellery, mostly Scythian and from the ancient Greek colonies around the Black Sea, but also from ancient Georgia, or Colchis, where Jason went to find the Golden Fleece. It is a stunning collection, and should not be missed, although it is sobering to realise that the art of jewellery ever since has simply been to reinvent the designs of the ancients.

Winter Palace, first floor

This is where the tour is more stately-home than art gallery, the first floor containing the grand formal rooms of the palace, as well as the Imperial living quarters, and some of the great art treasures. The layout is very complex, but broadly, the long **southern wing** of this floor contains western European art, and the other three wings contain formal rooms, the grandest furnishings, and Russian art.

The **south-east corner** was used as a guest suite for distinguished visitors. The German Kaiser and the King of Italy stayed here, and these rooms now house some of the finest works of art in the whole collection, although they are almost casually displayed and the guides tend to rush you through as if the paintings are assumed to be second division. In rooms 263–6 is the **German school**, of Cranach, Dürer and Holbein. Rooms 273–80 contain the **French school**, including Poussin, le Nain and Claude, and up to Watteau and Fragonard. Rooms 298–302 contain a well-chosen collection of **British paintings**, from Reynolds to William Morris.

In the far **south-west corner** are the rooms where Tsar Alexander II lived and where he was brought to die after the terrorist bombing of 1881. There is a striking gem collection in the **Gold Drawing Room**.

From the Gold Drawing Room take the tapestry-hung Dark Corridor to the **northern wing**, through the Rotunda, and there in the **north-west corner** are the rooms used by the last Tsar, Nicholas II, on his visits to the capital from Tsarskoye Selo. Do not miss the neo-Gothic **Library of Tsar Nicholas II**, alongside the Rotunda. The northern wing also contains the famous **Malachite Hall**, where in 1917 Kerensky held his last Cabinet Meeting as the Red Guard assault began. Kerensky escaped, disguised as a woman, but his Cabinet were all arrested in the White Dining Room next door.

To the east of Malachite Hall is the vast **Nicholas Hall**, where up to 5,000 would attend the Imperial balls, after a sumptuous champagne and caviar buffet in the Fore Hall and Rotunda. The formal dinner itself would be held in the **Hall of St George**, halfway down the east wing, the bridge between the Winter Palace and Small Hermitage, which was also the Great Throne Room. The ante-room to the Hall of St George is the stunning **Gallery of 1812**, filled with portraits of the victorious Russian officers, all inspired by the Waterloo Chamber at Windsor Castle, and mainly painted by the English artist George Dawe. At the southern end of the Gallery of 1812, is the Palace's own Cathedral, a sizeable chapel lost in the grandiose scale of the Winter Palace.

These northern and eastern wings of the Winter Palace were the formal stage upon which the public ceremonies of Tsarism were enacted. Their pivot was the huge and grand **Jordan Staircase**, at the north-east corner of the Palace. Named after the riverine ceremony held each 6 January when the Tsar descended to bless the waters of the River Neva, the Jordan Staircase, designed by Rastrelli, is a vastness of marble. From the head of the staircase, the long stretch of formal rooms to the south were known as the Great Enfilade, and the halls which extended along the north wing of the Palace towards Tsar Nicholas's private quarters were known as the Neva Enfilade.

Small Hermitage, first floor

Once the heart of the collection, this is now one of the few places one can stride briskly through with a clear conscience. It contains the **Hanging Gardens** of Catherine the Great and at the northern end, overlooking the Neva, the splendid **Pavilion Hall** with its marvellous chandeliers. The long galleries that run from north to south on either side of the gardens used to contain the personal possessions of Peter the Great and Nicholas II; they now house western European applied arts, and a comparatively weak selection of Netherlandish art.

Large Hermitage, first floor

This is the pride of the art collection, run by the Department of Western European Art. The **northern wing**, along the bank of the Neva, contains **Italian** Old Masters, including a Botticelli 'Annunciation'. There are two Leonardos in room 214. Venetian paintings run along the inner corridor of the north wing, with Veronese and Titian in room 221. Titian's 'Danae' is still being restored, after an attack by a deranged Baltic nationalist in 1985.

The **eastern wing** contains the 'Loggia of Raphael', a copy of the Vatican original. But next door, in room 229, which runs parallel to the 'Loggia', is Raphael's painting of the Holy Family. Special exhibitions are held in room 224 at the south-east corner, and then along the **southern wing** of the Large Hermitage is **Flemish** art, with Van Dyck in room 246, and Rubens in room 247. The galleries running from north to south along the **western wing** of the building house the **Dutch** art, with a profusion of twenty-six Rembrandts in room 254. On a quiet day, they seem to be very well, almost intimately, displayed, but with the usual Hermitage crowds, the Rembrandt room can feel like rush hour in the Metro.

There is also a **central gallery**, running west–east from the southern end of the Rembrandt room. It begins with El Greco in room 240, and then contains Murillo and some fine Goyas in room 239, before the lofty central hall with its vast works by Tiepolo and Canaletto. The next hall, still in the central gallery, contains Veronese and Tintoretto.

Winter Palace, second floor

Of the State Hermitage complex, this is the only part of the second floor which is open. These rooms were once the up-market staff quarters of the Winter Palace, for maids of honour and young nobles working as pages, rather than for the scullery wenches and footmen. These were also the discreet rooms for royal mistresses. Tsar Alexander II housed his Princess Yuryevskaya here.

The **western wing** contains **oriental** art. Princess Yuryevskaya's boudoir now houses Chinese porcelain, and the suite of rooms in the north-west corner, where Tsar Nicholas I, the gendarme of Europe, used to sleep, these days contains an exquisite collection of Persian miniatures.

The **north wing**, overlooking the inner courtyard, contains the **coin collection**, which numismatists say is one of the world's finest.

The **southern wing** contains the Hermitage's celebrated collection of **French** art of the nineteenth and twentieth centuries. The best way to approach is from the Cathedral on the first floor. As you enter the Cathedral, immediately to the right is the porcelain collection of room 269, and the staircase is just beyond. The stairs bring you into the rooms of David, Delacroix and Ingres, and then a better collection of Corot and Courbet than you will find in the Musée d'Orsay in Paris.

Room 320 is Degas and Renoir. Room 319 is Claude Monet. Cézanne and Pissarro are in room 318, and van Gogh and Henri Rousseau in 317. Gauguin has room 316, and Rodin's sculptures are in 315. Turn back into the Gauguin room, and go through the corridor to the southern wing and rooms 343–5, which house the Matisse collection. There are thirty-five works by Matisse, several of them bought for 1,000 francs each. 'The Dancers' was commissioned by Shchukin in 1910. The collection of Matisse sculptures was donated by Lydia Delektorskaya in 1971, and in room 345 there are two fine portraits of Lydia, his constant model in the late 1930s and 40s. She is also the model for the gently but powerfully erotic 'Seated Nude' at the Pushkin Museum in Moscow.

The Hermitage list of post-Impressionist riches continues with Picasso, his blue and rose periods, in rooms 346–7, and Bonnard, Vuillard and Derain in rooms 348–9. The collection then rather tails off into 'other' twentieth century, of which Rockwell Kent's donation of American work is the most interesting.

Tour two: The heart of Leningrad

The heart of the city is the junction where the two arms of the River Neva divide to pass north and south of Vasilyevsky Island. The junction is dominated from the north by the Peter-Paul Fortress, and to the south by the Winter Palace and the Admiralty. The Admiralty also lies at the centre of the four concentric rings of canals that run through the southern half of the city. From the Admiralty building run three great highways of the city: **Nevsky Prospekt** to the southeast; **Ulitsa Dzerzhinskovo** to the south, leading to Vitebsk Station; and **Prospekt Mayorova** to the south-west, leading to Warsaw Station. The Admiralty is also surrounded by the three great squares at the city centre. To its east is the Palace Square, with the Winter Palace and great curving façade of the General Staff building; to its west Decembrists' Square; and to the south-west, beyond the great domed cathedral, Isaac's Square.

Decembrists' Square (Ploshchad Dekabristov) is the old parade ground where the liberal officers launched their abortive coup in December 1825. Four years later, the Italian architect Rossi began building the classical group on the west face of the square: the old Senate, the supreme court of justice under the Tsars, which is joined to the Synod, the old centre of church administration, by the arcade above Krasnaya Ulitsa.

Overlooking the river, in the centre of the square, is the city's great symbol, Falconet's **Statue of Peter the Great**. Commissioned by Catherine the Great, it stands on a single block of granite which weighs 1,625 tonnes, and is immortalised by Pushkin's verse as 'The Bronze Horseman':

> Whither do you gallop, great horse?
> And on whom will your great hooves fall?
> Great prince of destiny
> Is this how you rode Russia,
> With iron control, making her rear up high
> Above the very gulf of disaster?

On the southern side of the square is **St Isaac's Cathedral**. Open daily from 11 a.m. to 7 p.m., closed on Wednesdays and the last Monday of each month. Designed in 1818 by the young French architect Montferrand, it holds over 10,000 worshippers and took forty years to build. There is a splendid view of the city from the top of the dome, some 91 m above the ground. Photography is not permitted. After the Revolution, it was for many years a museum of atheism, and the great pendulum which proves the rotation of the earth still swings.

Isaac's Square (Isaakiyevskaya Ploshchad) lies south of the cathedral. The equestrian statue commemorates Tsar Nicholas I. To its east, on the corner of **Gogol Street**, stands the old Angliya Hotel (now the Leningradskaya) and opposite, the house where Dostoyevsky lived until his arrest in 1849. **Gertsen Street** is the next to enter the square at the Astoria Hotel, where an over-confident Hitler planned his victory banquet, and even printed the menus. Opposite the hotel, on the other corner of Gertsen Street, is the old German Embassy. These two streets, running east to Nevsky Prospekt, were the heart of the fashionable quarter before 1914.

On the south side of Isaac's Square is the **Blue Bridge** (Siniy Most) over the River Moika, and beyond that, the **Marinsky Palace**. It was built for Grand Duchess Marie, the lame eldest daughter of Tsar Nicholas I for whom they designed gentle ramps rather than stairs.

Nevsky Prospekt

'There is nothing finer than Nevsky Prospekt – in St Petersburg, it is everything.' (Gogol)

The great road to Moscow, Nevsky Prospekt was famous in Tsarist times as the cleanest street in Russia. Prostitutes arrested in the night were sentenced to sweep it clean at dawn. From the Admiralty to Moscow Station at Ploshchad Vostaniye, the city's great thoroughfare runs for 3 km, and makes a pleasant stroll.

It begins at **Palace Square** (Dvortsovaya Ploshchad), and the first stretch is the old financial heart which was known simply as The City. On the corner of Gogol Street was the Private Commercial Bank, a building modelled on the Doge's Palace in Venice. **Gogol Street** is named after the author, who lived at no. 17, and Tchaikovsky died of cholera after drinking the water at no. 13. Nevsky Prospekt continues to Gertsen Street past a mixture of eighteenth- and nineteenth-century buildings and, on the eastern side, a stencilled notice dating from the Second World War warning that this was an exposed spot during artillery bombardments. **Gertsen Street**, leading down to the Imperial Yacht Club and the Astoria Hotel, was the height of Tsarist fashion; Fabergé's shop was at no. 24.

The River Moika is crossed by the **People's Bridge** (Narodny Most), and on the left is the 1830s' **Dutch Church**. With Finnish, Anglican and Lutheran churches nearby, this stretch was known as 'Street of Tolerance'. Opposite the Dutch Church is the green and white **Stroganov Palace**, built by Rastrelli in the 1750s. Next on the left is the Leningrad **Palace of Trade** department store, built in 1910 as the Guards' Economic Society. Ulitsa Zhelyabova runs down to the site of the old royal stables. Turgenev and Nijinsky lived at no. 13, and Rimsky-Korsakov at no. 11.

Kazan Square

Nevsky Prospekt now opens out into the fine Kazan Square, dominated by the **Cathedral of Our Lady of Kazan**, and in 1876 site of the city's first workers' demonstration, complete with a red flag. The Revolution of February 1917 began with a series of spontaneous demonstrations and hunger protests here. The cathedral was built from 1801–11 by Voronikhin; it takes its colonnade from St Peter's in Rome, and its central portal from the Duomo in Florence. It has been the Museum of Atheism since 1932. Opposite the Kazan Cathedral, and set back from Nevsky Prospekt is the pale yellow Lutheran **Church of Saint Peter**, built in 1832. **School 22** next door used to be the eighteenth-century Peterschule, where Mussorgsky was a pupil. One of the great landmarks of the city is the huge globe above **Dom Knigi**, the house of books. It used to be the showroom of the Singer sewing machine company, and the globe was their trademark. It stands on the corner of Nevsky Prospekt and the quay that runs alongside the Griboedev Canal. Turn left along the quayside to the **Church of the Saviour of the Spilled Blood**, built on the site of the assassination of Tsar Alexander II in 1881. Modelled on St Basil's in Moscow, it looks incongruous in the spare and classical setting of St Petersburg.

Back on Nevsky Prospekt, you cross the Griboedev Canal by the **Kazan Bridge** (Kazansky Most). On the corner above the Nevsky Prospekt Metro station is the **Glinka Hall of the Philharmonic**. Originally built by Jacquot in 1829, Rubinstein made his debut here in 1843. The eighteenth-century Catholic **Church of St Catherine**, by Vallin de la Mothe, is in the shape of a Latin cross, and holds the tomb of the last Polish king, Stanislas Poniatowski. On the far side of Nevsky are the **Silver Rows**, the old Silversmiths' Bazaar, and at no. 33, the old **Town Hall**, originally built by Quarenghi in the 1780s, but now much changed. The tower used to hold a telescope for semaphoric communication with the summer palace at Tsarskoye Selo. In October 1917, the municipal council tried in vain to organise resistance to the Bolsheviks from here. The porticoes alongside, the old shopping complex of the Perinny Ryad, now house the main theatre ticket office. Next is the **Gostinny Dvor**, the long yellow and white building which is now a single department store. Originally built in the 1780s by de la Mothe, it was remodelled in the 1880s and again in the 1960s.

Brodsky Street

Opposite the Town Hall, Brodsky Street, the old Ulitsa Mikhailov-skaya now renamed after the painter, was one of the great streets of the old city, part of a marvellous grouping of urban design by Carlo Rossi in the 1830s that leads down to the famous Arts Square. The street begins on the left with the **Sadko Restaurant**, and further down is the **Evropeyskaya**, one of Europe's grand hotels before 1914, which claimed to have the finest champagne cellars in the world. Opposite, the **Shostakovich Concert Hall** used to be the Club of the Gentry. The famous premier concert of Shostakovich's Seventh Symphony took place here under fire in August 1942.

Arts Square

This square (Ploshchad Iskusstv) is one of the finest in the city. It is dominated by the old **Mikhail Palace**, commissioned by Tsar Alexander I for his young brother. Built by Rossi in the 1820s, this grand yellow façade with its classical Greek portico now houses the **Russian Museum** (see p. 209). On the west side of the square is the **Maly Theatre**, and next door the **Brodsky Museum**, named after the painter who lived there, Ivan Brodsky, but the gallery hangs a wide range of nineteenth- and twentieth-century artists. On the south-east corner of the square, adjoining Ulitsa Rakova, is **Viyelgorsky House** (Dom Viyelgorskovo), which belonged to a famous patron of the arts who organised private concerts where Liszt and Berlioz would play.

The Nevsky Prospekt continues with the blue and white **Armenian Church** on the left (1770s), and the long arcade and narrow arcade, comprising the **Passage Department Store**, which merge into Ulitsa Rakova. In swift succession along Nevsky come the **Puppet Theatre** at no. 52, **Yeliseyev's Grocery Store** at no. 58 (the Harrods of Tsarist times but now a grim state Gastronom), and in the same building, the **Comedy Theatre**. Then the Prospekt is crossed by another of Leningrad's great thoroughfares, Ulitsa Sadovaya. On the far side of Sadovaya is the **Saltykov-Schedrin National Library**. The old Imperial Public Library, it contains over 20 million books, including the private library of the French Encyclopaedist Diderot, bought by Catherine the Great. One of the finest libraries in the world, it was badly damaged by fire in 1988.

Ostrovsky Square

The avenue then opens out into the Ostrovsky Square (Ploshchad Ostrovskovo), with a statue of **Catherine the Great** amid the gardens. Behind Catherine is the **Pushkin Theatre**, built by Rossi from

1828–32. To the rear of the theatre lies **Architect Rossi Street** (Ulitsa Zodchevo Rossi), designed by Rossi as a single and precisely calculated city-scape. The street is 21 m wide, and its symmetrical buildings are 21 m high. It is best seen from the far end, in Lomonosov Square. On the far side of Ostrovsky Square is the **Anichkov Palace**, now the Pioneers' Palace. (The Pioneers are the members of the Soviet-wide official and compulsory organisation for children, a Leninist version of the Scouts.) Built by Rastrelli, with later additions by Quarenghi, Catherine the Great gave it to her favourite Potemkin, and it later became the dwelling used by heirs to the throne. Beyond the square is the fine three-arched **Anichkov Bridge** (Anichovsky Most) across the River Fontanka with its prancing horses at each corner. The Fontanka marks the end of the finest stretch of Nevsky Prospekt, but the street continues another 900 m or so to the Moscow Station, and then for another 1.5 km to the **Nevsky Monastery**.

Fontanka and the Summer Gardens

If you are feeling energetic, turn left from Nevsky Prospekt at the River Fontanka, and take the quayside route. A pleasant stroll of about 3 km will take you past the Summer Gardens and to the bank of the River Neva, almost opposite the mooring point of the battleship *Aurora*. The name Fontanka comes from the Fountains of the Summer Gardens.

On the left is the Shuvalov Palace, now the **House of Peace and Friendship** (Dom Druzhbi i Mira), where foreign guests are entertained. On the far side of the river, the grand building with the classical columns and portico was the **Catherine Institute**, a school for noblewomen, built on the site of Catherine's Italian Palace. Next door is the long, yellow **Fontanka Palace**, erected in the 1750s by a Russian pupil of Rastrelli called Slava Chevakinsky. It has housed for many years the Institute of Arctic Research. Beyond the next bridge, the Most Belinskovo, is the **State Circus**. On the far bank stands a series of former palaces, which belonged to the Golitsyns and the Pashkovs, and then at no. 16 is the site of a notorious building, the home of the Third Section, the secret police of Tsar Nicholas I, the KGB of their day. It was torn down, brick by brick, in 1917.

The quayside now opens out on the left into a remarkably spacious area for the heart of a city. It is, in effect, the grounds of two palaces, which then open upon the Field of Mars and the Summer Gardens, which in turn continue to the River Neva. The farther of the two palaces is the **Mikhail Palace**, or the Russian Museum (see p. 209), which is usually approached from Arts Square. The nearer is the **Engineers' Castle**. Originally Tsarina Elizabeth's Summer Palace stood here, but the mad Tsar Paul announced that the Archangel Michael had appeared to him in a dream, ordering him to build a classic castle, complete with moats and battlements, where he would be safe from his enemies. He was murdered in one of the rooms six weeks after it was completed. In 1822, it became a college of military engineering and Dostoyevsky, among others, studied there.

Beyond lie the **Summer Gardens**, originally laid out by Peter the Great with lakes, fountains and pavilions to echo the formal French gardens of his day. In winter, the statues are enclosed within small protective wooden frames, to prevent frost damage. Just before the great entrance to the gardens from the embankment on the River Neva is the **Summer Palace**, a small building for pleasure and dalliance, not a royal dwelling, but Peter the Great lived there in the early years of the city. Now a museum, it contains Peter's own workshop, contemporary furnishings and kitchen utensils, and makes a plain and almost intimate contrast with the grander palace-museums for which the city is famous. Open daily from 11 a.m. to 7 p.m., closed on Tuesdays and the last Monday of each month.

Just west of the Summer Gardens is the **Field of Mars** (Marsovo Pole), the site of an old marsh drained by Peter the Great, which then became a parade ground. In 1917, those who died during the Revolution, and later in the civil war, were buried here. The vast building which flanks it is the **Pavlovskiy Barracks**, built as the home of the Pavlovskiy Guards who were recruited by mad Tsar Paul exclusively from men who shared his pug nose.

The main tourist sites

Peter-Paul Fortress (Petropavlovskaya Krepost)

Nearest Metro: Gorkovskaya. Open daily from 11 a.m. to 6 p.m., Tuesdays 11 a.m. to 4 p.m., closed on Wednesdays and the last Tuesday of each month. Entry into the grounds is free, but to visit the prison, the fortress itself, the commandant's house and the church, tickets must be purchased just inside the main gate.

From the centre of Leningrad, by the Winter Palace, you may get to the fortress by walking across the Kirovsky Most, a dramatic spar some 550 m long, and then turning left over the small bridge at Revolution Square (Ploshchad Revolutsyi). In winter, this gives you the best view of the winter bathers, who call themselves walruses. They break the ice in the river below the fortress and plunge into the freezing waters, claiming this is good for the health. The main entrance of Ivan Gate is located in a preliminary bastion. The entrance to the fortress proper is through the Peter Gate, between the Tsar's and Menshikov's Bastions.

History

The fortress was built from 1703–10, when Tsar Peter the Great saw it as his bastion against the Swedes. It was designed in accordance with the classic military principles of the day, with low, thick walls to absorb cannon fire, and arrow-shaped towers from which flanking fire could be brought upon enemy infantry who tried to scale the ramparts. Peter's victories made the fortress militarily redundant before it was complete, and it then became the Russian Bastille, the infamous prison whose brooding presence in the heart of the capital acted as a warning, if not a deterrent, to all political activity.

The main prison is in the Trubetskoy Bastion, and contains sixty-nine cells and two dungeons. Its first victim was Peter's own son, Alexis, imprisoned and tortured to death here in 1718. The Decembrists, the Zemlya i Volya, the Narodnaya Volya, the anarchist Bakunin, Lenin's elder brother Alexander – all the revolutionary groups of the nineteenth century were imprisoned here. And in 1917, the Tsar's Ministers, and later Kerensky's Ministers, were to follow them. Since 1922, the prison has been a museum where successive generations of guides have managed a fine sense of outrage at the wickedness of Tsarism for imprisoning its opponents, while the Soviet Union's own record in this field passes without comment.

Church of
Saints Peter
and Paul

The church was designed by Trezzini in 1713, damaged by fire and rebuilt by Rastrelli in 1750. The tower is nearly 122 m high, the slim golden spire alone being 58 m. After the fire, the interior of the church was rebuilt in Italianate Baroque. The tombs of all the Romanov Tsars, save Peter II and the last Tsar, Nicholas II, are to be found here. They are all in white marble, except for Alexander II and his wife, who chose Siberian stone, rhodonite from the Urals and jasper from the Altai Mountains.

Artillery
Museum

On the mainland opposite the small island on which the fortress stands are the Lenin Park and Zoo, and the Artillery Museum in a subsidiary fort. This is the main military museum in Leningrad, with a series of exhibits on the 900-day siege of 1941–4. Open daily from 11 a.m. to 5 p.m., closed on Mondays and Tuesdays.

Cabin of
Peter the
Great
(Domik
Petra)

Nearest Metro: Gorkovskaya. Open daily from 11 a.m. to 7 p.m., closed on Tuesdays and the last Monday of each month.

On the embankment between the Peter-Paul Fortress and the mooring point of the battleship *Aurora*, this log cabin was knocked together in three days by soldiers in May 1703. With just two rooms, a dining room and study, it was Peter's home for the next six years, while the work of laying down the city's foundations went on. It was given the protection of stone walls in Catherine's time, and then Tsar Nicholas I made the study into a religious shrine.

Alexander
Nevsky
Monastery
(Alexander
Nevskiy
Lavra)

At the far south-eastern end of Nevsky Prospekt, where the thoroughfare reaches the river. Nearest Metro: Ploshchad Aleksandra Nevskovo.

This is the third largest monastery in Russia, after those at Zagorsk and Kiev. Built from 1710–16, Peter the Great thought this was the site of Alexander Nevsky's riverside victory over the Swedes in 1240 which earned him the title 'Nevsky' ('of the river'). In fact, the battle was some miles upstream, but Peter had Nevsky's remains brought here from Vladimir and reburied.

The monastery grounds contain seven churches and three cemeteries, and this is still a working centre of the Orthodox Church, although it shares the place with a state museum. Whether seen from Nevsky Prospekt or from the river, it looks like a fortress. The main entrance through a classical domed archway leads to the **St Lazarus Cemetery**, where Pushkin's wife and the scientist Lomonosov are buried. To the right is the old **Tikhvin Cemetery**, now a park, but the tombs of Dostoyevsky, Glinka, Tchaikovsky and Mussorgsky are here. Then comes a tiny bridge over the narrow River Black, before the rectangular centre of the monastery itself.

You enter beside a tower which contains two churches, one above the other. The lower **Church of the Annunciation** contains the tomb of the great General Suvorov. Thanks to the array of richly-carved tombstones, testifying to the nineteenth-century fashion of burial here among the local nobility, this is now the **Museum of Urban Sculpture**. Open daily from 11 a.m. to 7 p.m., closed on Tuesdays. The main church of the monastery is **Holy Trinity**, still open for worship, a classical structure in largely Baroque surroundings.

Smolny

Suvorovsky Prospekt. Nearest Metro: Ploshchad Vosstaniya, then by bus. Open daily from 12 to 6 p.m., closed on Wednesdays.

The site of the old Swedish fort of Sabina long before the city was founded, Smolny gets its name from the Tar Courtyard (Smolny Dvor), built here by Peter the Great's Navy.

Smolny Convent

It was the Tsarina Elizabeth who decided to built a convent here where she might spend her declining years. Rastrelli, her favourite architect, designed the marvellous blue, white and gold confection we now see. But funds ran out before it was finished, so the work was not completed until the 1830s. It is now a museum of 'Leningrad; today and tomorrow', which is not recommended.

Smolny Institute

Attached to the south of the convent building, the Institute was established by Catherine the Great as a boarding school for the nobility. This almost drab (by comparison) three-storey building was the stage for the Revolution of October 1917. It was the meeting place for the city Soviet, and also the HQ of the Bolshevik Central Committee. It was here that Lenin announced the seizure of power in the name of the Congress of Soviets and from these buildings that the struggle for the city was organised. You might say that it was here the Revolution was finally betrayed; in 1934, the Leningrad Party leader Sergei Kirov was assassinated in its corridors, the event which started Stalin's purges. Still used by the Leningrad Party organisation, it is not open to the public.

inland Station (Finlyandski Vokzal)

Ulitsa Komsomola. Nearest Metro: Ploshchad Lenina.

The rail terminus for Finland, there is little here to recall Lenin's return to the city in 1917. Indeed, not many contemporaries saw in this event the beginning of the October Revolution. Lenin's enemies sneered at the way he had depended on the German government to travel from exile in Switzerland to Russia. With the war still on, the Kaiser's advisors reckoned – with brilliant prescience – that Lenin was likely to stir up trouble for the Russian enemy. There is a **Statue of Lenin** to commemorate his return, but the Finland Station, after heavy damage in the Second World War, was rebuilt in the 1960s, and the British-built Austin armoured car from which he addressed the crowd is now in the Lenin Museum. The American-built Baldwin locomotive in which Lenin, disguised as a fireman, returned to the city for the second time, in October 1917, is on display inside the station.

Aurora

Pirogovskaya Naberezhnaya. Nearest Metro: Ploshchad Lenina. Open daily from 11 a.m. to 6 p.m., closed on Tuesdays.

If you stay in the modern Leningrad Hotel, the battleship *Aurora* is moored just beneath your windows. In fact, she is no battleship. Built in 1903 as a cruiser, she sailed round the world with the rest of the Baltic Fleet to fight the Japanese in 1904, but luckily avoided the massacre of Tsushima Straits. Already obsolete by the time war broke out in 1914, the *Aurora* was in dock for modernisation in 1917, where the sailors were swiftly radicalised by the anti-war and anti-Tsarist mood of the city. On the night of 25–6 October, with resistance still continuing from the Winter Palace, the *Aurora* fired a single blank shell from her six-inch forward gun to intimidate the defenders. Moored that night nearly 3 km downstream from the Winter Palace, that warning did its job. When war came again in 1941, the ship was sunk in shallow water near Oranienbaum, and raised again after the war. Now an interesting museum, it contains almost as much material on the cruise to Tsushima and the sinking of 1941 as on the Revolution.

Theatre Square (Teatralnaya Ploshchad)

Best approached along the Kryukov Canal, which runs north and south between the Fontanka and the River Neva. Theatre Square is halfway along this canal, and may be approached from either direction.

Another of the best-known squares of the city, its original eighteenth-century name was Carousel Square, for the roundabouts and fairground that were here. On the eastern side is the **Conservatory**, a rather grim and graceless 1890s' building on the site of what was the Bolshoy Kamenny Teatr, the Big Stone Theatre of the 1780s. It is flanked by statues of Rimsky-Korsakov and of Glinka, whose 'Life for the Tsar' opera had its première in the old building. On the western side of the square, the site of the old circus, burned down in a fire, the Marinka Theatre was built in 1860. Now formally known as the **Kirov**, and home of the great ballet, Leningraders still call it the Marinka. The auditorium is splendid, a great array of plush and gold; to enter is an event in itself.

Strelka

Vasilyevsky Island, best reached by the Palace Bridge (Dvortsovi Most) from the Winter Palace quay.

208

Opposite the Winter Palace, the River Neva forks into two streams to run north and south of Vasilyevsky Island, which in Peter's time was to be the intellectual centre of the city. It is named after the lieutenant of artillery who commanded the guns here in Peter's day, Vassily Korvhmin. On the island's south-east corner, facing the Peter-Paul Fortress to the north and the Winter Palace to the south, some of Peter's old administrative centre remains. But most of the rest of the large island has been residential for many years; before 1917 many foreigners lived here and it was known as the 'German quarter'.

The administrative tip of the island is known as the Strelka, and was originally the main merchant dockyard. The Strelka, dominated by the two rostral columns which were erected in 1810 as a guide to shipping, is a marvellous viewpoint for the rest of the city. The main building at the front is the old Stock Exchange, now the **Central Naval Museum**. Open daily from 11 a.m. to 6 p.m., closed on Tuesdays. Its main exhibit is the first boat of Peter the Great, the *Botik*. It is flanked by two porticoed buildings, originally warehouses, now the **Museums of Zoology and Agriculture**. The star exhibit of the former (open daily from 11 a.m. to 6 p.m., closed on Mondays) is a huge mammoth, found deep-frozen in Siberia in 1902, and now thawed out, stuffed and rather seedy.

To the north of the Strelka, the domed classical building is the old Customs House, now the **Literary Museum**. To the south, curving round to face the Admiralty across the Neva, are the **Anthropology Museum** and the **Academy of Sciences**, which Peter founded in 1725 with the help of German scholars. The streets running north and south across the island are known as Lines, and the first of them contains the famous **Twelve Colleges**. Planned by Peter as the great building which would house each of his twelve new Ministries, the design was put out to competition. It runs for a half kilometre in length, and took so long to build that by the time it was finished both Rastrelli and Quarenghi had helped finish the design, the bureaucracy was too big to fit, and it was made into a university.

Russian Museum

Located in the old Mikhail Palace in Arts Square, the collection of ancient and modern Russian art spreads confusingly through three buildings, the Palace, the Rossi wing, and the Benois. Open daily from 10 a.m. to 6 p.m., closed on Tuesdays.

The Palace

In the Palace itself, only the first floor is of great interest. Rooms 1–4 contain icons. Room 1 has the strikingly modernistic 'Golden-haired Angel', which dates from the twelfth century; room 2 houses the outstanding 'Battle between Men of Suzdal and of Novgorod'; and room 3 contains some attributed to Andrey Rublyov. Room 5 presents a life-mask of Peter the Great, and begins an array of eighteenth-century portraits. The best of these are by Levitsky, 'Russia's Gainsborough', in room 10. The next room, no. 11, is the White Hall, grandest in the palace. This early nineteenth-century period of Russian art has few admirers, but I rather like Karl Bryullov's 'Last Day of Pompeii' (1833) in room 15, and Ayvazovsky's seascapes. The ground floor of the Mikhail Palace has some good portraits by Venetsianov and his school in rooms 19–21. Again, few share my view that Nikolay Gay has painted a highly distinctive and realistic 'Last Supper' (1863), displayed in room 26. Room 35 has Konstantin Savitsky's epic 'Off to War' (1888).

Rossi wing

The adjoining building is known as the Rossi wing, and it may be galloped through, except for the display of handicrafts on the ground floor, west side, which has some very good Palekh boxes and traditional costumes.

Benois building

Through a passageway, you reach this separate building, whose ground floor has paintings of the Soviet period, and not very good ones at that. Deyneka's militaristic 'Defence of Sevastopol' has a certain comic-book charm. Yevsey Moiseyenko's 'Sweet Cherries' is a very much more considered image of the war.

The first floor of the Benois building is the jewel of the collection. Rooms 67–70 contain the works of Repin, his 'Volga Boatmen' and 'Zaporozhets Cossacks' being the best known. Room 71 contains Vasnetsov's brooding 'Knight at the Crossroads' (1882), which says, or implies, all you need to know about the Slavophile movement and the revival of Russian nationalism in the late nineteenth century. Rooms 72–3 contain Vasily Surikov's happier echoes of a similar sentiment, while room 74 has Levitan's landscapes. Rooms 76–7 house Valentin Serov's stunning portraits, of which Olga Orlova is my favourite. Room 78 presents the weird genius of Mikhail Vrubel, and room 80 has Leon Bakst's almost psychiatric portrait of Diaghilev and his old nanny. In room 82, Boris Kustodiev's plump wives of merchants will restore your equilibrium.

Then come the rooms where they began discreetly replacing the works of those formerly frowned on by the Party philistines. There is a marvellous Robert Falk 'Woman in a White Shawl' in room 88, and room 89 has Nathan Altman's shattering portrait of the poetess Anna Akhmatova in 1914, looking young, stylish and sexy. And then you think how her husband was shot by the Bolsheviks, her son imprisoned by Stalin and how she wrote *Requiem*, the great tragic poem of the purges, and you shiver. In room 90 are two paintings by Malevich, and in room 92 are the works of the much under-estimated Petrov-Vodkin. His 'Death of a Commissar' shows you why he was acceptable to the regime, even though it could never comprehend the subtlety of his work. His best-known painting, the 'Petrograd Madonna' (official title 'Petrograd 1918'), is the most innocently subversive. It hangs in the Tretyakov Gallery in Moscow. But the Russian Museum has finally had the guts to hang his long-suppressed portrait of Anna Akhmatova (1922).

River trips

In summer, the best way to see the city is to stroll it, but the second best and laziest way is to take a cruise boat. The power of Amsterdam's inspiration upon Peter the Great will then become apparent. The cruise boats of the River Neva can take you from the Pier by the statue of the Bronze Horseman all the way to Smolny for 15 kopeks.

The best boat trip follows an 8-km rectangular course along the rivers and inland canals. There is a quay at the **Anichkov Bridge**, where the River Fontanka crosses Nevsky Prospekt. There are queues in good weather, but you may through Intourist book a seat on a boat with an English-speaking guide by paying in advance. The boats head west along the Fontanka to the Kryukov Canal, where they turn right past the Kirov Theatre to the River Moika. The boats then follow the Moika east to the Engineers' Castle and the Summer Gardens, where they turn right again on to the Fontanka.

Where to stay

Pribaltiyskaya, 14 Ulitsa Korablestroitelei (tel. 356-5112); nearest Metro: Primorskaya. This is very grand modern hotel architecture – acres of marble, and prices to match. The first time I stayed, in 1984, this was the most expensive hotel in the country, at 90 roubles for a single room. This seemed a lot for a hotel in whose lift a naked, drunken Finn slept undisturbed all night. Or at least, the porter explained that since the drunk was a Finn, he could not be wakened. Miles from anywhere except the port, with that lifelessness that infects over-large, over-marbled modern buildings, I do not recommend it. They also 'lose' your reservation when somebody else waves a lot of cash. It happened to Soviet rock star Alla Pugacheva, who was bounced from her room for a Georgian millionaire. When she made a fuss, the hotel tried to blame her for causing a scene. Not a nice place, except for the restaurants. Their fast self-service snack bar serves the best breakfast in Russia. Suites 170 roubles a night; rooms from 80–95 roubles.

Astoria, 39 Ulitsa Gartsena (tel. 219-1100); nearest Metro: Nevsky Prospekt. This is faded grandeur, the silk damask on the lamp shades worn away to gossamer, but the bathrooms would fetch a fortune in a London antiques market. The entire building is an Art Nouveau gem. The food is good by local standards, and the service tries to live up to the old traditions. You could not be more central, nor in a grander part of town. Suites 170 roubles a night, rooms from 80–95 roubles.

Yevropeiskaya, 1/7 Ulitsa Brodskovo (tel. 211-9149); nearest Metro: Nevsky Prospekt. Like the Astoria, only more so. This was the Hotel de l'Europe before the Bolsheviks came along to spoil it. Built in the 1870s in Third Empire whorehouse style, and then spruced up just before 1914 with a touch of late Art Nouveau by the same architect who designed the Astoria. It is the kind of place you want to enter smoking a fat cigar, escorting a lady in sable. Then you see the Finnish tour groups and reality sets in. Suites 170 roubles a night; rooms from 80–95 roubles.

Moskva, 2 Ploshchad Alexandra Nevskovo (tel. 274-9505); nearest Metro: Ploshchad Alexandra Nevskovo. A modern hotel, whose best feature is its location, right beside the Nevsky Monastery, and overlooking the upper part of the river. In summer, it is a pleasure to take a river boat down to the Winter Palace, but in winter you may feel a bit remote. The rooms are small, but clean and adequate. The food is functional, but the staff smile more than most. Suites 170 roubles a night; rooms from 80–95 roubles.

Leningrad, 5/2 Vyborgskaya Naberezhnaya (tel. 542-9123); nearest Metro: Ploshchad Lenina. This is a modern hotel, decorated in half-hearted Scandinavian style with lots of pine. The place where British tour groups are usually booked in, and handy for the battleship *Aurora*, which is moored on the river below. But it is a long walk past the Finland Station and across the Liteiny Bridge to the Winter Palace and Nevsky Prospekt. Alternatively, you have to cross two bridges and go past the Peter-Paul Fortress to the centre. This is no problem in summer, but in winter you may feel too isolated to wander freely away from the Intourist guides – which would be a shame. No suites; rooms from 80–95 roubles a night.

Karelia, 27/2 Ulitsa Tukhachevskovo (tel. 226-5701). Student groups are sometimes put up here, and do not speak well of it. Rooms from 40–55 roubles a night.

Where to eat

Pushkin Palace

The best hotel in Leningrad is the relatively new Pribaltiyskaya, and its **Neva** dining room works very hard at keeping pace. The result is an unhappy mix of Russian classics, like caviar and blinys alongside the flambé school of international cuisine. It also features an orchestra of Russian folk instruments. (14 Ulitsa Korablestroitelei; tel. 356-0158.)

The **Sovyetski** restaurant, in the hotel of the same name, is standard Soviet fare and all the better for being less pretentious. This 13-storey hotel is one of the main Intourist centres; it has a large Beriozka shop, and is often full of drunken Finns. (43 Prospekt Lermonetova; tel. 216-0032.)

There are two notable restaurants in the eponymous Yevropeiskaya Hotel, just off the Nevsky Prospekt. First is the large **Sadko**, and then the **Yevropeiskaya**. A grand nineteenth-century building, this used to be the Hotel de l'Europe. (Ulitsa Brodskovo; tel. 211-9149.)

The restaurant in the **Astoria Hotel** has the distinction of being chosen by Adolf Hitler for his victory banquet when Leningrad fell. He even had the menus printed in advance, and they were subsequently found by the advancing Red Army. The claim that this is one of the city's best restaurants rests upon tradition, decor and Intourist status, rather than on intrinsic merit. (39 Ulitsa Gartsena; tel. 219-1100.)

Beside the Armenian church at 46 Nevsky Prospekt is a double: the **Sever café** and pastry shop on the ground floor, with the **Neva Restaurant** above. The Sever's coffee is terrible, but they do excellent macaroons, and the Neva is recommended for its fish. (Tel. 153-490.)

The **Kavkazky** is a Georgian restaurant, and a reliable place for a good and slightly exotic meal. The *satsivi* (poultry with walnut sauce) and the *khinkali* (very peppery mutton dumplings) are recommended. They usually have a decent stock of Georgian wines, which seem to travel better to Leningrad than they do to Moscow. You can buy *lavash*, the flat Georgian bread, to take away. The coffee is probably the best in Leningrad. (25 Nevsky Prospekt; tel. 146-656.)

The **Fregat** used to have a good reputation for fish. On Vasilyevsky Island, behind the Frunze Naval Academy, it has a nautical flavour, and sometimes stocks the very rare Admiralty vodka. (39/14 Bolshoy Prospekt; tel. 326-176.)

The **Petrovsky Zal** in the Leningrad Hotel offers traditional Russian food and a Russian folk orchestra. A modern building on the quayside opposite the battleship *Aurora*, the Leningrad is usually filled with western tourists. (5/2 Vyborgskaya Naberezhnaya; tel. 542-9123.)

The **Karelia** restaurant in the new Karelia Hotel specialises in the cuisine of the Karelian Autonomous Republic, which used to be part of Finland. This means fish, sometimes elk, and delicious ice-cold red berries in winter. (27/2 Ulitsa Tukhachevskovo; tel. 226-5701.)

Outside Leningrad but worth an excursion

Pushkin Palace

The royal estate of Tsarskoye Selo (literally, Tsar's Village), lies 24 km south of Leningrad. It is now an estate-museum. The train from Vitebsk Station in Leningrad to the local station of Dyetskoye Selo takes half an hour, and then buses 371 and 382 go regularly to and from the palaces. Intourist excursions from your Leningrad hotel include coach travel and an English-speaking guide, and are strongly recommended. (The coach goes past the Pulkovo Observatory, and these modest heights, about 61 m above sea level, saw some of the most bitter fighting of the war during the 900 days the Germans besieged the city.) Open daily from 10 a.m. to 6 p.m., closed on Tuesdays and the last day of each month.

Originally owned by Peter the Great's wife, this great estate of palaces began to take shape in the reigns of Elizabeth (1741–61) and Catherine the Great (1762–96). It became a fashionable resort for the upper classes in the nineteenth century, with a school being built for their sons. The first Russian train went from here to the city, and it was the first town in Europe to be lit entirely by electricity. The road enters the town of Pushkino through an Egyptian-style gate. The town itself is pleasant, and the road then enters the formally sculpted park, dotted with pavilions and grottoes.

Catherine Palace

The heart of the estate is this palace, built by Tsarina Elizabeth and named after her mother, wife of Peter the Great. Just as the great churches of the Moscow Kremlin were designed by imported Italian architects, so Leningrad also was built by imported talents. The Catherine Palace was designed by the great Italian, Bartolomeo Rastrelli, whose success here led to his being commissioned to design the Winter Palace itself. A Baroque masterpiece, with a façade almost 304 m in length, much of the interior was almost gutted in the reign of Catherine the Great, to be redesigned by the Scots architect Charles Cameron in the fashionably austere neo-classic style. The building you now see is very modern. Almost completely (and deliberately) destroyed by the Germans in 1941–4, it has been lovingly restored, although gaps in the parquet floors betray a certain clumsiness.

Some things can never be restored. The famous **Amber Room**, originally made for the King of Prussia but donated to Catherine the Great for political reasons, used to be the great treasure house of the palace. The decorations and contents were looted by a new generation of Prussians in 1944, were traced to Königsberg, and then disappeared in the chaos of the collapse of the Third Reich. Every year, the Russian papers and magazines carry new speculation about the fate of the Amber Room, with dark hints that it has been rebuilt in some South American jungle hide-out, or kept from its Russian owners in some mean millionaire's vault.

Rastrelli's **Great Hall** is a stunning rococo mixture of gold and pure light, the windows on both sides concealing the unusual narrowness of the building. The **Picture Hall**, also by Rastrelli, and containing one of the great Dutch tiled stoves that dot the palace, was the first room to be restored. It presents a dramatic contrast with Cameron's rooms. The Scotsman's finest design is probably the **Green Dining-Room**, which is rather like being inside a piece of Wedgwood pottery, but the **Butlers' Room** and the **Blue Drawing-Room** are also magnificent. The whole complex of Pushkin is shot through with Chinese influences. The park contains a Chinese theatre and a Chinese village, but Cameron's **Chinese Drawing-Room** with its silk wallpaper is probably the most memorable. The most Russian room in the entire palace is the **Chapel**, but it is one of the lightest churches in the country, glowing in royal blue and gold. Put all these Scottish, Italian, Chinese, Dutch and Classical influences together, and we may conclude that the rulers of Russia were never more culturally remote from their own people than when at Tsarskoye Selo.

Thermae

To the south of the palace, and running at right angles, is Cameron's Thermae, a complex based upon the design for a Roman bathhouse. His greatest challenge was to find some non-vulgar way of using the almost too magnificent materials lavished upon him by his patron. The result was the Agate and Jasper rooms, extravagance tamed by design. Cameron's colonnades are perhaps the Scots architect's greatest triumph. There is a joke hidden among the colonnades' array of bronze busts of the great men of classical times. The distinguished English politician of the late eighteenth century, Charles James Fox, has a bust to himself simply because he was the opponent of Prime Minister William Pitt the Younger, whom the Tsarina hated.

Catherine Park

The park itself is a delight. There is a Turkish bath modelled on an Istanbul mosque, a Palladian bridge copied from Wilton House, some deliberate ruins and an island concert hall designed by Quarenghi, and a cemetery for Catherine's pet dogs. In summer, a rowing boat may be hired.

If arrangements are made through Intourist for lunch to be taken at the red brick **Admiralty Restaurant**, then the day may pleasantly be spent at Pushkino. There is still the **Alexander Park** to be seen, with its yellow and white **Alexander Palace**, built by Quarenghi when Tsar Alexander I was crown prince. The last of the Romanovs, Tsar Nicholas II, lived here with his family almost permanently after the 1905 Revolution fuelled his aversion to St Petersburg. To the west of the Palace is the **Children's Pond**, with its small island that was the playground for the royal children. Further north was a miniature Kremlin, called the **Fyodorovskii Gorodok**, designed as a small barracks for the Tsar's bodyguard. Finally, the **Pushkin Dacha**, where the poet and his wife spent the summer of 1831 is on Ul Vasenko in the town, and is now a small museum. Open daily from 11 a.m. to 6 p.m., closed on Mondays and Tuesdays.

Pavlovsk

Roughly 5 km south and east of Pushkin. Bus 280 makes the journey at highly irregular intervals. From Leningrad, Pavlovsk Station can be reached by train from Vitebsk Station, and the walk from there to the palace is less than 1.5 km, or take bus 283 or 493 from the station. If visiting Pushkin on an Intourist excursion, this may be combined with a trip to Pavlovsk. Open daily from 11 a.m. to 6 p.m., closed on Fridays and first Monday of each month.

A gift to her son from Catherine the Great, the palace is really the creation of Paul's widow, Mariya, who lived on here forty years after his murder. The palace was built as the Baroque style was giving way to neo-classicism, and the building is an unusually happy blend of the two. Designed by the Scots architect, Charles Cameron, it reminds many visitors of Jefferson's celebrated Monticello, 8,000 km away. The semi-circular arcades give the building a grandeur which is matched by the varied interiors, the work of different designers. Again, the palace was devastated during the German occupation, but fully restored by 1970. Cameron designed the rooms on the northern side of the ground floor, Carlo Rossi designed the corner drawing room, Quarenghi the Pilaster Study, Voronikhin the Lantern Study, and Brenna the Old Study. Brenna was also responsible for the arcades. The finest rooms are on the first floor, with the **Hall of War** (for Paul), and the **Hall of Peace** (for his wife) flanking the **Grecian Hall**. The palace also houses an **Exhibition of Porcelain**, and a **Exhibition of Nineteenth-century Russian Interior Design**.

English park

The best feature of Pavlovsk, the park was designed by Cameron along the banks of the River Slavyanka. This is landscaping at its most sumptuous, with small grottoes and pavilions suddenly emerging from bends in the stream, and vistas opening from a carefully planned gap in the trees. There are artificial ruins and miniature fortresses and what are meant to be peasant cottages which contain small art galleries. This was built at the time when the French Queen Marie Antoinette was pretending to be a shepherdess on a carefully sculpted farm at Versailles, and this park is the Russian equivalent.

Petrodvorets

The best way to reach this summer palace of Peter the Great, some 28 km west of Leningrad, is by hydrofoil from the pier at Makarova Embankment, on the Malaya Neva, the arm of the river that flows north of Vasilyevsky Island. The hydrofoil only runs in summer, from 3 May to mid-September, and takes 40 minutes. The train from Leningrad's Baltic Station goes to Novy Petergoff Station, and you then take bus 350, 351 or 352 to the Great Palace entrance. Open daily 11 a.m. to 6 p.m., closed on Mondays and the last day of each month.

History

Petergoff, the original name of the palace, is the transliteration of the German word Peterhof, or Peter's Hall. But the German occupation in 1941–4 did so much damage that after the building was liberated its name was changed to the Russian Petrodvorets – Peter's Palace.

Peter the Great began to live here when he was building the great naval base of Kronstadt, the island just visible to the north-west. But after visiting Versailles in 1717, he was inspired to build a great palace of his own. The seafront Palace of Monplaisir and the great fountains had been completed by the time of Peter's death. But the grand palace he had built was thoroughly remodelled by Rastrelli some forty years later, with new wings and an extra storey added. The 270-m façade retains some of the restraint of the early Baroque.

First floor | Most of the state rooms are on the first floor, and are open to the public. The tour usually begins at the eastern end, in the **Cavaliers' Room**, which is lined in red silk. One of the great views now unfolds as you look along the enfilade of rooms, through golden doorway after golden doorway, each one perfectly framing the next in a series of careful perspectives that runs the full length of the palace. The finest rooms are in the central core of the palace, beginning with Velten's **Partridge Room**, named after the birds which decorate the walls and hangings. The two **Chinese studies**, originally built in the 1760s, are marvels of restoration. They flank the central **Cabinet of Fashions and Graces**, a picture gallery of 365 paintings, one for each day of the year, with three more for the Graces. The models were ladies of Elizabeth's court.

Great Cascade | From the palace down the hill to the sea is one of the world's outstanding series of fountains, and the best single reason to come here in summer. In winter, the cascade is frozen. Among the statues, the central figure of Samson represents Russia's victory over the Swedes. The lower park leads to a series of smaller palaces and pavilions, of which the best is Peter's own **Monplaisir**, with its wide view of the Gulf from the study. Said to be the place where he interrogated his son Alexis before sentencing him to death, its charm lies in its simplicity.

Note: There are two further country palace estates which have not always been open for Intourist visits. There are plans for permanent opening, but you should check locally whether excursions are currently being offered. They are:

Lomonosov (Oranienbaum) | Located about 10 km west of Petrodvorets and on the coast, it was originally built by Peter the Great's favourite, Prince Menshikov. Situated on a hill facing the Gulf of Finland and the island fortress of Kronstadt, the palace later became the seat of Peter II, who had a vast parade ground constructed on which to drill his beloved soldiers. There is a fine park where Catherine the Great built her private roller coaster, and where she also had built a **Chinese Palace**, with its great ceiling painted by Tiepolo. The park contains the small palace of Peter III, designed by Rinaldi, and built in the 1760s.

Gatchina | Some 50 km south-west of Leningrad, this was the estate Catherine the Great gave to her favourite Grigory Orlov. He built an English park, and a palace designed by Rinaldi. When he fell from favour, Catherine gave the estate to her son Paul, who established his own court here and gave full play to his military fantasies. He built forts, bastions and a huge parade ground, and drilled his soldiers constantly. Paul treated them as toy soldiers, and the other sovereigns of Europe would scour their kingdoms to find giants who could be sent to Paul's special regiment of tall soldiers.

The **park** is the glory of Gatchina, with its network of lakes, canals and islands, where wild animals were bred in Paul's day. It also contains a **Catholic Priory**.

217

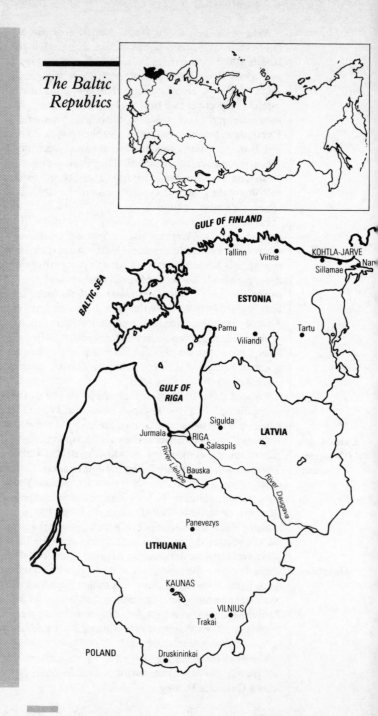

The Baltic Republics

GULF OF FINLAND

BALTIC SEA

ESTONIA

Tallinn   Viitna   KOHTLA-JARVE

Sillamae   Nar

Parnu

Viliandi   Tartu

GULF OF RIGA

Sigulda

Jurmala   RIGA

Salaspils

LATVIA

Bauska

River Lielupe

River Daugava

Panevezys

LITHUANIA

KAUNAS

VILNIUS

Trakai

POLAND   Druskininkai

The Baltic Republics

Route Three of the Motorists' guides on p. 313 takes you through parts of the Baltic Republics.

Introduction

History We tend to think of the three Baltic Republics – Lithuania, Latvia, Estonia – as a single entity, but historically, Lithuania has a very different experience of nationhood. It is a Catholic nation, which can look back to the days when it was the centre of a considerable empire. Latvia and Estonia, on the other hand, adopted the Protestant faith when Swedish rule replaced the German overlords in the sixteenth century. The two lands, whose history was shared to the degree that they were long known by the single name 'Livonia', have almost always lived under the domination of one or other of the neighbours. In the eleventh century, during the reign of King Canute of England and Denmark, the coastal regions of Livonia came under Danish sway. But the steady encroachments of German traders were accompanied by missionary monks from the Archbishopric of Bremen. Attacks on the monks were used as a pretext for a Crusade, and the two famous military-monastic orders were founded, the Teutonic Knights in what later became Prussia, and the Knights of the Sword in Livonia. In Livonia, their feudal grip was never really loosened. They remained landowners and gentry, and went on to become the Baltic barons who provided Tsarist Russia with so many of its Generals and Ministers.

The Knights of the Sword knew how to adapt, quickly transforming their fortresses of Reval (Tallinn) and Riga into prosperous trading ports of the Hanseatic League. They knew how to survive the tumults of the sixteenth-century religious wars, when Livonia became a Swedish province, and how to retain their lands and privileges during the Russian conquests of Peter the Great in the early eighteenth century. They were a ruling class of a different nationality and language from the Latvians and Estonians, a caste distinction that lasted well into the twentieth century. In the battles of 1918–19, when the Baltic nations won their independence from Moscow, the names of their leaders were almost all Germanic. But the names of the Latvian Red Riflemen, who provided Lenin's bodyguard and some of the Revolution's most reliable troops, were overwhelmingly Latvian.

In twelfth-century Lithuania, the local ruling elite under the tribal leader Midovg (Mindaugas) were able to fend off the threat of Crusade, partly by converting to Christianity, and partly through their own military skills. Lithuania flourished under a succession of able princes, from Gediminas, who conquered all of Byelorussia and half of the Ukraine, taking Kiev in 1321, to Olgerd, who pushed the Lithuanian Empire to the shores of the Black Sea. His son, the Grand Duke Yagailo (Jagiello), became King Wladislaw V of Poland, had his Lithuanian subjects baptised en masse into Catholicism, and the fate of the two countries was entwined. The dismemberment of Poland in the eighteenth century between Russia, Prussia and Austria, saw most of Lithuania carved off as Russia's portion.

It was not so much the Revolutions of 1917 which provided the opportunity of independence from Russia, as the use the Kaiser's German Army made of them. The collapse of the Russian armies allowed the German troops to flood through the Baltic provinces, and for the whole of 1918 they were under German occupation. Germany's defeat in November 1918 left the Baltic States vulnerable, and Britain sent warships, military advisors and officers to support their independence from Soviet Russia. (Among them was the later Second World War Field Marshal, Viscount Alexander.)

The three Baltic Republics had known barely two decades of independence before they were absorbed into the Soviet Union in 1940, under the secret codicils of the Non-Aggression Pact which Stalin and Adolf Hitler signed in August 1939. Under its terms, Nazi Germany and the USSR were each to swallow half of Poland, and Stalin was to be given a free hand in the Baltic States. There is, understandably, a great deal of nostalgia about this brief period of independence in the 1920s and 1930s. In fact, it was no golden age. Massive unemployment led to large-scale emigration to the USA, and by the late 1930s, all three republics were being run by semi-fascist, authoritarian and nationalist regimes. The small urban working class therefore had some slight reason to look to the Soviet Union with hope, and Stalin exploited this unmercifully when his armies rolled over the republics in 1940. Some workers' demonstrations, strikes, unrest and government crises were the pretext for later Soviet historians to claim that the republics had been 'liberated' by the Soviet Union at the request of the people. In fact, it was an act of conquest, and in the brief year of Soviet rule before Hitler's armies invaded, the members of the officer corps, the commercial and political establishment and the more prosperous farmers were arrested, deported, and in many cases killed. And after 1944, when the advancing Soviet armies reconquered the Baltic States from the Germans, Stalin's purge intensified, with tens of thousands deported in massive sweeps. Anyone with enough social authority to act as a potential political leader was simply liquidated. The nations were beheaded.

Recent unrest   The first real sign of the seriousness of the now surging hope for national independence came in March 1988, when Party and Latvian government members joined in a public meeting to commemorate one of the great Stalin deportations. This was the first act of nationalist defiance of Moscow which had the public backing of the men Moscow counted on to rule the Baltic colonies. I was there when it happened, and it would be impossible to exaggerate the flood of emotion in the crowd that gathered at the cemetery and shrine where the nation was recovering its soul. By the winter of 1988, Estonia was openly defying the authority of Moscow, passing resolutions in the republican parliament that said Moscow's laws only had authority in Estonia if they were endorsed by the Estonian parliament. Latvia and Lithuania played their hand more cautiously, winning a great deal of economic autonomy in return for soft-pedalling the demands for political independence. They want the right to run their own trade with foreign countries, rather than go through the Moscow Foreign Trade Ministry, which keeps the lion's share of hard currency, and the right to issue their own currency, a hard rouble that would be convertible with the Swedish crown and Finnish mark, just across the Baltic Sea. They want the right to stop Russian immigration, and reverse the trends towards cultural Sovietisation. They hope for a status rather like that of Hong Kong, attached to the Communist giant, trading with it, but not quite dominated by it.

This is one of the most dangerous of the results of Mikhail Gorbachev's promises of reform. It is possible, but unlikely, that Gorbachev and his team of reformers are content to watch the dismantlement of the new Russian Empire which Stalin conquered. He may be ready to see eastern Europe slip into the economic, and then the political, embrace of western Europe. But to give up Soviet power in the Baltic States is to see the erosion of the homeland, and would carry alarming implications for the traditionally Muslim republics in the USSR's Deep South. It would also worry the armed forces. The prospect of a stern new assertion of Soviet power, by Gorbachev or by a tougher-minded successor, cannot be ruled out. So any western tourist heading for the Baltic States in the foreseeable future should be aware of these political undercurrents. There is an exhilaration among the local people, and a palpable sense of unease among the large numbers of Russian immigrants whose presence has been a major cause of the renewed national sentiment. Some shops will refuse to speak Russian, and ignore Russian customers, but will become instantly and effusively co-operative when it is clear you are from the west. On 22 August, date of the signing of the Hitler–Stalin Pact, you can expect street demonstrations, which sometimes turn ugly. Do not change the date of your holiday on this account; just be aware that you are entering a highly delicate political situation.

Intourist tour

It is now possible to take a week-long Intourist coach tour from Minsk, via Vilnius in Lithuania, to Riga in Latvia. The road from Minsk to Vilnius follows the old Tsarist postal route past the ruined castle of Medininkai, but the real advantage of this tour is the unusual opportunity to see something of the interior of Lithuania and Latvia. As well as the two days in Vilnius and Riga for sightseeing, it includes an overnight stop in the Lithuanian provincial centre of Panevezys, which has a famous theatre, although few historic buildings of note. But the route to Riga goes past the restored Rundale Palace at Bauska, designed by Rastrelli.

Note: If your holiday will be in mid-summer, check with Intourist for the date of the Song Festival, and whether it is being held in Estonia, Latvia or Lithuania. It is an occasion not to be missed.

Latvia

Getting there

Until the roads are opened to foreigners, the old Hanseatic port of Riga may be reached by train, from Moscow, Tallinn or Leningrad; or by air; or by ferry, from Sweden, Finland and Leningrad. I have a fondness for sleeping carriages on overnight trains, which also save on a night's hotel bills, and for the moment rail is probably the best way to tour the Baltic cities. The foreign visitor is more restricted in Latvia than in almost any other Soviet republic. Only Riga and its coast, and two short excursions into the interior, are open to the western tourist. This is unfortunate, because the Valley of the River Daugava and the central heights around the town of Ergli are most picturesque, leading into the heartland of a country which contains 770 rivers and over 3,000 lakes.

Riga

The city was officially founded in 1201, by Bishop Albert of the Teutonic Knights. It quickly became one of the most prosperous of the Hanseatic League's Baltic ports, largely because of the easy access to the hinterland provided by the River Daugava. Occupied by the Poles and the Swedes before being absorbed into Peter the Great's Russia in 1720, it prospered steadily. In the nineteenth century, it was the second port for the export of grain after Odessa, and it developed a powerful industrial capacity. The first Russian car, the first Russian tank and the first Russian aircraft engine were all developed and built in Riga. With a population of almost 900,000, it is now one of the country's main industrial centres, with a leading role in high quality consumer goods like stereos and TVs, and in high-tech sectors of computing and precision machine tools. One US Pentagon study suggests that the Soviet armed forces so depend on the factories and design shops of Riga and the other Baltic cities that their missile guidance systems and their tank laser-sights would never work without them. Maybe; but watch the Russian tourist leave Riga's airport and train station laden down with tape recorders, radios and stereos, and you instantly appreciate the importance and rarity value of the high quality consumer goods of the Baltic States.

What to see The old town of Riga is a pleasure to stroll through. Starting from the main Intourist hotel, Latvia, at the junction of Kirov and Lenin Streets, take **Lenin Street** in the direction of the park. This takes you past a statue of Lenin on your left, and a nineteenth-century Russian Orthodox church on your right, which is now a planetarium and lecture hall, occasionally used for small graphics exhibitions. At the far end of the park on your right is the Latvian Art Gallery (see p. 225).

Continue down Lenin Street towards the tall monolith in the centre of the road. This is the 1935 **Statue of Freedom**, which is these days the regular site for nationalist demonstrations. **Rainis Boulevard**, the main street of bourgeois Latvia, runs to the left and right. To the right, one after the other, were the great embassies of Britain, France and Germany in the days of the independent Latvia in the 1920s and 1930s. Those were the days when Riga was the great listening post upon the Soviet Union, full of diplomats, exiles, western journalists and spies, the intrigue and the gossip making for a potent brew. The old embassies, now rather prosaic buildings like the State Procurator's Office, face the **Basteikalns Park**, with the city canal landscaped to look like a river curving through it. Beyond the park, and the Padomiyu Boulevard, begins the old town. At the junction of Lenin Street and Padomiyu Boulevard, on the right hand corner, is the best bookshop in town, and the **Café Luna**. To your right, the imposing neo-classical pile is the excellent **Opera and Ballet Theatre**. Continue down Lenin Street, and on your right, at no. 11, is the **Conservatory Concert Hall**, and on your left, at no. 24, the **Allegro Café**, with a youthful clientele, and occasional jazz concerts.

Old city Beside the drama theatre on your right is an archway leading to the maze of streets that make up the old city. Now being restored, with the houses to be made into inns and guesthouses for foreign tourists, they were in the early and mid-1980s filled with the garrets and art studios of young artists. Do not be afraid of getting lost. The old town is small enough, and at every corner you will see the great spire of the Dom, St Peter's Cathedral. The easiest way to reach the cathedral is to continue down Lenin Street to the junction with Skarnu Street and to your left is the first street of the old town to be restored. This is what you see in the tourist brochures, a row of medieval town houses, a jumble of styles and centuries, with echoes of Queen Anne English alongside sixteenth-century Amsterdam.

St Peter's Cathedral To your right, Skarnu Street leads you into the Dom Square, dominated by the splendid church. St Peter's was founded in 1211, but has been much rebuilt down the years. The central hall of the church was raised in the sixteenth century, and the Gothic lateral apsidioles added, just in time for the faith to change from Catholic to Lutheran Protestant. The 115-m timber tower was destroyed by lightning in 1721, rebuilt and destroyed again in the Second World War, and now rebuilt yet again. The church contains one of the great organs of Europe, with 6,668 pipes, and you should not miss the opportunity to attend an organ concert. Made into a music and occasional concert hall under the Soviet regime, one of the great symbols of liberalisation under Gorbachev came in the summer of 1988, when a religious service was held here for the first time since 1944.

Dom Square   The square is now officially known as the Square of the 17 June, the date Latvia is supposed to have volunteered to join the Soviet Union. The occasion used to be marked by official celebrations and parades. These days, there are protest demonstrations at the Statue of Freedom. On the southern corner of the square, close by the church, is the popular **Kresli 13 Café**, and if the queue is too long, stroll down the adjacent Tirgonu Street, to the **Zilais Putns Café**.

Most of the buildings around the square date from the nineteenth century, but at the northern corner, where Mars-pils Street enters it, is a row of fifteenth-century town houses, known as the **Three Brothers**. Follow this street down to the rear of what looks like a red brick Victorian English church. This was indeed the church used by the English, testimony to the importance of the English trade. In the days of Lord Nelson, most of the masts for the Royal Navy's ships came from the Baltic, and many of them through Riga. The building is now used as an occasional exhibition and concert hall by the youth section of the Latvian Union of Artists; an avant-garde fashion show, featuring post-punk wedding dresses and electronic music was featured here during the 1988 Riga Arts Festival. The front of the church looks on to the River Daugava, and from here you can follow two routes:

Route One   Turn right along the Daugava Embankment and you come to the old **Riga Castle**, begun in 1330, but much altered since. In the inter-war years of independence, this became the Presidential Palace. It now houses the **Museums of History and Literature**, and there is a pleasant sculpture garden. The History Museum is interesting on medieval Riga. Both open from 10 a.m. to 6 p.m., closed on Mondays. Behind the Palace is Pioneers' Square, and Tornya Street, which leads off to the east, passes the nineteenth-century arsenal complex, with the church of **St James** to the rear. It began in the thirteenth century as Romanesque, and was completed in the Gothic style. Crossing Komsomol Street, but staying on Tornya Street, you will pass the **Swedish Gates**, part of the old city wall, leading into a medieval trade and warehouse complex. At the end of the street is the **Gunpowder Tower**, the best preserved remnant of the seventeenth-century city wall. Straight ahead is the Basteikalns Park, and turning right alongside the park will bring you back to the Statue of Freedom.

Route Two

Turning left along the Daugava Embankment, you stroll on Komsomol Embankment to the **October Bridge**. On your left is an open square and the monument to the Latvian Red Riflemen, among the most loyal troops of the Revolution. Since the bulk of the Latvian people were not passionate supporters of the 1917 Revolution, and are less than devoted to the Soviet system it eventually brought, the Party's cultural commissars thought it advisable to play up the historical role of those Latvians who did support the Revolution. The Red Riflemen are therefore portrayed as epic heroes, and behind their monument is a rather interesting **Museum** in their honour. Open daily from 10 a.m. to 6 p.m., closed on Tuesdays. Next to the square is the **Church of St Jura** (St George), the oldest stone building in the city. It was originally the chapel of the Order of Knights of the Sword, attached to their castle. And just off the square, stretching back to Skarnu Street, is the **Church of St Jan** (St John), founded in the mid-thirteenth century as the chapel of the Dominican monastery. The main building dates from the fifteenth to sixteenth centuries, and the altar is eighteenth-century Baroque.

Back at Red Riflemen Square, continue south along Komsomol Embankment. On the left, in the narrow riverside park, is a monument to the demonstrators of 1905 who were shot down on this site. You then come to a great square that opens to the left, with the railway bridge crossing the river to your left, and the Pilsetas Canal entering the River Daugava just beyond. Turn left up **January 13 Street**, a wide and tree-lined boulevard that leads to the railway station. On the corner of Padomiyu Boulevard is the **Metropole Hotel** and restaurant. Continue along Padomiyu Boulevard, past the Opera Theatre, and you come to the newly restored **Riga Hotel**, now also available to foreign visitors through Intourist. The Statue of Freedom is just to the rear of the hotel.

Museums

The Latvian Art Gallery, 10a Gorky Street, in a late nineteenth-century building. Open daily from 10 a.m. to 6 p.m., closed on Tuesdays. This should not be missed, because Latvia is currently going through a golden age of women's painting. Look in particular for the works of Maya Tabaka, including her stunning self-portrait, Aija Zarinas, Lilija Dinere and, above all, Djemma Skulme. Leader of the Latvian Artists' Union and an important political figure in the campaign for more autonomy, Djemma Skulme is an artist of great power. She has also been the main force behind the organisation of the *Makslas Dienas*, the Riga 'days of art' every April. It is now the best art festival in the USSR, and the special four-day excursion which Intourist organises each year is strongly recommended.

The Open Air Ethnography Museum. In a pine forest on the shores of Lake Jugla. Open daily from 10 a.m. to 6 p.m., 3 May to 30

September, closed on Tuesdays. This is the rather pompous title for the museum of traditional and rural Latvian life. Peasant huts, farm buildings, inns, blacksmiths' forges, potteries and churches have been reassembled here from villages all over Latvia, and furnished in period style. In summer, folk dance and song concerts are held in traditional costume.

Where to stay   **Hotel Latvia**, run by Intourist, 55 Kirov Street (tel. 280-547); **Hotel Riga**, newly restored, 22 Padomiyu Boulevard (tel. 221-622).

Where to eat   The hotels above have reasonable restaurants, and the **Latvia Hotel** has an express bar, just across the access road from the hotel entrance, which serves snacks throughout the day. **Kaukazs**, 8 Merkela Street, in a side street opposite the railway station, serves Georgian food, with good *shashliks*. **Scecina**, 260 Maskavas Street, some 3 km up-river from the city centre, specialises in Polish food. **Daugava**, 24 Kugu Street, on the quayside just across the river from the old town. The food is standard Soviet fare, but this is the best view in Riga. In Andeyn Street is the excellent new **Palette** café, opened for members of the Artists' Union and the first post-modernist café decor in the Soviet Union.

Excursions from Riga   Just 8 km to the west of Riga, the holiday resort of Jurmala runs through the woods along the coast, and along the banks of the River Lielupe. There are local train and bus services from Riga.

Jurmala   One of the most popular summer holiday resorts in the Soviet Union, Jurmala is filled with holiday hostels and rest homes run by trade unions, and small dachas. But the 32 km of golden sands give plenty of room, and from mid-June the sea is warm enough for bathing. The organisers of the Jurmala cultural programme are among the most imaginative in the country. They pioneered the disco-dancing competition for one end of the market, while running the Soviet ballroom dancing contests for a rather different clientele. The town itself is delightful, with turn-of-the-century wooden buildings and pedestrian areas. The most modern building is the multi-storey **Jurmala Hotel**, which can be booked through Intourist although it is not listed in the brochures. The hotel boasts one of the best cocktail bars in the Soviet Union, and even produces decent hamburgers. It would be possible to use the Jurmala Hotel as a base for visiting Riga, except for the possible difficulty in getting to and from the city in the absence of Intourist car hire facilities, although the hotel can book taxis, which all cost 5–8 roubles, and there are the trains and buses.

The Salaspils Memorial   Just 16 km from Riga, the memorial may only be visited with Intourist. The site of a Nazi concentration camp where over 100,000 people were exterminated, mainly Jewish people from the Ukraine, Byelorussia and the Baltic States. There are memorial statues in the shape of tall, gaunt stone figures, and the place reeks of evil and morbidity. It is a moving experience to visit Salaspils, but a deeply depressing one, the more so when you think how many Latvians were marched off to prison and labour camps in the Soviet Gulag.

Sigulda

Some 48 km north-east from Riga. The heart of the Gauja National Park, where you can visit the thirteenth-century ruins of the **Sigulda** and the **Turaida Castles** on the banks of the very pretty River Gauja. The Sigulda Castle began as a forward bastion, the first thrown up by the Teutonic Knights as they pushed out from Riga. But it was rebuilt several times after many sieges, before assuming its odd double shape of two castles, separated by a 15-m deep moat. It changed hands frequently between Knights, Poles, Swedes and Russians. The **Gutmania Ala cave** is also worth seeing. But the highlight of the trip should be a visit to the **Senite Restaurant**, which serves excellent Latvian food, from country beer to locally hand-made sausages, smoked chicken, and roast boar.

Lithuania

The Lithuanians have good reason to be a proud people. Still the largest of the three Baltic Republics, their medieval Empire once rivalled that of Russia. And whereas Estonia and Latvia fell quickly under the iron hands of the Knights of the Sword, Lithuania fought off the feudal invasions to establish its own national sovereignty. The Lithuanians' university made the country one of the earliest centres of learning in eastern Europe; and, like the Russians, they can claim two capital cities. The main city of Vilnius, the centre of the Lithuanian court since the fourteenth century and seat of the university, is the true capital. But in Lithuania's twenty years of independence before 1940, Vilnius was in the hands of the Poles, and the capital was established in the second city of Kaunas.

With a population of 3.5 million, of whom only 75 per cent are native Lithuanians, it remains one of the smallest of the Soviet republics and yet like Estonia and Latvia plays a much larger role in scientific research and high-tech industrial manufacturing than its small numbers would suggest.

Vilnius
History

The archaeologists have traced back human habitation at this confluence of the Rivers Neris and Vilnia over 2,000 years. But the official date of the city's foundation is 1323, when the Grand Duke Gediminas transferred the seat of his power from Trakai Castle. Constant raids and attacks by the Teutonic Knights inhibited development, but their defeat in 1410 allowed the city to prosper as a trading centre. A manufacturing base was quickly established, including a mint, and glass, paper and weapons workshops. By the end of the fifteenth century, Vilnius had a 2-km city wall against Tartar attacks, a water pipeline and a sewerage system. Early in the sixteenth century, it began printing its first books in Lithuanian, and its importance as a cultural centre extended well beyond its own borders; in 1525 it published the first books in the White Russian (Byelorussian) language.

In 1579, after the Poles formally annexed the Lithuanian Grand Duchy, the Jesuits founded the academy which was to become the university. The final partition of Poland in 1795 brought Lithuania under the Russian Tsars, and any sign of nationalism was sternly repressed. After the Polish and Lithuanian risings of 1830–1, the university was closed by the Russians, and not reopened until 1919. After the next rising in 1863, the Lithuanian language was virtually banned, schools were closed and publishing forbidden. By the beginning of the twentieth century, with a population of over 150,000, the city was a major industrial centre.

Vilnius is a friendly and welcoming city, thanks partly to a large student population and a cosmopolitan tradition, whose people prides itself on speaking several foreign languages. There are few places in the Soviet Union where you will find it easier to strike up local acquaintances. This process is helped by the plentiful cafés and beer bars in the old town.

The old town of Vilnius is now undergoing a lengthy, slow and highly ambitious restoration programme. But enough work has already been done to make this one of the most rewarding cities in the Soviet Union. Like the rest of the Baltic Republics, living standards are several notches higher than in the Russian republics, but the quality of life is also better. There is more in the shops, the restaurants and cafés are concerned about service and quality, the bars and public lavatories are clean, and there is an atmosphere of civility on the streets that is rooted in civic and national pride.

What to see The centre of the old town is the fourteenth-century octagonal brick fortress built by Gediminas upon Castle Hill. Its tower has been restored, and now houses an interesting **Historical Museum**, with a fine collection of medieval arms and armour. Open daily from 10 a.m. to 6 p.m., closed on Tuesdays. The view of the city from the castle's observation platform is excellent, surpassed only by the view from the top-floor restaurant of Intourist's Lietuva Hotel, where you will almost certainly be staying.

The hill dominates **Gediminas Square**, the park-like heart of the city, and the start of Intourist's sight-seeing tours. The eighteenth-century classical building, the former cathedral, is now the art gallery. It was designed by the gifted Lithuanian architect, Laurinas Stuoka-Gucavicius, who also designed the city's neo-classical town hall. Organ recitals are given in the picture gallery, every Sunday evening from 1 October to 1 May, and on Wednesday evenings in the summer months, usually at 7 p.m. The handsome bell-tower now houses the city's tourist office.

The astonishing red-brick Gothic building is the early sixteenth-century **St Anne's Church**. The experts have counted that thirty-three different shapes of brick were used to give this building its look of gossamer and spun sugar. The doors are also very fine, and look for the tiny faces worked into the knockers. The church and its associated Benedictine monastery, now the **Fine Arts Institute**, are the striking buildings of this eastern side of the old town.

The Old Town

From Tiesos Street, take the narrow **Piles Street** to the wooden balconied house where the Polish poet Adam Mickiewicz lived in the early nineteenth century. This brings you into the heart of the old town of Vilnius, mostly now a pedestrian precinct. The old buildings and many of the old shops have been restored, and several of the streets paved again with brick in the traditional way. Look out for the painted shutters in **Stikliu Street** and its handicraft shops, and the happy streetscape jumble of architectural and national styles on **Gira Street**. This knot of old lanes is less complex than it seems and will eventually lead you into the old town's main thoroughfare, **Gorky Street**, which houses many of the city's monuments. The fifteenth-century Gothic **Church of St John** was later rebuilt in Baroque style and the interior shows how magnificently they could blend together. Its 60-m bell-tower is one of the city landmarks. Gorky Street also contains the old Town Hall (now an art gallery), the rather ugly early twentieth-century Philharmonic concert hall where Soviet power was first proclaimed in Lithuania, and a number of sixteenth-century dwellings, including the excellent **Medininkai Restaurant**, which specialises in Lithuanian food.

At the top of the hill, the street is closed by the Ashros Gates, above which sits a late Renaissance church, the **Chapel of the Gate**, one of its rooms covered in votive offerings – silver hearts, silver legs that were restored miraculously to life, and even an army officer's silver epaulettes, saying thank you for the promotion. The room is normally filled with devout Lithuanians, who are much offended that their own splendid Church of St Casimir has for so long been turned into a Museum of Atheism. Closely linked to Poland by language and geography, the political phenomenon of Solidarity had a powerful impact upon Lithuania, where many Poles still live, and where the Catholic religion is also of great importance. Part of the reassertion of Baltic rights in 1988 was the decision to start holding religious services again in St Casimir's, and other former churches. One church which was never requisitioned for state or Party purposes was the seventeenth-century Baroque masterpiece in the Antacalnic district, **St Peter and Paul**. To go inside is like being transported into the heart of a perfectly-iced wedding cake, all white and ornate, a stucco to end all stuccoes. It contains over 2,000 sculptures in plaster, and when the sun shines through the window, the effect is quite dazzling.

University

Just off Gorky Street is the university, now over 400 years old, and its buildings a well-restored national monument. The thirteen linked courtyards of the university embody the region's architectural history since the late sixteenth century. The oldest is the Observatory courtyard, dominated by the twin-pillared tall building, and the largest is the Philological Faculty, and is named after the poet Mathias Sarbievus. The much restored east wing houses the centre for Lithuanian studies, which has played an extremely important although discreet part in the revival of national sentiment in the 1980s.

Where to stay and eat

Hotel Lietuva, the main Intourist hotel, 20 Ukmerges Street (tel. 393-486). A modern multi-storey building.

The best restaurants are all to be found in the old town, in restored basements or the ground floors of old buildings, and specialise in traditional Lithuanian food of pork and game. In summer, when tourist traffic can be intense, it is best to book ahead through Intourist: The **Medininkai**, Gorky Street; The **Trakkai**, Gira Street; **Senasys Rusis**, Stikliu Street; **Bociai**, Gira Street.

Excursions from Vilnius

Trakai Castle

Some 24 km from Vilnius. Open daily from 10 a.m. to 7 p.m.

The island castle of Trakai was the seat of the medieval Duchy of Lithuania. The town of Trakai lies on a narrow peninsula, but the red brick castle itself stands on an island in the middle of Lake Galve, reached only by a narrow causeway. Once on the island, there was still a 10-m wide moat between the outer defences and the Ducal Palace. Often attacked by the Teutonic Knights, Trakai was never captured. Once inside the courtyard, you are at the bottom of a deep well in the heart of the 48-m keep. It is a most impressive building. Built in the fourteenth century, the castle was ruined in the Polish and Swedish wars of the seventeenth century. But even thereafter, it was the meeting centre for the local nobility, and a prison. It has now been thoroughly restored, and houses an excellent museum of the history of the castle and of the medieval Duchy. Not only the main defensive fortress of the Duchy, it was also the palace, where ambassadors from Renaissance Europe were formally received.

Where to eat

A hotel, called the **Galve**, has now been built in the town, but is not normally open to tourists, although it does provide snack meals. You are much better advised to go to the **Kibinine Café** on Melnikaite Street, where you can taste the hot mutton pasties which are the specialities of the Karaite people. Brought from the Crimea as personal servants and bodyguard to the Grand Dukes, the Karaite had the secret of making the most excellent meat pies, using a pastry which does not go soggy. Be careful when you bite into the pie, and hold it carefully upright, or about half a pint of red-hot mutton fat and gravy will spill all over you.

Kaunas

This second city of Lithuania is worth a lengthy visit, even though more than half of it was destroyed in the Second World War. Some 96 km west of Vilnius, Kaunas was founded in 1280 as a fortified settlement at the junction of the Rivers Nemen and Nerisa. The ruins of the castle may still be seen. Kaunas remained a relatively small town until 1920, when the seizure of Vilnius by the Poles made Kaunas into the national capital.

The heart of the old town is the sixteenth-century **Town Hall Square**, which has been carefully restored as a tourist precinct, with apothecary shops, cafés, restaurants and souvenir shops. The town hall itself is now the wedding palace. Just across the square is the white seventeenth-century Baroque **Jesuit Church**. Towards the river, the tall brick spire rises from the fifteenth-century Gothic **Vytautas Church**. The river embankment is itself a delightful stroll.

The second rewarding area of Kaunas is the **Laisves Avenue**, a 1.5-km long pedestrian precinct lined with trees and fountains which holds two-thirds of the cafés and restaurants, all of the city's five theatres and most of its thirteen cinemas. It also contains the Merkrijus department store, so modern and well-stocked (by Soviet standards) that when filming spy thrillers, Soviet movie directors would always film western urban sequences here, as the nearest they could get to the fleshpots of capitalism.

Jewish Memorial

Kaunas was badly hit during the war, and over 100,000 people died in Vilijampole Jewish ghetto, and in the death camps at the two prison complexes called the 9th and 6th Forts, just outside the city, where a very powerful memorial may be seen.

Where to eat

The **Ugne Café** and bar, and the **Gildija Restaurant** are both to be found in the old town square, and can be recommended as the best in the city.

Estonia

The northernmost and smallest of the Baltic Republics, part of its territory lies on several islands. Native Estonians make up two-thirds of the republic's population, accounting for the vast bulk of the rural population, and of the coastal fishing communities. But in the capital of Tallinn, almost half the population is composed of Russian immigrants, or 'colonists' as Estonian nationalists dub them. The Estonians have one of the lowest birth rates in the Soviet Union, well below replacement levels, and the nationalists blame the depressive effect of the Soviet occupation for this 'voluntary genocide'. Certainly, Russian immigration is unpopular – few Russians become fluent in Estonian and there is little intermarriage.

Tallinn
History

The first that we know of Tallinn comes in the gazetteer of the twelfth-century Arabian geographer Idris, who called the settlement Qaluwany. When the Danes conquered the place in 1219, they called it Reval, the name by which it was known until the twentieth century. The name Tallinn comes from the old Estonian phrase for 'Danish fortress'. The port flourished as a trading centre between Northern Europe and Novgorod and Pskov, the Russian towns of the interior. In 1285, the city joined the Hanseatic League, the north European trading confederation which dominated the commerce of the Baltic and the North Seas. Tallinn exported furs, leather, flax and seal fat, and imported wool and salt. In 1346, the King of Denmark sold the city to the Teutonic Knights, and a year later they sold it again, at a profit, to the Knights of the Sword. The town developed around two centres. The upper town, in the heart of the castle, was the preserve of the bishop, the Knights and the political power. The lower town was run by and for the commerical power, the tradesmen and merchants, who steadily assumed greater political authority. Tallinn prospered until the Swedish conquest of 1561, which brought heavy taxation with much of the trading profits taken over by Swedish rivals. Peter the Great's conquest in 1710 was followed by an outbreak of the plague, which killed over 5,000 people in a city that tax records showed to have a population of less than 10,000. Tallinn was later outstripped by Riga, which enjoyed better river communications into the Russian interior. But with the coming of the railway in the nineteenth century, Tallinn began to boom again, and by 1914, the population was 150,000.

What to see   Today, Tallinn is one of the best preserved of the old North European Hanseatic towns. It is one of the few Soviet cities where you can be woken by church bells, and stroll through a delightful old town following the smell of fresh pastries and real coffee until you reach a charming café. The best place to begin your strolling tour of the town is at the incongruously tall, modern **Viru Hotel**, which is run by Intourist, and where you will most probably stay. Turn left out of the hotel, and across the square lies the **Viru Gate**, two medieval towers of grey stone topped with cones of red brick tiles. Proceed along Viru Street, and after less than 90 m it brings you to **Raekoja Square**, dominated by the splendid fourteenth-century **Town Hall**. The square has been carefully restored, and it takes little imagination to think that you might be in any German or Swedish medieval town, which helps to explain why the Estonians reject the idea of Soviet or Russian nationality and perceive themselves as Europeans. On top of the town hall spire (a seventeenth-century Baroque addition) is Old Tom (Vana Toomas), a windvane that has been atop the town hall since 1530. On the ground floor is a small exhibition of historic Tallinn costumes, and the Magistrates' Hall on the first floor, formerly used as a court-room, contains a stunning 15-m frieze of hunting scenes carved from wood. The area in front of the town hall was used for public executions; the last major batch being seventy-two members of a peasants' uprising in 1806.

Lower town   To tour the lower town, walk towards the far right-hand corner of the square as you leave the town hall, to the old Apothecary's Shop. It dates from 1422, and for much of the time since, was run by the Burchard family, originally from Hungary. Just beyond is an archway into **White Bread Passage** (Saiai Kaik). Only 45 m long, it contains a jewellery shop, a small art salon, two flower shops, one tobacconist's, a café, and the **Church of the Holy Ghost**, which dates from 1306. The interior contains fine fifteenth-century wood carvings, and on the façade is the oldest clock in Estonia. You come out on to **Pikk Street**, where the wealthy merchants lived and the great trading and craft Guilds had their buildings. Opposite the Church of the Holy Ghost was the **House of the Great Guild** (1410), now the history museum. Only members of this Guild were eligible to sit on the Town Council, and almost all were German. House no. 26, with the striking reliefs on the façade, was for the Guild of Blackheads. These were the unmarried merchants, mainly foreigners, who formed their own regiment to defend the city, and whose patron was St Mauritius, the Moor – hence Blackheads. Next door was the house of St Olau's Guild, which brought together many of the town's craftsmen and artisans. The Guild system was the outward form of a very rigid class system. Members of St Olau's Guild, for example, did not have the right to wear velvet, taffeta or silk, nor to wear gold chains. Further down the street on the left is **St Olau's Church**, at 137 m the tallest in the Baltic and the wonder of the northern seas when it was built in the thirteenth century. After a devastating fire in 1820, it was rebuilt just a little shorter. Pikk Street ends with the **Fat Margaret Tower**, built in the early sixteenth century to withstand cannon fire – the walls are 4 m thick at the base. Beside Fat Margaret is the **Great Coast Gate**, with a part of the newer city beyond.

There are two ways to return to the Town Hall Square. The first is to turn right down Rennamae Tee, and then take the first street to the right, called Olevimagi, which instantly brings you to the Bremen Tower of the city wall. Take the right fork, down a street named Vene, which takes you along the rear of the city wall, and past the thirteenth- to sixteenth-century **Dominican Monastery**. It now contains a branch of the city museum, and open-air concerts and plays are given in the courtyard on summer weekends.

The other way to the Town Hall Square from Fat Margaret is to turn left, and then to take the first road to the left, Lai Street. This brings you past a number of medieval dwellings and warehouses, and then brings you to a fork. Go straight on along Rataskaevu Street, take the first right and you are back in the central square. But take the right fork, up the narrow uphill lane, and you are heading for the castle on the upper hill of one of the most famous streets of old Tallinn, called **Pikk Jalg**. Halfway up the hill there is a small café on the right, opposite a medieval, covered gateway on the left. This **Pikk** café does good cream cakes. Straight ahead is **Toompea Castle**, with its 45-m high keep, the 700-year-old tower called Tall Hermann (Pikk Hermann).

To the right is the **Dome Cathedral**, founded in the thirteenth century, but almost wholly rebuilt in the 1680s after a fire. The pink and white Baroque building is an eighteenth-century addition, now used as the government and ministerial offices of the Estonian Republic. The **Alexander Nevsky Russian Orthodox Cathedral** is an incongruous nineteenth-century addition. There are a series of vantage points around the castle walls from which you can view the old commercial town below, one of them just beside the **Toomkooli Bar**, where you can get a reviving drink before heading back down to the lower town. Toomkooli is the name of the street that runs between the castle and the Dome Cathedral. The bar is on the corner of the street that turns off to the left, towards the Observation Point.

To return to the Town Hall Square, go back down the Pikk Jalg hill, but turn right through the medieval gateway into Luhike Jalg, and the steps bring you out to the **Church of St Nicholas**, or Niguliste, as the Estonians say. Founded in the thirteenth century and rebuilt in the fifteenth century, what we now see is a very good job of late twentieth-century restoration of 1940s' war damage. The Romanesque northern gate is largely original. The crypt of the church was the merchants' security vault. In the western pediment was a hatch through which a pulley system raised and lowered valuables into the stronghold. The interior of the church has the stark impact that comes from emptiness, but some of the treasures were saved from war damage, including the startlingly morbid 'Dance of Death' by the Lubeck artist Bernt Notke.

From the church, turn left along Kulassepa to return to the Town Hall Square, or turn right towards the modern **Victory Square** (Voidu Valjak). This was the scene of the Soviet-inspired Workers' Demonstration of 21 June 1940, which led to the fall of the Estonian government and paved the way for the arrival of the Red Army. Recent attempts to commemorate this day by Party faithful have provoked counter-demonstrations from the Estonians. On the side of Victory Square nearest the old town is the main art exhibition hall, and opposite, the Russian drama theatre. The main street off to the left, called **Parnu Maantee**, leads down to the nineteenth-century Opera Theatre, past some of the main department stores. The first street to the left, Vana-Posti, contains the showrooms of Mode, the leading Estonian fashion designers.

Outskirts of Tallinn

Pirita

From your Tallinn hotel room you will probably see across the bay a strange pyramid shape. This is the remaining gable wall of the ruined fifteenth-century **Convent of St Brigitte**. Just across the road from the convent is the **Olympic Centre**, used for the 1980 games. Now the yacht and rowing club, it also leads to the long sandy beach of the **Gulf of Tallinn**. The best view of the old city is to be had from this beach. You may be disturbed by the sound of high-revving car engines. The car racing track, where the Soviet national championships are held, is just off the road at Pirita.

Kadriorg

The Kadriorg Park is a short tram ride from the city centre along the Narva Chaussee from the city centre.

Filled with boulders left by the last ice age, the park was laid out on the orders of Peter the Great. Topsoil was imported to cover the sandy earth, and seedlings of rare trees shipped here to create the park named after his wife Ekaterina (hence in Estonian, Kadriorg). On his visits to Tallinn before the great palace in the park was complete, Peter lived in a small cottage, which is now the **Museum**, decorated much as it was in his day. It includes a pair of boots said to have been made by Peter himself. Open daily from 9.30 a.m. to 7.30 p.m., closed on Tuesdays.

The **Kadriorg Palace** is now the Estonian Art Museum. Open daily from 11 a.m. to 6 p.m., closed on Tuesdays (tel. 426-240).

The finest room inside is the **White Hall**, a classic Baroque reception area. But the art collection is not distinguished. One section of the wall seems unfinished, where the bricks show through. These are the bricks said to have been laid by Peter himself.

Baltic Song
Festival

Kadriorg also contains the vast choral stage which is used for the national Song Festival, held every five years, and attended by up to 200,000 people. There are few events on earth quite like the Baltic Song Festivals. You will never hear quite so many voices singing as one. Each town and village sends its choir, dressed in distinctive and traditional costume. The Song Festival is an important national and political symbol. In the nineteenth century, under the strict Tsarist policy of Russification and suppression of Estonian culture, folk songs became a way to defy Moscow and to celebrate the traditions of the Estonian nation. It also was one of the activities which the Estonian gentry could share with the peasantry. The first Song Festival took place in Tartu in 1869, and the first in Tallinn's Kadriorg Park was in 1880. The huge shell-shaped stage, which was built in 1960, can hold 30,000 singers at a time, and the natural amphitheatre on the slopes of Lasnamagi can hold over 150,000. With the political and patriotic symbolism of the Song Festivals being given renewed significance, these are amazing events, and should not be missed if you are here in midsummer.

Rocca al
Mare

Some 10 km from the city, this was built by a rich nineteenth-century mayor of Tallinn who wanted to remember the Italian riviera on this cool northern cliff. It offers a stunning view of the enchanting skyline of Toompea Castle and the spires of the old churches. But the place should also be visited for the **Open-Air Museum**, where medieval and more recent rural buildings from all across Estonia have been reassembled. On summer weekends there are folk song and dance performances by people in traditional costumes.

Where to stay

Viru, 14 Viru Valjak (tel. 652-081); **Tallinn**, 27 Gagarinipuiestee (tel. 444-264); **Olympia**, 33 Kingissepa (tel. 602-436); **Kungla**, 23 Kreutzwaldi (tel. 421-460).

Camping

The **Kloostrimetsa** site lies on the coast road east of Tallinn, beyond Pirita, at Kloostrimetsa 56A (tel. 434-171). It has 200 plots, 100 available for your own tent, and 100 with a tent provided. Book early, and note that it has few facilities, just a bar and a grim restaurant. Open 1 June–15 September.

Where to eat

The best restaurant is at the old-fashioned-looking **Tallinn Hotel** (see p. 235), where they serve excellent game dishes and steak tartare.

Vana Toomas, 8 Raekoja Plats. This restaurant on the Town Hall Square specialises in Estonian dishes; **Gloria**, 2 Muurivahe, as much night club as restaurant, serves a Soviet version of an international menu.

Viru – the restaurants in the Viru Hotel are nothing special, except for the night club where you will see the sexiest and most complete strip tease in the Soviet Union. Or at least, you might see it if the drunken Finnish 'vodka tourists' permit.

Palace, Victory Square. Standard Soviet fare, but also serves decent fish dishes. Try the local Estonian Saku beer. Just up the steps from Voidu Valjak (Victory Square), and tucked into the old city walls is a basement bar where they serve Hoogwein, the delicious traditional mulled wine.

One of the best places to eat, if you can persuade Intourist of your interest, is the **Kirov Collective Fishery**, just along the Pirita road at Merivalja. One of the richest collective farms in the Soviet Union, it almost makes you wonder whether the system might not be made to work after all. The apartments and bungalows are classic Scandinavian in design, the sports facilities first rate, the package holidays include Bulgarian riviera and Mediterranean cruises, and the cafeteria gave me a very good meal indeed. The Kirov, like several of the rich Baltic collective farms, is enthusiastically seizing the opportunities of the Gorbachev reforms. It is planning its own bank, and building its own hotel and restaurant. Intourist in Moscow is fighting tooth and nail to maintain its monopoly of foreign tourism. Intourist in Tallinn, which suspects that competition might be a good thing and that local folk could do a better job of responding to the growing western demand for Soviet holidays, is watching developments with interest. The Intourist office in Tallinn is in the Viru Hotel, tel. 650-770.

Excursions from Tallinn

There are a limited number of permitted excursions from the region of Tallinn. To the south, on the road to Riga, are the sea bathing resort of **Parnu** and the inland forest resort and health spa of **Viliandi**.

Tartu

About 160 km to the south-east, on the road to Pskov.

This is an ancient university town, where a rock music festival is held each year in July. The first known building was the fifth-century fort of Estu, and in the eleventh century, Prince Yaroslav of Novgorod established a town here, which the local Est tribes quickly destroyed. The Danes and Teutonic Knights rebuilt and strengthened the fortress commanding the River Emajogi, and built the Church of Toomamagi Hill. In 1632, the first Academy was established here, which in 1803 became a full university. It has one of the great libraries of northern Europe, which thanks to Peter the Great's expedition and the North Sea and Baltic trades, has the finest collection of sixteenth- and seventeenth-century Dutch books outside Holland. The eighteenth-century **Town Hall**, and the neo-classic **University** buildings make it a pleasant town to visit.

Narva

This old fortress town, 195 km from Tallinn, is a reminder of how long the peoples of Russia and Estonia have been connected. The town was founded in the twelfth century, and the first fortress was built by the Danes. In the sixteenth and seventeenth centuries it changed hands repeatedly between the Russians and the Swedes. In the late seventeenth century, to force the Swedes back within their fortresses and deny them the exploitation of the land, Peter the Great sent in Tartar and Siberian troops like Bashkirs and Kalmuks to devastate the countryside – an early example of the scorched earth tactic. In 1700, when Peter's forces were besieging the town, Sweden's King Charles suddenly attacked their camp in winter and, although heavily outnumbered, inflicted a shattering defeat. Thousands of Russians drowned as a bridge across the river collapsed beneath them. Four years later, Peter was back, and this time Narva remained a Russian fortress until 1918.

What to see

In the nineteenth century Narva became the centre of a thriving textile industry, and the Krenholm mills, founded in 1852, were the largest in Europe, producing one-tenth of all Russia's cotton. Although the town was badly damaged during the Second World War, there are still a number of relics of the martial past. **Narva Castle** was begun in the thirteenth century and dates back to the Knights of the Sword. The tall **Herman Tower** was built in 1535, just before the Russians conquered the town for the first time. The seventeenth-century Baroque **Town Hall** has been much restored.

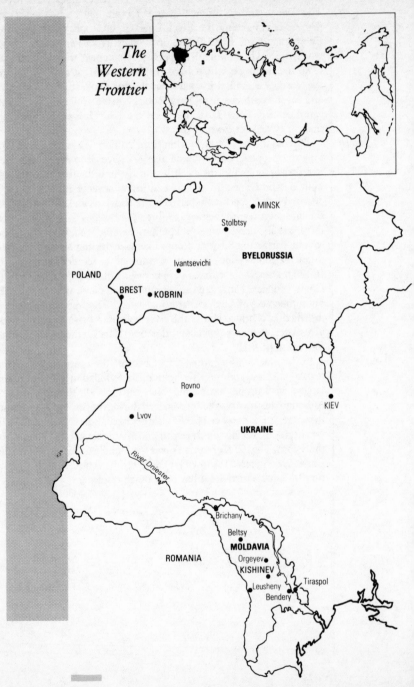

The
Western
Frontier

● MINSK

Stolbtsy

BYELORUSSIA

Ivantsevichi

POLAND

BREST ●KOBRIN

Rovno

KIEV

Lvov

UKRAINE

River Dniester

Brichany

Beltsy

MOLDAVIA

Orgeyev
KISHINEV

Tiraspol

ROMANIA

Leusheny

Bendery

The Western Frontier

Introduction

Much of Russia's tangled history with its western neighbours is rooted in the unavoidable fact that it has no natural frontier. Between the River Vistula, which runs through Warsaw, and the River Dniepr, which runs through Kiev, is a vast and flat border land of forest and the Pripyat marshes. At various times, this border land has been part of the Polish, the Lithuanian, the Swedish and the Russian empires. In this century, the frontier has shifted back and forth several times between the core territory of Poland around Warsaw and that of the Ukraine around Kiev. Indeed, for nearly twenty years after the 1917 Revolution, Kiev itself was so near the frontier that Kharkov, over 320 km to the east, was the official capital of Soviet Ukraine. These days the frontier has shifted far the other way, so that the old Polish city of Lvov is part of the Soviet Ukraine. And until Stalin's triumphant Army rolled the frontier westwards in 1945, the Soviet Black Sea port of Odessa was almost a border town. The absorption of Moldavia into the Soviet Union as a separate republic shifted the border some 320 km to the west, but brought yet another nationalist complication into the complex ethnic stew of the USSR. The different language groups of the peoples who live in this vast border zone between the Russian heartland and central Europe form distinct national cultures that are recognised in the Soviet republics of the Ukraine and Byelorussia.

Byelorussia

Route One of the Motorists' guides on p. 304 takes you through parts of Byelorussia.

Origins

Byelorussia (the name, literally, means White Russia) is the border land between Poland, Lithuania, the Ukraine and Russia itself and, in the traditions of such march lands, the precise boundaries are very hard to ascertain. There has been a distinct Byelorussian language since the sixteenth century, when it first began to be printed. But the first books were published in Vilnius, the capital of Lithuania. It could be argued that the Byelorussians were Russians who spent so long as members of the Lithuanian-Polish medieval state that they became something different from the mainstream Russians. Learned scholars and impassioned nationalists debate this matter of the origins of the Byelorussians bitterly, and only the expert or the foolhardy take sides. But we can say there are some 10 million Byelorussians in the Soviet Union, most of them living inside their republic, and for 80 per cent of them Byelorussian is the mother tongue. It is a language easily understood by Russian-speakers. Their capital is Minsk, and the other main towns are Brest, Gomel, Vitebsk and Mogilyev.

History

Historically, Byelorussia was part of the Lithuanian-Polish Empire until Poland was absorbed into Russia in 1795. In 1918, with the advance of the German armies against an enfeebled revolutionary Russia, Byelorussia was first occupied, then declared an independent republic. But in 1921 the Poles conquered and occupied western Byelorussia, and the eastern remnant rejoined the Soviet Union in 1922. With the Nazi–Soviet pact of 1939, the Soviet Union reclaimed the area Poland had seized, and rather more into the bargain. And in 1941, when the Nazis invaded the Soviet Union, some Byelorussians co-operated with the Germans in the hope of being allowed once again to establish an independent state. They were given enough encouragement to provide police forces and some army volunteers to serve under the Germans, but effectively they remained part of the Reich Kommissariat Ostland, the Slav colony of the Nazi Empire. Byelorussia was among the greatest victims of the war, its towns, villages and population being decimated as the armies rolled back and forth across the land.

About twice the size of Austria, Byelorussia is one of the most efficient of Soviet republics, with a higher than average industrial and agricultural production. About a third of the republic is covered by forest; it is a predominantly flat land, often marshy, and contains over 4,000 lakes. The forests are full of game, including wolves, bears, wild boar, elk and deer. The main natural resources are peat, used as a fuel, and potash. It also produces the widely exported Belorus tractor.

Minsk
History

The capital of Byelorussia, with 1.3 million inhabitants, Minsk was one of the great cities of Jewish culture. In the 1890s, the Jewish Bund was the leading socialist organisation in the region, and the first secret congress of the Social-Democratic Workers' Party was held here. In the 1930s, over 40 per cent of the population was Jewish but the Nazi occupation saw massive deportations to the death camps. There was a puppet Byelorussian regime under the Nazis, and since *glasnost*, books and articles have begun to appear that acknowledge how many of the local people in Byelorussia and the Ukraine were prepared to welcome

Hitler as a liberator. Indeed, there were Ukrainian and Byelorussian troops fighting for the Germans in Normandy when the Allies invaded in 1944, and a tiny proportion became concentration camp guards.

Khatyn

However, Nazi cruelties provoked a powerful partisan and guerrilla movement, attacking German lines of communication. The Nazi reaction was brutal. Just outside Minsk was the village of Khatyn, which was burned along with all its inhabitants by the Nazis. Now it is a deeply moving memorial, symbolic piles of stone where the village houses and walls used to be, its bells tolling day and night, and ashes from another 186 burned-out Byelorussian villages are also here.

What to see

Although it has now grown to be one of the major industrial centres in the country, Minsk itself was badly damaged by the Second World War. Only the seventeenth-century Catholic cathedral and an eighteenth-century tower remain of the old town. On the left of **Victory Square** is a single-storey building, now a museum, where that secret first congress of the Social-Democratic Workers' Party was held in 1898. A rebuilt city that embodies the assertive confidence of post-war town planning, with its huge squares and avenues, and industrial and housing estates, Minsk is softened by abundant parks and a large number of colleges and institutes. There are over 130,000 students in Minsk, and a lively cultural life. It is one of the leading regional centres for music. But the growing interest in the old Byelorussian language and culture is politically delicate. Moscow has traditionally firmly discouraged any interest in Byelorussian culture, which even threatened to become a political movement for separatism, most recently in the 1970s. But under *glasnost*, there are stirrings again.

Where to stay, and eat

You will be staying at one of the four hotels: **Yubileinaya Hotel** (run by Intourist), 19 Masherov Prospekt (tel. 298-024). **Minsk Hotel**, 11 Lenina Prospekt (tel. 292-363). **Planeta Hotel**, 31 Masherov Prospekt (tel. 238-416). **Minsky Motel**, Brest Highway, by the camp site (tel. 226-380). The camp site is the **Minsky**, Brest Highway (tel. 29-68-219).

Brest
History

Brest was founded in 1017, was invaded by the Mongols in 1241, and taken by Lithuania in 1319. Two centuries later it was Polish. From 1795 to 1917 it was Russian. Then until 1939 it was Polish again. The city not only dominates the crossing of the River Bug, but also the point where the River Mukhavets joins the Bug.

Brest Fortress

When Hitler's Wehrmacht launched their surprise attack on 22 June 1941, the Soviet armies reeled back, broken by the tactics of blitzkrieg. They kept on reeling until they stopped at Moscow. But at the Brest Fortress, the garrison of 7,000 men under General Pyotr Gavrilov held out for four weeks, even while the German artillery bombardment had caused fires so hot that the very steel was melting. Foreshadowing the tenacious defence of Stalingrad the following year, the heroic defence of Brest was the first sign that the great retreat of the Soviet Army did not mean that the country's resistance had finished. The fortress dates originally from the eighteenth century, but in 1971 the moving and informative museum complex was added, with the 90-m obelisk, shaped like a bayonet.

There is a petrol station in the city, but little else worth seeing.

Where to stay, and eat

The **Intourist Hotel**, 15 Ulitsa Moskva (tel. 510-73) is signposted as you drive into the city, and is on the same street as the museum.

Moldavia

Route Five of the Motorists' Guides on p. 321 takes you through parts of Moldavia.

History

Bordering on Romania, Moldavia has suffered the fate of most border countries. Fought over between Russians and Turks in the eighteenth century, it was the scene of bitter fighting again in the Second World War. In 1940 the Moldavian Soviet Socialist Republic was created by the merger of the former Moldavian ASSR with Bessarabia, ceded by Romania.

The Soviet Union insists that the Moldavians are a distinct national group, with a language and culture subtly different from that of the Romanians. Most western scholars disagree, and so do most Romanians and Moldavians, when they talk freely. The concept of Moldavia is a Russian fiction, designed to justify Russia's determination to seize Bessarabia. This is the standard western view of the matter, and certainly the Russian imposition of their Cyrillic script upon the Moldavian language cannot disguise the fact that it is indistinguishable from the Romanian tongue spoken just across the River Prut. All Romanians (and many Moldavians) will tell you that they are directly descended from the Roman legions who occupied their part of the world when it was known as Dacia, and that they speak a version of Latin to this day. There is something in this. One can converse with Moldavians, or at least get the gist across, in schoolboy Latin with a few French words. A great deal of goodwill and sign language are also required.

The Moldavians are a delightful people, generous and hospitable and with a pleasing sense of life's priorities, as most wine-growing folk tend to be. Moldavia has the highest population density of any Soviet republic, in spite of a tiny population of 3 million in a land roughly the size of Holland. Highly fertile black soil lowland, marshy except where drained by the River Dniester, is dotted with foothills and slopes for the vines, and some very pretty villages. The capital is Kishinev, and the other main towns are Tiraspol, Bendery and Beltsy.

The Moldavians have been slow to take advantage of the opportunities which are theoretically available in the Soviet Union.

The numbers of Moldavians receiving a university education, or becoming scientific workers, or even Party members, are disproportionately low, and since *glasnost* there have been growing rumbles of complaint about the numbers of Russian immigrants to the republic, and their alleged preferential treatment in the queues for urban housing. But there are limits to the yearnings for the reunification with the Romanian motherland; Romania's President Ceaucescu heads one of the most unpleasant regimes in Europe.

Kishinev
History

First mentioned in the fifteenth century, when it was founded around a monastery, Kishinev was in Turkish hands in the sixteenth century, and then sacked by the Tartars. But it revived in the eighteenth century, largely through the efforts of the Armenian merchants who settled here. In 1712, the town was ceded to the Good Friday Monastery by the *hospodar* of Moldavia, was burned down in 1739 as the Turks retreated from Bessarabia, as the province was known, and was wrecked again in the Russo-Turkish war of 1787-91. Most of the fine buildings date from the revival that came with the Russian occupation of the early nineteenth century, including the cathedral and triumphal arch, whose 13-tonne bell was cast from captured Turkish cannon. The poet Pushkin was exiled here from 1820-3, and it was here that he wrote *Prisoner in the Caucasus* and *The Gypsies*. But Kishinev remained a provincial backwater, even after the coming of the railway and in 1918 it was transferred to independent Romania. In 1939, the year before the Red Army marched in, the largest factory was a tobacco plant which employed 300 men. The most picturesque parts of Kishinev date from this period, when many of the houses were built from the local limestone, which encouraged decorative sculpture.

Kishinev today

Today's Kishinev is not an attractive city, having been rebuilt too hurriedly after the devastation of the Second World War, and with a great deal of the pompous 1950s-style Soviet architecture that was then thought fitting for the capital of a Soviet republic. Some of the blame should go to Leonid Brezhnev, who as First Secretary ran the new republic of Moldavia during Stalin's last years from 1950-2. Moldavia was an important springboard for Brezhnev's career and was where he gathered the group of aides and officials who were to share his rise to power.

Kishinev is now heavily industrialised and its population of almost 600,000 enjoys a higher than average standard of living. In summer, the gardens and parks are delightful – it is famous for its roses, and it lies in the heart of one of the prettiest regions of the USSR.

Where to stay, and eat

There is a small (non-Intourist) camp site with a café at the village of **Vadul-lui-Vode**, 33 km from Kishinev on the road to Goyanny. If driving, you will probably be put into the **Strugurash Motel**, run by Intourist, on the Kotovsky Chaussee (tel. 217-850). Most foreign tourists are assigned to the 16-storey **Intourist Hotel**, 4 Prospekt Lenina (tel. 529-083).

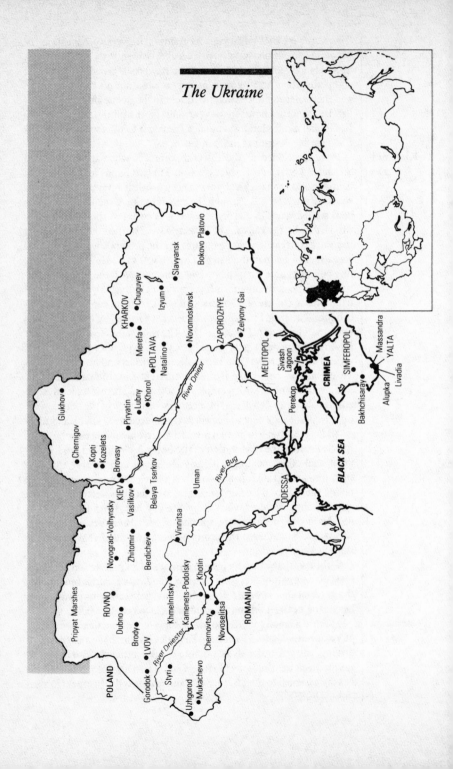

The Ukraine

The Ukraine

Routes Four, Five, Six and Seven of the Motorists' guides on pp. 316, 321, 326 and 332 take you through parts of the Ukraine.

Introduction

The third largest of the Soviet republics, after Russia itself and Kazakhstan, and one of the four original republics that formed the USSR in 1922, the Ukraine is a distinct nation of over 50 million people. It stretches some 1,300 km from east to west, from the Polish border to the Donets Valley, and nearly 800 km from the Pripyat marshes in the north to the Black Sea in the south, including the peninsula of the Crimea. It is the second largest republic in population and industrial might.

The name 'Ukraine' is a nineteenth-century invention; it means frontier, or more precisely, the Marches, in the sense that the word is used for the lands on the borders between England and Wales. Although the Russian and Ukrainian language shared a common alphabet and a common root in the years before the Mongol invasions, the long centuries of separation from the flourishing Russia around Moscow, and the Polish–Lithuanian dominance of Kiev, had produced two distinct cultures by the time they were reunited in the seventeenth century.

This could have been a source of enrichment for both, but the nineteenth-century Tsarist autocracy dreaded nationalism, and sought to suppress it through a programme of enforced Russification. Publications in Ukrainian were banned in 1876, while cultural nationalism was growing fast. The symbolic figure of the day was Taras Shevchenko (1814–61), the poet and father of Ukrainian letters, who was born and raised as a serf. The painter Bryullov auctioned off one of his paintings for 2,500 roubles to get the money to buy Shevchenko's freedom, but Shevchenko's revolutionary politics made him doubly dangerous; the Tsar ordered his arrest and exile in 1847.

The tensions between Russia and the Ukraine have never really subsided since. As the breadbasket of the nation, the Ukraine suffered terribly from the forced collectivisation of agriculture, and millions died of starvation in the 1930s. Like so many border lands, the Ukraine suffered the depredations of both neighbours. Barely had it begun to recover from Stalin than Hitler assaulted from the west. In the post-war years, any sign of Ukrainian nationalism was swiftly suppressed by Moscow, but the Ukrainian cultural and literary heritage was given some room to operate. As fellow Slavs, who can understand Russian, Ukrainian nationalism is not yet the disruptive kind of surge for independence which now grips the Baltic Republics. But the disaster at the Chernobyl nuclear power station in 1986, only 144 km north of Kiev, reminded many Ukrainians of how many decisions that affect their lives are taken in Moscow, with little regard for their interests. And as in most other parts of the country, *glasnost* and *perestroika* have given Ukrainians the opportunity to discuss and assess their grievances, while so far offering few clear remedies.

Kiev

Kiev is not only a great city, and the cradle of Russian culture, it is also the capital of the Ukraine, and the third largest city in the Soviet Union. It is built on the steep western banks that dominate the River Dniepr, a natural dwelling and fortification site that has known human habitation for at least 20,000 years. The name is thought to come from a Slavic Prince Kii, according to the legends of the 'Chronicle of Past Time', the great history of Kievan Rus that was written by the monk Nestor in the early twelfth century. Nestor was a member of the great Monastery of the Caves, the Kiev-Pecheri Lavra.

History
    The city and its great monuments have been repeatedly devastated. Almost nothing is left of the Kiev of the tenth to eleventh centuries built by the Princes Vladimir and Yaroslav, save for the stunning interior of the Church of St Sophia. The first Mongol attack of 1240 left little standing. In 1482 the Mongols came again and swept away what had been rebuilt. In 1718 the Monastery of the Caves suffered a dreadful fire, and lost its entire library. In 1941–3 the city suffered cruelly in the war, losing 200,000 dead, and Soviet historians claim 6,000 buildings were destroyed, from churches to museums to apartment blocks. Many of them were deliberately blown up by the Germans – including the twelfth-century Cathedral of the Assumption in the Lavra.

    Heroic efforts to rebuild and to restore what was lost cannot disguise the sad fact that Kiev is now overwhelmingly a drab, modern Soviet city. But the treasures that have been preserved are truly splendid. The climate of Kiev is also kind. Never as cold in winter, nor as humid in summer as Moscow, the city is filled with parks and trees, and summer stretches well into September. Its huge student population also makes Kiev a young city, and a friendly one.

Touring the city
    The required stroll in Kiev is along Kreshchatik, which the more fanciful locals will claim is their version of the Champs Élysées in

Kreshchatik Paris. Almost exactly 1.6 km long, it is a wide and grand thoroughfare, and has been the main street of Kiev since the 1830s, when the wealthy decamped from their traditional quarter because the army was building a vast barracks there. The Kreshchatik was a shallow valley through the plateau on which the city is built, and the street runs from south-west to north-east. To the north and west is the historic town, with the Church of St Sophia and the ruins of the Golden Gates. To the south and east is the Monastery of the Caves, with the River Dniepr beyond.

At the far north-east end of the Kreshchatik is **Komsomol Square**, formerly Stalin Square, where the main Intourist hotel, a gloomy Stalinoid building of the early 1950s called the Dniepr, is located. The road then curves around to that not-to-be-missed jewel of Baroque architecture, St Andrew's Church.

The Kreshchatik is intersected by three large squares. Going from north to south, the first is **October Revolution Square**, with the Moskva Hotel opposite the telecommunications building. This joins **Kalinin Square**, which used to be known as Goat Fen, and was a gate in Prince Yaroslav's city wall in the eleventh century. There was a famous Cossack charge into a crowd of unarmed anti-Tsarist demonstrations here in 1905, which was later recorded by the novelist Paustovsky, who had been a child in the crowd. The Kreshchatik then continues past the **Tchaikovsky Conservatoire**, built in 1899 and much restored after 1945. The great arch between apartment blocks leads to the arcade of the Passage department store. At no. 19, the huge Metro Restaurant is in the building above the Kreshchatik Metro station. The street then has a series of official buildings, the Ministries of Culture, of Agriculture and of Posts, before reaching **Bessarabskaya Square**, named after the pre-1914 market.

Shopping Kreshchatik is still the best street for tourist shopping, with a number of stores worth examining:

No. 15, Dyetski Mir (Children's World), the toy shop

No. 19, Perlna, jewellery store

No. 24, Mistetstvo, art books, posters and postcards

No. 30, Druzhba, books in foreign languages – Polish, German and Vietnamese more than English, but you will find some novels of Hemingway, Steinbeck, Melvyn Bragg and other approved authors, most of whom are set books for students

No. 44, Dom Knigi, the bookshop. Again this has an English language section

These are all rouble shops. The hard currency Beriozka store that sells jewellery is called 'Kashtan', and is at 2 Taras Shevchenko Boulevard.

The Kreshchatik we now see is a post-war creation. The Germans flattened the old buildings. The result is a remarkably coherent cityscape of totalitarian architecture, and the world being what it is, this style will doubtless become highly fashionable again sooner or later. The squatness and stolidity is explained by the shortage of metal when they were built. Reinforced concrete was in short supply, so the strength had to come from brick and stone alone. The wide pavements, fountains and trees are pleasant, but there is something grimly regimented about the colour of the stone, and the official blandness of the buildings.

By contrast, to get a flavour of the way the city used to look, walk down the hill from St Andrew's Church. **Andrivsky Uzviz** is one of the oldest streets remaining in Kiev, still paved in the traditional cobbles and with old fashioned street lights. And in the lower town, **Zhdanov Street** retains something of the city's pre-war character.

From Komsomol Square, at the northern end of the Kreshchatik, the complex of parks and terraces that overlook the river and lower town really begins. The 18-m high bronze pedestal is topped by Prince Vladimir, the tenth-century Prince who established Christianity by forcibly baptising his pagan subjects in the river.

St Andrew's Church

23 Vulitsya Andriivsky Spusk. Open daily from 10 a.m. to 6 p.m., closed on Thursdays. At 4 p.m. on Saturdays and Sundays there are hour-long recitals of ancient Russian and Ukrainian music.

This enchanting blue, white and gold confection atop the hill was designed by Rastrelli, architect of St Petersburg's Winter Palace, and was built between 1748–53. A tricky feat of engineering in its day, it has differential foundations, 12 m deep on the river side and only 2 m deep on the land side. It has been greatly, although faithfully restored. Wonderfully light within, it shows off well the paintings by Alexei Antropov, the founder of the realist school of Russian portraiture. He painted, 'The Last Supper in the Sanctuary', 'The Lord God on the Cupola', and 'The Sermon on the Mount' beside the pulpit – itself an unusual feature of a Russian church. He was also in charge of the design for the iconostasis, and painted its 'Assumption of the Virgin'.

State Museum of the History of the Ukraine

2 Vulitsya Volodimirskaya. Open daily from 10 a.m. to 6 p.m., closed on Wednesdays. From St Andrew's Church, go down the hill of Andriivsky Spusk to the south, until at the bottom of the hill you reach a junction dominated by this museum.

Halls 4–9 cover the early history of the Slav culture and the rise and flowering of Kievan Rus, and are worth a quick look. There is some charming jewellery, a fine bone chess set, and an interesting collection of medieval armour. Thereafter, Halls 15–27, which show the emergence and triumph of Ukrainian socialism, will be of interest only to a specialist.

Church of St Sophia

24 Vulitsya Volodimirskaya. Open daily from 10 a.m. to 6 p.m., Wednesdays 10 a.m. to 5 p.m., closed on Thursdays.

Do not be dismayed by appearances. You were not expecting this rather ordinary early Baroque building of nineteen cupolas and a second storey, but this is not what Prince Yaroslav founded in AD 1037.

Once inside the great glow of gold, you are seeing pretty much what Prince Yaroslav saw – the uniquely Russian mixture of mosaics and frescoes, including the portraits of his children. These rather domestic images are a delightful addition to the formal religious mosaics. The hunting scenes and drawings of life in Yaroslav's court, with his jesters and musicians, are faded but quite charming; they were long covered by whitewash and seventeenth-century oil paintings, and were only found by chance in the 1850s.

The most striking single feature is the **Oranta**, the huge (5 m) Virgin Mother of God mosaic on the vault of the main apse. There are over 10,000 tiles in the head alone, and the gradations of gold in her shawl, her halo and the vault itself, together with the skin tones of her face, are of great subtlety. As you walk towards her, the lightness of the central fold in her dress makes it look as if she is wearing man's trousers, hence the undignified nickname among local students, of 'Virgin in blue jeans'. No such levity about the **Pantocrator**, Christ the Ruler of all, in the main cupola.

Golden Gates

Just down Vulitsya Volodimirskaya from St Sophia, at the corner of Yaroslavov Val Street, are the remains of the Golden Gates, the main entry way through Yaroslav's wall. They were famed throughout Europe in their day for being covered in beaten gold. Even in ruin, they carry a potent mythical charge. In 1648, when the great national leader Bogdan Khmelnitsky liberated the Ukraine, he rode in triumph through these gates.

The Monastery of the Caves

21 Vulitsya Sichnevoho Povstannya (January Uprising Street). Open daily from 9.30 a.m. to 6 p.m., closed on Tuesdays. Entry to the caves in excursion groups only. If not going on an Intourist tour, this monastery is some 4 km from the centre of Kiev, and can be reached by Trolleybus 20, asking for the stop Lavrsky Provulok.

Founded in AD 1051 by the monks Antonius and Theodosius, the monastery began with a group of hermits in the deep caves in the cliff. Being close to the residence of the Grand Prince of Kiev, it soon attracted ambitious monks, scholars and artists, which in turn attracted wealth. And with wealth, they began to build great churches and establish the monastery as the great cultural centre of Kiev.

The main entrance is the **Trinity Gate Church**, ornate and grand above the entrance arch. It was built in the twelfth century, and reconstructed in the eighteenth. The interior is very striking, a chased gold iconostasis around mainly red paintings, by very talented local artists who have broken well clear of the usual rigid subjects of the icon form. The floor is made of cast-iron slabs. The single-storey buildings to either side of the church are the monks' cells, which now house museum exhibits of sixteenth- to eighteenth-century engravings, *objets d'art*, and a series of architectural plans and designs for the monastery complex.

Straight ahead are the ruins of the eleventh-century **Cathedral of**

the Assumption, which survived the Mongols, only to fall victim to twentieth-century barbarians when the Nazis deliberately blew it up on 3 November 1941.

Most of the buildings that may be seen are early Baroque, from the period of Kiev's revival after the seventeenth-century reunification with Russia. To the left of the ruins are **All Saints Church**, built in the 1690s, and the imposing yellow and white bell-tower, built in the 1740s. The **Refectory** and **Refectory Church** are late nineteenth century.

There is a separate museum, called the **Historical Treasures**, in the Kovnir Building, immediately behind the ruins of the cathedral. The first three halls on the first floor contain a stunning collection of Scythian gold jewellery, including items from the Ordzhonikidze royal burial mound, discovered in 1971, and one of the finds of the century. The tomb's main burial chamber had been plundered centuries ago, but the modern archaeologists found hidden tombs beyond.

The Caves   The caves after which the monastery is named provide natural conditions for mummification, keeping a constant temperature and low humidity. They were not only useful as shelter and for storage, but were used for burial. The 'miraculous preservation' of the bodies led to pious pilgrimages, and the bodies still attract religious enthusiasts to this day, some of whom harangue tourists with strange prophecies and accounts of sightings of the Virgin Mary. This activity rose sharply after the Chernobyl nuclear disaster. The word Chernobyl in Ukrainian means Wormwood, and in the Bible's Book of Revelations, the Day of Judgement is heralded by a Star named Wormwood falling blazing into the waters of the earth and making them bitter. It may seem fanciful now, but with a nuclear reactor raging out of control not far north of Kiev, this passage attracted considerable local interest.

There are two sets of caves, and each labyrinth is some 228 m in length. The mummies are not as well preserved as they might be, with fingers and toes dropping off, but the underground churches are striking. In the Far caves, the **Church of St Theodosius** and in the Near, the **Church of St Balaam**, each boasts a remarkably intricate eighteenth-century iconostasis. The Far caves have the finer group of buildings, which meld happily with the wooded slopes overlooking the river. The seventeenth-century **Church of the Nativity of the Virgin** has an unusual arcade and terrace, and the bell-tower is beautifully proportioned. In summer, the kilometre long stroll along the heights above the river to the Far caves is very pleasant.

Museum of Folk   In the south-west outskirts of the city; take Trolleybus 11 or 24 to
Architecture   VDNKh (Exhibition of Economic Achievements) and then take bus
and Rural Life   24. Open daily from 10 a.m. to 6 p.m., 1 May to 6 November only, closed on Wednesdays.

Not on the usual Intourist circuit, this is one of the more rewarding outdoor trips. The museum presents over 200 rural farmhouses, barns, windmills and cottages from all across the Ukraine, from the Crimea to the Carpathians. They are dotted pleasantly along the 11-km trail. There are homes of poor peasants, and of rich, and inside are displays of traditional furniture and clothing. Some are woodmens' huts in forest glades, complete with bee hives. It is all very charming, and a great deal more attractive than the associated display of modern collective farm architecture, which proudly displays the brick structures where the farm workers now live.

Where to stay

The main Intourist hotels are:

Dniepr, 1/2 Kreshchatik (tel. 914-861); **Lybid**, Pobeda Square (tel. 742-066); and **Dyesna Hotel**, 46 Milyutenko sy (tel. 584-090).

Two new Intourist hotels are being built, but foreign guests are sometimes accommodated in the **Moskva**, the largest hotel in the city, 4 October Revolution Square (tel. 292-804).

Hotel Bratislava, 1 Andrey Malysko, beside the Darnitsa Metro station (tel. 57-7233). The newest hotel in the city, and named after the Czechoslovak city of Bratislava with which Kiev is twinned. It has dining rooms specialising in Ukrainian and Slovak cuisine.

For motorists, **Prolisok Motel**, 1 Brest-Litovsky Prospekt (tel. 440-093).

Where to eat

Ukrainian food:

Dubki, 1 Ulitsa Stetsenko; **Khata Karasya**, at the Prolisok Motel, 1 Brest-Litovsky Prospekt; **Mlyn**, at the Hydropark; **Natalka**, 202 Kharkovskoye Chaussee; and **Vitryak**, 147 Prospekt Sorokaletiya Oktyabrya.

Standard Soviet cuisine:

Kiev, 26/1 Ulitsa Kirova; **Leningrad**, 4 Taras Shevchenko Boulevard; **Goloseyevsky**, 93 Prospekt Sorokaletiya Oktyabrya; **Slavutich**, 1 Ulitsa Entusiastov; and **Teatralny**, 17 Ulitsa Lenina.

Odessa

Odessa was named on the mistaken assumption that this was the ancient Greek settlement of Odissos. When the Russians took the place in 1789 it was the Turkish fortress of Khadji-Bey, and a strategic rather than a commercial base. Most ports are built at the estuaries of rivers. Not Odessa. The Rivers Dniepr, Bug and Dniester which flowed into the Black Sea nearby each had rapids that made navigation difficult. But General Suvorov saw the need for a naval base that was combined with a commercial harbour. The steady growth of the Black Sea shipping trade helped Odessa to prosper, but it was the coming of the railways which allowed the town to become the major entrepôt for the Ukrainian grain trade.

Odessa is a mysteriously attractive town. There are no fine old buildings, or at least, nothing older than the nineteenth century. But the relatively low and human scale of the roofline, the abundance of trees and shade, the balconied houses and the liveliness of its streets and markets make it a delightful city. It was always the most cosmopolitan of Russian cities, filled with the traders of the Levant and the Balkans, Turks and Armenians, Jews and Greeks.

Pushkin

Russians love Odessa; the very name is redolent of the warm south, boat trips and golden beaches. For this, Pushkin takes much of the blame. While exiled here in 1823–4, he wrote parts of *Eugene Onegin* and *The Fountains of Bakhchisarai*, and poems of Odessa where he sang of the Turkish coffees and Balkan tobacco, and the wines that came to Odessa from Italy and France. Odessa was also identified with the vastly popular nineteenth-century policy of expansion in the Balkans, to free fellow Slavs from the heel of the infidel Turk. At least, that was how the policy was justified. And Odessa was also a base for the Hetaeristi, the campaigners for Greek independence from the Turks. Liberation movements, Slavic destinies, Pushkin and the warm south all went to concoct a heady mixture for the Russian imagination. And something of this atmosphere remains in the older quarters, although Odessa now is a vast port city of over a million people.

What to see

The most famous structure in the city is the Richelieu Steps, leading from the Governor's Palace to the seafront, which starred in one of the great moments of cinema in Eisenstein's film *The Battleship Potemkin*. They are now called the **Potemkin Steps**, and are an architectural marvel, being twice as wide at the bottom as at the top, although the two sides seem parallel. They were originally named after the French aristocratic exile, the Duke of Richelieu, who was the first governor of Odessa and helped assure its commercial success by running it as a free port.

The seafront of Odessa should be strolled, from the **Vorontsov Palace** at one end (restored after 1945) to the 1880s' **Opera House** at the other. The cannon on the terrace of the embankment is from the British frigate *Tiger*, which was sunk just off the Middle Fountain (the main esplanade) by Russian coastal guns during the Crimean War in 1854.

Inland, the old town is a pleasure to walk around. From the **Suvorov Esplanade**, stroll up the street named after Garibaldi to the main street of traditional Odessa, the **Deribasovka**. At number 16 is the Richelieu College, where Pushkin was a student, and where Mendeleyev, the great physicist who drew up the periodic Table of the Elements, used to teach. The Deribasovka crosses Pushkin Street, and to the left at number 13 there is a museum to Pushkin.

Catacombs

The town was built of the limestone on which it stands, quarried from beneath the city. The resulting catacombs, a veritable labyrinth, became a base for the resistance to the Germans. Visits to them can be arranged through Intourist.

Beaches

The beaches of and around Odessa are crowded and polluted, but remain popular. The best known are Arkadia, Otrada, Luzanovka, Chernomorka and Fontanka. Tram 5 or 17 goes to Arkadia, and there are hydrofoils to all the beaches from the main harbour.

Just outside Odessa, the resort of **Karolino-Bugaz** was developed in the 1960s with accommodation for 50,000 people. Avoid it unless you love really down-market package tours, canteen food and bathing in used soup.

The **Kuyalnik canal resort** depends on the medicinal properties of its mud, in which Russians are great believers. Coal miners from the Donetsk basin swear by it, and their trade union has built a large sanatorium here. As an act of international solidarity, these facilities are on occasion offered to fellow miners in the west who do not always appreciate, it should be said, the sacrifice made for them. British miners' families, treated to the restorative effects of Kuyalnik mud during a brief break from the miners' strike of 1984–5, declared themselves mystified by the treatment, and not altogether grateful for the experience.

Where to stay, and eat

There is a very good Intourist camp site at Odessa (see p. 111), a motel and three Intourist Hotels: **Odessa Hotel**, 11 Primorsky Boulevard (tel. 225-019); **Krasnaya Hotel**, 15 Pushkin Street (tel. 227-220); and **Chernoye More (Black Sea) Hotel**, 59 Lenin Street (tel. 242-025), largest and most modern, with air conditioning.

The Crimea

Route Six of the Motorists' guides on p. 326 takes you through parts of the Crimea.

The Crimea lies in the south of the Ukraine and virtually forms an island in the Black Sea. It is joined to the mainland by a thick neck of land – the Isthmus of Perekop – to the north-west, and by the Chongarsk Bridge, across the extremely salty Sivash Lagoon, to the north-east.

The northern part of the Crimea is steppe, and was less fertile than the rest of the Ukraine until the building was completed in 1975 of the irrigation canals from the River Dniepr. The southern Crimea comprises valleys, mountains and coastal resorts and contains some spectacular scenery. The mountains help create the micro-climate of the region which keeps it warm and temperate throughout the year, and protected from the hard winters imposed to the north. It is a vast resort area and boasts a large wine-making industry.

Yalta

Founded in the twelfth century, Yalta is both a major port and health resort. Despite pebble beaches, overcrowding, pollution problems and the usual deficiencies of Soviet catering and night life, it is also the best of the country's sea and summer resorts, because there is so much to do in addition to sunbathing. With 2,300 hours of sunshine a year, Yalta is as sunny as the south of France, and in July the sea temperature is an almost soupy 27°C. It is comfortable to bathe between May and October, and even in mid-October the daytime air temperature ranges between 15°–20°C. In July the air temperature averages 25°C, slightly cooler than the sea.

What to see　　The **Chekhov House-Museum**, 112 Kirov Street. Open daily from 10 a.m. to 6 p.m., closed on Tuesdays. This fascinating museum is where Chekhov wrote *The Cherry Orchard* and *The Three Sisters*, and where he met Tolstoy and Gorky.

Children will be terrified by '**Polyana Skazok**' (the glade of fairy tales), an open air museum on Kirov Street where roots and deformed trees are carved into grotesque fairy tale shapes. There is a thesis to be written on the sheer awfulness of the characters of most Russian fairy tales, from the witch Baba-Yaga to the wicked warlock Kashchey the Immortal, or the Grey Wolf and the bandit Solovey-Razboinek, half-bird and half-man. After a childhood being brought up on this lot, Ivan the Terrible and Joe Stalin probably came as light relief.

Wine　　To the east of Yalta is **Massandra Park**, the base of the Massandra vineyards. This is the centre of Russian (as opposed to Georgian or Moldavian) wine making, and it has suffered badly at the hands of the Philistines who administered the anti-alcohol campaign of the 1980s. (See p. 124.) The real brain of the industry is at the Magarach Institute of Viticulture, where there are some enchanting gentlemen who love and understand their wine. If the new Puritans permit it, Intourist may run tours there again. Intourist guides will boast of the 1970 International Wine Contest, when Massandra wine won twenty-four of the twenty-five Gold Medals. What they will not tell you is that the contest was held here in Yalta, and therefore the objectivity of the judges was less than absolute, and that the big winner of two Gold Medals, the white muscat of Krasny-Kamen, was so sweet a wine that not even the Sauternes could compete. Given a chance, the men of Magarach will civilise the Soviet palate yet.

The **Yalta Wine-tasting Pavilion**, 1 Litkens Street (just across the park from the Oreanda Hotel). Open daily from 11 a.m. to 6.30 p.m., closed on Mondays.

Here you will be given a short lecture on Crimean wines and a tasting session. Most of the wines are so sweet they make your tongue curl; however, there are some decent dryish whites – try the Aligote Zolotaya Balka, which is flinty rather than dry. The Alkadar Riesling and the Sylvaner use the German grapes, but lack the delicacy of the Rhine and Moselle wines. Try also the local attempt at a claret, called Aluschta, which sniffs better than it drinks.

Where to stay　　The two Intourist hotels are:

The massive (1,200-room) **Yalta Hotel**, 50 Drazhinsky Street (tel.

350-150), from where you have a fine view of the port of Yalta. The small **Tavrida Hotel**, 13/2 Lenin Embankment (tel. 327-784).

Oreanda Hotel, 35/2 Lenin Embankment (tel. 325-794), was recently restored by the Finns, and is now managed under a joint venture agreement designed to bring the hotel up to high western standards. It is small, with fewer than a hundred rooms, and probably the best hotel in the Soviet Union.

There is also a camp site at Polyana Skazok on Kirov Street (tel. 395-249).

Where to eat

The best restaurants in Yalta are chosen for location rather than food. Try the **Gorka** on Darsan Hill, which can be reached by cable car, and the **Lesnoi** at Lake Karagol (no. 6 bus goes direct), or the **Vodopad** at the Uchan-Su waterfall (no. 6 bus again). The **Yakor** fish restaurant inside the main port is not bad, but the best food is to be had at the **Oreanda Hotel** restaurant. Try also the new co-operative restaurant, **Sitil**, on 35/6 Ulitsa Balaklavskaya.

Excursions from Yalta

The Crimea is full of interesting excursions, but if staying in Yalta, it is more fun to take the cruise boats to the various coastal resorts rather than to drive. This is one of the few parts of the Soviet Union where parking is sometimes a problem.

Bakhchisaray

The old Tartar capital should not be missed. The Khan's palace is still standing, and now houses a local history museum and the famous courtyard with the fountain which inspired Pushkin's poem. You used to be able to hunt in the game reserve, but these days hunting permits are rare.

Another excursion is to the **Swallow's Nest**, a delightful neo-Gothic folly of a castle perched on the rocks above the sea. Built in 1911, it now houses a small café.

Livadia

This great park, sanatorium and museum, just west of Yalta, also deserves a visit. Built in 1913 as a summer residence for the Tsar, in the style of the Italian Renaissance, it was the scene of the Yalta Conference in 1945, where Stalin, Winston Churchill and the invalid President Roosevelt carved up the post-war future of Europe. They agreed to a Soviet sphere of influence in eastern Europe and in the Balkans, and although Churchill and Roosevelt are sometimes wildly accused of surrendering half of Europe to Stalinism, since the Red Army was already in place, while their western Allies were still stalled on the Rhine, it is not clear that they had much choice.

Vorontsov Palace

The neo-Gothic palace at Alupka is another interesting excursion. Designed by an English architect, Edward Blore, and built by serf labour, it is now an art museum, containing the cream of the art treasures from all the other royal and aristocratic stately homes along the coast. It was the residence of Churchill and the British delegation during the Yalta Conference. The surrounding parks are magnificent, dotted with 'stone wives' – the statues of women placed in the graves of steppe warriors in the twelfth century.

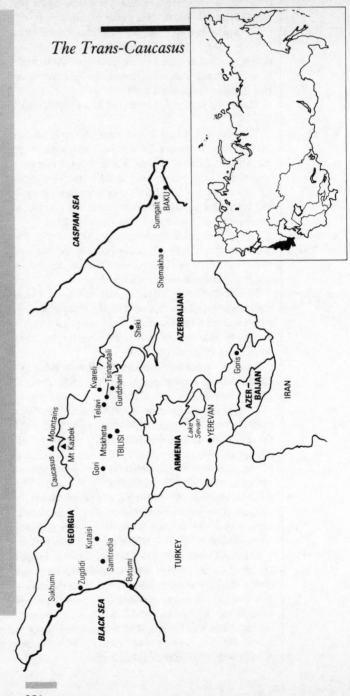

The Trans-Caucasus

CASPIAN SEA

BAKU
Sumgait •
Shemakha •

AZERBAIJAN

Sheki •

Kvareli
Telavi • • Tsinandali
Gurdzhani

Caucasus ▲ Mountains
Mt Kazbek

Goris •

AZER–
BAIJAN

IRAN

Lake
Sevan

YEREVAN •

ARMENIA

Gori • Mtskheta
TBILISI •

GEORGIA

Kutaisi •

Samtredia •

Batumi •

Zugdidi •
Sukhumi •

BLACK SEA

TURKEY

The Trans-Caucasus

Route Seven of the Motorists' guides on p. 332 takes you through parts of the Trans-Caucasus.

Introduction

Lying between the Black Sea, the Caspian Sea and the Sea of Azoz, this region comprises three separate republics – Georgia, Armenia and Azerbaijan.

Getting there
Large tracts of all three republics are open to foreign visitors. Although there is a rail link to Iran, this border is not open to passengers. Despite the fact that there is a rail link with Turkey, it is difficult to make the border crossing as Turkey is a member of the NATO alliance and the border is thus a top security zone. Foreign drivers may drive only on the routes along the Black Sea riviera to Tbilisi, south to Yerevan and north again along the Georgian Military Highway.

Religion
The historic nations of Georgia and Armenia have a Christian culture that is far older than that of Russia, and fills the region with ancient churches and monasteries. Armenia was the first nation to become Christian, in the year AD 303, followed by the Georgians in 330, shortly before Constantine declared it the official religion of the Roman Empire. Traditionally, Azerbaijan has its roots in both Turkish and Persian cultures. Its Azeri-Turkish language comes from the former (although with a lot of Farsi influence) and its predominantly Shi'ite Muslim religion comes from the latter.

The Caucasus Mountains make this a scenically beautiful region, and, with an excellent climate and the beaches of the Black and Caspian Seas, it is a natural tourist centre. The mountains ought to be a natural frontier. They are high and steep, and can be easily crossed only at the edges, where they run into the Black Sea in the west and the Caspian Sea in the east. The only way through the centre of this mountain chain is by the beautiful but difficult Georgian Military Highway.

History
If political boundaries were ruled by geographical logic, the Caucasus Mountains might equally have formed a natural frontier with Turkey and Persia. But south of the mountain ranges were the Chris-

tian nations of Georgia and Armenia. The mountains themselves were blocked by Muslim tribesmen whom the Russians fought a series of tough nineteenth-century campaigns to subdue. The Georgians and Armenians had nowhere to retreat from the Persian and Turkish advance, with the result that in the eighteenth century Georgia appealed to the Russians for protection. If the relationship smacked of the Imperial, it was voluntarily chosen by the Georgian monarchy because the alternative of being swallowed up by the Muslim Turk or Persian was worse. The same brutal logic held good for the Armenians. The lesson of the Armenian massacres of 1915 was that the Armenian nation could only survive within Tsarist or Soviet Russia.

The case of Azerbaijan is different. Originally a Persian province, the Arab expansion with Islam challenged the Persian authority. Ruled by the Seljuk Turks, with whom the later Mongol invaders happily merged, it was then an independent Khanate, but in the seventeenth to eighteenth centuries Azerbaijan became increasingly a battleground between Ottoman Turkey and Safavid Persia. Just as Russia had moved across the Caucasus to swallow Georgia, and when naval bases on the Caspian and Black Seas, and the Military Highway through the mountains, had given the Tsarist armies the physical capacity to intervene, Persia provided the opportunity. The Tsar's Ambassador to Tehran, the writer Alexander Griboedov, was assassinated in 1829. Russia declared war, won, and annexed northern Azerbaijan. The southern half of the country around its inland capital of Tabriz was left to Persia, where it remains. Spasmodically claimed as a Soviet sphere of influence, it was occupied by Soviet troops from 1941-5, while British troops occupied southern Iran, to guarantee safe passage for British and US munitions and Lend-lease equipment to the Soviet ally. The Russians subsequently withdrew to the traditional border.

Recent conflict This complex history, and the rivalries of religion, help to explain the sudden outburst of ethnic tension and violence between Armenians and Azerbaijanis in 1988. The region of Nagorno-Karabakh had been over 90 per cent Armenian when it was rather casually assigned to the Republic of Azerbaijan in 1925 after a very confused period of war and invasion and counter-revolution. By the 1980s, Nagorno-Karabakh was less than 70 per cent Armenian, and clearly an underprivileged region, with the Azerbaijani authorities in Baku, the capital, not too concerned to provide nurseries, medical facilities and school books in Armenian. The new mood of the Gorbachev reforms encouraged the Armenians of the Nagorno-Karabakh enclave, and in Armenia itself, to campaign and demonstrate peacefully for a change of the borders. Hundreds of thousands of Armenians went on strike and marched in Yerevan in the biggest political demonstrations the Soviet Union had known since 1917. What had been inevitably an Armenian national challenge to Azerbaijan now began to look like a challenge to the authority of the Soviet state too. There were some scattered outbreaks of violence, enough to alarm many of the several hundred thousand Azerbaijanis who lived in Armenia. Some of them fled to Azerbaijan for refuge, where public opinion reacted very angrily, and more demonstrations followed. In the industrial city of Sumgait, just across the peninsula from Baku, young Azerbaijani thugs launched a pogrom against the many Armenians who lived in the city, killing thirty-two and forcing the Soviet Army to intervene and restore order after two days of riot and murder.

None of this was quite as simple as it looked. First, the Party leaders of both Georgia and Armenia were controversial, facing accusations of corruption, and fearing the sack from Moscow. They both played rather equivocal roles in the early stages of the trouble, perhaps hoping that a quick national crisis would mobilise public support behind them. Second, Sumgait itself was a classic example of the social problems building in the run-down and polluted Soviet slums. Many of the rioting Azerbaijanis were living in what amounted to a shanty town, having not long arrived from the countryside. And the Armenians they went hunting for were living in decent apartments. That played a role. Third, the real problem was that the republican borders meant little. Armenians and Azerbaijanis lived among and with each other, as they had for generations, in reasonable harmony. It was the very success of their relations that put so many of their communities at risk when the explosion came. How this will eventually be solved is unclear. The situation is at impasse, with the Supreme Soviet of Armenia demanding reunification with Nagorno-Karabakh, and the Supreme Soviet of Azerbaijan refusing, and Moscow facing a very difficult problem of arbitration that will have important implications for its relations with national minorities in other republics too.

Georgia

The Black Sea coast, the route through Gori and Mtskheta, and the Georgian Military Highway are described at length in Route Seven of the Motorists' guides on p. 332.

Georgia is one of the most welcoming of the Soviet republics, with a powerful tradition of hospitality, and a climate and national temperament that reminds many western visitors of the Mediterranean lands. It produces the best wines in the Soviet Union, and can claim perhaps the most distinctive cuisine. The people are handsome and friendly, and the whole republic exudes an atmosphere of colour, fun and *joie de vivre* that is not quite Soviet as we have come to understand it in Moscow. The Russians are the first to acknowledge the difference, nicknaming it after the formal title for West Germany, the FRG – the

'Federal Republic of Georgia'. They claim that the station announcer always says every evening 'The train now leaving platform one for the Soviet Union . . .'. There is a note of jealousy in this, a suspicion that every Georgian is a millionaire, that they use their fertile soil and abundant sunshine to grow the fruit and vegetables that they can sell at fancy profits in the Moscow markets. Certainly, Georgia is visibly more prosperous than most of the USSR, and has a higher proportion of car ownership. But many of the attractions of the place can be attributed to a delightful country and a delightful people. It became a single country during the twelfth century, under King David the Great, who united what had been since ancient times two separate kingdoms. Western Georgia, on the shores of the Black Sea, was known as Colchis, the land of gold visited by Jason and the Argonauts. Eastern Georgia was Iberia, and the ancient Greek geographers describe the two countries as civilised and prosperous, with trade routes and bridges.

Tbilisi

The capital of Georgia, its name means warm springs. The local people shun the old Persian name of Tiflis, and call it 'kalaki' – the town. The legend says that King Vakhtang of Iberia shot and wounded a deer while hunting. It jumped into the warm sulphur springs, magically recovered and darted away. Deeply impressed, King Vakhtang decided to move the capital from nearly Mtskheta to the warm springs. In fact, the prosaic archaeologists have established that there were settlements in this part of the Kura Valley around 3000 BC, and there was a fortress by AD 360. But King Vakhtang and his successor Dachi began the construction of the city, building the Shuris Tsikhe citadel on top of Sokolaki Hill and the Metekhi Church on the far bank of the river, now marked by the equestrian statue of King Vakhtang.

History

For over a century, Tbilisi prospered, but then came attacks from Persia, and later the city was taken by Byzantines, and in 721 it fell to the Arab expansion. In the next four centuries it was destroyed by the Khazars, the Arabs, the Persians, and twice by the Seljuk Turks before the twelfth-century renaissance under King David who recaptured the town and began rebuilding. King David died in 1130, but from 1171–98 Queen Tamara presided over a great cultural flowering of architecture and sculpture. At the Queen's brilliant court, Rustaveli wrote his epic of the land *The Knight in the Panther's Skin*, and Georgia's jewellers, metalsmiths, and mosaic and enamel artists produced masterpieces which you may still see in the Museum of Georgian Art. But then in the thirteenth century came the Mongols, and Tamburlaine followed in the fourteenth, and the Ottoman Turks in the fifteenth, who divided the country into weak principalities. The city that Marco Polo praised as a lovely town, surrounded by picturesque fortresses, had almost disappeared. But there was a final blow to come. In 1795, the Persian Shah Aga destroyed the city and banished the entire population. King Herakles, of the Bagrati dynasty which had ruled in Tbilisi for a thousand years, appealed to the Tsar for protection. The Russian armies came, and the city began to recover – although few Georgians returned to live in it, save for in the Avlabar quarter around the Metekhi Church. The city's population was mainly Armenian artisans and merchants and Russian officials.

What to see

The devastation of 1795 means that only isolated buildings of the ancient city remain, but the old town itself has been excellently restored on both sides of the river. It is now a strolling town, around the old fortress walls which have a coffee shop and wine-tasting cellar built into their thickness, into the riverside bakery where the flat *lavash* bread is slapped on to the sides of the huge subterranean oven while a portrait of Stalin beams benignly down, and just inland from the bakery is the entrance to the public baths which Pushkin made famous. If the legend of King Vakhtang and the deer has any truth in it, then these are the warm springs.

Rustaveli Avenue

Up the hill is the city's impressive main street which makes a pleasant walk. It filled from end to end with angry demonstrators in 1976, when the new Soviet constitution seemed to hint that there might be some reduction in the official status of the Georgian language. The **Rustaveli Theatre**, one of the finest companies in the Soviet Union, with a remarkable facility for Shakespeare, is based here, as is the **Tbilisi University**, also renowned for its Shakespearian scholars. On this main avenue, too, is the **Kashveti Cathedral**, a twentieth-century copy of the eleventh-century original. And try to find Stalin's face in bas-relief on the Institute of Marxism-Leninism.

Museums

The Tbilisi museums are among the best in the Soviet Union. The **State Museum of Georgia** on Rustaveli contains personal effects and household items. The **Museum of Georgian Art** on Lenin Square contains gold jewellery from ancient Colchis, the magnificent enamels of the twelfth-century renaissance under Queen Tamara, and the remarkable primitive paintings of Niko Pirosmanashvili, Georgia's Henri Rousseau.

Where to stay

In Tbilisi tourists are accommodated in the **Hotel Adzharia**, 1 Constitution Square (tel. 362-716), and at the **Hotel-Motel Ushba**, 4th km, Georgian Military Highway.

Where to eat

Some of the best *shashlik* bars are to be found in Tbilisi, and on the riverfront there are restaurants that serve the Georgian speciality *khachapuri*, a cheese-filled bun. Or try the **Iveria** and the **Mukhrantubani** restaurants for a Georgian feast.

Just opposite the Theatre on Rustaveli Avenue is a lively basement café, **Pirosmani's**, decorated with copies of the marvellous primitive paintings by Niko Pirosmanashvili – the originals being in the Museum of Georgian Art. A splendid and convivial place for supper after the opera or theatre, it is presided over by a buxom waitress nicknamed Queen Tamara.

Excursions from Tbilisi

Mtatsminda

Take the cable car to this, the sacred mountain, site of the old Monastery of St David. The view from the summit is stunning and on a good day you can see the 4,500-metre Mount Kazbek. There is now a pantheon to the playwright Griboedov, who was the first Russian administrator of the city and much loved, and whose assassination in Tehran sparked off the war which conquered Azerbaijan. He has been joined by other tombs of celebrated Georgian writers, and by Stalin's mother. The restaurant there is good.

Kakhetia

The excursion into eastern Georgia is worth taking. This goes into the valley of the River Alazan, the best of the wine-growing districts, past Badiauri, Gurdzhani and Tsinandali, which between them make the best Soviet wines. Drunk here, or in Tbilisi, it is very good indeed, but beware the difference back in Moscow as the Georgians tend to keep the best vintages for themselves. The road climbs over another ridge of mountains to **Telavi**, the ancient capital of Kakhetia, with an excellent restaurant in the main square and an Institute of Viniculture. Just north of the city on the bank of the river is the tenth-century Alaverdi Cathedral. The sixth-century Ikalto Monastery, where Rustaveli studied, is 6 km from Telavi. On the road to the town of **Kvareli**, also celebrated for its wines, is the pleasant old town of **Gremi**, seat of the Kakhetian princes of the sixteenth century.

Armenia

The Armenians tell a story about the day God assigned land to all the peoples of the earth. But the Armenian in the queue saw a friend and started chatting and lost track of events and suddenly the land distribution was all over, and God was about to leave. The Armenian said he was sorry, but he had been distracted, and was there any land left. 'Just these stones and pebbles,' said God, brushing them from His lap. And that was the land of the Armenians.

It is rocky, and 90 per cent of its territory is above 900 metres. Less than half the land is cultivable, and it is the smallest republic in the Soviet Union, with a population of 3.5 million. But another 1.5 million Armenians live elsewhere in the Soviet Union, and at least another million live scattered around the rest of the world. A remarkably talented people, with a flair for commerce that has contributed to the prosperity of medieval Poland and modern California – to name but two – they are an ancient nation. Darius the Great of Persia mentioned them as one of his conquests in 521 BC. Another legend says they stem from the branch of Noah's family that decided to stick around Mount Ararat after the Ark beached. Archaeologists reckon they come from the Thracian-Phrygian peoples who began in the Balkans and moved into Turkey, breaking the Hittite Empire.

History | Alexander the Great brought Armenia into his short-lived Hellenic Empire, and the kingdom subsequently flourished. By the first century BC it had spread to dominate most of what is now the Middle East, until defeated by the Romans. Armenia prospered rather more modestly under Rome and Byzantium, embraced Christianity and developed the distinctive alphabet, and began to learn the difficult art of survival between a declining Byzantium, aggressive Arab Islam, and the looming Persian neighbour. And yet this period was the outstanding age of Armenian architecture when the great churches were built. There was another golden age in the tenth century, when the southern capital of Ani was founded in what is now Turkish territory.

Disaster followed over the next seven centuries at the hands of the Arabs, the Mongols, the Turks and the Persians. Somehow, the Armenians maintained their faith, their language and their culture and, perhaps infuriated by their sheer endurance, the Persian Shah Abbas deported the lot far to the south around Isfahan. As the Russians began to probe beyond the Caucasus, the Armenians seized every opportunity to return to their rocky homeland. The Turks became even more infuriated with the endurance of the Christian Armenians on what they claimed as Turkish territory, and in the 1890s and in 1915, embarked on a series of massacres that have become known to history as a genocide. At least a million Armenians were slaughtered. With the 1917 Revolution and the collapse of Russian power, the Turks invaded, planning to conquer Armenia, while the Armenians themselves dreamed of an independent nation. They soon settled for Russia, as the only shield against the Turks. And to this day, the symbol of Armenia, the twin peaks of Mount Ararat, dominates the capital of Yerevan, but lies inside the Turkish border.

Following the political troubles over Nagorno-Karabakh in 1988 and after the earthquake in December of the same year, tourism to Armenia was suspended. It will be revived, but it is advisable to check the latest situation with Intourist.

Yerevan | The ancient city fortress of Erebuni (hence Yerevan) was founded in the year 783 BC, by King Argishti I of Urartu, according to a stone title deed, inscribed in cuneiform, the city's proudest possession. The fort of Erebuni was built on a hill in the southern part of the city of Arinberd, where there is an intriguing museum decorated with copies of old Urartu wall paintings. It is now a Soviet city, but a handsome one, built, of pink-brown volcanic tufa, on a radial pattern.

What to see | The centre is the handsome **Lenin Square**, where the Intourist hotel, the Armenia, the Historical Museum, and the main Government building are found. To the north is the great square in front of the Opera House, scene of the demonstrations for Nagorno-Karabakh.

Looming above the centre of the city is the **Matenadaran**, one of the world's great libraries, filled with Armenian, Latin, Greek, Persian, Arabic, Georgian, Russian and still unidentified and untranslatable manuscripts that record the history of half the ancient world. It is a working library, but the permanent exhibition is worth a visit. The **Sarayan Museum**, housing Martiros Sarayan's paintings, is a gem.

Karmir-Blur　To the south-west of the city is this Urartu fortress dating from the seventh century BC. On top of the hill was a massive building with over a hundred rooms, some of them 30 metres in length. Many of the storerooms, containing the bones of domestic animals, earthenware jars and provisions, were found intact, because the roof beams burned through and collapsed when the fortress was taken by the Scythians in the sixth century.

Beside the great lake known as the Yerevan Sea, there is an open air **Museum** of traditional Armenian buildings, and artisan workshops.

Overlooking the city from above the River Razdan is a deeply moving monument to the victims of the Armenian genocide – a tall thin obelisk with a splinter sheered off to symbolise the lost lands, and around an eternal flame, a ring of massive blocks that lean in towards the flame in mourning.

Where to stay, and eat　There are three Intourist hotels in Yerevan:
Armenia, 1 Amiryan Street (tel. 525-383); **Ani**, 19 Sayat Nova Street (tel. 523-961); and **Dvin**, 40 Paranyan Street (tel. 534-851).
The best ethnic restaurant is in the Ani Hotel.

Excursions　*See also Route Seven of the Motorists' Guides on p. 332 for the route north to Lake Sevan.*

There are a number of excursions without which no visit to Armenia would be complete.

Cathedral of Echmiadzin　Some 20 km from Yerevan, this is the seat of the Catholicos, the head of the Armenian Church. Founded in the year AD 303, the current church was rebuilt in the seventh century, and has been much restored. The belfry is seventeenth century. The church contains some striking paintings, but the most important relics are in the **Treasury**, including some wood from Mount Ararat said to be from Noah's Ark. Carbon-dating has established that it comes from the fourth millenium BC.

Churches　The cemetery of Echmiadzin is dominated by the **Church of Gayane**, which dates from AD 630. The ruined **Church of Zvartnots**, and the nearby seventh-century **Church of St Ripsimeh** add to this complex of church architecture for which the Armenians of the period developed a whole new technology, working out how to build domes on top of squares or crossed naves, to mount a cone above a dome, and to build other shapes that had baffled the Greeks and Romans.

Garni　Some 35 km from Yerevan, a classic Roman temple rises from a mountainside to dominate the Azat Valley. It was built by the Romans in the first century after they had captured and demolished the Armenian royal residence and fortress in the campaign of AD 59. It later became a summer residence of Armenian kings, but was destroyed by a seventeenth-century earthquake. The Roman temple building has been thoroughly restored, and restoration work is now under way on the third-century royal baths, with their striking mosaics.

Gegard Continuing on the same road from Yerevan takes you to this stunning rock monastery, carved into the mountainside. The oldest visible building dates from the thirteenth century, but some are thought to be much older. Monastic cells, churches, tombs and Khachkar commemorative crosses are hewn from solid rock. The churches are still working, and sacrifices of sheep sometimes take place on the occasion of a baptism.

North-west Armenia The main buildings of the medieval period are in the north-west of the republic. The tenth- to thirteenth-century **Sanahin Monastery** by the River Debed is perhaps the most dramatic with its five churches.

A special excursion may also be made to the far south-west of Armenia, to the fortified **Monastery of Tathev**, perched inaccessibly on a spur of the Zangezur Mountains, with two ninth-century churches and an eleventh-century Church of the Virgin. The nearby village of **Goris** is carved into the mountainside at a height of 3,000 metres.

Azerbaijan

The city of Baku, capital of Azerbaijan, fascinated visitors for centuries because of the way the land leaked fire. Marco Polo reported 'fires that cannot be put out' on his visit to the city, and to the *Zorastrian* fire-worshippers, the oil-soaked land was a holy place. It remains a bizarre landscape, the endless jetties stretching hundreds of kilometres into the Caspian Sea to bring in the oil. You can still smell petrol from the embankment at Baku, even though the focus of the Soviet industry long since shifted north to the 'second Baku' around Tartaria and now the third great oil district of western Siberia.

Baku The city gets its name from the phrase 'bad kube', or town of winds. Its great period was from the ninth to thirteenth centuries, until the Mongols came and sacked the city and, more damagingly, destroyed the vital irrigation system in the surrounding countryside.

The sharpest contrast is between the historic Islamic city and the sudden eruption of the buildings of the nineteenth-century oil boom. The Azerbaijani people could not meet the sudden demand for workers in this new industry, and an instant proletariat rushed in, Russian, Armenian and American oil experts and British and French managers. Living conditions were appalling. 'When I think of the oil industry, I think of a black hell painted by a brilliant artist, the workers' huts huddled close to the ground around the chaos of oil rigs, the long barracks quickly knocked together from red stones, piled one on top of the other as they were found, these barracks looked like nothing so much as the lairs and caves of prehistoric man,' wrote Maxim Gorky. The workers' strikes of 1902, 1903 and 1905 were important events in the shaping of a working class consciousness in the years before the Revolution, times when Bolshevik activists like Joe Stalin suddenly found the workers flocking to hear their speeches.

The 1917 Revolution saw a struggle for the oil wealth of Baku. The town was first seized by Whites (counter-revolutionaries), who enlisted the support of the British, who had been fighting their way to control of the Iraqi oilfields against the Turks throughout the First World War. In August 1918, to break the power of the Bolsheviks among the Baku oil workers, the twenty-six leading Communists, the Commissars, were shipped to the far side of the Caspian Sea by the British authorities and then shot. Not that it did the British much good; the Whites of Baku were also negotiating with the Germans and Turks, Britain's wartime enemies.

What to see The most memorable single building of Baku is the twelfth-century **Gyz-Galasy**, the Maiden's Tower, built before the Mongols came. It is easily climbed, and the view is striking.

Up the slope of the hill from the Maiden's Tower are the thirteenth-century town walls, and then the palace complex and the surrounding town of the **Shahs of Shirvan**. Although the palace is a large and rambling building, it is designed to produce an intimate effect, of small courtyards and a labyrinth of shaded rooms. The palace now houses the **Baku Museum**. The main mosque of the complex is dated to AD 1441, and the acoustics were cunningly controlled by the hollow jars fixed into the dome. The stone carvings of the Turbe or mausoleum of the Shahs, and of the Divan Khaneh are marvellously detailed.

From the **Icheri-Szekjer**, the old fortress, the view along the Bay of Baku spells out the history of the city. After the Maiden's Tower come the nineteenth-century buildings from the era of astonishing boom when Baku was Petropolis, the fastest-growing city in Asia. And beyond them again is the modern city, of Intourist hotels, office buildings and esplanades, of Soviet Baku.

The **Museum of Carpets and Applied Arts** should not be missed, but on the whole, Baku is a town to stroll through and is Middle Eastern enough to have a life on the streets. There are open air cafés near the foot of the Maiden's Tower and endless games of chess are played along the Esplanades. Around the walls of the old town is a ring of pleasant boulevards, shaded by trees.

Where to stay The three main hotels are:

Intourist, 63 Neftyanikov Avenue (tel. 92-1265); **Moskva**, 1a 76 Mekhti Gussein Street (tel. 39-2898); **Azerbaijan**, 1 Lenin Street (tel. 98-9842).

Where to eat

The best place to eat is at the **Caravansaray**, a historic stone building in the old town with the look of a fortress. A ring of cells encircles an open courtyard, where each merchant could sleep with his goods and his attendants. Now each of the cells serves as a private room, with a single knee-high table. The doors are kept open so you can see the floor show of traditional Azerbaijani music and dancing. The food is the traditional Azerbaijani specialities of *pilau* and *dolm* and *lyula-kebab*. But try the *kutab*, pastries filled with greens or pumpkin. And Muslim it may be, but Azerbaijan has a significant wine and cognac industry. Good value cognacs are Gurgul and Shervan. The Sadilli white wine is terrible but the Matrassa red is drinkable.

Excursions from Baku

Outside Baku, there are a number of worthwhile excursions. You should not miss the **Surakhany Fireworshippers' Temple**, where an enterprising management has tried to bring a touch of Madame Tussaud's to the usual grim sobriety of Soviet museums. From here, you can go on to **Neftyaniye Kamni** (oily rocks), on the coast, and to the beginning of the great causeway to the oil rigs at sea.

Kobustan

Seventy km from Baku is an amazing array of over 4,000 prehistoric rock paintings of animals, men and women, snakes and lions, ships, galleys and battle scenes, the sun and heavens, and what seem to be ritual dances. A tourist attraction for a very long time, the rocks also bear the signatures and graffiti of some Roman legionnaires.

Shemakha

There is a special excursion to Shemakha, 130 km to the west, the carpet weaving centre, with its medieval fortress and Seven Domes Mausoleum. The tour then continues to the ancient town of **Sheki**, 250 km further on, which was an important trading centre. The main Persian cities of Isfahan and Tabriz each maintained their own permanent caravansaray here, which have been preserved. The town also contains the eighteenth-century **Palace of the Sheki Khans**, which is notable for the interior murals and wood-carving.

*Soviet
Central Asia*

KAZAKHSTAN

• Tselinograd

• Karaganda

Lake Balkash

ARAL
SEA

CASPIAN
SEA

Turkestan

Chimkent

Dzhambul

• ALMA-ATA

UZBEKISTAN

Urgench

FRUNZE

*Lake
Issyk-Kul*

KHIVA
Kara-Kum

TASHKENT

KIRGHIZIA

Tien-Shan Mountains

TURKMENIA

SAMARKAND

Osh

CHARDZHOU

Zeravshan
River

BUKHARA

Leninabad

Bakharden

River
Amudara

Pendzhikent

CHINA

TADZHIKISTAN

ASHKHABAD

Kopetdag
Mountains

DUSHANBE

Pamir Mountains

IRAN

AFGHANISTAN

Soviet Central Asia

Introduction

From the Caspian Sea to the Chinese border, the five Soviet republics that make up the vast region of Central Asia – Turkmenia, Uzbekistan, Kirghizia, Tadzhikistan and Kazakhstan – used to be known in Tsarist days as Turkestan. It is a stunningly impressive region, a sub-continent of its own, with vast mountain ranges, huge deserts and inland seas and the marvellous buildings of a civilisation whose roots go back to ancient times.

It is also one of the outlying regions where the claim of the USSR to be a truly and happily multi-ethnic union will be most severely tested. The current total population of the five republics is 45 million, of whom fewer than 30 million count themselves as of Turkmen, Uzbek, Kirghiz, Tadzhik or Kazakh nationality and thus, by implication, from a traditionally Islamic background. And yet the growth rate of these national groups has been dramatically higher than that of the Russians and other non-Islamic groups of the USSR. In the 1970s, the population of the Russian Federation grew by 6 per cent, whereas the population of Tadzhikistan grew by 31 per cent, and of Uzbekistan by 29 per cent and of Turkmenia by 28 per cent. These sharply differing growth rates are already becoming more visible in each annual intake of conscripts to the Red Army, with delicate political implications while the Afghanistan War was under way. After an initial poor performance from the local reserve divisions from Central Asia, who were mobilised for the first phase of the invasion of Afghanistan in 1979–80, the war was mainly fought by white boys from the north.

In December 1986, the corrupt and elderly Party boss of Kazakhstan, Dinmukhamed Kunayev, was sacked on Moscow's orders and replaced by a Russian, Gennady Kolbin. This sparked off three days of anti-Russian riots in the Kazakh capital of Alma-Ata, with at least two deaths, pitched battles with the police, looting of shops and burning of cars, and hundreds of arrests. In retrospect, it seems more to have been the angry reaction of one Kazakh tribe, the Djiuzi, who saw their privileges disappearing with the era of their fellow tribesman, Comrade Kunayev, than a purely nationalist, still less Islamic, outburst. But it served as a powerful warning to Moscow. 'Demography is our domestic problem number one' Mikhail Gorbachev told the French Communist newspaper *l'Humanité* the month after the riots.

Corruption, pollution and religion come close behind as Kremlin concerns. In the Brezhnev years, the Central Asian Republics were given a great deal of autonomy, and corruption became widespread. Rashidov, the Party Chief of Uzbekistan, ran the republic like a feudal fiefdom. One of his cronies ran a private underground prison camp in a remote collective farm, and while the republic each year proudly announced yet a new record for the cotton crop, in fact the statistics were being doctored. The cotton crop was actually falling. The fraud squads from Moscow have been busily at work since Brezhnev died and the photo magazines have been full of pictures of the hordes of gold coins confiscated from former Ministers and local police chiefs. But Moscow's enforcers face an uphill battle. In Uzbekistan, death threats to them were commonplace and they would routinely switch car number plates after arresting some bigwig to stop the Uzbek police from staging a rescue.

Ecological crisis

Pollution may be the more serious concern in the long run. The level of the Caspian Sea seems to have stabilised after many years of sinking, but the Aral Sea is now almost dead. It has lost 60 per cent of its water, and its main fishing port, which used to provide 11 per cent of the Soviet fish catch, is now 60 km from the water. The sharply-increased salinity of the soil is not only threatening the crops, but is starting to increase infant mortality rates among the children of the local Karakalpak people. The cause has been the extraction of too much water for irrigation from the two great rivers which flow into the Aral Sea. This is bad enough, but the Aral Sea has been a weather kitchen for the rest of Asia, and it now seems that its slow disappearance is starting to affect the climate in the rest of the region. Indian climatologists have been worriedly studying its effects upon Himalayan snow fall, and thus upon the water levels of the great Indian rivers, the Ganges and Indus.

Religion

The role of Islam remains powerful in the region, and the growth of fundamentalism in neighbouring Iran has raised the alarming possibility (for Moscow) of a similar phenomenon on their side of the frontier. Certainly, Radio Tehran has been broadcasting solid religious propaganda, and there has been a sharp rise in the numbers of unofficial *mullahs*, itinerant preachers and Koran teachers who operate outside the tightly-controlled official Islamic Church. But only in Azerbaijan, on the western side of the Caspian Sea from Central Asia, does one find a sizable Shi'ite community of Soviet Muslims. Soviet Islam is, on the whole, a fairly relaxed Sunni religion, with some sharp regional differences.

The water
dispute

Indeed, Central Asia is so big and its five republics so different in size, geography and tradition that they seem to have little in common. But there is one powerful issue which is beginning to persuade the five republics to act, or at least to campaign, as one in Moscow. It is not religion, but water. The fastest-growing population in the country is stuck in the driest region, and even the run-off waters from the Pamir and Tien-Shan mountain ranges cannot slake the region's thirst. Farms and factories are just as thirsty as people, and the future growth of the region will depend on getting new water resources. The Siberian rivers are the obvious source of supply, and for over a decade there has been a bitter controversy between the Central Asians who say they face a disaster unless the flow of the Siberian rivers can be reversed to bring them water, and the Siberians who say that such a reduction of the fresh water supply into the Arctic would lead to a global disaster, with the Arctic ice cap advancing hundreds of kilometres into Siberia.

The dispute has spilled over from the academic institutes into the public arena, and there have been some ugly whiffs of racism about the way certain Russians object to their clean water going to help the Central Asian Muslims continue with their high breeding rates. The issue also became a political symbol of the tension between conservatives and reformers in Brezhnev's day. Brezhnev and Chernenko came from the generation when Soviet power had been symbolised by mammoth projects, and the grandiose river reversal was to be theirs. The plan was also heavily supported by Brezhnev's allies, the Central Asian Party chieftains like Rashidov and Kunayev. The scheme was bitterly and publicly opposed by reformers like Dr Abel Aganbegyan, now Gorbachev's economic advisor, as well as by most of the journalists and writers who have been in the forefront of *glasnost*. So it was no surprise when two years after Gorbachev came to power the scheme was officially dropped.

But citing the ecological disaster of the Aral Sea as new proof of their desperate need for water, the Central Asians have demanded that Moscow study the project yet again. It is looming as a clear-cut clash of interests between the Russian north and the Central Asian (or Muslim) south, and at a time when some very tough decisions will have to be made.

Most Soviet raw materials are in the north and east. Most of its factories are in the west, in old European Russia and the Ukraine. More and more of the future workforce will be coming from the south, and the vast distances between people, factories and natural resources are one of the major difficulties faced by the Soviet economy. And the peoples of Central Asia have shown a very marked reluctance to leave home and find new work in Siberia or in Moscow. Migration has mainly been the other way, with Russians so keen to move south that they now outnumber Kazakhs in the Kazakh capital of Alma-Ata. But to build the factories of the twenty-first century in Central Asia will mean ensuring new water supplies. The politics of water are going to be very important to the future of the Soviet Union as a multi-ethnic economic community.

Turkmenia

Although large in size, Turkmenia has the smallest population of the five republics, just over 3 million people, of whom two-thirds are of Turkmen nationality. Most of Turkmenia is desert, the Kara-Kum (black desert) being the largest, which creeps up to suburbs of the capital city of Ashkhabad. Just across the 3,000-metre peaks of the Kopetdag mountain range, which rears above Ashkhabad, is the border with Iran. Other than the oil and gas industry by the Caspian Sea, the main economic activity is based on cotton and, as in the past, on livestock. The republic breeds some of the finest horses in the country, the Arganaks, and indeed it claims that the famous Arabian breed began in these oases. Turkmenia is best known for its Karakul sheep, and is the main source of astrakhan.

Kara-Kum Canal

The economics of the region were transformed by the canal, which was completed in 1962, bringing water 800 km from the River Amur-Darya, known to the ancients as the Oxus. This is the water that fills the public fountains, lakes and roadside canals which keep the city and nourish its avenues of plane trees. Although the grandiose irrigation project has allowed cotton fields, orchards and vegetable crops to flourish in the desert, the ecology is now taking its revenge by drying up the Aral Sea, into which the Oxus used to flow.

Traditions maintained

The most striking feature of Turkmenia is the remarkable strength of the old customs in the rural areas, even after seventy years of Soviet power and schools and literacy programmes. Several times a year there are reports in the Soviet Press of young Turkmen women setting fire to themselves either because they have not got a husband or they have failed to satisfy their husband's family. The payment of *kalym*, a traditional dowry or bride price, is universal, although almost all of the young people are nominally members of the Komsomol, the Party youth league. The practice is stoutly defended by local Party officials as leading to much greater marital stability. Although women have stopped wearing the veil, the traditional *koinek* (long dress) is still common.

Ashkhabad

The capital was founded in 1881 as a Russian fort at a crossroads of caravan routes at the oasis of Akhal-Tekhinsk. Never a city of distinguished buildings, it was largely destroyed by an earthquake in 1948.

Getting there

Although it is on the railway line that goes from Tashkent to the Caspian Sea, tourists are recommended to travel to Ashkhabad by air.

What to see and do

Intourist organises tours of the **Ashkhabad Carpet Factory**, where the finished products have stopped celebrating the coming of the tractor and now echo the classic designs of the seventeenth to eighteenth centuries. However, they are not cheap.

Boat trips on the Kara-Kum Canal may be arranged, and also camel rides at the Ashkhabad Race Course, where some of the traditional '*kara-oy*', the portable felt tent of the desert nomads, have been erected.

Where to stay

In Ashkhabad, Intourist runs the **Hotel Ashkhabad**, 74 Svobody Prospekt (tel. 903-14), on the airport road. There is an Intourist office at 19 Ulitsa Gogol (tel. 569-32).

Excursions from Ashkhabad

The best single excursion is to the underground lake of **Bakharden**. This warm-water mineral bath is better than a tonic. They claim it contains over thirty different chemical elements, and they all seem to do one good.

Nisu

The main attraction of the area is the ruins of this ancient Parthian capital, 15 km to the west of Ashkhabad, which flourished from the third century BC to the second century AD, in the fringe of fertile land between mountains and desert. Advertised by Intourist as Turkmenia's Troy, it is impressive mainly to the archaeologist. There are two cities, Old Nisu, which as a royal residence was a closed precinct with temples and tombs, and New Nisu, which is in fact the older although it was discovered later. Known as Mihrdatkart, it shows considerable Greek influence, particularly the marble sculptures, an influence which dates back to the period of Alexander the Great. Its brick walls are nearly 9 metres thick.

At **Dzheitun**, 30 km north-west, the archaeologists have found a new Stone Age site which they claim marks the spot where man stopped being a nomadic herdsman and began to settle – the earliest example of a settled farming culture in Asia.

Chardzhou

Foreign tourists are also permitted to visit the second city of Ashkhabad, Chardzhou, and there are plans to open the ancient city of **Merv**, with its celebrated ninth-century Hamedani mosque.

What to see

Chardzhou's main attraction is the **Repetek Wildlife Preserve**.

Where to stay, and eat

Tourists are accommodated at the **Hotel Polyot**, which is at the airport.

Uzbekistan

With nearly 20 million people, Uzbekistan is the most populous of the Central Asian Republics, and by far the most rewarding for the tourist. The three ancient cities of Samarkand, Bukhara and Khiva are breathtaking, and they give Uzbekistan an overwhelming presence of history as an almost tangible force.

History

Near Samarkand archaeologists have found traces of man dating back for 100,000 years, and at Khiva, they have excavated an urban settlement that is 5,000 years old. A mere 2,500 years ago, Cyrus the Great, King of Persia, was killed in Sogdiana, near what is now Tashkent. Two centuries later, Alexander the Great captured Samarkand, then known as Marakanda, which was already a great city whose walls stretched 8 km around.

Few westerners have ever heard of the Battle of Talas, in AD 751, but it was here, just east of Tashkent, that the Arabs beat back a Chinese invasion, marking a frontier between these two great civilisations which has proved durable. One famous Asian dictator, Genghis Khan, devastated the region, but another, Tamburlaine, established the seat of his power at Samarkand. It was one of the great medieval trading centres, a place where the caravan highways – of the Silk Route from China, the trails to India and to Marco Polo's Europe, and later the Gold Route from Siberia – all met and crossed.

Tashkent

Getting there

Tashkent is the transport capital of Central Asia, the hub airport with the most frequent flights to Moscow and to the other republics. Although cars may be hired from Intourist for local journeys, it is not permitted to drive here from western Russia, and despite the fact there are passenger trains, they are slow and not recommended.

History

Tashkent claims an ancient origin, of which there is little remaining sign. In the nineteenth century, it was ruled by Khan Kokand, and then conquered by the Emir of Bukhara as part of the endless tribal conflicts among the Uzbeks that had weakened the once powerful empire that Tamburlaine had founded. By the mid-nineteenth century, it was a soft target for the Russian Empire. Its expansion was less a determined act of policy laid down in St Petersburg than a series of opportunist campaigns and land grabs by ambitious Russian Generals on the spot. But Tashkent itself was important enough, and well-placed enough, for General Cherniayev (disobeying orders) to besiege and take the place in 1865. The Russians established a protectorate over the Emirates of Bukhara and Khiva, which gave them a nominal autonomy, while Tashkent was built up as the forward base of the Tsarist Empire.

Rather like the garrison cities of the British Raj in India, Tashkent embodied apartheid in town planning. There was the new Russian town of railway station, barracks, bungalows and church, all laid out on a grid pattern. And then there was the native quarter, a great jumble of bazaars and mosques, mansions for the rich and mud huts for the poor, all crammed together around narrow streets.

Rapid growth

As the centre of the new Imperial Province, Tashkent grew rapidly, to a population of 150,000 within thirty years of General Cherniayev's conquest. By 1966, the city had grown to over a million people, when the great earthquake devastated Russian and native town alike. It is now a modern city of wide boulevards and high-rise apartments, rather more attractive than the average Soviet city because of the range of architectural styles. After the earthquake, every other republic and city in the USSR pledged assistance, and built part of the new housing. The grandiose era of Rashidov in the 1970s left the city with some lavish public buildings and monuments, museums, Metro stations and concert halls, although the most lavish of the lot, the planned mausoleum of Rashidov himself, has been cancelled.

What to see   What remains of the old town is clustered around the sixteenth-century **Barak-Khana Medrese**, the headquarters of the Islamic faith in Central Asia. There is a garden circled by small rooms or open cells arranged in a square, rather like cloisters, where church officials and scholars work in agreeable surroundings.

Opposite the restored Medrese is an undistinguished mosque whose congregation spills over to fill the entire square on religious festivals, and a magnificently decorated library with a number of antique Korans.

A short stroll away is the **Tomb of Abu Bekr**, the apostle who brought the teachings of Islam. Shorn of its tiling, it is an unimpressive brick structure, but it dominates the entrance to the largest Muslim seminary in the Soviet Union. To the south, on Komsomol Square, is the visually more impressive **Kukeldash Medrese**, which has kept more of its tiles.

There is little point in spending much time in Tashkent. It is the springboard to the historic cities.

Where to stay   Intourist guests are booked into the **Hotel Uzbekistan**, 45 Karl Marx Street (tel. 334-327), a skyscraper in what used to be the Russian colonial town, some of whose buildings can still be seen around the small park in front of the hotel.

Where to eat   Two of the better *Stolovaya* (cafeteria) are to be found in Tashkent. The first is on the corner of the second street to the left as you cross the park in front of the Uzbekistan Hotel; and the second is in Riga Square in front of the railway station. When I was last there they wiped down the tables between customers, most of the crockery and cutlery were clean and dry, and the food much better than average.

There are two good co-operative restaurants in Tashkent, the **Vermisazh**, in the basement of the city art gallery on Lenin Street, and the **Tulpan Café-Rendezvous**, on Pushkin Street, with an ambitious semi-oriental menu. The Bayan-Shirei local rosé wine is not bad if well chilled.

Samarkand
Getting there   Samarkand is a short journey from Tashkent by air (270 km), and at a height of 600 metres on the slopes of the Chupan-Ata, is cooler than the other towns of Uzbekistan. However, in mid-summer the temperatures soar above 30°C. Spring comes at the end of February, when the honeysuckle and apricot trees begin to blossom.

History   The city you see today is the creation of Tamburlaine and his grandson Ulug-Beg. The city that Alexander the Great captured had long disappeared, and by the year AD 1220, the Turko-Arabian city which had developed was wiped out by Genghis Khan. Its buildings were almost all demolished and its remaining population deported and enslaved. Samarkand was rebuilt after AD 1370 by Tamburlaine, and in the next century the work was continued by his grandson, a scientist and philosopher who built an observatory and studied navigation. Soon afterwards, the Shaibanid dynasty shifted their capital to Bukhara, and Samarkand began a slow decline that lasted until the arrival of the Russian Empire.

What to see
There are five great complexes of buildings in Samarkand that must be seen. Perhaps the most impressive, because it unfolds slowly rather than overwhelms you at once, is the **Street of Tombs** (Shahi-Zinda). This group of mosques and mausoleums of Tamburlaine's family, his companions in arms, and his women, all stretch along a narrow passage and stairs. The colours are unforgettable, the blue of the domes merging into the sky, and the mixtures of colour in the colonnades – red and purple among the green and blue – subtly delicate yet outrageously bold.

The **Registan**, the main square, is stunning. Three magnificent buildings on three sides of the square whose pillars, arches and domes explore perfection in shape, while the colours somehow manage both to glow and to embody coolness at the same time. On the west side is the **Ulug-Beg Medrese**, and opposite is the early seventeenth-century **Shir-Dor Medrese** (it means decorated with tigers), and to the north is the **Tillja-Kari Medrese**. A Medrese was an Islamic college, a place of religious higher education, and in a way we can think of this square as a Muslim equivalent of Oxford or Cambridge. Inside the Ulug-Beg Medrese you can see the cells surrounding the courtyard where the *mullahs* lived and taught.

North along Tashkent Street you reach the **Mosque of Bibi Khanum**, the largest in Central Asia. It was built with the money and loot Tamburlaine brought back from his Indian campaigns, and named after his beautiful Chinese wife. There is a marvellous legend that she planned the mosque as a gift to await Tamburlaine on his return from India, and work proceeded well, but the architect fell in love with her. He refused to continue unless she agreed to accept his kiss. She refused, and showed him a white, a brown and a speckled egg. They all taste the same, she said, however different they look. The architect should find another woman. He countered by showing her two glasses of colourless liquid. One was water, the other alcohol. Other women were tasteless; she was intoxicating. She agreed to the kiss, and the mosque was completed, but so fervent was his passion that it burned a brand upon her cheek. When Tamburlaine came home, he liked the mosque but had the architect tortured to death and his Chinese wife hurled from the minaret of the mosque she had built. And so ever since then, the story tellers continue, Central Asian women wore veils so that men would not be tempted to make a wife betray her husband.

Gur-Emir
Mausoleum

Tamburlaine himself, his two sons and Ulug-Beg are all buried in the **Gur-Emir Mausoleum**, to the south of the Registan, the most gloriously decorated of the buildings, and one which will probably be instantly recognisable from tourist posters. Tamburlaine's green jade tomb is in the crypt, his throne in the courtyard.

The last of the buildings that must be seen is on the road out of town. Go past the mound at Marakanda, which is the site of the city Alexander the Great took, and just across the river are the remains of what was the huge, nearly 30 metres tall **Observatory of Ulug-Beg**, with its giant sextant.

Where to stay

The Intourist hotel is the **Hotel Samarkand**, 1 Gorky Street (tel. 20-82).

Excursions
from
Samarkand

There are several organised excursions. Two of particular interest are to **Shakhrisabz**, 85 km south, the birthplace of Tamburlaine, and to **Pendzhikent**, which is just across the frontier in Tadzhikistan, but most easily approached from Samarkand. It is the massive archaeological excavation of a pre-Islamic city that flourished in the sixth to seventh centuries and was destroyed by the Arab invaders. Some of the jewels and the remarkable frescoes are now in the Hermitage in Leningrad, and in the Tashkent Museum.

Bukhara

The name is thought to come from the Sanskrit for monastery – '*vihara*' – but it was also a trading centre, with fifty specialist bazaars, including one for moneychangers, and forty caravansarays. Its splendid 45-metre Kalyan minaret was the symbol of Bukhara the devout and the wealthy. It served God when the faithful were called to prayer, Mammon when convicted criminals were hurled to their deaths from its gallery, and it also served commerce, since it was the great landmark by which the caravans steered their course. It was also a pestilential hole, famous for its plagues and epidemics. These were caused mainly by the eighty-five '*khauz*', small canals and ponds from which the people drew their water supply. Bukhara was sited away from the River Zeravshan, and it was served by the Shakhrud Canal.

History

Bukhara's great days began in the ninth to tenth centuries when it was the seat of the Samanid dynasty; and even after their fall it remained an intellectual and commercial centre. Bukhara then flourished whenever Samarkand was in decline, and vice versa, except when they were both devastated by Genghis Khan. Bukhara held out for twelve days and was then sacked, but recovered so fast that fifty years later the Mongols sacked the place again. It was quickly rebuilt, prospered, and in 1316 the Mongols came back for a third time. On this occasion Bukhara took over two centuries to recover, until the Shaibanid dynasty shifted their capital from Samarkand.

What to see

The city is too rich to describe in detail. The whole of the old town is a constant feast of old and beautiful buildings, many of them hard to find in the warren of streets. However, begin at the centre, with the **Ark**, the citadel whose 18-metre walls dominate the main square. The foundations are still the ninth-century castle that held off Genghis Khan, but the fortified gateway is fourteenth century, and contained dungeons.

South and east of the Ark, and going on foot through the old town, you will find the tall **Kalyan Minaret**, built in 1127, and soaring from a large square. Climb it for the view, and also because at the top you will see the first known use of the famous glazed blue tiles that were to become so characteristic of the region.

Back on the ground again, on the eastern side is the sixteenth-century **Mir-Arab Medrese**, stunning in its decoration and colours, and on the western side is the vast **Kalyan Mosque** with its enormous dome. It could accommodate a congregation of 10,000 people.

Continue walking east on Ulitsa Kommunarov, under the large dome of the **Taki-Zargaron** which covers the street junction. This was the covered market used by the jewellers. Straight on for about 90 metres, and on both sides of the street are two Medreses, the beautifully proportioned **Ulug-Beg** to the north, and the superbly decorated **Abdul-Aziz Khan** to the south. Retrace your steps to the covering dome of Taki-Zargaron and turn left. Go under the dome of another Taki at the crossing with Pushkin Street, and on to the next Taki, of the moneychangers, at Lenin Street. The Shakhrud Canal flows below. Some 90 metres to the east was the pond of Lyabi-Haus, surrounded by a modest tomb, a caravansaray, a Medrese and teahouses. This is how the ordinary Bukhara used to look.

At the far side of the old town, back beyond the Ark, in the Kirov Park, is the late ninth-century **Mausoleum of Ismail Samanid**, a cube topped with a dome. Utterly simple in proportion and yet complex in decoration, with receding doorways and chequered façade, it is a building of squat solidity that is also light and clean in its lines.

Where to stay   The Intourist **Hotel Bukhara** is at 40 Years of October Street (tel. 37-37).

Excursion from Bukhara   About 10 km outside the town is the nineteenth-century **Sittore-i-Makhi-Khasa**, the summer palace of the Emir of Bukhara, which should be seen if only because the last Emir, Said Alim Khan, had one of the great harems of 300 girls. When he felt romantic, tambourines would play – a signal for all the men to disappear and the latest candidates for harem status to start splashing and bathing in the small lake below the loggia. The Emir would climb into the loggia, enjoy the scene below, and toss an apple to the lucky lady.

Khiva   Khiva is the least known of the historic Uzbek cities, over 320 km north from Bukhara up the Valley of the Oxus. There is neither hotel nor airport at Khiva. It is a ninety-minute flight from Tashkent and you land and sleep at the nearby city of Urgench, which has nothing to recommend it.

The Khanate of Khiva flourished in the sixteenth century, thanks to its location on the trade route to the Volga when it made its fortune by selling Russian slaves. And it enjoyed another period of prolonged prosperity in the nineteenth century, before the Russian occupation of 1873.

What to see   Khiva is impossible to navigate without a guide, being too jumbled and twisting. A charming old town to stroll through, few of the buildings are in themselves stunning. The great charm of Khiva is the totality of it, the view of the place. From any angle, the skyline miraculously hangs together. At sunset, it is an image from The Arabian Nights. The best place for the view is from the fortified palace, the **Kunya-Ark**, or from the minarets. Many of the buildings of the old town are nineteenth century, including the windowless **Palace of the Harem**, and the throne room and prayer hall of the Kunya-Ark. The slim **Islam-Khodza** minaret, with its marvellous bands of tiles, was built in 1908. And the unfinished minaret, the **Kalta-Minor**, dates from the 1850s. It was almost certainly completed as planned, but is called unfinished because of the legend that Khan Mohammed wanted to build a minaret high enough to see Bukhara, 400 km to the south.

The most famous building of Khiva is the **Tomb of Pahlavan Mahmud** with its blue dome and richly decorated mausoleum chamber. The large **Dzhuma** (Friday) **Mosque** is eighteenth century, but 15 of the 213 columns inside are carved wood from the original tenth-century mosque on the same site. The **Medrese of Allaluli Khan** is now a museum dedicated to Avicenna, the great surgeon. The façade of the building is magnificent, and the museum contains the oldest known example of trepanning, a skull operation that dates from the first century.

Where to stay   The Intourist hotel in Urgench is the **Khorezm**, 8 Al-Buruni Street (tel. 47-29).

Kirghizia

The word Kirghiz has two meanings, stemming from the two ethnic strands that went to make the Kirghiz people. One strand were Turkic peoples from the Yenisey river basin of Siberia, who were driven back to the Kirghiz mountains by the surging expansion of the Mongols. In their language, Kirghiz means 'forty clans'. Once in their refuge, the forty clans from the Yenisey merged with the local aboriginal people, in whose language Kirghiz means 'the indestructible'.

Kirghizia is nearly all mountains and glaciers. Almost the size of West Germany, the republic would be flooded to the depth of 3 metres if all its glaciers were to melt. The capital, Frunze, itself 760 metres up, is dominated by the 4,500-metre range of the snowcapped Ala-Tau mountains to the south. But the Ala-Tau mountains are but one arm running from the mighty Tien-Shan, which rises to 6,700 metres along the Chinese border.

To anyone who likes mountains, Kirghizia is one of the most awesome of lands, magnificent in its high and jagged peaks and lush valleys. A place of superlatives, Kirghizia's herdsmen go hunting with golden eagles on their wrists. Its great folk legend, **The Manaz**, is several times longer than *The Odyssey* and *The Iliad* put together, and old bards still go through the mountain villages, singing it all from memory.

When they built the great Toktogul dam to tap the power of the River Karyn, the Kirghiz had to establish an alpine mountaineering school before the construction workers could dare approach the gorge where the 200-metre-high dam was to be built. One-fifth the length of Siberia's River Ob, the Karyn can generate six times as much power – it drops over 3,000 metres as it runs through the mountains.

Specialist holidays The interest of Kirghizia to tourists is mainly in the specialist holidays for mountaineering and hunting that can be arranged through Intourist. The warm water Lake Issyk-Kul is now a vacation resort. The claim that its water has curative properties is strengthened by the tremendous size to which trout can grow when transplanted into Issyk-Kul. Trout from Lake Sevan in Armenia, which normally grow to a maximum of 45 cm, proceeded to grow to 1.5 metres in Issyk-Kul. You need salmon rods to catch them.

Frunze The capital has no buildings older than 1917, although it now has a population of over 600,000. The second city of **Osh** is rather older, and is built on the site of a fortress that dates back to the time of Alexander the Great. But the changes and modernisations brought to these mountain people by the Soviet system have been dramatic. The record is impressive. In 1917, there was 96 per cent illiteracy, and male life expectancy in this largely nomad culture was forty-three. Today, illiteracy is unknown, life expectancy is seventy-two, and there are factories, power stations and universities. It is a Soviet success story, and a favourite theme for propagandists. The most gifted exponent of this theme is Tingiz Aitmatov, the Kirghiz novelist whose works sustain Soviet-Kirghiz culture. Short stories are made into ballets, novels are made into films and plays. The latest Aitmatov bestseller, *The Scaffold*, is being made into a film by the brilliant Kirghiz director Bolot Shamshiev.

What to see The racecourse in Frunze is great fun, since the Kirghiz traditionally learned to ride before they could walk. They play the celebrated horseback game of Ulak-Tartysh, a sort of polo which uses a goat instead of a ball. The riders grab the goat by the hair, throw it like a ball, wrestle each other for it and, finally, score goals with the poor creature. Although traditionally Muslim, they take a relaxed view of religion. One favourite horseback sport is called 'catch the girl', and if the young man catches her, he can claim a kiss. If he cannot catch her, she can then chase him, belabouring the wretch with her horsewhip. This is not the kind of role that women are meant to adopt in fundamentalist Islamic lands.

*Where to stay,
and eat*

The only hotel for foreigners is the **Ala-Too**, 1 Dzerzhinsky Prospekt (tel. 338-24), whose dining room claims to be the best in town. It has a frontier charm, the kind of place where bats occasionally fly through the room just above the diners' heads, and where on a convivial Saturday night well-connected customers suddenly dart from the table to wrestle the waitress amorously to the floor. The hard currency bar has a deceptively impressive display of dummy packs of western cigarettes and empty bottles of Scotch whisky.

The **Nasin** restaurant on Kievsky Prospekt now has a 'variety' floor show on Friday evenings, and a new co-operative café has opened, the **Vityaz**, on the corner of Kievsky Prospekt and Ulitsa Sovyetskaya. These events have transformed the night life of Frunze.

There is a co-op Korean restaurant on the outskirts of town, called the **Kuksi**, manned by Koreans whom Stalin shifted from the Far East to the Far South as a precaution.

As a visitor, you will almost certainly be offered *kumyss*, fermented mare's milk. Breathe through your mouth and just swallow – it smells worse than it tastes, and it is very good for your stomach. Be warned that it is slightly fizzy.

Tadzhikistan

Almost all mountain, the Republic of Tadzhikistan contains the USSR's tallest peaks, and the world's biggest glacier – over 70 km long. Unlike the other peoples of Soviet Central Asia who are of Turkic-Mongol stock, the Tadzhiks are part of the Iranian people, and their language, dari, is very similar to Persian. They claim Omar Khayyam as the Tadzhik national poet, but in the most isolated valleys along the Afghan and Chinese borders, there are villages which still speak the ancient Soghdian dialect, the language that Alexander the Great heard when his conquests brought him to these mountains. The second city of Tadzhikistan, Leninabad, is believed to stand on the site of a city he founded, Alexandra Eschate.

The most striking feature of Tadzhikistan is the riotous sense of colour. The national clothing of both men and women, the decoration of guest rooms and the interiors of public buildings are bright and jazzy. Bold primary colours jostle and clash together on jackets, skull caps and dresses. The crockery is sometimes so brilliantly coloured that it merges into the tablecloth in a confusing camouflage of bold patterns.

If you ask the Tadzhiks about this, they look mystified, wondering how anyone can possibly think their use of colour unusual. The inspiration seems to come from the high alpine meadows in springtime, when the wildflowers are a riot of colour. In small doses, this is great fun and Tadzhik robes make wonderfully improbable dressing gowns as souvenirs. Too much of it, like the sight of a room full of Tadzhiks wearing local costume in a restaurant where the ceiling, crockery and wall hangings all look like an explosion in a dye factory, can start to induce a nagging headache.

Expeditions

Independent travellers may organise hunting, mountaineering and wildlife expeditions through Intourist, but credentials from a mountaineering club will be expected. These are peaks for serious expeditions, not casual fell-walking. The wildlife of Tadzhikistan is the richest in the whole USSR. There is a very wide geological range between the wormwood scrub of the lowland and the high peaks, but there are deserts as well as alpine meadows at 4,500 metres in the Pamirs, high altitude snakes, and very rich birdlife. The snow leopard is now too rare for hunting, but Bukhara deer and several breeds of wild mountain goat are common.

The Tadzhik National Plan calls for a steady development of the leisure and recreation industry in the 1990s. Sanatoria and mountain rest homes have already been built, and the spectacular Varzob Gorge, north of Dushanbe, is already on the Intourist trail. Ski resorts are also being developed for winter sports. The most popular sport remains the traditional wrestling bouts, known as *Gishtingiri*, for which the prize is a lamb. Whenever *Gishtingiri* bouts are screened on TV, the power stations' engineers claim that a surge in electicity demand can be predicted.

Dushanbe

For tour groups, only the capital is open, with daily excursions to particular sights, although there are plans to open the ski resorts to foreign holiday-makers. Dushanbe was a very humble village until the 1920s. The word means 'Monday', and the city is named after the weekly market which used to be held here. From 1929–61, it was called Stalinabad. The city began to grow when the railway reached Dushanbe in 1929. Located in the Gissar Valley, the mountains to the north of Dushanbe, above which the Aeroflot planes to Moscow have to climb, are nearly 4,900 metres. They protect the city in winter, when the mean temperature does not drop below freezing, but in summer it soars to 28°–30°C. Now an industrial city of 600,000 people, almost half its population are Uzbeks, Russians, Kirghiz and Turkmen. The most important economic activity in the republic is hydro-electricity. Irrigation has made cotton into a major crop, but the abundant flowers have also made Dushanbe a centre of the Soviet perfume trade.

What to see

Dushanbe is an undistinguished city and the organised tours of the University and 1930s' Opera House are of limited interest. The tour of the textile factory which makes the characteristic '*tyubiteika*' headgear, the square, black skull cap, is more fun. The **National Museum** and the medieval illuminated manuscripts in the **Firdausi Library** emphasise the traditional link with Persian culture. You will certainly be taken to the famous Chaikhana, or central tea house, called the **Rokhat** (pleasure), on Putovsky Square, to sample green tea in a modern Intourist version of traditional surroundings.

Where to stay, and eat

Tourists are accommodated in the **Hotel Tadzhikistan**, 22 Ulitsa Kommunisticheskaya, and there is an Intourist bureau at Ulitsa Lenin (tel. 245-92).

Excursions from Dushanbe

There are excursions to the **Nurek Dam**, a feat of engineering, and to the mildly radioactive waters of the spa town of **Obigarm**, used to treat eczema. The most interesting excursion is to the eighth-century Buddhist monastery of **Adzhina-Tepe**, where the archaeologists found a 12-metre reclining Buddha. The ancient city of Pendzhikent, although on Tadzhik territory, is most usually visited from Samarkand (see p. 277).

Kazakhstan

Kazakhstan is the second largest republic of the USSR after the Russian Federation, and so big that it is normally listed separately, rather than treated as a part of Central Asia. But this vast region, over four times larger than the Ukraine, has a smaller population than Uzbekistan. The very low population density and the vast expanse of desert and empty steppes account for the location here of the Semipalatinsk Nuclear Weapons Testing Centre in the north-east of the republic, and the Baikonur Space Centre just north of the aptly-named Hungry Steppe.

Each of the republics of Central Asia has been rapidly modernised in the seven decades of Soviet rule. Illiteracy and feudalism have given way to mass education and universities, and epidemics have given way to a modern, if still flawed, health care system. The leading scientists and intellectuals often boast of their origins, born into the families of illiterate peasants; and what was once empty desert is now humming with industry and development. Kazakhstan has been for many years a showcase of the Soviet system, the classic example of the way a system of centralised planning could modernise an undeveloped and backward land. Asian and African leaders are proudly escorted to Kazakhstan to be shown what Communism can achieve. Arabs are steered to the Caspian Sea town of Shevchenko which depends on a nuclear reactor for its irrigation and drinking water, distilling the salt water of the Caspian.

When a country the size of the Soviet Union decides to invest mas-

Virgin Lands Scheme

sive resources in a single region, the effects can be dramatic. It was in 1954, the year after Stalin's death, that the Party planners in Moscow decided the capacity of the Ukraine to feed a growing population had been exhausted and that new farm land had to be developed. They decided to cultivate Tselino, the virgin land in the northern Kazakh steppes and, in classic Soviet style, whipped up the propaganda chorus of a great national venture to which every city and republic was expected to contribute. To this day, the vast state farms are named after Moscow, Leningrad and Kharkov, from whence came the eager young Komsomol volunteers.

That first winter, they froze, living in tents and sleeping in fur hats and mittens. But the crops of the first few years justified every expectation, and made the reputations and careers of Nikita Khrushchev, who had pushed the Virgin Lands Scheme, and the Party official in charge of the project on the ground, Leonid Brezhnev. But within four years, the yields began to fall disastrously as the thin steppe soil began to erode. It took another ten years to find the combination of irrigation, contour ploughing, windbreaks and fertiliser to keep the topsoil from blowing away, and to restore the crop yields to reasonable levels.

Mineral wealth

The exploitation of Kazakhstan's minerals has been equally intense, and is already starting to throw up the problems of environmental damage that nearly wrecked the Virgin Lands Scheme. There is growing concern about the impact of copper foundries on Lake Balkhash, and the fate of the River Ural that flows into the delicate ecology of the Caspian Sea.

The flood of new labour into Kazakhstan means that the original Kazakh population is now a minority in the republic. But the raw materials are plentiful, and the Soviet economy needs them. The republic is also a leading coal-mining region and the huge Ekibastuz open cast mine produced its billionth tonne of coal in 1985.

Intourist tours

The Soviet authorities are so proud of the industrialisation of Kazakhstan that several of the brash new cities are on the tourist trail. Intourist runs lengthy tours to: **Karaganda**, centre of the new iron and steel industry; to **Tselinograd**, capital of the Virgin Lands area; and to **Dzhambul**, a chemical centre that retains a small fragment of its old town of Taras, some twelfth-century baths and an aqueduct. There are also tours to **Chimkent**, centre of Kazakhstan's cotton-belt, which has some eleventh-century remains, from where an excursion can be made to the ancient city of **Turkestan**, with its celebrated fourteenth-century Khodzha mausoleum.

Where to stay

There are Intourist hotels in the following cities (hotel telephone numbers unavailable):

Karaganda: **Hotel Kazakhstan**, 49 Sovyetsky Prospekt, and **Hotel Karaganda**, 66 Sovyetsky Prospekt. Tselinograd: **Hotel Ishim**, 8 Ulitsa Mira. Dzhambul: **Hotel Taraz**, 75 Ulitsa Trudovaya. Chimkent: **Hotel Voskhod**, 1 Ulitsa Sovyetskaya.

Alma-Ata

The main tourist centre of Kazakhstan is Alma-Ata, which means 'father of apples', and the apricots and apples from the orchards around the city are legendary. Built at the mouth of a fertile valley, on a 760-metre high plateau, Alma-Ata is dominated by mountains that range up to 4,500 metres.

*History and
what to see*

Founded in 1854 as the Russian military outpost of Verny, the city still contains some of the buildings from that colonial period. The War Memorial Park on Gogol Street contains both the old **Officers' Club**, and the **Zenkov Cathedral**, built without a single nail and still, at 48 metres, the tallest wooden building in the USSR. It is now used as an art gallery and concert hall.

The city was used in the Tsarist period and after the Revolution as a place for political exiles. Leon Trotsky was the most eminent exile, sent here from 1927 until 1929, when he was banished from the Soviet Union. The house where he lived has been demolished, but older citizens recall that he spent most of his time hunting, wore thigh-high fishing boots and was accompanied by an enormous dog. Mornings he would spend sitting in the bookshop, reading but never buying. This section of town is now ironically the heart of the thriving new private sector, where the clothing co-operatives sell their home-made jeans and pseudo-western clothing with forged labels at exorbitant prices. The other booming co-operative business is bootleg tape cassettes of western pop and heavy metal music.

Alma-Ata is a modern town built on a grid pattern, but with trees, parks and roadside canals to make the streets bearable in the heat of summer. The main new square, the focus for the grand new museums and Party HQ used to be called Brezhnev Square until 1988, when they discreetly took down the street signs and renamed it New Square.

*Mount
Koktyube*

It also leads to Mount Koktyube (Green Hill), with its state guest house where Brezhnev used to live when he ran Kazakhstan, and to the cemetery where Kazakh big-wigs flaunt their wealth with lavish tombs. From the top of Mount Koktyube there is a celebrated view of the city, and the **Azul** Restaurant, built in the shape of the traditional yurt felt tents of the Kazakh nomads. The complex also contains a tea house, and a second restaurant that specialises in *shashlik* and other Kazakh dishes. The summit can be reached by road or cable car.

Further into the mountains, which are marked by barriers to protect the city from the regular mud slides, is the high altitude Medeo winter sports centre and ice skating rink. On the way is the excellent **Samal** restaurant, a semi co-operative sponsored by Intourist.

Ayak-Kalkan

The strangest excursion from Alma-Ata is a day-trip to the health resort of Ayak-Kalkan, which is famous for its 'singing sands' as the wind buffets the sand dunes and produces great hoots and bellows rather like a ship's siren.

Where to stay

Visitors to Alma-Ata stay in Intourist's **Hotel Otrar**, Gogol Street (tel. 30-00-39).

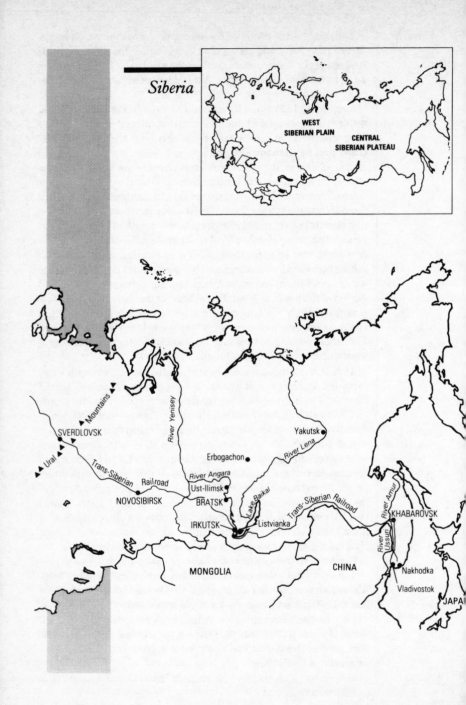

Siberia

WEST SIBERIAN PLAIN

CENTRAL SIBERIAN PLATEAU

Ural Mountains

SVERDLOVSK

Ural

Trans-Siberian Railroad

River Yenisey

NOVOSIBIRSK

River Angara

Ust-Ilimsk

BRATSK

IRKUTSK

Erbogachon

Lake Baikal

Listvianka

Yakutsk

River Lena

Trans-Siberian Railroad

River Amur

KHABAROVSK

River Ussuri

Nakhodka

Vladivostok

MONGOLIA

CHINA

JAPAN

Siberia

Introduction

Tourism in Siberia is still for the moment limited to the route of the Trans-Siberian railroad, and excursions to the regions around the famous freshwater Lake Baikal and the Bratsk power station. This is unfortunate, because so much of Siberia is remarkably beautiful, and all of it shares in the deeply impressive grandeur of a place so big, so empty, and so very cold. Siberians are to other Russians like Texans to other Americans: they think on a much grander scale. There is a saying that to a Siberian, a hundred roubles is not money, a hundred *versts* (about 96 km) is no distance, and a mere hundred grams of vodka is not a drink.

But Siberia tends to impose the big perspective. It is without doubt the richest collection of raw materials on earth. The Middle East may have a little more oil, and South Africa more gold, but in the range of its wealth and resources, Siberia has no rival. Lake Baikal is so big that if it were suddenly emptied it would take all the rivers in the world a year to fill it again.

History   The journey to cross Siberia by train takes a week, and given the vastness it is remarkable how quickly the Russian colonists explored and settled the place. The process began in 1581, when the Cossack adventurer Yermak, together with his band of mercenaries, crossed the Urals to Isker. Yermak had promised the Tsar to commute his conquests in exchange for a pardon for past crimes, which he duly did. Although Yermak was killed in 1584, within six years the town of Tobolsk, on the River Ob, had been founded as a fortified trading post. Twenty years later, the Cossacks and colonists had reached the River Yenisey at Turukhansk, and in 1633 Yakutsk, on the River Lena, was established. Irkutsk, by Lake Baikal, was founded in 1652 and by the end of the century they had crossed the Pacific Ocean at Kamchatka and begun to colonise Alaska. (The Tsar finally sold Alaska to the United States for seven million dollars in gold in 1867.) The Russian expansion met little resistance or fighting from the primitive tribes although the Buriats, local tribesmen in the Buriat Mountains, kept up a guerrilla harassment of Irkutsk for a decade in the 1650s, and in 1696 the old enemy, the Mongols, besieged Irkutsk before being beaten off.

The exploration and settlement were accelerated by the rivers.

Even though they are frozen for up to six months of the year, river traffic plays a crucial role in Siberian transport. The spring thaw sees a furious bustle at the Siberian river ports as the barges load to carry food and industrial supplies up the rivers to the vast regions where there are no railroads. To this day, the rivers and inland waterways carry 135 million passengers a year, and air transport only 112 million.

Siberia begins at the Ural Mountains, which run for 3,000 km from north to south, but they are not an impressive mountain range. Their maximum height in the far north is just over 1,500 metres, and to the south, where the railroad climbs to a maximum height of 420 metres to cross the Urals range, they are little more than modest ridges.

East of the Urals runs the taiga, the frozen forest and tundra of the north, and, more to the south, is the biggest bog in the world, the Urmany. The West Siberian gas and oil fields are located here, and their exploitation in the 1970s and '80s was a remarkable feat of engineering, as difficult in its own way (and thus as costly) as the extraction of oil from the North Sea. Whole drilling rigs simply disappeared into the bogs. There was little point in trying to lay down rail tracks or permanent roads. Hovercraft and amphibious military vehicles had to be used. Permafrost in winter, slush in spring and autumn, mosquito-infested bog in summer, it was an oilman's nightmare – which is why salaries were three and four times higher than usual.

The rail line itself, and the ribbon of towns and cities, runs far to the south, skirting the firm steppes to the River Yenisey, where a different geology begins, the Central Siberian Plateau. Averaging from 400–900 metres, this plateau of primary rocks is rich in coal and copper, and it is permafrost land. The top 2 metres thaw in summer, but the permanently frozen ground beneath can be up to 1.6 km thick, which complicates the design of buildings. They have to be erected on insulated piles, or they would slowly melt the permafrost and sink. From Central Siberia all the way east to the Pacific, the pine trees give way to endless larch forests. Beyond the River Lena, and stretching to the Pacific, is a series of mountain ranges of up to 3,000 metres, and beyond them are the still active volcanoes of Kamchatka, part of a seismic zone that stretches south to Japan.

Climate   The climate is not quite so bad as it sounds. There are places of intense cold. Om-Yakon, in the north-east mountains near Yakutsk, is the coldest place in the northern hemisphere, with temperatures down to 67°C below freezing. Unwary passengers descending from the aircraft hear the crack of the synthetic soles of their boots. Film shatters like glass inside their cameras. Triple glazing is commonplace, and the engines of working trucks are kept running throughout the winter because, without a heated garage, it is too difficult to start them again.

There are compensations. When it is this cold, as you exhale, the water vapour in your breath freezes instantly and falls tinkling to the ground, a quite magical sound which Siberians call the whispering of stars. And then there is the great consolation of vodka. But Siberians who drink (and most of them do) prefer spirt to vodka. Spirt is rocket fuel, virtually raw alcohol, and the Siberian trick is to mix it with water – the quantity depending on how far north you are when the bottle is opened. At 50N, you mix it half and half. At 66.6N, you add two-thirds spirt, one-third water and so on. Spirt has the great advantage of not freezing when carried in a backpack into the taiga. Vodka freezes solid.

The Siberian cities are mainly located too far south for quite such intense cold. In Irkutsk, the mean January temperature is 25°C below freezing, and at Novosibirsk, a positively balmy 18°C below. The cold snaps, however, can plunge towards 40°C below, but they are rare. One of the main reasons for Siberia's climate is a highly stable system of anticyclones around Lake Baikal for up to eight months of the year. But in glorious July, Irkutsk has the same mean temperature as Paris.

The Trans-Siberian rail journey

Unless you are besotted with trains, or are deeply committed to this journey, or need to catch up with your reading, avoid this train. Or at least, do not spend up to ten days of your life pottering slowly across an eternal and unchanging landscape of which you will see very little. For most of the journey, mile-long trains carrying coal and iron ore will chug slowly past your window in an endless chain, blocking your view. This is a working railroad, more than a tourist line. The smart way to travel the Trans-Sib is to cheat a little. Fly to Irkutsk, and then catch the train for Khabarovsk on the River Amur. This takes you through the most scenic part of the route, around Lake Baikal and through the Buriat Alps and the Yablonovy Mountains to the Rivers Ussuri and Amur. And once at Khabarovsk you are only eight hours from Moscow by air. If you want to travel on to other countries, you can catch the train from Irkutsk to either Beijing, or Nakhodka on the Pacific coast where there are regular ferries to Japan. And if you possibly can, book on the Chinese train that runs once a week. It is cleaner, more comfortable and the food is better. If you are stuck with a Russian train, the first-class one called *Rossiya* has the best reputation. Take lots of food and drink because you will not be impressed by the restaurant.

Current prices are 350 roubles (in hard currency) for a place in a four-berth cabin on a second-class train on the ten-day trip to Nakhodka, with a transfer to Yokohama. A place in a two-berth cabin on a first-class train is 635 roubles. There are package tours that include a stretch on the Trans-Siberian line, but to book on your own behalf means that Intourist will want a minimum of six weeks' notice to arrange your 'independent travel'. And then you face a waiting list for the train itself. There is a highly readable account of the journey in Eric Newby's book *The Big Red Train Ride*.

The tourist cities of Siberia

Sverdlovsk By the time you read this, the Urals industrial city of Sverdlovsk may be open to western tourists. Founded in 1721, the settlement's first ironworks began work within five years, and heavy industry has hardly stopped since. The proximity of raw materials explains the early growth of the city, whose name used to be Ekaterinburg. This is where the Tsar and his family were executed in 1918 by the local Soviets, who feared the town was about to be recaptured by counter-revolutionaries. Sverdlovsk grew even faster in the 1930s and then during the war, when the Urals industries were usefully out of range of German bombing. The centre of the biggest engineering combine in the country, Uralmash, the population is now 1.4 million. A major base for the aircraft, rail and ball-bearing industries, Sverdlovsk has also more recently been a cradle for Soviet politicians. Prime Minister Nikolai Ryzhkov came out of the technocratic Uralmash management team, and the outspoken radical reformer Boris Yeltsin, who was fired from his job as Party Chief of Moscow in 1987 after attacking conservatives in the Kremlin, made his political career as First Secretary of Sverdlovsk.

Novosibirsk This is the largest city in Siberia, and an industrial and food processing centre that is also a major rail junction for the Trans-Sib line, and for the Turk-Sib railroad down to the Kuzbas mining region. It is the middle of the area where your view from your carriage will be blocked by freight trains.

Novosibirsk was founded in the 1880s as the town of Novonikolayevsk, and owed its growth to a current population of nearly 1.5 million, to the railroad, which needed a place to cross the River Ob and for which there were secure granite riverbanks here. The first stone building rose in 1910, but since then growth has been explosive. There are no great buildings, but it boasts the biggest opera and ballet theatre in the country.

Akademgorodok Thirty km south is the science city of Akademgorodok, founded after a decision of the 20th Party Congress of 1956 to develop the scientific and technical expertise for the intensive exploitation of Siberia. Perhaps the world's biggest think-tank, with specialist research institutes in almost every topic and elite schools, its impact has not been as dramatic as its founders hoped. But it is now coming into its own as the think-tank behind the Gorbachev reforms. Dr Abel Aganbegyan, Gorbachev's economic advisor, and the influential sociologist Dr Tatyana Zaslavskaya, both made their names at Akademgorodok, with research into ways of overcoming social and economic problems that would have been too radical for Moscow, where academic life was more closely monitored by the Central Committee.

Irkutsk This modern city of over 500,000 people was founded in the seventeenth century, and the town centre retains many of the neo-classical and wooden buildings from pre-revolutionary days. Now an industrial zone on the River Angara, scene of one of the world's most ambitious hydro-electric schemes, Irkutsk owed its early growth to the Tsar's secret police and penal systems. The aristocratic rebels of the Decembrist movement of 1825 and the Polish nationalists of 1830 helped make Irkutsk into a major cultural town. By 1862 it boasted sixteen schools, a Catholic, Protestant and twenty-six Orthodox churches, six hospitals, and with a population of 25,000 was one of the largest towns in Russia, and the commercial centre to the nearby Altai gold mines. In winter, the market still sells milk in frozen chunks.

What to see   The modern centre of the town is **Kirov Square**, surrounded by the large Angara Hotel, a Stalin-era Party HQ, and the **Spasskaya Church**, built by exiled Poles, which is now a museum. On the way to the river bank you pass the eighteenth-century **White House**, formerly the Tsarist Governor's residence, and now part of the university. Beside the small River Ushakovka, a tributary of the mighty Angara, is the nineteenth-century **Znamensky Monastery**, with the tomb of the Princess Trubetskaya, who caught the imagination of nineteenth-century Europe by choosing to follow her Decembrist husband into exile.

Where to stay,   **Intourist Hotel**, 44 Gagarin Boulevard (tel. 91-335, 91-338);
and eat   **Angara Hotel**, 2 Kirov Square (tel. 91-498).

Baikal   One-fifth of all the fresh water in the world is in Lake Baikal. Up to 1.6 km deep, containing as much water as the whole Baltic Sea and as big as Belgium, it is 25 million years old and a unique geographic phenomenon. Of the 1,800 living species scientists have identified in the lake so far, over 1,200 of them are unique to Baikal. One of the most striking is the Golomyanka fish, which lives deep down and is no more than a vertebra surrounded by fat. When brought to the surface, it bursts. There are seals whose ancestors swam down from the Arctic Ocean and adapted to fresh water. The water is delicious and very clear. It should stay that way, after an unprecedented public protest movement began in the 1970s, demanding the closure of the cellulose plants which were beginning to pollute the lake. It took seventeen years, but in 1988 the plants were finally banned from releasing anything into the lake. The first Soviet mass movement to force a change in government policy and to defeat the bureaucracy, the political implications of the Baikal protest movement are profound.

Getting there   Day excursions are arranged from Irkutsk by road or by fast hydrofoil, and at the village of Listvianka, where the Baikal Museum
Where to stay,   is worth a visit, there is now a modern lakeside hotel, **Hotel Baikal**
and eat   (tel. 96-234). Many of the small dachas near the river bank have their own saunas, and through Intourist you may be able to arrange to take a hot sauna bath, followed by a sluice down with water from the lake, an experience to be relished at evening as the light from the sinking

sun plays red and gold on the snow-capped mountains across the lake.

Bratsk

There are 336 rivers which flow into Lake Baikal, and only one, the Angara, which flows out. From Irkutsk north along the Angara a whole new industrial zone has built up over the last thirty years, around the electric power generated by the chain of dams built to tap the River Angara. The first dam is at Irkutsk, and produces 4 billion kilowatt hours a year. At Bratsk, the dam produces six times as much power, and its building in the 1950s was an epic venture, which state propaganda hailed as that generation's equivalent of the first Five-Year Plans. Most of the builders were young people, Komsomol members, who began by living in tents on the virgin taiga. They froze in winter and were eaten alive by mosquitoes in summer as they built the dam, the new town and the surrounding factories virtually all at once. There were 35,000 lumberjacks employed simply in felling trees. These days, there is a population of 250,000, and further up river at Ust-Ilimsk is another dam and an even newer town, which already has its opera and ballet theatre where you can see the local schoolchildren perform *Swan Lake* on a spot where only wolves howled ten years ago. Further up river again begins the BAM, the Baikal-Amur-Mainline, the second Trans-Siberian railroad, built far to the north of the first, and able to tap the remote new iron core and copper deposits found far to the north of Lake Baikal.

Where to stay

The hotel in Bratsk is the **Taiga**, 35 Mir Street (tel. 43-978/9).

Erbogachon

This is a hunting village of log cabins about a 1,600 km north of Lake Baikal, on the Lower Ingusk River, where hunting parties may sometimes be arranged through Intourist. Many of the local professional hunters are Evenks, indigenous Siberian tribesmen who still travel through the winter taiga on reindeer-drawn sleighs. They hunt sable, wolf and fox for the valuable skins, eat elk, and watch Moscow TV news via satellite. Erbogachon can be reached by helicopter and, if you can get there, it is a quite magical place. But avoid the great melt of the spring, when everyone in town is conscripted into the great loading and unloading of the river barges on which the village depends.

Where to stay

Accommodation is provided in a wooden dormitory or in the local hunters' huts.

Khabarovsk

Founded in 1858, and named after the seventeenth-century explorer of Siberia, Khabarovsk is now the main industrial centre of the Soviet Far East, with a population of some 550,000. It is built on seven hills that overlook the confluence of the Rivers Ussuri and Amur, which both mark the border with China. It is a grimly functional and mainly modern city, too hilly to walk with pleasure, and its lack of amenities and desperate housing shortage have led to a steady loss of population over the past decade, even though the population of the Far East as a whole has increased. On a visit there in 1986, Gorbachev complained that the Far East was not justifying the investment it was receiving from Moscow, and that the economic performance would have to improve. The way to do it, Gorbachev argued, was by more trade and contact with the neighbours – China, Japan and even Australia were recently invited to hold a trade fair in the Soviet Far East. Gorbachev's policy seems to involve a transformation of the traditional one in this region of tightly sealed borders, massive security zones with sealed-off areas and big military bases. Also in 1986, Gorbachev promised that the port (and big naval base) of Vladivostok would 'soon' be open to western travellers. Two years on, and Vladivostok is still closed.

Where to stay, and eat Visitors stay at the **Intourist Hotel**, 2 Amursky Boulevard (tel. 33-7634, 33-6507).

The Golden Ring

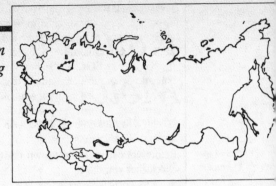

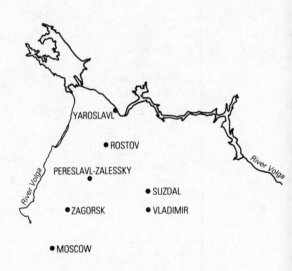

YAROSLAVL

ROSTOV

PERESLAVL-ZALESSKY

SUZDAL

ZAGORSK

VLADIMIR

MOSCOW

River Volga

River Volga

Routes for Motorists

See also Motoring and Camping on pp. 106–11.

Before your first encounter with Soviet immigration guards, double check that you have:

- Passports with visas.
- International driving licence with an insert in Russian.
- Car registration document.
- 'Instructions for Motorists' issued by Intourist in the country where you booked your tour and where your visas were issued.
- Sticker for your car indicating country of origin.
- Petrol vouchers, also issued by Intourist.
- List of hotels and/or camping sites, and vouchers for overnight accommodation throughout your stay. This will also include your authorised route.
- If you have not taken out insurance before departure (and note that very few western companies will insure you for the Soviet Union), you may do so at the border post.

Follow Soviet traffic regulations; do not overtake when there is a solid white line on your side of the road.

Petrol stations in the Soviet Union often lack the high octane fuel required by western cars, so always refuel whenever it is available.

The Golden Ring
(Zolotoye Koltso)

Moscow to: **Zagorsk**, 70 km; **Pereslavl-Zalessky**, 140 km; **Rostov**, 200 km; **Yaroslavl**, 260 km; **Vladimir**, 186 km; **Suzdal**, 216 km

The ancient Russian cities to the east and north of Moscow – and some of them were once rivals as potential capitals – are known as the Golden Ring. They are hauntingly beautiful, visibly run down in spite of recent efforts at restoration, but they embody the great traditions of Russian culture. The Golden Ring is where you can still discern what Russia was before the Tartars came to conquer. And this is Russian history made flesh, where you can understand the way the Orthodox

Church subordinated itself to the Russian state and the cause of national survival.

This ought to be a most pleasant three-day excursion by car, driving out through Zagorsk to the River Volga at Yaroslavl, and then turning south to Suzdal, and returning to Moscow via Vladimir. In practice, Soviet security makes this impossible. For some baffling reason, it is not permitted to drive the 80 km from Yaroslavl to Suzdal, and so you must retrace your steps to Moscow, and then drive 190 km east again to reach Vladimir and on to Suzdal. Intourist hotels are available in three of the six main towns of the Golden Ring: Yaroslavl, Vladimir and Suzdal.

You will need some careful planning to enjoy the Golden Ring. One way to tackle it is to spend the morning and have lunch at Zagorsk, drive on to Rostov and spend the afternoon there, then drive on to Yaroslavl to spend the night. You can see Yaroslavl the following morning, have lunch at the hotel, and then motor back to Moscow, stopping off for an hour to stroll around Pereslavl-Zalessky. After an overnight stay in Moscow, drive out to see Vladimir the next day, sleep at the Suzdal Motel, see Suzdal the following day and drive back to Moscow in the last afternoon. If you have limited time, the trip to Suzdal and Vladimir is the most rewarding, so long as you can spare a morning for a separate trip to Zagorsk.

Zagorsk
What to see

The Trinity Monastery of St Sergius (Troitse-Sergiyeva Lavra) lies 64 km north-east of Moscow, and the approach by road is breathtaking, the great bell-tower, the golden domes of the monastery churches and the battlements of its protective fortress emerging over the brow of the final hill, defiant and beautiful. Until 1988, when the seat of the Patriarch was allowed to return to Moscow's Danilovsky Monastery, Zagorsk was the centre of the Russian Orthodox Church for most of the Soviet period. The Patriarch lived within the Monastery, which also housed the main seminary to train future priests, and acted as a national shrine for the faithful. It was given the prosaic name of Zagorsk in 1921.

The monastery was founded in the 1340s by the remarkable monk Sergei Radonezhsky (St Sergius), who launched a movement for national unity and revival while the Mongol yoke still lay heavily on the land. His disciples quickly established a total of twenty-three monasteries around north-eastern Russia, which was to be the heartland of resistance to the Mongols. Sergei believed that Russia had fallen to the Mongols because its princes were divided among themselves, so he preached unity under Moscow – and declared formal religious anathema against any prince who argued. It was Sergei's campaign, his injection of religious fervour into the national crusade, that enabled Dmitry Donskoy to lead the Russian armies to their first victory in the field against the Mongols at the Battle of Kulikovo.

Sergei himself is buried under the **Trinity Cathedral**, the oldest building within the monastery complex, and the furthest church from the entrance. Its single gold dome rises above a tall central drum and a somewhat dumpy base which more clearly than many church buildings shows the debt Russian architecture owes to the Byzantine basilica. Sergei's grave remains a shrine for the devout and for Russian nationalists alike. The iconostasis used to contain works by Rublyov and by Daniil Cherny, but the growing pressure of tourism means that they have been shifted to the Tretyakov and other museums including Zagorsk's own **Museum**, in the long low building beneath the Kelarskaya Tower. The devotion of the faithful can take strange forms. The Russian Orthodox Church has always been a haven for the mentally ill, and with the long state abuse of Soviet psychiatry for political ends reducing public confidence in mental hospitals, many families understandably take their afflicted to the church. The result is sometimes almost medieval scenes of families crawling on their knees to the churches begging for divine intercession, splashing each other with holy water from the well just opposite the tomb of Boris Godunov, roaring out hymns as they stamp or limp around the courtyard, and sometimes fighting and wrestling for precedence to kiss a particular shrine.

One of the great treasures of a museum that is filled with priceless relics, is the embroidered portrait of Sergei, dating from the very beginning of the fifteenth century, which once covered his plain wood coffin in the church. The Trinity Monastery was one of the richest in all Russia, a beneficiary of the wills and bequests of countless devout nobles. The monastery owned large tracts of land and over 120,000 serfs, and the jewelled chalices and icon frames on display testify to its wealth. The monastery museum also contains an excellent collection of icons, mainly of the Moscow school, and a folk art section.

The Church of the Holy Ghost, a smaller and much more refined building that rises to its single blue and gold spire, is one of the great masterpieces of Russian architecture. Built by craftsmen from Pskov in 1476, it was the first brick structure in the monastery. The detail on the frieze of the church is very fine. The large and central church is the **Cathedral of the Dormition** (1559–85), built after Ivan the Terrible had begun raising and reinforcing the walls of the fortress. The seventeenth-century iconostasis and the dazzling frescoes make the interior extraordinarily lavish, as if locked inside a jewel box. The defensive walls were begun in the 1540s, and strengthened yet again to their current height of some 12 m just before the Time of Troubles, when the monastery withstood a sixteen-month siege of 30,000 Polish–Lithuanian invaders. In the later seventeenth century, a further period of building saw the construction of the Tsar's **Chertogi Palace**, the all-white **Church of Saints Zosima and Savvaty** with the high tent roof, and the splendid **Refectory** with its chequerboard and tiled façade and balcony.

Peter the Great came here regularly and used the monastery as a base for hunting expeditions, an activity commemorated by the **Utichya (Duck) Tower**, just to the right of the main gate. Above the gate in Peter's reign was built St John the Baptist's **Church of the Gates**. The 76 m bell-tower was designed by Dmitry Ukhtomsky in 1740, and took thirty years to erect.

The town of Zagorsk is also famous for its craftsmen producing wooden toys, and contains two Matrioshka factories, the nests of wooden dolls which fit inside one another. The **Zagorsk Art Production Workshop**, in the main square beside the monastery, claims to be the biggest creative collective in the Moscow region, and produces most of the toys that you will find in the Beriozkas. The **Zagorsk Toy Museum**, just off the main square, is open daily from 11 a.m. to 6 p.m., closed on Mondays.

Where to eat The **Zolotoye Koltso** Restaurant is five minutes from the monastery main gate, just across the Podol, the low-lying ground alongside the river under the fortress walls. Bookings may be made through Intourist at your Moscow hotel. Package tours of the Golden Ring organised through Intourist will usually include lunch here before going on to Pereslavl and Rostov.

Pereslavl-Zalessky Founded by Prince Yuri Dolgoruky in 1152, five years after he founded Moscow, the monastery town of Pereslavl-beyond-the-woods occupies a stunning position alongside Lake Pleshcheyevo. A border town in the thirteenth-century rivalries between Moscow and Tver, it was from here that Alexander Nevsky set out to do battle with the Swedes in 1240 and with the Teutonic Knights in 1242. The town enjoyed a golden age in the sixteenth and seventeenth centuries, both as a centre for Ivan the Terrible's secret police and bodyguard, the *Oprichniki*, and as a centre for the trade route to western Europe via Archangel and the White Sea. The young Peter the Great began his boat-building here, one of which is on display in the local museum, and the town consequently claims to have founded the Russian Navy.

What to see Most of the twelfth-century buildings have gone, but the sturdy and fortress-like **Cathedral of the Transfiguration of the Saviour** was built in the 1150s and still survives on Krasnaya Ploshchad in the centre of the town on the south bank of the River Trubezh. Opposite is the sixteenth-century **Church of St Peter the Metropolitan**, one of the first churches to copy the tent-roof style of the simple wooden churches of the villages, but using stone.

The town is surrounded by monasteries. To the south-west, atop the low hill between Sovyetskaya Street and the lake, is the seventeenth-century Goritsky Monastery, which is now the **History and Art Museum**. Its main building is the fine green-domed **Cathedral of the Dormition**, which contains a magnificent carved iconostasis of the 1750s. Its acoustics are among the best in Russia. The entrance to the monastery, through the Holy Gates, is marvellously ornate.

One of the richest regional museums of the country, it has a fine collection of Russian nineteenth-century paintings, and some outstanding sixteenth-century icons. Open daily from 11 a.m. to 6 p.m., closed on Mondays and the last day of each month.

On the far side of Sovyetskaya Street, surrounded by green fields and the river, stands the sixteenth-century **Monastery of St Daniel**. Although badly run down, it contains the remarkable miniature **Church of All Saints** (1687) and a bell-tower which once housed the bell that now hangs in the central span of the belfry of Ivan Veliki in the Moscow Kremlin. On the outskirts of the town, surrounded by a long white wall with roofed turrets at each corner, is the newly restored **Monastery of St Necetas**, begun in the sixteenth century, and completed in the nineteenth. It looks better from a distance than close to.

Rostov

Traditionally known as Rostov the Great (Rostov-Veliki), this is one of the oldest towns of northern Russia, first mentioned in the Chronicles in AD 862. Some 64 km further than Pereslavl-Zalessky on the Yaroslavl road, it stands on the banks of Lake Nero. Its greatest age was far in the past, as the centre of the Rostov-Suzdal principality from the tenth century, and from 1207 as capital of the independent principality of Rostov itself. Almost destroyed by the Mongol attacks, it was finally absorbed within the expanding influence of Moscow in the 1470s.

What to see

Under Ivan the Terrible a programme of rebuilding began with the **Cathedral of the Dormition** which virtually obliterated what few traces the Mongols had left of the older medieval city. On the ancient cathedral's south door you will see handles in the shape of a lion's head, which are twelfth-century originals. The basement and pillars of the five-domed cathedral use the original stone. The bell-tower, built in the 1680s, is one of the most famous in Russia. The biggest 32-tonne bell was named Sysoy, after the humble village priest who was the Metropolitan's father. Berlioz came to Rostov to hear the chimes, Mussorgsky tried to put them into his operas, and they can be heard for over 30 km.

The Kremlin

Rostov is unusual in that this main Cathedral of the Dormition is not included within the Kremlin, which was built nearly a hundred years later, in the seventeenth century, by the Metropolitan Iona Sysoyevich as his residence. This Kremlin, decorative rather than defensive, has two great ceremonial gateways, each flanked by churches. All of the buildings may be reached from the walls; the centre of the courtyard is left empty and contains only trees and a small lake. The five-domed **Church of the Resurrection** (1670), which stands above the holy gates, is filled with stunning and unusually light frescoes, of which the white-turbaned Pilate washing his hands is my favourite.

The jewel of the Kremlin churches is the cube-shaped and single domed **Saviour in the Vestibule** (Spas-na-Senyakh) (1673), with its dramatic raised interior and stone iconostasis. Its fresco of the Last Judgement, painted by the local priest Timothy, Dmitry Stepanov of Vologda and the brothers Karpov, is one of the great masterpieces of Russian art. Note the Russian garb of the righteous who are being saved, and the pointedly foreign dress of the damned.

The Museum This is in the Metropolitan's house, nearest the lake, and spreads into the **Prince's Chamber** and the impressive **White Chamber** (1675), its vaulted roof supported on a single pillar of great girth. The museum contains one striking fourteenth-century icon, of the Archangel Michael, some delightful fourteenth- and fifteenth-century wooden primitive sculptures, and the celebrated enamels. Rostov is famous for its enamels, which became the main support of the town in its eighteenth-century economic decline, when Peter the Great had weakened the power and consequently the income of the Church. Open daily from 11 a.m. to 6 p.m., closed on Mondays and the last Tuesday of each month.

Yaroslavl Less than 64 km beyond Rostov, the city of Yaroslavl stands where the River Kotorosl flows into the mighty Volga. It takes its name from Prince Yaroslavl of Rostov, who conquered the primitive earlier settlement here and named after himself this new port with its strategic access to the trade of the River Volga. In the thirteenth century, when the Monastery of the Saviour was founded, Yaroslavl was the capital of a powerful principality, but after Mongol devastation it was absorbed by Moscow in 1463. In the Time of Troubles at the beginning of the seventeenth century, with Moscow occupied by the Poles, Yaroslavl became briefly the national capital, the centre of the uprising, and this period launched the town's golden age.

Yaroslavl, which contains chemical plants and synthetic tyre factories, has the reputation of being one of the most polluted of all Russian cities. The first factory ever closed and fined for breaking pollution laws was in Yaroslavl.

What to see The best way to see the town is on foot, beginning at the beautiful white **Church of the Prophet Elijah** (1650) in the great square just a block north of the river. This is where the Intourist buses park. Catherine the Great was so struck by this church that she ordered the surrounding shops and houses to be cleared so it could be seen. This was tough on their owners, the Skripkn family of merchants, who had given the money to build the church in the first place. The murals on the galleries, with their cycle running from the Creation to the Apocalypse, should not be missed.

Walk east from the church along the great square, at the end turn right for the river, and on the Volga Quay stands the **Church of Nikolay Nadein** (1620). The first of the town's stone churches, its iconostasis is thought to have been designed by Fyodor Volkov, father of Russian theatre. Then start walking westwards along the embankment. This takes you past the **Church of the Nativity** (1644) with its pyramidal tower, to the **Volga Tower**, which stood at the corner of the old Kremlin. Turn right between the **Church of St Tikhon** on your right, with the restored seventeenth-century **Metropolitan's Palace** on the left, and walk straight on to the **Church of the Saviour** (1672), with its remarkable murals, fantasies of how the cities of Jerusalem and Byzantium were supposed to be. Beyond and to the north is the seventeenth-century **Church of Archangel Michael**, with its commercial warehouse on the ground floor.

Monastery of the Saviour

Then comes the walled Monastery, much restored after being badly damaged in the civil war in 1918. It was here that the manuscript of the Lay of the Host of Prince Igor, the epic which began Russian literature, was found in the eighteenth century. The Cathedral of the Saviour dates originally from 1516, but only the east front is unchanged from that period. The **Museum** is housed in the old seminary, and contains some fine icons, including the Smolensk Mother of God, and a collection of old peasant distaffs, beautifully carved and painted. Open daily from 11 a.m. to 6 p.m., closed on Mondays and the last Tuesday of each month.

Immediately north of the Monastery is the very fine red brick and green-domed **Church of the Epiphany**, of the 1680s. The bridge then crosses the River Kotorosl, and it is well worth making a detour to the suburb of **Korovniki**, and the **Church of St John Chrysostom** (1648–54), perhaps the finest single building in the city. It stands beside the **Church of the Mother of God of Vladimir**, and the complex is held together by a pyramid tower. From a distance, the red brick church looks ordinary. Close to, the detail of the tile work around the amazingly shaped altar window makes you think you have stumbled on the very earliest origins of Art Nouveau. Inside, the late seventeenth-century iconostasis is splendid.

Volkov Theatre

Yaroslavl also claims to have founded the Russian drama. Inspired by the Italian and French plays and operas he saw in St Petersburg, Fyodor Volkov came back to Yaroslavl in 1748 and founded the first professional repertory company. Although starting with Racine, he went on to produce and direct the first Russian plays, some of them his own adaptations of folk tales. The present Volkov Theatre was built in 1911 and, backed by its own drama school, has one of the best reputations of the provincial theatre. From the Church of the Epiphany, instead of turning left across the bridge, turn right past the arcades of the Gostinny Dvor bazaar to the modern Intourist Hotel Yaroslavl, which stands opposite the Volkov Theatre.

Where to stay
Vladimir

Hotel Yaroslavl, 40/2 Ushinskaya Street (tel. 212-75); 150 rooms.

Founded in 1108 by Vladimir Monomakh as the power of Kiev was declining, Vladimir became the capital of the new Principality of Vladimir-Suzdal in 1157. In spite of the ravages of time, the depradations of the Mongols, and the jealousy of Moscow, many of the twelfth-century glories of Vladimir remain. The first that you see as you enter the town from the Moscow road are the **Golden Gates**, built by Vladimir's grandson, Andrey Bogolyubsky, in 1164. They were modelled quite deliberately on the gates of Kiev, just as the great Cathedral of the Dormition was meant to echo and then outdo the Cathedral of St Sophia in Kiev, the city against which any ambitious northern princeling had to measure his achievement.

Cathedral of the Dormition

Craftsmen from the whole of Russia (except Kiev, as an act of policy) were brought in to build the cathedral, including some Germans sent by Emperor Frederick Barbarossa. All the princes of Moscow and Vladimir, starting with the son of Moscow's founder, Prince Yuri Dolgoruky, ascended the throne here, Alexander Nevsky and Dmitry Donskoy among them. It was regarded as the classic building of medieval Russian architecture, and the Italian architect of the cathedrals of the Moscow Kremlin was sent here for inspiration. What he saw was not quite the real thing. Very badly damaged by fire in 1185, it was repaired over the next five years and propped up with a thick curtain wall, and four more domes were added. It was damaged further by the Mongols, when the town was briefly abandoned. Andrey Rublyov was among those sent to restore the cathedral in 1408, and Rublyov's 'Last Judgement' is painted above the choir.

Cathedral of St Demetrius

Built by Vsevolod III between 1194–97, this is a gem of the classic period of Russian architecture. Beautifully carved of white limestone, there are over 1,000 bas-reliefs on the walls. From a moderate distance, it looks spare and elegant, clean in line. Close to, the carvings appear fantastical, even down to the feet of pillars shaped like the claws of animals digging into the ground. The frescoes of the interior are much faded. The lion's head carving on the pillars was the coat of arms of Prince Vsevolod. Just east of St Demetrius are the remains of the **Monastery of the Nativity**, founded in the twelfth century, and burial place of Alexander Nevsky.

Bogolyubovo

Some 9 km from Vladimir, this village is the site of Prince Andrey's Palace. The main building is now a run-down nineteenth-century cathedral, but some remains of the original palace may be seen, although the staircase tower has sunk over a metre into the ground. The real purpose of the expedition to Bogolyubovo is to go 1½ km further across the water meadows, approaching the loveliest single building in all Russia, the **Church of the Intercession on the Nerl**. Built in 1165, the proportions of this soaring, single-domed chapel are quite perfect. Erected on a man-made hill, which seems to float on the waters as you approach, the church is marvellously carved when seen close to. The scenes of beasts savaging one another are meant to be allegorical, telling of the need for Russia's princes to unite and cease their fratricidal warfare.

Where to stay, and eat

Hotel Vladimir, 74 Street of the Third International (tel. 30-42), 85 rooms.

Suzdal | Some 40 km north-east from Vladimir, across the fertile fields that were the granary of the Principality of Vladimir-Suzdal, lies the ancient city of Suzdal. It was first mentioned in the Chronicles in the year 1024, but it began to flower in the twelfth century during the reign of Moscow's founder, Yuri Dolgoruky. In spite of the fortification of the Kremlin and a second line of earthwork defences, Suzdal was pillaged and burned down by the Mongols in 1238. Quickly rebuilt within the protective curve of the River Kamenka, it remained the capital of its Principality until absorption into Moscow in the fifteenth century. Suzdal is one vast museum and tourism complex, a high-minded if somewhat funless Soviet version of Disneyland. The whole of traditional Russian life is here, the churches, the private houses of townsfolk and peasants, the wooden carvings, and an astonishingly complex wooden building, constructed without a single nail.

The Kremlin | In the centre of the town, with its blue-domed **Cathedral of the Nativity**, the Kremlin assumed its present form, after several collapses and rebuildings, in the 1520s. The south and west doors, etched and gilded with Old Testament scenes, were part of the original cathedral. Next to the cathedral, the **Archbishop's Residence** is a group of fifteenth- to eighteenth-century buildings, now a museum. The icons of the Suzdal school make up the pride of the collection, and this is a rare opportunity to see an entire school develop and mature from the first tightly formalised designs. The best examples are the fourteenth-century 'Eleusa' and the fifteenth-century 'Shroud', and are displayed in the magnificent **Chamber of the Cross**, one of the largest unsupported vaults in Russia. The Kremlin also contains two smaller parish churches, the 1650 **Church of the Dormition**, and the 1739 **Church of St Nicholas**. The dual chambers of the churches were a standard form in northern Russia, a warm church for winter, and a cool one for summer.

Going north from the Kremlin into **Soviet Square**, you come to the long rows of the Gostinny Dvor, the shopping arcades, which now house a tourist restaurant and souvenir shop. The central church is another double structure, the summer **Church of the Resurrection** and the winter **Church of Our Lady of Kazan**. They both date from the 1730s. The street continues to the north, past the **Church of St Nicholas**, and to the **Monastery of the Deposition of the Robe** in the north of the town. Founded in 1207, with its sixteenth-century triple-domed church, the striking double gates were built by local craftsmen in 1688. The bell-tower is from the early nineteenth century. Opposite the gates is a house-museum of eighteenth-century domestic furniture.

Further north outside the town is the vast fourteenth-century fortress-**Monastery of the Saviour and St Euthymius**. Its whitewashed red-brick walls are nearly 6 m thick, and are made the more impressive by the twelve thick towers. Beyond the entry tower are the Holy Gates, topped by the seventeenth-century **Church of the Annunciation**. The central **Cathedral of Transfiguration** was completed in 1594, and the stunning murals were added later. There is an interesting display of contemporary folk art in the old **Archimandrite's House**, a graceful white building with elaborate carvings around the small windows. Adjoining it is the Refectory Church of the Dormition, and the Church of St Nicholas which contained a hospital, as well as a small prison used to detain religious and political dissidents. One cell was reserved for Leo Tolstoy after his excommunication, but for once the pen proved mightier than the Church's law.

On the far side of the river from the Saviour Monastery is the fourteenth-century **Convent of the Intercession**, which was long used as a prison for women of noble birth. Further down river, opposite the Kremlin, is the most distinctive single feature of Suzdal, the **Field-Museum of Wooden Architecture**. Old wooden churches, manor houses and windmills from all across northern Russia have been dismantled and brought here to be re-erected in the grounds of the Monastery of St Demetrius. The most distinctive is the **Church of the Transfiguration**, with its fish-scale domes, from the village of Kozlyatyevo.

Where to stay, and eat   **Motel Suzdal**, Ivanovskaya Zastava (tel. 211-37), 85 rooms. Also **Hotel Suzdal**, at the same address, 211 rooms. This purpose-built modern tourist accommodation complex is the pride of Intourist. There is also a plan for small cabin-bungalows inside the Suzdal Monastery to be available for tourist stays, once restoration work is complete. Check with Intourist for availability.

Route One:

From Warsaw to Moscow, via Brest (1,265 km)

Warsaw — **Brest** (212 km) — **Kobrin** (50 km) — ○ (75 km) — ○ **Stolbtsy** (130 km) — **Minsk** (80 km) — ○ **Smolensk** (320 km) — **Gagarin** (218 km) — **Borodino** (60 km) — ○ **Golitsino** (95 km) — **Moscow** (25 km)

○ = petrol

This is the classic invasion route to Mosow, from Poland via Brest and Smolensk. You are following in the steps of Napoleon and Hitler. If you are booked to spend the first night in Minsk, leave Warsaw very early in the morning, certainly before 8 a.m. The Customs and immigration procedures at the Terespol border point are not quick. Your car tyres will have to go through a pool of disinfectant, and the car will be parked above an inspection pit. Door panels and rear seats may well be removed. All luggage will be removed and probably opened. This is usual.

It is worth spending a night in Brest, just inside the border, because of the Brest Fortress Museum. The road from the border point will take you straight into the city, and the museum is to the left along Moskovskaya Street.

Brest   See p. 241.

From Brest, you drive on a wide straight road that will be almost empty, through the flat Byelorussian countryside. Most of the landscape is forest, bog or farmland, and Byelorussia is one of the great centres of dairy farming.

Kobrin   About 50 km from Brest is the town of Kobrin, which has a small military museum in the house where the best of the Tsarist generals, Alexander Suvorov, lived for a while.

Ivantsevichi   There is a petrol station 75 km further, at the village of Ivantsevichi, and the next petrol pump is 130 km after this at the town of **Stolbtsy**. Minsk is 80 km further. If camping, watch for the camp site and motel sign in a pine forest, 62 km after passing Stolbtsy.

Speed traps   Beware speed traps on this road. Even if you do not understand the policeman, he will write a note on your visa, and the *straf* (a fine, usually 10 roubles) will have to be paid before you leave the country.

Minsk   See p. 240.

After 50 km, the road east from Minsk, to Smolensk and Moscow, crosses the River Beresina, near the spot where Napoleon's retreating Grand Army suffered a disaster, many of his troops falling through the ice to drown. Some 250 km from Minsk, you leave Byelorussia and enter the vast Russian Republic, that stretches all the way to the Pacific Ocean. Seventy km further, and there is a petrol and service station at the junction where the road turns off for Smolensk.

Where to stay   The nearby camp site of **Khvoiny** (not run by Intourist) is signposted, and so is the **Phoenix Motel**, where Intourist will usually assign foreigners (tel. 214-88).

Smolensk   This is an ancient city on the River Dniepr, an important point on the Water Road from the Baltic to Byzantium, under Kievan domination. After the Tartar invasion, it became part of the Lithuanian Empire. It was burned during Napoleon's advance in 1812, and badly damaged again in 1941 as the Germans advanced, and in 1943 as they retreated. The city guides will tell you 7,600 of the 7,900 dwellings were destroyed in the war.

What to see   But Smolensk retained many of its ancient buildings. On the right bank of the Dniepr is the old town, with some of the fortified walls, classics of sixteenth-century military architecture, and built by the same man who designed the white walls of Moscow. The twelfth-century **Churches of Saints Peter and Paul** (on the far bank of the river at Gorodyanka), and of **St John**, and the **Svirskaya** have been

305

restored and have enough similarities to suggest that there was a distinct Smolensk school at work. The seventeenth-century **Cathedral of the Dormition** is a fine example of the period, and is built on the site where the first (wooden) church was erected in 1101. The town has some interesting neo-classical buildings that date from the rebuilding after 1812, notably the **College of Medicine**, formerly the Assembly of the Nobility.

Gagarin

The road to Moscow is almost bare, but for filling stations. After 218 km, there is a petrol station, a small café and a signpost to Gagarin, the town named after Yuri Gagarin, the first man in space in 1961. The town has a museum to this local hero, who was born in the nearby village of Klushino in 1934.

Borodino

Sixty km after Gagarin, and shortly after the signpost to Mozhaisk, there is a turning on the right to Borodino, the site of the desperate battle between Napoleon's Grand Army and the retreating Russian armies under Marshal Kutuzov. At the time, it seemed like a French victory, because the Russians retreated, opening the way to Moscow, and Napoleon occupied the city. But he had paid too high a cost – over 55,000 men. The Russians lost rather fewer, because they had been defending a series of fortified redoubts. Kutuzov had chosen a good position, where Napoleon was unable to outflank him, and was thus forced into a series of bloody frontal assaults. Some of the redoubts changed hands several times in the course of the day. Kutuzov was able to make good his losses and keep his army intact, ready to fall on Napoleon again once the great fire and imminent winter had forced the French to retreat from the ashes of Moscow. Napoleon could not replace his casualties, and his gamble that the loss of Moscow would lead to a Russian surrender proved a failure. Allowing himself to be lured on deeper into the vastness of Russia by the chimera of victory proved disastrous, the beginning of his collapse, just as it proved the undoing of Hitler.

Battlefield and museum

Each year, on the first Sunday in September, there is a colourful re-enactment of the battle. But the battlefield is probably worth a visit, having changed little in nearly 180 years, and the attached museum, with an electrified model of the battle, is also interesting. Near the monuments you will see some granite gravestones. These commemorate Soviet troops who died here fighting the Germans in 1941.

To Moscow

Back on the road to Moscow, from the filling station at **Golitsino**, just before the Moscow ring road, on a clear day you can see the distinctive neo-Gothic spire of Moscow University. Turn off when you cross over a motorway. This is the Moscow outer ring road, Mozhaisky Highway, and the site of the Moscow camp site and **Mozhaiskaya Motel** (tel. 447-3435). Keep straight on for Kutuzovsky Prospekt, the 1812 Victory Arch, then the bridge beside the Ukraina Hotel and the aggressively modern thoroughfare of

Moscow

Kalinin Prospekt which will take you down to a junction. Ahead of you will be a red brick wall with a yellow ochre building behind. This is the Kremlin.

See p. 152.

Route Two:

From Finland to Moscow, via Leningrad (1,208 km)

Helsinki — **Vyborg** (307 km) — **Zelenogorsk** (120 km) — **Leningrad** (60 km) — ○ **Chudovo** (120 km) — **Novgorod** ○ (70 km) — **Vyshny-Volochek** (231 km) — **Kalinin** (**Tver**) (130 km) — **Klin** (80 km) — **Moscow** (90 km)

○ = petrol

Crossing the border by car at the Torfyanovka border point can be a lengthy process (see Route One). Leave Helsinki early for the two- to three- hour drive to the Soviet border and, with luck, you should be in time for lunch at the Finnish-built **Druzhba Hotel** in Vyborg (5 Ulitsa Zheleznodorozhnaya, tel. 247-60), the modern white building near the railway station. There is an Intourist bureau at Vyborg station where you may purchase car insurance if the booth at the border is closed.

Vyborg

Until the Winter War of 1939–40, when Stalin invaded Finland in order to push the frontier back from vulnerable Leningrad, all this part of Karelia had been Finnish territory. The Finns held out with great courage, inflicting a series of defeats upon the clumsy Red Army, until superior numbers finally told.

There had been battles in this territory between Finns and Swedes and Russians for centuries. The imposing castle was built by the Swedes and dates from the late thirteenth century, when they took over what had been a Russian trading post. It then became a Hanseatic League port, but always remained a fortress. In 1710, it was captured by Peter the Great in the Northern War against the Swedes, and the foundations the Russians built in the 1740s can still be seen. It remained Russian until 1812, when it was transferred to Finland. Finland retained its autonomy, with a separate legal system and separate army, but the Russian Tsar ruled as Grand Duke. The autonomy was real enough for this region to be outside the jurisdiction of the St Petersburg police. Lenin was to take advantage of this sanctuary in 1906 and again in 1917. The Finns seized the opportunity of the 1917 Revolution to declare independence.

The contrast between the well-kept roads, prosperous villages and shops of Finland and the potholes and drabness of the first Soviet city you see is striking. And from now on the roads will not be impressive, the petrol stations will be dirty, the lavatories a disgrace and the roadside shops and cafés will make you wonder how on earth this backward economy could be called a superpower. For the native Finnish-speakers who still live in this region as Soviet citizens, or for the many Finns who commute into the USSR to work here each day, the contrast must also be cruel. Nowhere else does the Soviet Union have a direct border with a prosperous western economy.

Zelenogorsk

From Vyborg the road runs inland through a quietly attractive region of pine trees, rocks and lakes for 120 km, until you reach the resort town of Zelenogorsk. From here all along the 60 km to Leningrad, you drive alongside the beaches of the Gulf of Finland, and past sanatoria, rest homes, holiday camps and a growing number of dachas, or country cottages. The Regional Plan calls for this flurry of building to continue into the 1990s, to develop this region still further as a recreation zone. But there is a growing local ecology campaign which says the region is already over-developed.

Penaty

Just outside Zelenogorsk, at Repino, is 'Penaty', the museum-estate of the great Russian painter Ilya Repin, who lived here from 1899 until his death in 1930. The museum is discreet about the point, but in fact Repin chose to go on living in exile from the Revolution after 1917. Burned down in the war, the rather attractive brown wooden house with its steep glass roof to catch the northern light was restored in the 1950s. Although he lived in exile, you could call Repin a premature social realist. His paintings are wonderfully hammed-up bits of history, sentiment dripping from the canvas.

Where to stay

Leningrad's Intourist camp site is located here, although a new one has been built at Olgino. Check availability through the Intourist office at Vyborg railway station (tel. 167-21).

Razliv

Further along the road are various Leninist shrines. There is Razliv, on the shores of Lake Razliv, where he went into hiding in July 1917, and a commemorative jetty has been built to mark the spot where he came ashore. A hut has been built to pay due homage to the original hut where he hid out and wrote *The State and Revolution*. There is also a small museum with some mementoes.

On a good day, you should now be able to see Leningrad, or at least the needle spire of the Peter-Paul Fortress. Inland is a hilly winter sports area known as the Russian Switzerland, which gets very crowded on winter weekends. You enter Leningrad via Kirovsky Prospekt. This leads into the very centre of the city, the Kirov Bridge, beside the Peter-Paul Fortress, from where you have a stunning view of the Winter Palace and the Hermitage on the far bank.

Leningrad

See p. 192.

Leaving Leningrad – what to see

You leave Leningrad by the rather more humble and modern route of Moskovsky Prospekt, past the Rossiya Hotel and the **Moscow Triumphal Gate**, which commemorates the defeat of the Polish uprising of 1830–1. Demolished in the 1930s, its cast iron was used in the wartime defences of the city, and it was rebuilt in the 1950s. This has always been the road to Moscow, but it used to be called Prospekt Stalina, and before that it was called Trans-Balkan Prospekt, in honour of the troops who followed this route to the Balkan wars against Turkey in 1877–8. The Soviet memorial is at **Victory Square**, the red granite obelisk to mark the defeat of the German siege of Leningrad from 1941–4, and there is a good museum of the siege beneath the monument. There was a harebrained plan in the 1930s to make this southern suburb, from Moscow Square to Victory Square, the centre of the new Soviet Leningrad, leaving the decadent Tsarist city to the north to wither on the vine.

There is a large fork in the road at the memorial, the right fork leading to Pskov, and the left to Moscow. You know you are on the right road if you shortly see a signpost for a road to the old Tsarist palaces of Pushkin and Pavlovsk turning off to the right.

The 190-km road to Novgorod is a disgrace, sometimes narrowing to two thin tracks. This is the part of the route where pigs sometimes potter across, where sudden jams clog around a railway crossing, and where you need lots of water in your windscreen washer reservoir to get rid of the mud thrown up by the lorries. There is a petrol station at **Chudovo**, 120 km from Leningrad, and another at the turn-off to Novgorod, a city where you should spend the night, because it is one of the great centres of medieval Russian culture, with some of the loveliest buildings in the country. You will need at least a day to do it justice.

Novgorod

First mentioned in 859, this spot on the River Volkhov and hard by Lake Ilmen became an increasingly important trading centre on the river road, and Yaroslav of Kiev gave the place a charter of self-government in 1019. Novgorod is a lovely old city, but it is fascinating also because the place is one of the great Ifs of history. If democratic Novgorod, ruled by its *Veche*, or Popular Assembly, had become the great city around which Russia coalesced, rather than autocratic and Tsarist Moscow, the world would have been a different place. The prospect so alarmed Ivan the Terrible that he did a rather more thorough job of sacking Novgorod than the Tartars ever managed. The Germans did their worst, however, from 1941–4.

What to see

There are four main groups of historic buildings. The first is the Kremlin, known here as the **Detinets**. Built in the eleventh century, and rebuilt in the fourteenth and fifteenth, the 9-m high red-brick walls and cone-peaked towers are striking in themselves. Viewed from the far bank of the river, the brick walls and their contents of churches, bell-towers and green and gold domes make up one of the great Russian historic townscapes. Under the great gold dome is the **Cathedral of St Sofia**, built in the 1040s on the model of Kiev's St Sophia, and still being restored. It looks splendid today painted white, but in the prime of Novgorod it was multi-coloured. The carefully carved bronze west doors were booty from the Swedish town of Sigtuna in 1187. Although extensively remodelled in the nineteenth century, the bell-tower remains a stunning building. And the great bell-shaped **Memorial of the Millennium**, cast in 1868, is a striking work of sculpture, and a reminder that Tsarist Russia felt quite as grandiose and messianic about Russia and her world role as its Communist successor.

Just beyond the church is the Law Court, and the Vladychny Dvor, the courtyard of the Archbishop, with its Hall of Facets. Modest on the outside, inside is the magnificently-vaulted formal reception hall for ambassadors in the days when the city itself was known as Lord Novgorod the Great.

Icons
There is a museum inside the Kremlin which must not be missed. It contains some magnificent early icons, and also the birch-bark manuscripts. These were the vehicle of literacy in a culture where parchment was rare. Many of them are private letters, mainly from the fourteenth century, which give a picture of ordinary life – and its surprising level of sophistication and education. One of the bark plaques contains a cartoon sketched by a boy called Omphim, seven centuries ago. But the icons are the real treasure. The Novgorod school was distinctive for its clear lines and silhouettes, its boldness with colour and the way it sought to idealise the humanity, rather than the divinity of saints. The outstanding single icon for the people of Novgorod is 'Our Lady of the Sign', which is said to have saved the city from a siege by the men of Suzdal in 1169. My own favourite is the fifteenth-century painting of the battle itself. (See also p. 61.)

Churches
The second group of old buildings lies outside the Kremlin, though on the same side of the river. The **White Tower** shows the line of the outer ramparts, and the nearby **Church of the Trinity** and the marvellously simple **Church of St Blaise** have been restored since the city was badly damaged during the German occupation of the 1940s. Further downstream, the churches of **St Thomas** and **Saints Peter and Paul** are good examples of the twelfth-century style. The **Trinity Church** of the Monastery of the Holy Spirit, all that remains of the monastery, was built in 1557, when Moscow's authority over Novgorod was complete. But even the coming of a Muscovite architecture is affected by the Novgorod sense of proportion, the balance between curves and sharp gables.

Business district
Across the river is a third group of buildings, known as the business district, and the stronghold of the guilds, each of which had its own church. Opposite the Kremlin itself is the **Yaroslav Dvor** or courtyard, all built around the city's main market. The churches of **St Nicholas** (twelfth century) and of **St Prascovia** (fourteenth to sixteenth centuries) are the most interesting. The frescoes in the crypt of St Nicholas are delightful, particularly what is left of 'Job Afflicted

with Boils'. Further inland is the classic fourteenth-century **Church of Our Saviour of the Transfiguration-in-Elijah-Street**, whose exterior is simply perfect. The southern façade achieves a mysterious symmetry of opposites, and the drum, the tower that supports the dome, is unusually well-decorated, but it works. The marvellous outside is more than matched by the contemporaneous murals (although only rediscovered this century) painted by Rublyov's teacher, Theophanes the Greek (see p. 61). Just beside it is the splendid seventeenth-century Znamensky Cathedral, with its classic five domes.

The final group of buildings runs along the banks of the river on the short 5 km to Lake Ilmen, but they suffered desperate damage during the German occupation, much of it deliberate. The **Church of the Saviour of Nereditsa** was a veritable museum of twelfth-century art, containing frescoes by Novgorod painters, but now almost all gone. The massive **St George's Church**, on the riverbank, is almost all that is left of one of the earliest monasteries. But the church is one of the finest buildings in Russia, the heaviness of it magically lightened by proportion. The frescoes inside were restored in the 1930s, but the sense of soaring height as you enter and gaze upwards is very powerful. Just beside St George's is the excellent **Museum of Wooden Architecture**. Wooden churches and peasant huts have been transported and rebuilt here, and the sense of simple rustic faith in the Kuritsko Church of the Dormition or the Tukholya Church is quite humbling. And whoever designed the perfect balance of interlocking planes that makes the Peredki Church was a genius.

Where to stay, and eat

The **Intourist Hotel**, 16 Ulitsa Dmitrievskaya (tel. 750-89) is spartan. There are two Russian hotels, the **Sadko**, 16 Prospekt Gagarina (tel. 951-70), and the **Volkhov**, 24 Ulitsa Nekrasova (tel. 924-98), but if they try to assign you to either, complain. There is also a non-Intourist camp site called the **Yuryino** (tel. 724-48), 12 km south towards Moscow, with a grim restaurant. Eat if you can at the **Detinets Tourist Restaurant**, inside the Pokrovsky Tower of the Kremlin. The food is not good, but the location is unbeatable.

Vyshny-Volochek

South of Novgorod, there is a long stretch of 231 km without a petrol station, before the old porterage centre of Vyshny-Volochek. The road passes through the picturesque birch woods and slopes of the Valday. This group of hills, which barely tops 300 metres, is the highest land in the great north European plain. The area is dotted with over 100 lakes, famed for their purity, and the region is being developed as a recreation zone. Vyshny-Volochek was one of the most important sites in medieval Russia, the porterage between the Volga and the northern river system of Novgorod. Peter the Great had Russia's first canal built here in 1709. The gap between the River Msta, which flowed into Lake Ilmen and to Novgorod, and the River Tvertsa, which flowed into the Volga, had to be bridged by a porterage, or *volok* in Russian, where the boats were hauled over a log track. It is now a textile town of 100,000 people.

Kalinin (Tver)

Another 130 km by road brings you to the city which dominates the spot where the River Volga is joined by the Tvertsa, the ancient city of Tver. Since 1931 it has been called Kalinin, after the old revolutionary whom Stalin permitted to be official head of state as Chairman of the Supreme Soviet.

History

Founded in the twelfth century by Novgorod settlers who saw its strategic location on the river route, within two centuries it had rivalled, and finally shifted its loyalties to Moscow. Tver became the nearest thing to an industrial base in medieval Russia and was famous for its forges, ironsmiths and churchbells, its craftsmen, jewellers and engravers and potters, and later for its gunsmiths and samovars. Perhaps its most famous son was Afanasi Nikitin, a merchant who wrote a journal of his expedition to India in 1466.

What to see

Badly damaged in the German occupation, and now an industrial city, its oldest surviving building is the **Belaya Troitsa Church**, built by Ivan the Terrible in 1564. The eighteenth-century **Palace of Catherine**, designed by Kazakov, is now the regional government building. The 1813 Church of the Ascension became an **Ethnography Museum**. There are some fine waterfront houses on Stepan Razin Quay.

Where to stay, and eat

If planning to stay overnight, there is an **Intourist Motel Tver** (tel. 556-92) and a camp site at the entrance to the city from the Leningrad road. If going into the city centre, the **Tsentralnaya Hotel**, 33/8 Ulitsa Pravda (tel. 381-57) serves reasonable meals. The main street, Sovyetskaya, is still known by locals as Millionaya, from the days when pre-revolutionary Tver was a booming industrial centre.

Klin

About 40 km south of Kalinin on the road to Moscow is a turn-off to the left which goes to **Zavidovo**, where Leonid Brezhnev kept a hunting lodge on the banks of the River Volga. And 40 km further is the small town of Klin, where Pyotr Tchaikovsky lived from 1885 until his death eight years later, and where he wrote (among other things) his *Pathétique*. His house is now an interesting museum. On 7 May and 6 November, his birth and death dates, leading musicians come here to perform his works.

War memorial

The 90 km between Klin and Moscow passes through the wooded landscape where the fate of Hitler's invasion was decided between October and December of 1941. Halfway to Moscow is a T-34 tank dominating the road, marking the spot where the Soviet counter-attack in December broke the German line and began their retreat. One km further is the peak of a hill with a memorial of crossed bayonets, where the main thrust of the panzers was stopped. The Unknown Soldier, whose body now lies at the corner of the Kremlin, was taken from the mass grave here. Soon on the left you will see a sign for Shermetyevo airport, and then on the right is a war memorial devastating in its simplicity, giant steel girders crossed in the shape of a tank trap. This point, 23 km from the Kremlin, is the nearest the Germans got, just near the terminus of the trams.

To Moscow The road continues straight, and after 12 km you go between two large football stadiums, Dinamo on the left and TsSKA, the Army sports club, on the right. You then pass on the right a fairy tale building in turquoise green and white, the Belorussky Railway Station, continue straight down what is now Gorky Street, Ulitsa Gorkovo, and the Kremlin and Red Square lie ahead.

Moscow See p. 152.

Route Three:

a) From Leningrad to Tallinn (320 km)
b) From Leningrad to Minsk, via Pskov and Vitebsk (909 km)

a) **Leningrad** — **Krasnoye Selo** (25 km) — **Kingisepp** ◯ (125 km) — **Narva** (25 km) — **Sillamae** (20 km) — **Kohtla-Jarve** (32 km) — **Viitna** (80 km) — **Tallinn** (64 km)

b) **Leningrad** — **Luga** (148 km) — **Pskov** (142 km) — **Ostrov** (65 km) — **Vitebsk** (264 km) — **Orsa** (122 km) — **Minsk** (168 km)

◯ = petrol

Note: In principle, Intourist and the Soviet authorities will shortly be opening the northern tour route. This should enable you to go by car from Leningrad through Estonia to Tallinn, along the Baltic coastline to the old Hanseatic League city of Riga, capital of Latvia, then inland to Vilnius in Lithuania, and on to join the main Warsaw–Moscow road at Minsk. This would greatly improve the attractions of a motoring holiday through the USSR. The roads in the region are among the finest in the Soviet Union, partly because of the very high incidence of car ownership, and partly because of a major road building programme which took place in time for the 1980 Olympic Games, when boating events were held on the Baltic. It is a far more attractive and interesting itinerary than the usual straight dash to Moscow via Minsk and Smolensk. In a three-week or month-long motor tour, one could go through the Baltic Republics to Leningrad, and then return through Moscow and Kiev and back into central Europe. This would be a drive of some 3,500 km, and would take in the most interesting and attractive cities of the European Soviet Union. But in spite of Intourist promises that this Baltic route is 'imminent', the delicate political situation in the three Baltic Republics may well keep these roads closed to foreigners well into the 1990s.

a) From Leningrad to Tallinn

The distance from Leningrad to Tallinn is some 320 km, and if you have already visited the Tsarist palaces at Pushkin, Petrodvorets and Pavlovsk, there is little enough on the route to detain you. The journey is easily managed in a day. From the centre of Leningrad, you follow Mosskovsky Prospekt south to Victory Square (Ploshchad Pobedy) and then turn right on to Leninsky Prospekt, which becomes Petergofskoye Chaussee, the road which takes you to Tallinn. Or you may leave Leningrad by the south-west route, taking Ulitsa Dekabristov from Theatre Square, crossing the River Fontanka at the Starokalininskt Bridge to Gaza Prospekt, which takes you to Petergofskoye Chaussee.

Kingisepp

You pass through **Krasnoye Selo**, where the road forks off to Pavlovsk and Pushkin. A long and straight road through flat and wooded countryside takes you to the old fortress town of Yamburg, on the River Luga, where there is a petrol station. Now called Kingisepp, after an Estonian Communist leader, the fortress was originally founded in the fourteenth century to protect Novgorod. Parts of the city wall still stand, but there is little of interest to see. The **Cathedral of St Catherine** dates from the nineteenth century. The **Gostinny Dvor**, a market and shopping arcade, dates back to the eighteenth century.

The real significance of Kingisepp is that you are entering the phosphorite pollution zone, one of the most contentious issues between Estonia and Moscow. From the River Luga for the next 160 km to the village of Viitna, you are going through country that is being strip-mined, pillaged, polluted and exploited to breaking point. When the phosphorite mining stops, the oil-shale industry begins, one of the world's dirtiest and least efficient ways of producing energy. Acid rain is visibly eroding Estonia's forests, but it is also affecting the forests of Finland across the Gulf, and of Karelia. The Estonians want to phase out the industries; Moscow says the nation needs the output. Uranium has also been found beneath the phosphorite deposits, and in the old days before *perestroika*, Moscow would simply have ordered the mines to be sunk and the deposits exploited, and any local opposition would have been dealt with strictly. These days, there is a vocal protest movement, and Moscow is treading cautiously, but the phosphorite industry continues. As the flat land around Leningrad gives way to the more picturesque and hilly country around the Estonian border, it is sobering to realise the ecological damage that has been inflicted.

About 20 km beyond Kingisepp is the River Narva, the boundary between Estonia and the Russian Republic. There is a vast reservoir to the south of the town, and a hydro-electric power station at the dam. On the Russian side of the river is the fortress town of **Ivangorod**, founded in 1492. The stone walls and towers have been through a number of sieges. It was twice taken by the Swedes in the sixteenth century, before Peter the Great won it back in the campaigns of 1704.

Estonia   Just across the river is the Estonian city of **Narva**, and you are likely to be struck by the cleaner streets, the better dress of the people, a general air of neatness. There are shop signs in Estonian, as well as Russian. See p. 237.

From Narva, the road turns in towards the Gulf of Finland and the new industrial town of **Sillamae**. The coast here is deeply scarped and gullied, falling to bays and inlets, with steep terraces known locally as 'glints'. The road then skirts the coastline for 32 km before reaching the centre of the oil-shale industry at **Kohtla-Jarve**. The industry began in 1916, and now mines some 30 million tonnes a year. It is the basis of the local chemical industry, almost equally polluting, which produces pesticides, leather tanning agents and varnishes. There is a museum devoted to the oil-shale industry, but the pungent smell of industry throughout the town does not encourage the visitor to linger.

The road continues towards Tallinn through forests and farmland, and after crossing the River Kunda, some 32 km west of Kohtla-Jarve, the drive becomes increasingly picturesque. The small village of **Viitna** is distinguished by an elderly wooden inn at the side of the road, which I have yet to see open to the public. You may be luckier. Another 64 km brings you to the city of Tallinn, dominated by the hill on which stands the old castle of Toompea.

Tallinn   See p. 231.

b) From Leningrad to Minsk

A new route for independent drivers has been opened to go from Leningrad to Minsk, via Luga, Pskov, Ostrov, Vitebsk and Orsa.

Pskov   One advantage of this route is to see the ancient city of Pskov, about 160 km from Leningrad. On the junction of the Rivers Pskova and Velikaya, Pskov was far enough from the Mongol attacks to retain some of the look and feel of a medieval Russian town. The oldest building is the twelfth-century **Mirozhsky Monastery**, but the thirteenth-century **Kremlin** is the most impressive, the building from which Alexander Nevsky set forth for his great battle with the Teutonic Knights. A border town that came within the orbit of Novgorod the Great, Pskov knew a second phase of prosperity and building as a base during the Livonian wars of the seventeenth century. It was in this period that the **Holy Trinity Cathedral** and **Pogankiny Palace** were constructed.

Route Four:

a) From Hungary to Moscow, via Lvov and Kiev (1,653 km)
b) From Poland to Lvov, via Shegini and Gorodok (74 km)

a) **Chop** — **Uzhgorod** (23 km) — **Mukachevo** (40 km) — **Styri** (160 km) — **Lvov** (70 km) — **Brody** (109 km) — **Dubno** O (55 km) — **Rovno** O (45 km) — **Novograd-Volhynsky** O (110 km) — **Zhitomir** (77 km) — **Kiev** (130 km) — **Kopti** (92 km) — O (200 km) — **Orel** O (200 km) — **Tula** (180 km) — **Serpukhov** (80 km) — **Chekov** (35 km) — **Podolsk** (30 km) — **Moscow** (17 km)

b) **Shegini** — **Lvov** (74 km)

O = petrol

a) From Hungary to Lvov

This is probably the most attractive land entry to the Soviet Union, through the wooded slopes of the Carpathian Mountains from Hungary. The border is just short of the small town of **Chop**, attractively located with the mountains rearing behind. If you have bookings for the night in the Soviet city of Lvov, almost 300 km from the border, you should arrange to go through the frontier early in the morning. The mountainous roads will take at least six hours to negotiate safely.

Uzhgorod

But it is possible, although not comfortable and indeed discouraged by Intourist, to spend the night in the attractive small city of Uzhgorod.

History

Uzhgorod is the regional capital of a very confused part of the world, at least in historical geography. The Carpathian Mountains have traditionally been a natural (although disputed) border between the Ukraine, Poland, Czechoslovakia and Hungary. The ancient town of Uzhgorod was founded in the eighth century, and was part of the Kievan Federation until the twelfth; it then came under Magyar control, although in effect it was the virtually autonomous centre of the White Croat tribe. By the eighteenth century, it had become part of the Austro-Hungarian Empire, remained so until 1919, when it became briefly Hungarian, and then Czech. In 1938, as part of the general loot of Czechoslovakia after the Munich Agreement, it became Hungarian again, but in 1945 it was absorbed into the USSR by right of conquest, ratified by a treaty with the Czechs.

What to see

Uzhgorod therefore contains a number of architectural styles, but the thirteenth- to fourteenth-century crenellated castle is outstanding, with its moats and Baroque palace, begun in 1598. This is western, rather than Slavic architecture. The university library, built for a Jesuit monastery in the seventeenth century, is also rather fine. The neighbouring cathedral was later turned into an Orthodox church. That change symbolises the crucial religious issue in this part of the

Western Ukraine, the status of the Uniate Church. Although traditionally Roman Catholic, it has been absorbed within the Russian Orthodox Church, and the Catholic Church is virtually underground. This is the major outstanding dispute between the Vatican and the Kremlin, or at least the Orthodox Church.

In summer, when the rose gardens are in bloom along the river banks, Uzhgorod is a delightful sight, and the celebrated vineyards around the town produce a wine that is hard to find in Moscow. If you cannot track down a bottle, which goes well with the local trout, you can make do with the health-giving waters, which have made Transcarpathia a traditional spa region. The waters of Naftusya and Svalyava are prized. The region is now being developed for recreation, and in winter is popular for winter sports holidays with the relatively affluent people from the Baltic Republics.

Where to stay, and eat

Given enough notice, Intourist can make a booking at the **Uzhgorod Hotel**, 2 Bogdan Khmelnitsky Square (tel. 350-65), which claims to have six de luxe double rooms; or at the **Hotel Zakarpatye**, 50 Lyet USSR Square (tel. 363-70).

Mukachevo

Forty km beyond Uzhgorod is the town of Mukachevo, dominated by the fourteenth-century Palanok Castle on its grim hill. The views on the road beyond Mukachevo are very fine, and you do not start to leave this mountainous country until you have crossed the 850-metre Veretsky Pass, marked by a restaurant and viewing platform. After 200 km from Uzhgorod, you reach the industrial and natural gas centre of **Styri**, 70 far less picturesque km from Lvov.

b) From Poland to Lvov

It is possible to skirt the Carpathians by driving through Poland on the E-22 Motorway and crossing into the Soviet Union at **Shegini**, 74 km west of Lvov.

Gorodok

The only town on the route of any interest is Gorodok, with a fifteenth-century Catholic church, a sixteenth-century Orthodox one and a seventeenth-century wooden church to John the Baptist. As the churches suggest, this too is a region of Uniate controversy. It is also a region of great religious fervour, with a series of claimed sightings of the Virgin Mary here in the 1980s, which led the alarmed Soviet authorities temporarily to seal off certain churches.

Lvov

History and what to see

This city, named after Prince Lev who was to become King of Galicia, was founded in 1256 as a stronghold against the Tartars. It fulfilled its military function, withstanding regular raids and sieges, but steadily prospered as a commercial centre, thanks in part to the flourishing Armenian community, whose fourteenth-century cathedral added an exotic flavour to what was by then a Polish city. The jewellers, goldsmiths and blacksmiths of Lvov won a wide reputation. The city was a cultural centre, giving a home to Ivan Fyodorov, printer of the first Russian books, who settled and was buried at

Lvov's **St Onuphrius's Monastery** in the 1570s. The prestigious **University of Lvov** traces its roots back to a seventeenth-century Jesuit academy. The **Catholic Cathedral** is classically Gothic, but there was a school of Italian architects here, imported by the Italian bankers and merchants, whose blend of eastern and Italian styles can best be seen in the Benedictine church, the Valacca Greek-Catholic church, and the Campiani and Boimi chapels.

In 1772, as part of the first partition of Poland, Lvov was swallowed by the Austrian Empire and given the German name of Lemberg. It remained a great fortress city against the Russians until the First World War, when in spite of the disasters the Russians suffered at the hands of the Germans, they managed to take Lemberg from the Austro-Hungarians. After 1919, Lvov became part of newly independent Poland. A census in 1931 showed a population of 316,000, of whom 63 per cent were Poles, and the rest Jewish, Ruthenians and Germans. In 1939, Lvov was badly battered by the Germans before being handed over to the Soviet Union as part of the Non-Aggression Pact between Hitler and Stalin. In 1941, the Germans took it again during their invasion of Russia but the Russians regained the city in 1945. Today it is a city of 700,000 people, and a very large student population, many of them attending what is now called Ivan Franko University, after the Ukrainian poet and revolutionary. Lvov is a modern industrial centre, producing TV sets, fork-lifts, buses and electronics.

Where to stay, and eat

The 98-room **Intourist Hotel**, 1 Mickiewicz Square (tel. 726-751), has a decent restaurant. The **Lvovsky Camping Site** (tel. 721-373) is 13 km out on the road to Kiev.

Brody

There is no petrol station in the 109 km between Lvov and Brody, and halfway along the road crosses the River Bug. Brody was founded in the twelfth century, and contains a sixteenth-century Catholic

Dubno

church and a seventeenth-century castle. Fifty-five km further is the town of Dubno, where King Charles XII of Sweden, retreating from Peter the Great, buried twenty-eight bronze cannon, which are now on display in the town.

Rovno

This flat land of marshes and dank woods is all border country, fought over for centuries. The town of Rovno, 45 km onwards from Dubno, was founded in the thirteenth century, at about the time of an important battle when Prince Alexis of Volhynia defeated the Lithuanians. Volhynia had been a province of the Kievan Federation until the decline of Kiev and the coming of the Tartars threw Volhynia back upon its western neighbours. It was then ruled until the seventeenth century by successive great Polish warlord families, the Ostrovskys, who built a strong castle, and then were succeeded by the Lubomirskys, who softened the fortress into a rococo palace. (This was largely destroyed in the Russo-Polish war of 1921.) In the 1795 partition of Poland, Rovno was swallowed by Russia and its Catholics subjected to a policy of Russification. The Orthodox Cathedral was built at the Tsar's personal expense in 1890. In 1921, Rovno became part of independent Poland. The eighteenth-century wooden **Church of the Dormition** is of interest. There is no Intourist hotel.

Novograd-Volhynsky

The road passes through the Pripyat marshes, through a countryside whose gloom only lifts in the brightest sunshine. There is a café at the town of Korets, but no petrol station until Novograd-Volhynsky, 110 km from Rovno, where the ruins of a fourteenth-century castle of the Ostrovsky family can be seen.

Zhitomir

Some 77 km further east is the city of Zhitomir, founded in the ninth century as part of the Kievan Federation. It became Lithuanian in 1320 and Polish in 1569, before being absorbed by Russia in the partition of Poland in 1793. During the civil war of 1918–21, and in the Russo-Polish war, and again in the German invasion, there was bitter fighting here. Virtually all the historic buildings were destroyed, but the seventeenth-century town hall has been restored.

Two hours' drive through some pleasant but unkempt villages and wooded country will take you the 130 km to the Ukrainian capital of Kiev. As you see Kiev in the distance, the nuclear power station of Chernobyl is directly to the north, about 90 km up the River Pripyat.

Kiev

See p. 246.

The main road for Moscow crosses the River Dniepr by the Paton Bridge, and runs almost due north past the huge inland Sea of Kiev through the small towns of Brovasy and Kozelets to Kopti. Take the right fork at Kopti for the Moscow road, but it is possible to make a diversion to the ancient city of Chernigov, 50 km north. Founded in the ninth century, it prospered until the Tartars sacked it in 1239. In the fourteenth century it was taken over by the Lithuanians, and in 1499 was absorbed into the Muscovy of Vassily III.

Chernigov

What to see

It contains a number of striking buildings. The eleventh-century **Church of the Transfiguration**, the **Church of St Elijah**, rare in its absence of columns, and the twelfth-century **Cathedral of the Annunciation**, with its mosaic floors, are all notable. Another wave of building followed the city's absorption into Russia in the seventeenth century. The **Military Chancellery** and the **Eletsky** and **Trinity Monasteries** all date from this time, as does the house of Mazeppa, Hetman or leader of the Cossacks, who supported King Charles XII of Sweden against Peter the Great. To return to the Kiev–Moscow road, take the road back to the Kopti junction.

Ukrainian steppe

From Kopti to Orel, there is a 400-km stretch of fast straight road, with a petrol station at the turn-off to **Vertiyevka**, and at **Glukhov**, after 200 km. This is the flat and endless Ukrainian steppe, the most fertile soil in the USSR. But in harvest time, the road will be splashed and sticky with the crops that have fallen from the trucks hauling themselves on to this one decent road from the rutted tracks that make up the country's rural road network. In harvest time again, watch for

319

the coaches that bring schoolchildren, conscripts, factory and white collar workers into the fields to help collect the crops. Enormous efforts are made to gather the crops, but too little is then done to improve the means of getting the crops to the farm and railhead, and of storing them without rotting or vermin attack. Beware speed traps on this road.

Kursk

The turn-off to **Zheleznogorsk**, 360 km from Kopti, marks the biggest iron ore deposits in the country, the Kursk magnetic anomaly. At Kursk itself, south of the road, took place the world's biggest ever tank battle, in the summer of 1943, when the Germans tried to recover the initiative they had lost at Stalingrad with a massive armoured assault in the Soviet centre. The Red Army knew they were coming, built massive defensive lines and prepared the armoured reserves for the counter-attack. When the German offensive stalled, the Russian counter drove the battle line back into Byelorussia. This region, where the main road from Krakov and the Crimea joins from the right, is a fertile district renowned for its orchards and for its apple brandy.

Orel

Founded by Ivan the Terrible as a fortress town, Orel paid the price of exposure, being sacked repeatedly by the Tartars, destroyed by the Poles and also destroyed by fire in 1573. But its location was too important for the town not to recover. It was the collection point for the Ukraine grain to be shipped north to Moscow along the River Oka.

What to see

Badly damaged during the war, the city is noteworthy now for its association with the novelist Turgenev, who described its woods and countryside in *A Sportsman's Notebook*. There is a Turgenev museum in Orel itself, and at the lodge of the Spasskoye country estate where he was brought up.

Where to stay

The **Shipka Motel** (tel. 307-04), along with a petrol and service station, is on the outskirts of town on the Moskovskoye Highway.

Yasnaya Polyana

The road north to Tula runs through an area around the new town of **Schekino**, which is polluted by mining for lignite, the sulphurous brown coal. Just before Tula is a turn-off to the left to Yasnaya Polyana, the museum-estate of Leo Tolstoy, where the great novelist was born, and spent the bulk of his life. Here he wrote the great novels *War and Peace* and *Anna Karenina*. Tolstoy's modest green hump of a grave lies in a shadowed grove in the delightful wooded estate where he had played as a boy and looked for the 'green stick' that held the secret of universal happiness. The estate was ransacked and the house burned during the German occupation of 1941–2. It has been extensively restored, and there is a restaurant, but the estate is now in renewed danger from pollution. The nearby 'Azot' chemical works, in spite of repeated warnings and fines, continues to fulfil its plan and belch out so much sulphur dioxide in the process that the woods and avenues of limes and ash trees around Tolstoy's shrine are dying.

Tula

This city, just north of Yasnaya Polyana, dates back to the twelfth century, and for the next three centuries it acted as an advance fortress to defend Moscow and give it warning of Tartar raids.

What to see

The heart of the city is still the seventeenth-century **Kremlin**, but by the time it was built, Moscow's borders had moved safely to the south, and Tula was enjoying its golden age as a centre of industrial crafts. Guns and samovars were the specialities of the Tula ironsmiths, so favourably placed near the iron ore deposits. The **History of Firearms Museum** is fascinating, and the eighteenth-century **Church of St Nicholas** stands in the heart of the old gunsmiths' quarter.

Serpukhov

Eighty km north of Tula is the fortress town of Serpukhov, another outer bastion for Moscow, and the remains of its stone walls can still be seen. Turn left after crossing the River Oka to visit the town. After

Chekov

35 km, the small town of Chekov was named after the great playwright who practised in the nearby village of Melikhovo as a country doctor in the 1890s, and where he wrote *The Seagull*.

To Moscow

The road continues another 30 km to **Podolsk**, the main limestone quarry for Moscow, with its small museum commemorating the several weeks Lenin spent here in 1900. After 17 km, the road crosses Moscow's outer ring road, and there is a signpost to the Butovo camp site. At the ring road junction is the largest car service station in the USSR, but only for Soviet-made Lada cars. The road continues up the Warsaw Chaussee into central Moscow, up Pyatnitskaya Street and on to the bridge that leads into Red Square from the south.

Moscow

See p. 152.

Route Five:

From Romania to Kiev, a) via Vinnitsa (629 km)
b) via Kishinev and Odessa (1,024 km)

a) **Siret** — **Porubnoye** (5 km) — **Chernovtsy** (37 km) — **Novoselitsa** (40 km) — **Khmelnitsky** (176 km) — **Vinnitsa** (120 km) — **Berdichev** (82 km) — **Zhitomir** (40 km) — **Kiev** (130 km)

b) i) **Leusheny** — **Kishinev** (80 km) — *
   ii) **Siret** — **Novoselitsa** (as above) — **Brichany** O (80 km) — **Beltsy** (90 km) — **Orgeyev** (85 km) — **Kishinev** (45 km) — *

* **Kishinev** — **Bendery** (60 km) — **Tiraspol** (23 km) — **Odessa** (100 km) — **Uman** (230 km) — **Belaya Tserkov** (120 km) — **Vasilkov** (70 km) — **Kiev** (40 km)

O = petrol

a) The shorter option, via Vinnitsa

The border crossing between the Romanian town of **Siret** and the Soviet town of **Porubnoye** takes you across the River Siret and into the Bukovina, which translates as Beech-Tree Land. This region of the Carpathian foothills has been ruled at different times by all of its neighbours. There is evidence of Roman occupation here, and Attila's Huns passed through.

Chernovtsy

History

This city, 37 km from the border, was part of the Kievan Federation until the twelfth century, when it moved into the ambit of the Principality of Galicia-Volynia. It was invaded by the Tartars in the thirteenth century, and came under Hungarian rule in the 1350s, before being absorbed into the Turkish Empire. A border town, frequently attacked and plundered by Poles and Turks alike, it was taken over by Russia in 1768 during the reign of Catherine the Great. Seven years later, it was ceded to Austria, who renamed it Czernovitzy, and it prospered as the centre of the increasingly autonomous Bukovina.

During the First World War, the Russians occupied Chernovtsy in 1916, but from 1918–40 it was part of independent Romania, until the Red Army marched in. The following year, the city was badly battered during the German invasion, whose forces included a Romanian army bent on revenge as much as reconquest.

What to see

Few important buildings survived, but in the older part of town one can see traces of Turkish influence. The seventeenth-century **Church of St Nicholas** remains, and so does the nineteenth-century **Palace**, today the home of the university, but little else. The palace is part of the international school of nineteenth-century sub-Gothic design; it could be a Scottish country house, a Canadian hotel or an Australian city hall.

The city of Chernovtsy has for the past century and more been a centre of Ukrainian nationalism, largely because the Austrian authorities tolerated the development of the Ukrainian language and culture, while Tsarist Russia across the frontier repressed them as an act of the state policy of Russification. Whatever complaints may be levelled against the Soviet authorities over Russification, it has been mild compared to that of the Tsars.

Where to stay

There is a camp site just east of the city, and two spartan hotels, neither of which is run by Intourist, both located on the main street, Ulitsa Lenina. The **Hotel Bukovina** (tel. 382-49) is larger and slightly more comfortable and has a money changing office.

The attractive wooded and hilly countryside makes for pleasant driving on the 40 km from Chernovtsy to Novoselitsa, where the road forks. Left and north is the direct route to Kiev, right and east goes through Moldavia the 308 km to Kishinev and to Odessa. On the Kiev road, you pass the fourteenth-century fortress town of **Khotin**, commanding the crossing of the River Dniester.

Kamenets-Podolsky
History and what to see

The next town of Kamenets-Podolsky is worth a look. Founded in the days of Kievan Rus (see p. 18), Kiev's decline saw it absorbed into the emergent Principality of Galicia-Volynia, and in the fifteenth century into Polish and then Turkish hands, but many of the buildings have been preserved, and the resulting jumble makes the town an architectural history of the region. The old bridge across the River Smotrich was built by the Turks, and they also helped build the old castle, or at least restore the original fourteenth-century structure. There is a small historical museum in the grounds. The sixteenth-century churches of Saints Peter and Paul and the Dominicans reveal the Polish influence. The Dominican church combines Gothic style with a Turkish minaret.

Khmelnitsky
History

The next 100 km towards Khmelnitsky sees the landscape change into the characteristic low horizons of the Ukraine. More undulating than it looks, the countryside is lush and well-watered, which made it perfect for the Cossacks and their horses. Khmelnitsky is named after the Bogdan Khmelnitsky, the seventeenth-century Cossack leader who led the rebellion against Polish rule. After considerable success, he was forced on the defensive, and turned for support to Moscow. With the Treaty of Pereyaslav in 1654, he held off the Poles but began the process of steady erosion of Cossack autonomy by Moscow. In modern Soviet mythology, he is hailed as the wise and far-seeing liberator who believed in the reunification of the Ukraine with Russia. In fact, several of the Bogdan's successors as Hetman, including his son (who later became a monk), reversed his policy and made treaties with the Poles. The Hetman Doroshenko even offered allegiance to the Turks, which brought Russians and Poles into a Christian alliance against him.

This part of the Ukraine, perhaps because it was for so long border country, remained poor and backward well into the twentieth-century. Khmelnitsky itself had neither running water nor sanitation until after the Revolution.

Vinnitsa
History

The city dominates the crossing of the River Bug, 120 km east from Khmelnitsky. It was a kind of regional capital, but the first stone buildings did not begin to appear until late in the seventeenth century, a Catholic church and school which still stand today. The Tartars hit this region hard. Vinnitsa was founded in the fourteenth century around a wooden fort, a place of refuge from the Tartar raids, which then became a stronghold against the Poles. Today Vinnitsa is a centre of Ukrainian music and linguistic culture, and has a population of 350,000.

What to see

The eighteenth-century wooden **Church of St Nicholas** has been preserved, and the remains of the former Jesuit, Dominican and Capuchin monasteries from the seventeenth to eighteenth centuries may also be seen. Near the camp site, some 15 km from Vinnitsa, are the remains of the German High Command's forward HQ.

Where to stay

The Oktyabrskaya Hotel on Yuri Gagarin Square (tel. 265-60) and the **Lastochka** camp site on the road out to Zhitomir are not run by Intourist, but bookings may be made at their office.

Berdichev

After 82 km, the road passes the small town of Berdichev, with its seventeenth-century Carmelite building, half-fortress half-monastery. There are large catacombs dug beneath the town, used for storage rather than for burials. In 1850 Honoré de Balzac was married to Evelina Hanska in the Catholic church here. Madame Hanska's estate at the village of **Verkhovnya**, where Balzac lived from 1848, has a small museum in his memory.

Another 40 km takes you into **Zhitomir**, from where the route to Kiev and to Moscow is described in Route Four on pp. 319–21.

b) The longer option, via Kishinev and Odessa

There are two border crossings from Romania that go to Kishinev, capital of Soviet Moldavia.

The first and shorter route crosses the frontier on the River Prut at **Leusheny**, scene of a massive battle in 1944, in which eighteen German divisions were encircled. The journey to Kishinev takes about an hour and passes through the small town of **Kotovsk**, which contains the nineteenth-century palace of Manuk-Bey, a memory of the Turkish cccupation. Another 35 km brings you to Kishinev.

The second route to Kishinev from Romania goes via **Chernovtsy** (see the beginning of this section on p. 322) and only turns off to Kishinev at the town of **Novoselitsa**. The 300-km drive from Novoselitsa to Kishinev is one of the most pleasing in the Soviet Union, through picturesque villages and well-tended vineyards. The road runs along the Romanian border for the first 50 km, through the valley of the River Prut, and then skirts the Rossoshansky Forest and game reserve on the way to the village of **Brichany** where there is a petrol station. The next 90 km runs through hilly and wooded country before descending into what used to be the marshy land surrounding the sources of the River Reut around **Beltsy**. The word Belts means marsh, and the small settlement that was founded here in the fifteenth century was formally named a town only after the Russian occupation in 1818. The Cathedral of St Nicholas (1791) and the nineteenth-century Armenian church are worth a glance.

Orgeyev

South of Beltsy, modern drainage systems have made marshes into a fertile plain, some of the richest land in the country. The 85 km to Orgeyev passes through fields of wheat and maize, sunflowers and sugar beet. Moldavia is the least urbanised of all the Soviet republics, but the villages reflect the high population density on the land.

Orgeyev itself, the second biggest city of Moldavia, was a minor country town until the expansion of agriculture and agro-industry in the last thirty years. But archaeologists have established that there were human settlements here of the Getic culture in the fourth century BC. The seventeenth-century Church of St Demetrius, built from the easily-carved local limestone, is rather fine.

The 45 km to Kishinev is a delightful drive through the Sergiyevsky Forest, with an excellent picnic spot at the cliff where the cave known as the **Mygla** is signposted.

Kishinev   See p. 243.

The 180 km from Kishinev to Odessa is a pleasant drive that runs down the valley of the Dniester, with its orchards and vineyards. The first town is **Bendery**, after 60 km, which has been the site of a fortress commanding the Dniester crossings since the second century BC. The original twelfth-century fortress was built by the Genoese, who traded actively with the Black Sea ports, but it fell to the Turks in the sixteenth century. The rectangular fort with its citadel was Turkish-built in the 1530s. It was besieged several times by the Russians in the eighteenth century as part of their drive for Bessarabia, and all but destroyed in the German retreat of 1944.

Another 23 km brings you to **Tiraspol**, founded as a stronghold by General Suvorov in 1792, but named after the ancient Greek colony hereabouts of Tiras. Built in the grid pattern of eighteenth-century new towns, there are traces of the original fort, and some of the older houses, with their traditional Moldavian balconies, betray Turkish influence. Just outside Tiraspol, on the 100-km drive to Odessa, you pass the village of **Kuchurgan** and leave the Moldavian Republic to enter the Ukraine.

Odessa   See p. 251.

The road from Odessa to Kiev, 490 km over the steppes, is modern, straight and fast, across an oddly empty landscape. It will take about six hours, and you should either pack a picnic to eat on the move, or stop for a bite on the way. Beautiful at spring and autumn time, with a wide and almost sea-like horizon that makes the sky seem enormous, the road skirts the few towns along the way. After 230 km, there is a turn-off to the town of **Uman**, site of a great battle in 1941, and of a famous national park. Known as the Sofiyevka, it was presented to his wife Sophie by Count Potocky in 1793, and its 100 hectares contain nearly 400 species of plants and trees, imported from all over the world. The rarest are the Amur cork tree, the iron tree, the marsh cypress, the bear nut tree and the tulip tree. There is a buffet café, and a stop here makes a pleasant break in the journey.

Another 120 km brings you to the town of **Belaya Tserkov** (White Church), built in the fourteenth century on the site of the older town of Yuriev, which was destroyed by Batu Khan's Tartars. It was called White Church after the only building the Tartars left standing. It is known now for mineral springs and an eighteenth-century park, which is also the site of the Botanical Gardens of the Ukraine Academy of Sciences.

After another 70 km, you pass the ancient town of **Vasilkov**, founded by Prince Vladimir of Kiev in 998, and after another 40 km, you enter Kiev along the avenue named after the 40th Anniversary of the October Revolution. This takes you past the permanent Exhibition Park of Ukrainian Economic Achievement, where there is a petrol and service station.

Kiev | See p. 246.

Route Six:

From Moscow to the Black Sea, via Kharkov to the Crimea (1,451 km)

Appendix: From Kharkov to Kiev (470 km)

Moscow — **Orel** (360 km) — **Kursk** (160 km) — **Obayan** (60 km) — **Belgorod** (40 km) — **Kharkov** (83 km) — **Merefa** (22 km) — **Natalino** O (120 km) — **Novomoskovsk** O (90 km) — **Levshino-Mikhailovka** O (70 km) — **Zaporozhye** (22 km) — **Zelyony Gai Motel** O (60 km) — **Melitopol** (60 km) — **Chongarsk Bridge** (100 km) — **Simferopol** (122 km) — **Yalta** (90 km)

Appendix: **Kharkov** — **Poltava** O (135 km) — **Khorol** (95 km) — **Lubny** (40 km) — **Piryatin** O (45 km) — **Kiev** (155 km)

O = petrol

The road south from Moscow is the Warsaw Chaussee, which leaves the inner ring road at Dobryninskaya Metro station. Follow the signs for the M4 highway, signposted to Butovo, Tula and Kharkov.

For the first 420 km, until the great road junction 60 km south of Orel, you are following in reverse the same route described in Route Four on pp. 320–1. At the junction, the Kiev road goes right and west, and you follow the road south to Kharkov. The characteristic countryside of the Ukraine does not begin until Belgorod, some 250 km south of the junction and the first 95 km, to the city of Kursk, are through undulating country, with woods and ill-kempt orchards. It is seldom that Soviet orchards appear to be properly pruned, which makes for abundant blossom in the spring, but rather small apples in the autumn.

Kursk
History | The city was founded in the tenth century, and some of its warriors took part in the battle against the Polovtsy which was made epic by the first great Russian tale 'The Lay of the Host of Prince Igor'. Kursk was so completely sacked by the Mongols in 1240 that it disappeared from history until it was refounded in 1586, just after the death of Ivan the Terrible, as a southern bastion against the Crimean Tartars, and was attacked by Poles and Tartars alike. But as the Ukraine came

under Moscow's control in the seventeenth century, Kursk stagnated until the discovery of the vast iron ore deposits led to its rapid industrialisation this century.

What to see

The museum to the great tank battle of Kursk of 1943, which effectively broke the offensive power of the Wehrmacht, is of some interest, but there is a far more impressive memorial 100 km to the south, where some of the original battlefield has been preserved. In Kursk there are two seventeenth-century churches, the Upper and Lower Trinity, to be seen, and an unusual example of a provincial design by Rastrelli, the architect of the Winter Palace and Tsarkoye Selo in Leningrad, and the magnificent St Andrew's in Kiev. His **Sernievo-Kazansky Cathedral** in Kursk is dramatic, both intensely coloured and striking in design, with what appears to be two churches on top of one another, topped by a dome and stepped belfry. Inevitably after the war damage, it is a restoration.

Where to stay

The **Solyanka camp site**, 150 Engels Street (tel. 508-71) which is not run by Intourist, is beside Intourist's motel, the **Solovyinaya Roshcha** (tel. 515-62), where money may be changed.

Sixty km to the south, you pass the town of **Obayan**, founded as a border fort in the seventeenth century, but destroyed in the Second World War. The Kursk battlefield memorial, 40 km further on, is signalled by a T-34 tank by the side of the road. It stands above a mass grave of Soviet tank crews. Without doubt the best tank of the war, heavily-gunned and easy to manufacture and maintain, the T-34 stunned the German panzers when they first encountered it. The tank was also a technological generation ahead of its rivals, its armour plate having been quickly welded into place on an assembly line in a revolutionary process developed by the Paton Institute of Kiev. The first stage of the Battle of Kursk was the slowing down and stopping of the German panzers by successive lines of Soviet artillery, and the memorial also features an anti-tank gun as a tribute to the 6th Guards Army, which took much of the brunt of the battle. The dugouts, trenches, tank-traps and even some of the sited weapons have been preserved, to keep the battlefield looking as it did in 1943.

Kursk Battlefield Memorial

The town of **Belgorod** (White City), 40 km from the battlefield, was named in the thirteenth century after the nearby hills of white chalk. It was entirely destroyed in the Second World War but has been rebuilt.

Where to stay

There is a small camp site in a larch grove just south of Belgorod and 1 km left of the highway.

After Belgorod, the great land sea of the Ukrainian steppe begins again – the wide fields separating the whitewashed villages and orchards. After 40 km, a roadside obelisk marks the boundary between the Russian Republic and the Ukraine at a point exactly 700 km from Moscow.

Kharkov

Founded in the 1650s as a frontier post on the empty steppe,

Kharkov was populated by emigrants from the Polish Ukraine who were attracted by land grants. It was a quasi-military system of land-holding, with the land divided according to the 'regiments' of men it was supposed to support. A number of such settlements, of Kharkov, Sumy, Izyum and others, made up the 'Ukraine of Townships' and, rather like the Cossacks, enjoyed considerable autonomy in return for guarding the frontier. But as the threat of the Tartars ended, the regiments and townships stagnated until the railways brought to the Ukraine both industrialisation and bulk transport for its grain. By the end of the nineteenth century, Kharkov was the second city of the Ukraine, and its main industrial centre before the Revolution, and thus the Bolshevik stronghold in the Ukraine. It was the republic's capital until 1934.

In the 1930s Kharkov was the site of the massive 'Hammer and Sickle' tractor factory and today, with 1.5 million people, the city is still a major industrial zone. The massive Dzerzhinsky Square, however, is dominated by the restored **House of Industry**, a classic building of the 1930s, one of the great icons of the posters hailing the first Five-Year Plans, and still imposing.

What to see

There are some pre-Revolutionary buildings. The seventeenth-century **Church and Monastery of the Intercession** overlook the River Lopan from their position high on its banks, and the sixteenth-century **Church of the Dormition** claims Rastrelli contributed to the design. Now part of the university, the **Palace of Catherine II** is also attributed to Rastrelli.

Where to stay

There are three Intourist hotels in Kharkov. The most modern is the 17-storey **Hotel Mir**, 27a Prospekt Lenina (tel. 322-330). The **Intourist Hotel** is at 21 Prospekt Lenina (tel. 308-785) and there is a motel, called the **Druzhba** (Friendship) at 185 Prospekt Gagarina (tel. 507-905). The **Lesnoy** camp site (tel. 225-200) is not run by Intourist, but can be found 16 km south of the city on the road to Zaporozhye and Simferopol.

Note: Kharkov is a major road junction. This route goes south to the Crimea, but it is also possible to turn west for Kiev and a brief route guide will be found in the appendix at the end of this section on p. 330. There is also another turn-off to the south-east for Rostov-on-Don and the Caucasus, which is covered in detail in Route Seven on p. 332.

Crimea

The road south to the Crimea from Kharkov is at first dotted with what seems to be colonies of overgrown garden sheds. These are dachas, or country cottages, belonging to the people of Kharkov. It is possible to buy a dacha, to build one's own, or to rent a dacha for the summer from one's trade union or factory, which will find it very much easier to obtain a lease on the land than most private citizens.

After the village of **Merefa**, which was once known for its distinctive pottery, the great plain stretches infinitely on, the horizon broken by the occasional patch of forest or line of trees acting as a wind-break. There is a petrol station after 120 km at **Natalino**, and another 90 km further at the town of **Novomoskovsk**, whose eighteenth-century wooden church has been turned into a local history museum. After 70

Camp site km, there is a petrol station and a camp site at **Levshino-Mikhailovka** (tel. 348-232), which serves the city of Zaporozhye, 22 km further south.

Zaporozhye The historic importance of Zaporozhye lay in the way the River
History Dniepr narrowed into rapids at this point. It was inhabited by Scythian tribes some 6,000 years ago, and in the later middle ages **Khortitsa Island** became the famous base camp of the Sech Zaporozhskaya, the Cossacks of the Dniepr, whose camp life is described in *Taras Bulba*. A detour can be made to visit the island, and the best way to get there is to leave your car at the Zaporozhye Hotel and take a no. 2B bus which goes direct.

In the nineteenth century, its location between the coal mines of the Don and the iron ore deposits of Krivoy Rog helped develop Zaporozhye as an industrial centre. But its real growth took place with the building of the great dam in the 1920s, the Battle with the Dniepr, which Moscow's propaganda elevated into the status of a national epic, a symbol of socialist modernisation, and Soviet man overcoming the elements. The dam began work in 1932 to an enormous fanfare, but only began producing full power in 1937. It was almost destroyed in the war, to be rebuilt by 1947, and an obelisk beside the dam commemorates the Unknown Soldier who prevented its complete demolition by the retreating Germans.

One of the city's most famous products is the Zaparozhyets car, possibly the most lethal automobile ever manufactured. Cheap and nasty, with an underpowered engine that sounds like a sewing machine on heat, even the Soviet consumer has to be bribed to buy one. Their price was halved in 1984 to a mere 3,000 roubles (or a year's pay for the average Zaporozhye worker) in order to reduce the stocks of them. They are slow, uncomfortable, unreliable, very hard to start in winter, and with extremely temperamental electric systems that go haywire in the damp.

Where to stay **Zaporozyhe Hotel**, 135 Prospekt Lenina (tel. 341-292).

Sixty km south of Zaporozhye, the road skirts the vast Kakhovka reservoir at a point marked by the aptly named **Zelyony Gai** (Green Country) **Motel** and its petrol station; western tourists, however, are not allowed to stay here. Another 60 km brings you to **Melitopol**, home of the best Soviet watermelons. The town is more famous for the fourth-century BC Scythian burial mounds, where nearly 5,000 gold ornaments were found in archaeological excavations in the 1950s. Their remarkable sophistication forced some academic rethinking of the nature of Scythian culture and their relationship to the world of Ancient Greece. The best collection of Scythian gold and other artefacts is to be found in the Hermitage Museum in Leningrad.

The Crimea

The road runs absolutely straight for 100 km to the **Chongarsk Bridge** across the Sivash Lagoon, whose mud is said to have medicinal value. On the right is the Isthmus of Perekop, the neck of land that joins Crimea to the mainland. It is marked by a massive man-made earth wall, the old defensive rampart of the peninsula, which now contains the bodies of the thousands of Soviet soldiers who died taking it from the Germans in 1944.

Simferopol

It is just over 110 km from the Canal and rampart across the plain to the main city of Simferopol, built on the site of the old Tartar township of Ak-Mechet (White Mosque), and before that, the site of the Scythian capital of Neapolis. The archaeological evidence bears out occasional references in Greek texts, including the geographer Strabo, and suggests that Neapolis flourished from the second century BC to the fourth century AD, when it was destroyed by the Huns. A necropolis and stone mausoleum, with tombs of over seventy nobles, have been excavated, together with city walls 8 m thick, including towers and a defended gate. The site of the forum has been established, and bronze and marble statues found. Open daily from 10 a.m. to 6 p.m., closed on Mondays and Tuesdays.

Southern Crimea

The road to Yalta, 90 km to the south, passes through the Salgir Valley and then into the spectacular scenery of the southern Crimean mountains. But your first impression will be an overwhelming scent of roses, from the plantations which feed the local rose oil factory, which produces half the rose oil of the Soviet Union. One kilo of rose oil takes 400,000 rose buds. The road climbs to the 700-m **Angarsky Pass**, between the Demerdzhi range and the cliffs of the Chatyr-Dag (Attic of Heaven) which rises to almost 1,500 m.

The road runs south to the sea past vineyards, and the resort of **Aluschta**. This was first a Greek, and then Byzantine settlement, and even when the Tartars occupied the Crimea, Aluschta remained a Genoese fortress. From Aluschta you can take either the new motorway direct to Yalta through the mountains, or the coast road through **Gurzuf**. Whichever route you take, try to distinguish the shape of a bear sipping from the sea in Mountain Medved (Bear Mountain) just before the childrens' holiday camp of Artek.

Forty km beyond Gurzuf, and past the Nikitsky Botanical Gardens, is the turn-off to the Intourist hotel where you will probably be staying.

Yalta

See p. 253.

Appendix: From Kharkov to Kiev

This is the route by which to explore the Ukraine, but if you have already driven through much of the Ukrainian steppe, only the cities on this drive will be a new experience. (It is, however, a faster way to

Kharkov from Kiev than going via Moscow, and any traveller who has already seen Moscow should take this route from Kiev to the Black Sea or the Caucasus.)

Poltava
History

From Kharkov, the 135 km to Poltava is a flat and dull route. Poltava was founded in the twelfth century, disappeared with the Tartar invasions and then its remains fell into Lithuanian and, after the treaty of 1569, into Polish hands, at least nominally. In fact, it was the headquarters of one of the regiments of the Zaporozhskiye Cossacks, and one of their winter quarters. It was burned in the seventeenth century by the Poles and by the Tartars, and in 1709, it became the site of the decisive battle between Peter the Great and King Charles XII of Sweden, who had marched south to join what he hoped were his Cossack allies. King Charles was soundly defeated, and he and his ally the Cossack Hetman Mazeppa had to flee to Turkey.

What to see

There is a museum in Poltava dedicated to the battle, and some obelisks on the battlefield, one inscribed 'To the Swedes from the Swedes' and the other 'To the Swedes from the Russians'. It is not much to commemorate such an important battle – one which ended Sweden's period as a great power and definitively launched Russia into the centre of European great power politics. In the town, the seventeenth-century Cathedral of the Monastery of the Exaltation of the Cross is a good example of Ukrainian Baroque.

Where to stay

Poltava Motel, 2 Ulitsa Sovnarkomoskaya (tel. 357-47).

Ninety-five km to the west, you pass **Khorol**, the site of the battle where Prince Igor and Svyatoslav of Kiev defeated the Polovtsy army of Konchak Khan. Forty km further from Khorol is the town of **Lubny**, the site, in the 1720s, of the Ukraine's first pharmacy. It sold the products of the local herb garden, which remains part of the Soviet Institute of Medicinal Plants.

To Kiev

The remaining 200 km to Kiev pass through woodland steppe, and the black earth fields are visibly fertile in their crops of wheat, interspersed with sunflowers and sugar beet. This area is a great centre for bee-keeping, and you can sometimes buy (for at least 8 roubles a kilo) the excellent thick and golden yellow local honey at the café beside the petrol station at **Piryatin**. The road into Kiev passes the the Borispol airport, and enters the Ukraine capital over the welded bridge named after its designer (also the man who invented the technology which produced the T-34 tank), Yevgeny Paton.

Kiev

See p. 246.

Route Seven:

From Moscow to the Caucasus, via Kharkov through Cossack country to the Georgian Military Highway (3,370 km)

Appendix: From Tbilisi to Yerevan (292 km)

Moscow — **Kharkov** (800 km) — **Chuguyev** (40 km) — **Izyum** ○ (90 km) — **Slavyansk** ○ (45 km) — **Bokovo–Platovo** ○ (126 km) — **Novoshakhtinsk** ○ (60 km) — **Novocherkassk** (50 km) — **Rostov-on-Don** ○ (40 km) — **Bataisk** (11 km) — **Kushchevskaya** ○ (45 km) — **Krasnodar** ○ (196 km) — **Novorossiisk** ○ (142 km) — **Sochi** ○ (296 km) — **Lykhny** (166 km) — **Novy Afon** ○ (20 km) — **Samtredia Junction** ○ (203 km) — **Batumi** (105 km) — **Borzhomi** ○ (197 km) — **Gori** ○ (96 km) — **Georgian Military Highway** (60 km) — **Tbilisi** ○ (30 km) — **Ordzhonikidze** (200 km)

Appendix: Tbilisi — **Krasny-Most** (60 km) — **Kazakh** ○ (35 km) — **Idzhevan** ○ (32 km) — **Dilizhan** ○ (40 km) — **Lake Sevan** ○ (27 km) — **Razdan** (32 km) — **Bedzhni** (16 km) — **Yerevan** ○ (50 km)

○ = petrol

This is the grand tour of Soviet motoring, made the longer by a round trip that runs along the Black Sea coast of the Soviet Riviera, to the Georgian capital of Tbilisi and back through the Caucasus Mountains. An extra excursion to Yerevan, capital of Armenia, will add another 560 km. You will need a minimum of ten days for this tour, but it really deserves much longer. The mountains and the spa towns are pleasant for walks and relaxation, and if you are taking a holiday rather than entering a motorsport rally, you ought to enjoy the Black Sea beaches and coastal resorts. Georgia itself is a republic to appreciate and relish at some length (see p. 259). Properly paced, this could be the driving holiday of a lifetime.

Intourist is not supposed to authorise driving trips that aim to do much more than 500 km a day, and you should be averaging less.

Moscow to Kharkov

The first 800 km of this trip, from Moscow to Kharkov, is described in Route Six on p. 326.

From Kharkov, take Moscow Avenue, past the vast Tractor Factory, and the road goes south-east to Rostov-on-Don. This is not a route to linger on as it is one of the busiest of the Soviet highways and heads into the huge coal and industrial belt of the Don basin. After 40 km, you pass the town of **Chuguyev**, birthplace of the painter Repin and with a disappointing museum. Chuguyev, and the town of **Izyum**, 90 km further, are both located on the River Northern Donetsk, scene of some of the most bitter fighting of the 1943 campaigns. After Izyum, you are driving along the Donetsk Ridge, the eastern flank of the huge Donbass coalfields, 600 km wide and 150 km long.

Once past the town of **Slavyansk**, you start to see the slag heaps and winding gear of the pits. The miners here are on average the best paid workers in the Soviet Union, but times are getting hard. The easy seams have long been worked out, and since the 1970s pressure to keep up productivity from the tougher and deeper seams has caused an alarming rise in accidents, according to unofficial union sources. These figures are not made public in the workers' state, even under *glasnost*. But *glasnost* has revealed a shattering problem of absenteeism, low morale and sick leave among the miners.

In spite of the evidence of mining, this is not the black country of northern France or colliery England. There are large stretches of farmland and woods between the mines, but with few of the roadside villages, and few of the babushkas selling buckets of vegetables that are a feature of other routes.

At **Bokovo–Platovo**, 300 km from Kharkov, there is a large petrol and service station, a regular truck stop where you can sometimes buy fresh-roasted *shashlik* and tea. You now cross from the Ukraine back into the Russian Federation, 377 km south of Kharkov, and pass **Novoshakhtinsk**, where the coal seams are so thick they began completely mechanising the pits in the 1960s.

Novo-cherkassk

Another 50 km brings you to Novocherkassk, and you are now in the heart of Don Cossack country, the setting of Sholokhov's novel 'Tikhi Don' – *And Quiet Flows the Don*. Novocherkassk was the administration centre for the Cossacks, the Don Voisko (headquarters) of the Cossack Army.

What to see

Novocherkassk has a fascinating museum devoted to the Cossacks, and you can still see the triumphal arches erected in 1817 for the welcome home of the Cossacks led by Ataman Platov, who had pursued Napoleon's troops all the way back to Paris. The museum also houses the famous Novocherkassk treasure, gold jewellery and ornaments dating from the second century AD, which were found in the tomb of a Sarmatian princess at the nearby Khokhlagh Hill.

Rostov-on-Don

Forty km south of Novocherkassk is the huge industrial centre of Rostov-on-Don. The route is pleasant enough, with farmland and fields on both sides of the river, lovely with flowers in the spring, and rich with sunflowers in summer. There is a camp site just before you enter the town, opposite the airport (see p. 334).

What to see

Although founded in the eighteenth century as a harbour and customs post, there are few buildings of interest in Rostov save for the nineteenth-century town hall. The city began to grow quickly only when the new railways of the nineteenth century combined with Rostov's access to the Black Sea down the River Don to make it a regional centre. It was badly damaged during the German retreat of

1943. Other than spending the night in the hotel, there is little reason for the tourist to linger in this industrial centre of a million people.

Where to stay, and eat

There is a large 17-storey **Intourist Hotel** at 115 Engels Street (tel. 659-065). The restaurant is good, and stocks the local wines from the vineyards that stretch along the lower Don from Tsimlyanskaya.

The camp site (tel. 704-44) opposite the airport is noisy, has no chalets and is not run by Intourist.

Excursions

There is an interesting excursion to the fourth-century BC Byzantine Greek town of **Tanas**, 40 km from Rostov, where a small palace and townhouses have been well preserved. There is also an excursion to **Azov**, 46 km downstream, at the mouth of the Don where it flows into the Sea of Azov. This was the fortress city which the Turks long held to keep the Russians from the Black Sea.

From Rostov, cross the bridge to the left bank of the Don and take the Ordzhonikidze road. After the first 20 km, until well past **Bataisk**, where traffic can be heavy, this is a pleasant drive through agricultural land.

Krai of Krasnodar

Some 45 km south of Bataisk, you pass into the Krai (territory) of Krasnodar, one of the great agricultural centres, as is the region of Stavropol to its south, another of the Cossack marches, which was also the home of Mikhail Gorbachev.

Drive 50 km south of the village of **Kushchevskaya** and you will come to a road junction. The left fork is marked for Ordzhonikidze. You take the right fork for Krasnodar itself. It is a straight road that runs between fruit orchards and long lines of poplars. The villages you pass are Cossack settlements, although of much later date than those of Novocherkassk.

Krasnodar

The city of Krasnodar was founded only in 1793 and named Ekaterinodar, after the Empress. An undistinguished modern city, it is visibly more prosperous than most.

Where to stay, and eat

Foreign tourists are usually booked into the **Yuzhny Motel**, 40 Ulitsa Moskovskaya (tel. 594-42), or the **Intourist Hotel**, 109 Ulitsa Krasnaya (tel. 588-97). The restaurant at the Yuzhny Motel is generally disappointing although the steak is good.

The road to Novorossiisk leads through an avenue of trees, heading towards the Caucasus foothills which can be seen in the distance. After the village of **Enem**, the road heads through the oil-producing region and then you start to climb from the plain, with the steppe to the right and the rising mountains becoming steadily clearer and more impressive to the left. Ninety km from Krasnodar you pass the site of the Blue Line, the massive German defences built to protect Novorossiisk in 1943. The road climbs steadily to the high pass of **Volchyi Vorota** (Gates of the Wolf), with its stunning view of the main Caucasian ridge, before descending to Novorossiisk.

Novorossiisk

This is a classic site for a harbour. The Genoese built a fortress here in the twelfth century, and the Turks built the castle of Sudjuk-Kale, which the Russians took in 1811. In Soviet times, the vast local deposits of marl ensured that the port grew as a major manufacturing centre for cement. The scene of bitter fighting against the Germans, Novorossiisk is unusually well-supplied with war memorials and museums. This is because Leonid Brezhnev was the Commissar with the army on this front, and the importance of the battle in which he was involved has been exaggerated by his memoirs and by sycophancy.

Soviet Riviera

A hard-working port, Novorossiisk is also the beginning of the Soviet Riviera, an 800-km strip of coastal resorts, holiday camps and sanatoria, which stretches all the way down to the Turkish border. Much of this coastline has been rapaciously overdeveloped, and capitalism, or at least greed, is alive and well here.

Sochi

The road clings to the coast, through resort after resort, climbing up to the Mikhailovsky Pass and the Pshada Pass, and going through steadily more imposing scenery until you come to Greater Sochi, the Soviet Costa Brava, stretching for 150 km to the Georgian border, and welcoming nearly 5 million holiday-makers every year. Sochi is a year-round resort, thanks to the protective Caucasus Mountains and the Black Sea. It gets chilly in winter, with an average temperature of 7°C, but that is still the average April temperature for Moscow. The parks are in bloom all year round.

Sochi is made up of a number of different districts. There is **Dagomys** with its tea plantations, and **Matsesta** and **Khosta** with their sulphur springs and medicinal baths. Sochi has its own hill resort, **Krasnaya Polyana**, reached via the enchanting road through the Akhtsu Gorge. Finally, there is the resort of **Adler**, where the new airport has been built, and where the Yuzhnye Kultury state farm specialises in growing flowers and ornamental trees and shrubs. There is even the **Eagles' Nest**, a restaurant on top of **Mount Aibga**, nearly 2,500 m high, so remote that it has to be reached by helicopter. They used to hand out diplomas to all the guests in recognition of their 'endurance and courage'.

You either love Sochi or you hate it. I cannot stand the place, because it suffers from the usual Soviet problems of overbooked hotels, grim restaurants, the state not providing anything and the private sector stepping in to rip off the punters. And any place as crowded and as dedicated to leisure and recreation as Sochi ought to do a better job of night life.

Where to stay

There are three Intourist hotels, and the big modern one, 19 floors and nearly 1,000 rooms, is called **Zhemchuzhina**, 3 Ulitsa Chernomorskaya, (tel. 934-355). The other two Intourist hotels are both on the main street, Kurortny Avenue (which translates as health place), the **Camelia** at 89 (tel. 990-398), and the **Intourist** almost next door at 91 (tel. 990-292).

Where to eat

The restaurants of Sochi are crowded and no more than serviceable. But it is worth making an effort to get to the **Gorskaya**

Derevnya (Village in the Mountains) restaurant, near the Agura waterfalls. Housed in a log cabin, it serves Caucasian food, spices the *shashlik* with peppers, and sells the excellent Georgian wines you will not see in Moscow (see pp. 123–4). On Mount Bolshoy Akun, one of the dominant sights of Sochi, is an observation tower with stunning views of the Caucasus Mountains, and the **Akun** restaurant. It serves both Caucasian and Russian cuisine, but the site and outlook are better than the food.

The **Primorsky Restaurant**, at 21/1 Primorskaya in Sochi, is good for fish. The **Goluboy Restaurant**, 8 Voikov Street, serves Georgian mountain food with Georgian music.

Abkhazia

On leaving Sochi, you enter Abkhazia, an autonomous republic within the Republic of Georgia. This system of autonomous republics is the traditional and sensible constitutional device to prevent sudden outbursts of tribalism or nationalism, of the kind which brought hundreds of thousands of Armenians on to the streets in the spring of 1988. National identities are even trickier in the Caucasus because they go back such a long way. Abkhazia was known to the Ancient Greeks as Colchis, the land to which Jason sailed in search of the Golden Fleece. Nor was he wrong. There was gold in the rivers, and a sheep's fleece was one reasonably efficient way to strain out the gold dust.

The Soviet Riviera continues in spite of republican boundaries. The holiday resorts stretch on along the coast, beginning with **Leselidze**, where there is a huge children's camp, and also the sports training centre the Soviet team used before the Moscow Olympics. In the resort of **Gantiadi**, the eighth-century Tsandripsh Church is not only striking as a building but is acoustically perfect, thanks to resonating hollows built into the walls. Above Gantiadi, the road clings perilously to the cliff for a stunning view of historic **Gagra**, the warmest place on the Black Sea. Apart from the remains of a fifth-century castle, Gagra also boasts the best-stocked sub-tropical park in the country.

Fourteen km beyond Gagra on the right is a road leading to the purpose-built resort of **Pitsunda**. Dwarfing the tenth-century Abkhazian Church, the resort is dominated by three skyscrapers rising incongruously from the golden beach, and backed by the world's only long-needled pine forest. Seven km after the Pitsunda turn-off is a road to the left that goes to lovely **Lake Ritsa**, hemmed in by mountains like a scene on an Alpine postcard. Even more striking is the smaller **Lake Goluboy** (light blue), which retains its bright colour whatever the weather or hue of the sky. By the viewing point overlooking the lake is a café, where you can buy some of the local honey which is produced by the prolific grey mountain bee.

Back on the main road, after the resort village of Gudauta comes **Lykhny**, site of the fourteenth-century palace of the old Abkhazian dynasty, and a tenth-century Byzantine church. A further 20 km brings you to the old Monastery of Novy Afon, founded in 1875 by monks from Mount Athos in Greece, but now the Psyrtskha holiday camp. From the monastery you can visit the huge Anacopia Cave, whose biggest chamber is 140 m long. It is open from Tuesday to Saturday. The tenth-century church beside the Vodopad (waterfall) holiday camp in Novy Afon used to be the seat of the Abkhazian bishop.

Where to eat

Drive a further 8 km and you will come to two restaurants which specialise in the local cuisine, the **Eshera**, and the **Apatskha**. Tourism is an intensive business in this region.

Sukhumi

The road then descends to the bayside city of Sukhumi, the Abkhazian capital, which claims to have been founded 2,600 years ago as the Greek trading post of Dioscurias, whose remains are now beneath the sea. Sukhumi has certainly proved a popular, or at least a strategic site over the years. The remains of a second-century AD Roman fort may be seen by the quayside. There is also a tenth-century castle, built by Georgia's King Bagrat, and the fifteenth-century Turkish fort of Sukhum-Kale. The Soviet contribution was to drain the marshes and eradicate the region's traditional curse – malaria.

What to see

Although the phrase has little meaning in the USSR, Sukhumi gives itself the air of being an upmarket resort. Certainly, Moscow intellectuals claim to prefer it to Sochi. Development for mass tourism has been slightly more restrained, and the delightful local wines seem to give a feeling of well-being without noise or aggression. There is little night life, but if given the opportunity, on no account miss the centenarians' choir. Abkhazia is one of the centres of the famous Georgians who live for well over a hundred years (most of them attribute longevity to the local yoghurt). Under the urgings of the Folk Art Centre, they have formed a choir of thirty ancient gentlemen. The oldest is 130.

Where to stay

The Intourist hotel is the small, three-storey **Abkhazia**, 2 Frunze Street (tel. 233-11). The Intourist-run **Sukhumi camp site** (tel. 295-68) is at Gumista, just north of the town.

From Sukhumi, the road turns inland and runs for 200 km across a plain towards Kutaisi. You pass through **Mingrelia**, home of another Caucasian tribe, and the birthplace of Lavrenti Beria, Stalin's last secret police chief and one who tried to succeed him, according to Nikita Khrushchev, until arrested in the middle of a Politburo session in 1953. Beria was later shot. The road passes the capital of Mingrelia, **Zugdidi**, where the palace of the ruling Dadiani dynasty is now a museum. It should not be missed. The Dadianis were related to Napoleon, and many of his personal possessions, books, weapons, china and personal utensils, somehow ended up here.

Dadiani museum

Batumi

At the Samtredia junction, a detour can be made by taking the road right to Batumi, a major oil port some 20 km from the Turkish border. Very hot, with almost tropical levels of rainfall, Batumi was Bathys to the Ancient Greeks, and Vati in medieval times, and was sacked by Tamburlaine. It remained Turkish until 1878, when its boom years began as the port to export the oil from Baku, at the far side of the Caucasian Isthmus. Batumi then became the first springboard for the political career of Stalin, who organised a major strike in 1902 when Rothschild sacked 400 workers from the Batumi oil refinery. Fifteen people were killed when the police fired on the demonstrating workers, provoking more protests and strikes across southern Russia. In a celebrated proclamation, Stalin called for the workers to unite to overthrow Tsarism. A state of siege was declared in Batumi, and Stalin was arrested and later sentenced to three years' exile in Siberia. These

What to see days, there is little to see save the busy port, the **Botanical Gardens**, the **Chorokh Gorges** and the thermal resort at **Kobuleti**, north of town.

You return to the main road and Samtredia junction the same way you came. The road then passes through **Khobi**, site of a twelfth-century monastery, before reaching Kutaisi, the second city of Georgia.

Kutaisi   Dating back to the third century BC, this was the capital of the King-
History and   dom of Colchis after the eighth century AD, and when the Turks
what to see   occupied Tbilisi, from the tenth to twelfth centuries, Kutaisi became the seat of the Georgian monarchy. On a hill in the west of the city is the tenth-century **Church of King Bagrat III**, and a striking chapel of green stone on a rock overhanging the River Rioni. The **Gelati Architectural Reserve**, just outside the city, contains the restored remains of a twelfth-century monastery, a classic collection of architecture from Georgia's golden age of King David. A detour can be made to the north-west of Kutaisi to the spa town of **Tskhaltubo**, whose mildly radioactive waters are used to treat arthritis and ailments of the bones and joints. This region is filled with orchards and vineyards, producing the local Vasizondansky and Vartsisky wines.

Where to eat   You pass a huge champagne winery on the road that climbs from Kutaisi to the 900-m **Rikoti Pass**, where there is a café which offers a stunning view of the main Caucasian range. Downhill from the pass into the forested valley of **Surami**, another spa centre, the road brings you to the town of **Khashuri**, where the road turns off for an excursion of 30 km to Borzhomi, one of the most famous spas in the Soviet Union.

Borzhomi   Borzhomi water is, with Narzan, one of the most popular mineral waters in the country. It tastes so salty it must be doing you good, and indeed if Soviet food has been blocking your insides, Borzhomi water will unblock them fast. Borzhomi, at a height of 800 m and surrounded by pine-covered mountains, nestles in the valley of the River Kura. The two natural springs bubble out at temperatures of 23°C and 20°C. It has been a popular spot since the Stone Age, some of whose tourists left axe heads and other souvenirs, now in the local museum which is located in a fifth-century monastery. The Gorges of

Borzhomi wind for 60 km through mountains that soar to 1,500 m. As well as a spa town, this is one of the country's leading ski resorts, with a huge ski jump, and is the site of several winter sports championships.

Gori

Returning to Khashuri and the main road to Tbilisi, after 50 km you reach the town of Gori, which is famous as the birthplace of Joseph Stalin, and the last place in the Soviet Union where there is still a museum in his honour. A vast 18-m statue of the old brute dominates the main square. To his left is the only Univermag (department store) in the USSR that sells Stalin souvenirs, plaques and photo-calendars. At the other end of the square is a small Greek-style temple enclosing the modest hut where the great man was born, the son of a cobbler. Behind that is an imposing building, and as you climb the first flight of stairs, there he stands, life size in white marble – the sculptor has managed to make him look both kindly and authoritative.

Stalin
Museum

The museum is one of the most amazing sights in the Soviet Union, a paean of praise to the old dictator. Built four years after Stalin's death, when Khrushchev's anti-Stalin campaign was under way, it reflects an entirely genuine local sentiment. In 1961, when Stalin was removed from the Red Square mausoleum and his statues were being dismantled across the Soviet Empire, the men of Gori organised a round-the-clock rota to guard their statue in the main square from Moscow's demolition men.

The first room is devoted to his childhood, his sensitive poems (!), his early pride in being Georgian, and his time in the seminary. Then comes the room devoted to Koba, the young revolutionary, terror of the Tsars, with a full supporting cast including one Lenin whose great claim to fame was that he spotted Stalin's talents early. Lenin's testament, warning the Party against Stalin, receives no mention. There is no reference to Trotsky, and even the historic photographs of 1917 have been doctored to cut him out. The most sickening room is the one displaying the gifts sent to Stalin on his seventieth birthday, the vases, mugs, pots and sand paintings, and embroidery and tapestry with his image, rather like the souvenir shops at Lourdes.

But there is one awesome room no visitor can ever forget. You leave the room dedicated to Stalin's victory over Hitler (with some help from the Soviet people, Britain and the USA), and suddenly you are in a darkened corridor. At the far end, a light shines on a painting of Stalin on his deathbed. You walk towards it, and a room opens to your right, lined throughout in black and deep purple velvet. The room is dark, and the only light falls on a large pit, from which rises, on a slim plinth, the bronze and glinting deathmask of Stalin. The pit is surrounded by a fence of narrow white pillars that go from floor to ceiling, except in the centre, where the pillars have been broken off at knee height to allow the visitor to peer in. The effect is like a broken cage, from which the beast may escape at will.

If you have the stomach to stay, Gori is also proud of its hilltop castle, and Leo Tolstoy claimed this was the stronghold which Caesar's great rival Pompey had to relieve in his Georgian campaign.

Where to stay The small (54-room) **Intourist Hotel** is at 24 Prospekt Stalina (tel. 226-76).

North of Gori is the beautiful autonomous region of **Southern Ossetia**, where hunting trips may be arranged. And the region around Gori is famous for its orchards and vineyards. The local people will tell you that most European fruit trees originated in Georgia. Indeed, no Georgian would entertain the thought that God might have been so misguided that He located the Garden of Eden anywhere but in Georgia. Certainly the apples, pears and pomegranates of Gori are succulent, and the wines light and dry. The farmers hereabouts are prosperous, and so committed to the great tradition of hospitality that the first call on their savings is to build a large dining room on the side of the family house in which to entertain guests.

Sixty km south-east from Gori, passing the sixteenth-century Ksanis Tsikhe fortress, built to repel the Turks, the road joins the Georgian Military Highway. This is the last stretch before Tbilisi.

Mtskheta Almost at once, you reach Mtskheta, the traditional capital of Georgia since long before that upstart Tbilisi became capital a mere 1,500 years ago. Over 3,000 years old, Mtskheta was known to the Greeks as Armosica, and was the capital of the ancient kingdom of Iberia. It has always traditionally been the religious centre, whether of the pagan cult Ormuzd, or the seat of the Christian Patriarch and the Cathedral. Mtskheta has grown around the valleys where the Rivers Kura and Aragvi meet.

History and what to see

The town is dominated by a mountain spur, on which stands the marvellously simple sixth-century **Church of Dzhvari** (The Holy Cross), an excellent viewpoint. Before the church was built a large wooden cross stood here. The Cathedral of Mtskheta, surrounded by a fortress wall, was built between 1010 and 1029, but destroyed by Tamburlaine, among others, and rebuilt in the fifteenth century. It is known as the **Cathedral of Svetitskhoveli** (the Tree of Life). The first building on the site is said to have been in the fourth century, on the spot where the robe of Christ was discovered. The Cathedral is the tomb of the royal Bagrationi dynasty. (One of its later sons, Prince Bagration, is buried over 1,600 km to the north, on the battlefield of Borodino outside Moscow where he was mortally wounded in fighting Napoleon's Grand Army.)

Where to eat There are a number of restaurants in Mtskheta, and you will be unlucky to have a bad meal in Georgia. The main state-run tourist restaurants are the **Ormuzd** and the **Mtskheta**, but go instead to the newer restaurant, the **Marani**, on the outskirts of town, on the road to Gori, built in the shape of a traditional semi-underground and domed house. This place was operating as a co-operative, with staff pay depending on profits, some years before the new co-op system was thought about, let alone legalised.

From Mtskheta the Georgian Military Highway will take you the few kilometres into Tbilisi.

Tbilisi

See p. 260.

From Tbilisi to Ordzhonikidze

Retrace your route to Mtskheta, beyond which the road runs closely along the bank of the Aragvi. After **Badorno** the strangely-shaped cliffs of yellowish rocks contain a number of caves, used as refuge from the Tartars. The next village is **Ananuri**, where the River Arkala joins the Aragvi, which is dominated by a steep hill topped by a double castle, containing two churches, and a famous six-storey rectangular tower known as The Intrepid. Then comes the stunning **Aragvi Gorge**, dominated by the Vhartali and Vashloba watchtowers, and you pass by the flat-roofed villages before reaching the spa resort of **Pasanauri** at the confluence of the White and Black Aragvi.

Mleti Hill

One of the toughest parts of the road lies ahead – the eighteen hairpin bends and tunnels that climb the 20 km of Mleti Hill to reach the Ossetian village of **Gudairi**, at over 2,000 m on the slopes of Mount Gud-Gora, with marvellous views. You then descend into the Devil's Valley, where the White Aragvi flows through a steep gorge and the route is almost impossibly picturesque, surrounded by alpine pastures and wooded slopes. Next comes the ascent, alongside a precipice, to the highest point on the Highway, **Krestovy Pass** (the Pass of the Cross) at 2,255 m. The descent goes through the **Baidari Gorge**, named after Toti Baidarashvili, an eighteenth-century Ossetian mountaineer who was sent to live here by King Irakli of Georgia and rescue snow-trapped travellers, a human version of the St Bernard's dog in the Swiss Alps. This is the section most at risk from avalanche, and the road passes through several reinforced tunnels. From here all the way into the Terek Valley, the minerals in the rocks have stained the hillsides and congealed into bizarre shapes. It makes for a fantastical landscape running into the jagged cliffs and glaciers that dominate the Terek Gorge. A harsh landscape, yet there are watchtowers and *auls* (mountain villages) and churches. And they were built with an eye to defence. The village of **Arsha** is dominated by its medieval fortress, but the plateau is also defended by a series of fortified houses and signal posts.

Kazbegi

The road descends to the village of Kazbegi, a mountaineering centre that is dominated by the 4,700-m mountain of the same name which legend says is the rock to which Prometheus was chained. The twelfth- to fourteenth-century **Tstminda Sameba** (the Church of the Holy Trinity on the left bank) is one of the masterpieces of Georgian architecture. Beyond, the mountain caves at a height of 3,600 m were inhabited by hermits until well into the last century. Some remains are in the local museum.

From Kazbegi, the road crosses back and forth across the River Terek, from ledge to narrower ledge which are known as the Devil's Gates, to the village of **Gveleti**. Perhaps the wildest part of the route is yet to come, the 12 km **Daryal Gorge**, where the river roars through a narrow ravine nearly 1,500 m deep. The gorge is dominated by an ancient fortress known after the twelfth-century heroine as Queen Tamara's Castle, although it is far older. Known in antiquity as the Sarmatian Gates, it seems inconceivable that the military engineers of 1801 could have built a road here, let alone the last Devil's Bridge that somehow spans this gorge.

Ordzhonikidze

As you leave the Daryal Gorge and the Terek Valley, you leave Georgia and enter the **North Ossetian** autonomous republic, one of sixteen within the Russian Federation. Its capital, Ordzhonikidze, is named after a Georgian revolutionary who died in mysterious circumstances at the time of Stalin's purges. It was founded in the 1780s as the military town of Vladikavkaz, Ruler of the Caucasus, and it was here in 1942 that the German advance into the Caucasus was stopped. It now has a population of over 300,000.

Excursions

There is an excursion to the **Alan Necropolis**, the tombs of the Sarmatian peoples who began as aggressive nomads, rather like the Huns, but settled in the north Caucasus from the second to ninth centuries AD. And from nearby Karmadon, there is another excursion to the **City of the Dead** in Kargav Gorge, which contains almost 100 sixteenth- to eighteenth-century tombs.

Where to stay

There are three Intourist hotels in Ordzhonikidze. Motorists are usually booked into the **Daryal Motel**, on the by-pass road at Redant village (tel. 573-78). The large and newish **Vladikavkaz Hotel**, which has nearly 200 rooms, is at 75 Ulitsa Kotsoyev (tel. 520-28). There is an elderly and small **Intourist Hotel**, with 16 rooms, at 19 Prospekt Mira (tel. 346-26).

Seventy km south of Ordzhonikidze you leave North Ossetia and enter the **Kabardino-Balkaria** autonomous republic, first annexed to Russia in the 1550s, although their language did not have a written alphabet until 1924. The republic contains the highest mountains in

Nalchik

the Caucasus, and the capital of Nalchik, 115 km from Ordzhonikidze, is one of the great centres of Soviet mountaineering, although there is so far no Intourist hotel or camp site nearby. But arrangements for bona-fide mountaineers to stay here can be made through Intourist. It is also an equestrian centre, with several stud farms producing the famous Kabardin breed, and there are annual riding championships.

Twenty-three km beyond Nalchik is the small town of **Baksan**, where the ruins of a Russian fortress built in the 1820s are a reminder that the Georgian Military Highway did not solve all the region's security problems.

Baksan is also the turn-off for **Mount Elbrus**, at 5,300 m the highest mountain in the Caucasus, where you can ski in summer. The Baksan Gorge along the way is a striking drive, and you can take a cable car to the Novy Krugozor viewing platform for a remarkable panorama of the peaks.

Where to stay

You may arrange to stay at the modern **Itkol Hotel** (tel. 74-730), which is not run by Intourist, if arranged well in advance.

You return to the main road again through the Baksan Gorge to the town of Baksan. Just beyond the town is the **Great Tambukan Lake**, whose mud is said to be medicinal and to relieve arthritis. You are now entering the Krai of Stavropol, home of Mikhail Gorbachev, but famous also for its mineral waters. After the Great Tambukan Lake, and the old Cossack village of **Goryachevodskaya** (hot water), you can see the white buildings of Pyatigorsk, on the southern slopes of Mount Mashuk, the centre of the Caucasian spa resorts.

Spa resorts

Intourist has not yet greatly developed foreign tourism in these Caucasus spas, but they are some of the most popular vacation resorts for the Soviets who often deem the necessity for some spurious medical reason to justify a holiday. The Russians are a deeply superstitious as well as hypochondriacal people, and the aura of folk medicine about mud baths and water cures suits them perfectly. This is also a lovely and restful part of the world, with clear air, good walks, and marvellous scenery. No wonder they feel better.

The best mineral water is Narzan, which comes from the Kislovodsk resort, and is so pure you can add it to Scotch or Campari.

Pyatigorsk

To be avoided in the rainy spring, Pyatigorsk (it means five mountains) is at its best in autumn.

What to see

The best buildings of the spa resorts are to be found here, with the Lermontov Baths, built in the 1820s, and the Pushkin Baths, which date from 1901. Lermontov, author of the influential romantic-psychological novel *A Hero Of Our Time*, is also the hero of Pyatigorsk, having been shot here in a duel in 1841. There is a museum to the man, in the house where he lived, and his name crops up everywhere. The charming Tsvetnoi (Floral) Park contains a Lermontov Grotto and a Lermontov Gallery as well as the Lermontov Baths.

Where to stay

There is an Intourist motel, the **Volna**, 39 Ulitsa Ogorodnaya, (tel. 505-28), with a non-Intourist camp site attached.

Zheleznovodsk

This is the most beautiful of the resorts, and nestles in a small valley between Mounts Beshtau and Zheleznaya. There is a very fine park, with the palace of the Emir of Bukhara at the entrance, and beyond a delightful avenue of chestnut trees leads to the hot spring (55°C).

The resort which doctors say is best for the health is the old Cossack village of **Yessentuki**, with its celebrated mud baths. They may or may not do you good, but you do feel much better when they let you out.

The road north from Pyatigorsk back to Rostov-on-Don is 505 km, a good day's drive through the Stavropol steppe on a road that avoids

Stavropol

towns. Intourist will normally discourage stops at the towns on this road, but the main city of Stavropol itself is open to foreign tourists. The name means 'Town of the Cross' and it was founded in the eighteenth century as a military bastion against the Muslim tribes of the Caucasus. The place where Gorbachev worked in the 1960s and 70s, the regional Party HQ on Lenin Square, and the fairly modest house around the corner where he lived and whence he walked to work may both be seen. His home village of Privolnoye is not open to tourism. Gorbachev has so far resisted the temptation to establish a cult of personality around himself, and told one visitor that he had to fight against sycophants who 'want to make me into a god'. There is no Gorbachev museum yet in Stavropol, and it will be a bad sign when one is established.

Where to stay   **Stavropolskaya Hotel**. 14 Ulitsa Lenina (tel. 22-241).

Appendix: From Tbilisi to Yerevan

This road was built by Tsarist military engineers between 1834–75. Not as spectacular as the Georgian Military Highway, it is nonetheless a striking and memorable drive, with enough interesting spots on the way to justify a full day's excursion. The road leaves Tbilisi through the Kura Valley, past endless vineyards and the large state hunting reserve, where permits may be obtained to hunt grouse in season. Some 60 km from Tbilisi, the road crosses the seventeenth-century **Krasnaya Most**, or Red Bridge, over the River Khrami, which is the boundary between Georgia and the traditionally Muslim Republic of Azerbaijan.

Kazakh

This western corner of Azerbaijan, the Kazakh region, is the oldest of the republic's oil-producing regions and is the only place in the world that still produces the medicinal oil, naphthalene. The town of Kazakh itself, some 35 km inside Azerbaijan, contains the remains of a temple which dates from the fifth century BC, and which was found above evidence of earlier Bronze Age settlement. Kazakh is now a centre of carpet weaving, and its Kazakh, Zily and Dashzal-Akhly styles of fleecy carpets are prized. The capital of a district known for its horses, the town dominates the confluence of the Rivers Akstafa and Dzhogas. There is a tea house on the right before the bridge which serves good *shashlik* and flat bread. However picturesque, this mountain area is visibly far from prosperous, and horses, carts and load-carrying donkeys are common sights.

Armenia

The road heads south through the Akstafa Valley to the border with Armenia, and the first Armenian town of **Idzhevan**, which was a caravansaray 1,500 years ago. This scenic route down the Akstafa Valley leads after another 40 km to **Dilizhan**, centre of the delightful region known as the Armenian Switzerland. Tucked into the Lesser Caucasian Range, Dilizhan has thermal springs, spa waters and sanatoria. The town itself is located in a fine gorge, and through the forest lies the exquisite Lake Parz-Lich. The very fine eleventh-century Agartsin Monastery is 18 km away. The churches here are striking, but the real masterpiece is the vast thirteenth-century refectory, two cube rooms divided by pillars and vaulted by crossed arches.

Lake Sevan

From Dilizhan, the road climbs steadily through steep woods to the Semyonovsky Pass, at 2,000 m, which leads down to Lake Sevan, the pride of Armenia. It has a stunning setting. Surrounded by mountains, and 1,800 m above sea level, the lake is 71 km long and averages 25 km wide, and is more than warm enough to swim in summer. On average, it freezes once every ten winters.

What to see

The church buildings on the small island in the lake date from the fourth to ninth centuries, but archaeologists have found evidence of far more ancient settlements around the lake. Tragically, incautious irrigation and hydro-electric schemes have brought about an ecological crisis, with the water level dropping steadily throughout the 1970s. Increasingly urgent efforts are being made to put it right without causing an economic crisis by stopping the irrigation and electric power generation which the republic needs. A respite was expected from the building of a new nuclear power station near Yerevan, but in the wake of Chernobyl, which inspired public demonstrations in Yerevan in 1987, the project is now under review – which means that the pressure is again on the waters of Lake Sevan. The ecological problems of the lake mean that it is unlikely you will be able to lunch on 'Ishkhan', the famous breed of salmon-trout which is unique to Sevan. But you may be lucky.

Where to stay, and eat

There is a man-made beach near the town of Sevan where you can picnic, and a restaurant at the adjacent **Sevan Motel** (tel. 922-67).

The town of Razdan, 32 km south-west of Sevan, was built on the industrialisation of Lake Sevan, growing with the hydro-electric stations. The local off-white quarry produced the marble which faces the Kremlin's Palace of Congresses. A road leads off from Razdan to Tsakhkadzor, the valley of flowers, a popular health resort for Armenians and a skiing resort in winter. The ruined eleventh-century Kecharis Monastery lies at the edge of the woods.

Razdan

From Razdan, the road descends to a series of plateaus spotted with villages of Russian Old Believers and other religious non-conformists. They were expelled here by the Tsarist government in the late nineteenth century, partly to preserve the purity of the Orthodox faith in Russia itself, but also as colonists in these newly-acquired lands beyond the Caucasus.

To Yerevan

Some 50 km short of Yerevan is the village of **Bedzhni**, on the gorge of the River Razdan, with a striking eleventh century Church of the Virgin. Twenty km further is the new town of **Aboyvan**, from whose ridge there are excellent views of Yerevan itself, backed by the majestic double peak of Mount Ararat, just over the border in Turkey.

Yerevan

See p. 263.

Useful Reading

The more you read about the Soviet Union and its history before you arrive, the more rewarding the experience will be. Few western tourists travel to the USSR for the sun, the beaches, the food, the service or in search of pampered luxury. It is a cultural-political-sociological experience, challenge and curiosity shop all rolled into one.

History

The best single-volume history remains the pre-war textbook, Sir Bernard Pares' *A History of Russia* (1955), partly because it is rooted so firmly in Klyuchevsky's classic history. Also very good is the whole *Companion to Russian Studies* series, edited by Auty and Obolensky. Vol. 1 *Introduction to Russian History* (1976), Vol. 2 *Introduction to Russian Language and Literature* (1977) and Vol. 3 *Introduction to Russian Art and Architecture* (1981) give an exceedingly thorough background. A very useful single-volume history of Soviet Russia since 1917 is Geoffrey Hoskings' eponymous paperback. *Holy Russia*, by Fitzroy Maclean, is a highly readable history-cum-tourist guide.

Arts and Culture

James Billington is the US Librarian of Congress and a scholar of astonishing erudition. His survey of Russian cultural history, *The Icon and The Axe* (1966), is breathtaking in its bold sweeps and generalisations, and in its grasp of detail. But only read it after you have read everything else, and thoroughly know your Hordes from your Habakuk.

On architecture, the best English book is Kathleen Berton's *Moscow: An Architectural History* (1977), a labour of love by a woman who went through a series of diplomatic postings to Moscow. I once joined one of her walking tours up Herzen Street and along Suvorovsky Boulevard, and she knew every brick. The exhaustive four-volume *Moscow Architectural Monuments* (1973–7) is usually available at the Book Beriozka just off Moscow's Ulitsa Kropotkinskaya.

On Leningrad, Audrey Kennett's *The Palaces of Leningrad* (1973) is an excellent guide and a great deal better illustrated than the rather dull and over-centralised *Architectural Monuments of Leningrad* (1969). Tamara Talbot Rice's *Concise History of Russian Art* (1963) is thorough, and Camilla Gray's *The Russian Experiment in Art* (1962) is a stirring argument and a good read.

Pictorial History of the Russian Theatre (1977) by Herbert Marshall is good. The collection of Stanislavsky's writings published by Progress is enjoyable. Natalya Roslavleva's *Era of the Russian Ballet* (1966) is good but dated, and the glossy book *Bolshoy Theatre* sold at Beriozkas is all right for the pictures. Any reliable book on the modern Bolshoy would have to be very critical.

Politics

Glasnost, *perestroika* and Gorbachev are such recent phenomena that there are few books on the market. Christian Schmidt-Hauer's *Gorbachev* (1986) was the first biography and a better job than the rather disappointing work by Zhores Medvedev. My own book on Gorbachev, his troubled inheritance and his reform plan *The Waking Giant* (1986), remains the only one of its kind. The paperback version takes events into the summer of 1987. Also my own *Martin Walker's Russia* (1988) is the most up-to-date account of Soviet life styles, and what it is like to live there. Most other accounts by western journalists date from the Brezhnev era, and it shows. Although Hedrick Smith's *The Russians* (1976) is the best known such work, I prefer Robert Kaiser's *Russia* (1976).

Academic Sovietologists tend to write more slowly than journalists, and perhaps more carefully. Then also tend to be slower to perceive change. The eminent American scholar Marshall Goldman writes fast, but his optimistic studies of Gorbachev's prospects followed hard on the heels of his pre-Gorbachev studies saying that the Soviet Union was falling apart. In the Reagan years, one dominant school of American Soviet experts wrote that the country was in a state of collapse, while the other dominant school argued that the Commies were coming to get us. Until he got to Moscow to see for himself, President Reagan seemed to believe both schools were right. The Russians themselves choose to read the mavericks among the western experts, such as Jerry Hough and Stephen Cohen. The latter's life of Bukharin was translated into Russian within the Central Committee and read by Gorbachev before Bukharin was finally rehabilitated.

Fiction

The best-seller *Gorky Park* by Martin Cruz Smith won deserved acclaim for his success in getting the feel of Moscow across to a western audience. But a far better thriller, because it was rooted in fact, was *Red Square*, by two Soviet émigrés, Topol and Neznansky. According to Soviet sources who ought to know, this account of the corruption and venality of the last years of the Brezhnev regime is virtually documentary, and there are some who say the account of an anti-Brezhnev *Putsch* is also true. Maybe, but at this level, the Kremlin keeps its secrets. The best of their follow-ups is *Red Gas*, a prophetic account of nationalist tensions in the Siberian oil and gas fields.

Because it was the first to break the publishing taboos, western journalists paid a lot of attention to Anatoly Rybakov's rather laboured fictional account of Stalin's purges, *Children of the Arbat*. Western publishers, keen to cash in on *glasnost*, got into an auction and paid large sums of money, which had to be earned back. Hence the massive hype campaign for a flawed novel, with a commonplace portrait of Stalin.

The point is that it is too soon for any Soviet fiction to have yet emerged that embodies the spirit of *glasnost*. Most of the books and poems Soviet intellectuals are thrilled about have been available in the west for years. And for most of those years, the trendy Soviet poets and writers have shown off their own contraband copies of these forbidden works. It is not that the Soviets are reading this stuff for the first time, but that it can be read openly in the Metro.

You are better off reading Yuri Trifonov's *House on the Embankment* for the moral choices and impossibilities inherent in Stalinism. Or to understand the minds of basically decent men trying to make a career in the moral slough of Brezhnev's years, try Yuri Bondaryev's *The Shore* and *The Choice*. The irony is that Bondaryev has now become the most respectable spokesman for the Russian nationalist, Ligachev-conservative point of view within the Establishment.

But the worst irony is that this culture which has produced some of the greatest writers of our time has been unable to live with them. Vassily Grossman's *Life and Fate* is probably the greatest novel to have come from the Second World War and far too good to be published in the USSR until 1988. The fate of Solzhenitsyn's novels remains a blot on the face of *glasnost*. Aksyonov's *Island of Crimea*, or Zinoviev's *Yawning Heights* or Voinovitch's satires or Brodsky's poems – these are all the stuff of exile. And by contrast, the product so far of the Russian writers who stayed has not touched greatness. There have been books of power and interest: Astafyev's *Sad Detective*, Tatyana Tolstaya's stories and Rasputin's novels of the honest, bewildered peasants of Siberia trying to understand what the Soviet system wants of them. But to read the single most important Soviet writer, you have to move to the outskirts of the Russian Empire, to the Kirghiz writer, Tingiz Aitmatov. He writes in Russian, and his *A Day Lasts Longer than a Century* has already been translated into English. An English edition of his latest novel *Plakha* (The Scaffold, or perhaps The Execution Block) is being prepared. Partly an account of the drug trail from the Soviet south to Moscow, and mainly a spiritual Odyssey, it was the novel that convinced many Soviet middlebrow readers that something important was starting to happen in their home-grown literature again.

Index